THE POTTERY INDUSTRIES OF THE ROMAN EAST

What was the social experience of work in the ancient world? In this study, Elizabeth Murphy approaches this question through the lens offered by a particular set of workers, the potters and ceramicists in the eastern provinces of the Roman Empire. Her research draws on the rich and growing dataset of workshops and production evidence from the Roman East and raises awareness of the unique features of this particular craft in this region over several centuries. Highlighting the multifaceted working experience of professionals through a theoretically informed framework, Murphy reconstructs the complex lives of people in the past and demonstrates the importance of studying work and labor as central topics in social and cultural histories. Her research draws from the fields of archaeology, social history, and anthropology and applies current social theories – communities of practice, technological choices, *chaîne opératoire*, cultural hybridity, *taskscapes* – to interpret and offer new insights into the archaeological remains of workshops and ceramics.

Elizabeth A. Murphy is Assistant Professor of Classics at Florida State University. Her research focuses on the crafts- and trades-people of the Roman and Late Antique worlds and uses the archaeological record to gain insight into the social lives and practices of working communities in antiquity.

THE POTTERY INDUSTRIES OF THE ROMAN EAST

CRAFT COMMUNITIES AND WORKING PRACTICES

ELIZABETH A. MURPHY
Florida State University

CAMBRIDGE
UNIVERSITY PRESS

CAMBRIDGE
UNIVERSITY PRESS

Shaftesbury Road, Cambridge CB2 8EA, United Kingdom

One Liberty Plaza, 20th Floor, New York, NY 10006, USA

477 Williamstown Road, Port Melbourne, VIC 3207, Australia

314–321, 3rd Floor, Plot 3, Splendor Forum, Jasola District Centre, New Delhi – 110025, India

103 Penang Road, #05-06/07, Visioncrest Commercial, Singapore 238467

Cambridge University Press is part of Cambridge University Press & Assessment, a department of the University of Cambridge.

We share the University's mission to contribute to society through the pursuit of education, learning and research at the highest international levels of excellence.

www.cambridge.org
Information on this title: www.cambridge.org/9781009514606

DOI: 10.1017/9781009514613

When citing this work, please include a reference to the DOI 10.1017/9781009514613
First published 2025

A catalogue record for this publication is available from the British Library

Library of Congress Cataloging-in-Publication Data
NAMES: Murphy, Elizabeth A., author.
TITLE: The pottery industries of the Roman East : craft communities and working practices, late 1st century BCE to 650 CE / Elizabeth A. Murphy.
DESCRIPTION: Cambridge, United Kingdom ; New York, NY : Cambridge University Press, 2025. | Includes bibliographical references and index.
IDENTIFIERS: LCCN 2024043774 (print) | LCCN 2024043775 (ebook) | ISBN 9781009514606 (hardback) | ISBN 9781009514590 (paperback) | ISBN 9781009514613 (epub)
SUBJECTS: LCSH: Labor–Rome. | Potters–Rome–Social conditions. | Pottery, Roman–Middle East. | Rome–History–Empire, 30 B.C.-476 A.D.
CLASSIFICATION: LCC HD4844 .M87 2025 (print) | LCC HD4844 (ebook) | DDC 338.4/76663937–DC23/eng/20241118
LC record available at https://lccn.loc.gov/2024043774
LC ebook record available at https://lccn.loc.gov/2024043775

ISBN 978-1-009-51460-6 Hardback

To my father

CONTENTS

FIGURES

CHAPTER 5. POTTING TRADITIONS, CRAFT LEARNING, AND PRODUCT INNOVATION

CHAPTER 6. SOCIALLY EMBEDDED TECHNOLOGIES AND LOCAL TECHNOLOGICAL STYLES

CHAPTER 7. INTERNAL SOCIAL DYNAMICS OF INDUSTRY CLUSTERS: COOPERATION AND COMPETITION

TABLES

ACKNOWLEDGMENTS

This book draws together a wide range of sources and archaeological datasets, and this scope would not have been possible without the advice and guidance of many scholars, as well as the generous support of several institutions.

I was first exposed to the world of potters as an undergraduate Anthropology student at Arizona State University. My mentor, Nancy Serwint, introduced me to the world of Mediterranean archaeology, and in a basement *apotheke* on Cyprus, she generously and patiently trained me to identify and analyze the techniques of ceramic production from artifacts. She set me on this path, and for that I am immensely grateful. As a master's student at the University of Leuven, I was introduced to the archaeology of workshops by Jeroen Poblome. He brought me to the Sagalassos Archaeological Research Project, and my time studying the potters there was transformative. The archaeological record of craft production that we uncovered in the Potters' Quarter is in my experience unmatched, and my years of excavation and material analysis at Sagalassos fundamentally changed how I see the archaeology of Roman labor and the potential for socializing these ancient workspaces. While at Brown University, my dissertation committee, Sue Alcock, John Cherry, Peter van Dommelen, and John Bodel, directed my research and thinking in ways that cast these workshops in new theoretical light and that integrated them into a wider world of ancient labor. I have been extremely fortunate to have had such supportive and knowledgeable advisors, and I sincerely thank them all.

Since my dissertation, fellowships at the Koç University Research Center for Anatolian Civilizations in Istanbul (a Postdoctoral Research Fellowship) and at the W. F. Albright Institute of Archaeological Research in Jerusalem (the Marcia and Oded Borowski Research Fellowship) provided opportunities to delve deeper into the published records of workshops across the eastern Mediterranean. My time in Israel was also supported by funding from the Institute for the Study of the Ancient World, New York University, and Florida State University (Council on Research and Creativity). Adi Ziv-Asudri of the Israel Antiquities Authority very kindly provided access and assistance in studying the material from the Binyanei Ha'uma excavations, and Rina Avner of the Israel Antiquities Authority generously discussed her work in the area. During my time in Israel, I was fortunate to collaborate with Haim Goldfus and Benny Arubas, both of whom generously spent many hours with me discussing the legionary kilnworks in Jerusalem. Our work together has been a pleasure, and I would especially like to thank Haim for helping me to navigate the Rabbinic sources discussed in this volume.

There are so many others who also have offered advice and information about their sites and material in meetings and correspondence. Ina Kehrberg-Ostrasz, Heike Möller, and Rubina Raja have helped me to better understand the important workshops and material of Gerasa (Jerash). Alex Knodell has offered me advice on the landscape of Petra. Jeffrey Blakely provided an extensive bibliography on Gaza Jars and the Hesi Region. Beth Greene and Rob Collins have helpfully discussed military labor. Jim Sickinger has offered interpretations of inscribed tools. I also benefitted intellectually from my time with the Deutsche Forschungsgemeinschaft Graduiertenkolleg on the Archaeology of Pre-modern Economies, and in particular my conversations with Martin Bentz, Michael Heinzelmann, and Tymon de Haas have shaped my thinking on matters of economy and production. An invited lecture series with the Centre for Urban Network Evolutions at Aarhus University with Rubina Raja and Søren Sindbæk also helped crystalize some central ideas for this volume.

Several individuals and institutions also have offered critical assistance in bringing this manuscript to final publication. Jeroen Poblome, Haim Goldfus, Benny Arubas, Sarah Craft, and Tom Leppard offered comments on all or parts of the text. Andrew Murphy and Tom Leppard helped prepare several of the figures. The Sagalassos Archaeological Research Project has allowed me to publish several images. Haim Goldfus and Benny Arubas gave me permission to revise figures from their excavations at Binyanei Ha'uma. Ayla Cevik, supported by the FSU College of Arts and Sciences Book Publication Fund, masterfully handled the indexing. My father, Patrick Murphy, who otherwise spent his days in comfortable retirement, took on the task of cleaning my shamefully messy bibliography, and while he unfortunately was not able to finish the project, Jen McLish capably saw it to completion. The monograph is dedicated to his memory. Finally, I would like to extend a special thanks to John Lund and the reviewers of the volume for their insightful suggestions on improving the manuscript, as well as to the editors and staff at Cambridge University Press for their expertise, patience, and diligence in seeing this to print.

ABBREVIATIONS

ARS	African Red Slip
CBM	ceramic building material
CRS	Cypriot Red Slip
ESA	Eastern Sigillata A
ESB	Eastern Sigillata B
ESC	Eastern Sigillata C
ESD	Eastern Sigillata D
GTS	Gallic Terra Sigillata
ITS	Italian Terra Sigillata
LRD	Late Roman D
MASL	meters above sea level
SRA	Service Régional de l'Archéologie
SRSW	Sagalassos Red Slip ware

CHAPTER ONE

INTRODUCTION

This book is about the social experience of work in the Roman world. It examines this experience through the lens offered by a particular set of workers – potters and ceramicists in the eastern provinces of the Roman Empire. It undertakes this examination via the material remains of these workers and their work that are still preserved today – the remains of cleaned clay lying on work floors, pots discarded due to cracks and warping, modest structures built of mudbrick and stone, and scorched kilns reddened and blackened by long firings – in order to understand how everyday Romans lived and worked. Too often, ancient potters have been outshone by their products. This book refocuses attention on Roman potters, their communities, and their material culture to show how work happened and how it was experienced as a fundamentally social practice.

Just as there is increasing archaeological recognition that pots can be studied and analyzed in myriad ways to answer a multiplicity of social and cultural questions, so this book draws attention to the social lives of their makers, both through their experiences of working clay in their workshops and as part of their local communities, in order to enrich and complicate our understanding of Roman society. The potters that will be discussed worked on estates, in villages, and on the urban fringes. They manufactured dishes and plates, cooking pots and casseroles, and transport containers, and they were consequently embedded in different markets and operated at variable scales of production. Yet what binds these diverse examples together is the shared demands and experiences of transforming clay into ceramic in order to make a living,[1] and what unites the analysis of these different contexts is a conceptual appreciation that "the social" and "the economic" are inseparable in a work setting. Through this exploration and analysis, the social structures and interrelationships, the economic ties, and the person–material connections are shown to underlay and interknit craft and labor in the Roman Empire.

This book draws together evidence from dozens of ceramic worksites from Asia Minor, the Near East, and Egypt – a record spanning over eight centuries (from the late second century BC into the seventh century AD). It represents one of the first attempts to integrate this material evidence into a social study. Archaeologists have employed the material record of ceramic workshops and their products for different means – most notably to analyze the organization of production and to reconstruct trade and ancient economy. Each of these archaeological applications employs the material record of pottery workshops and their production in different ways and to different ends. Clearly, ceramic workshops were undeniably economic places where goods were manufactured for distribution, and they were important as setting the starting point for the economic cycle of production, distribution, and consumption. However, they were also workplaces occupied for long hours by groups of workers, workers who lived within intersecting frameworks of tradition, work culture, labor practice, family, guild, friendships, and rivalries. A better understanding of the social and cultural lives of ceramics workers can offer a means of balancing and humanizing economic narratives. The workshop, from the perspective adopted in this book, is a locus for small-scale social encounters – as a place of social performances of status and hierarchy, economic competition, shared cultural practices, and community collaboration. Therefore, this book also promotes the social interpretation of archaeological workshops, beyond simply the Roman context.

As the following pages will show, many social dynamics could be at play in the ancient workplace. There are infinite combinations of relationships involved, but some particular examples have been selected as the evidence provides fresh perspectives on our understanding of potters and pottery for the period: the relationship between potter and workgroup; between potter and occupation; and the relationship between potter and pot within a wider community of potters. Some of these relationships can be interpreted through the traces of pottery workshops, the assemblages of their material worlds, and the human actors in them. What this relational approach demonstrates is not only how different workshop contexts were experienced but also how each

[1] While the majority of examples discussed in this book concern the production of pottery by potters, occasional examples of molded lamp, brick, and tile production are also referenced, and these should more accurately be referred to as ceramicists.

differing experience highlights the fundamentally social nature of working with ceramic. Taking this broad, synoptic, historicizing view – a view that also incorporates selected textual sources on potters, when available – allows the construction of a rich, theoretically robust exploration of how social work and labor was constituted in the Roman East.

SOCIAL HISTORY AND LABOR

Fundamentally, work unites people across time and space. At the broadest possible conception, work comprises those activities by which people sustain their lives (Harper and Lawson 2003, xi). The activities that are considered to be "work" are, however, culturally relative, and how work is recognized in terms of distinct professions distributed across different industries is therefore a fundamental means of structuring and characterizing society. This recognition is not novel for the scholarship of ancient work; while this book differs from many others in its approach and theoretical framing, it is not alone in attempting to socialize ancient work and labor – in the last two decades increasing attention has been paid by scholars (both archaeologists and historians) to the working lives of everyday Romans.[2] This social approach to the archaeology of Roman work and labor sits at the intersection of several ongoing conversations in the field of Roman studies. Some of these conversations concern the place of labor and craft professions in wider ancient society, whereas some reflect an archaeological interest in the products of labor – either in terms of their place in economic cycles or in material culture studies of consumer goods.

This current, modern interest in the everyday working lives of ancient Romans finds few parallels with most of the textual voices of that period, however. Many ancient authors probably would not have considered such modest ceramic workshops – or, indeed, workshops more generally – as warranting such attention. Some, in fact, were very candid in their views; neither Cato nor Cicero held craft workshops in high esteem, in spite of their willingness to profit from investment in such trades (D'Arms 1980; Reay 2005). In Cicero's well-known assessment of occupations (*De Officiis* 1, 150–51), craft workshops were not deemed places appropriate for men of standing and reputation (Lis and Soly 2012; Verboven 2014). Of course, the opinions held by Roman elites about those involved in the manufacturing professions certainly do not reflect the entirety of views recorded from antiquity (Joshel 1992;

[2] Roman work and labor, particularly of craft industries, is a driving topic as evidenced by several volumes appearing in recent years (Monteix and Tran 2011; Tran 2013; Bond 2016; Hawkins 2016; Wilson and Flohr 2016; Verboven and Laes 2016; Benton 2020; see Freu 2018 for discussion).

George 2006; Bond 2016; Lis and Soly 2016; Tran 2016). That said, because of the textual lens through which much of Roman society tended to be viewed in earlier scholarship, elite attitudes to manual work have received disproportionate attention (see Verboven 2014 for a fuller discussion). This has exerted a profound and distorting bias on how we understand work, its socialization, and its value in the ancient world, and it is key to move beyond this and understand the importance of craft industries in antiquity as critical in balancing historical narratives and experiences of antiquity – particularly modest professions, like ceramic work, that are best accessed through their material remains. The cultural anthropologist Herbert Applebaum, in his study of the anthropology of work, characterized its social role:

> Work is like the spine which structures the way people live, how they make contact with material and social reality, and how they achieve status and self-esteem. As anthropologists we are interested in work because of what it tells us about the rest of society, based on the viewpoint that basic institutions touch all institutions. (1992, ix)

Balancing and nuancing elite imaginaries of work, other bodies of ancient text provide clearer and more detailed evidence for the professional and personal lives of craftspeople of the period. Indeed, in some respects many dimensions of the socioeconomic experiences of these professions in the eastern Mediterranean have been successfully reconstructed by historians. Studies of professional associations have emphasized their sociability and civic activities (Kloppenborg and Wilson 1996; van Nijf 1997, 2002; Mees 2002, 217–18; Diosono 2007; Verboven 2016); how professionals worked collectively to foster and protect business interests (Mees 2002, 217–18; Venticinque 2010; Liu 2016); how the culture of such organizations reinforced a shared sense of identity (van Nijf 2002; Liu 2005); and how the local activities of such associations might vary in different urban contexts (Arnaoutoglou 2011; 2016). Contracts preserved on Egyptian papyri, for example, indicate how the training of new generations of craftspeople might be conducted through apprenticeship (Westermann 1914a, 1914b; Bradley 1985; Saller 2011; Freu 2015). Detailed analysis of occupational titles found on funerary stelae and in work contracts demonstrates how highly specialized the active work force was, even within single industries (Wissemann 1984; Zimmer 1985; Trombley 1987; Joshel 1992; Tran 2007; Iacomi 2008; Ruffing 2008; Hawkins 2016). Other texts have been useful in reconstructing business practices of the period through accounting records (Aubert 1994; Andreau 1999) and civic codes (Arnaoutoglou 2002; Aubert and Sirks 2002; Baldini Lippolis 2005; Riggsby 2010, 25–46). Yet still other texts concern workshop placement through construction recommendations (Saliou 1994, 1996) and private lease contracts (Berger 1948; Cockle 1981; Rowlandson 1998; Mayerson 2000; Martin 2001;

Du Plessis 2006). These sources provide bodies of evidence regarding the lives and activities of working professions that are otherwise extremely difficult to reconstruct from the archaeological evidence alone and that help to contextualize potters in a wider world of labor and working communities. The archaeological evidence presented in the following chapters therefore draws on such important textual comparanda.

WHY POTTERS?

In spite of this rich corpus of epigraphic and archival documents, few such records were written by or for "working class" audiences, leaving the lives of craftspeople largely without narrative from either personal or collective perspectives. Even references to craftspeople are relatively uncommon on stone or bronze inscriptions, and references to ceramicists and potters are especially uncommon – especially when compared to sources on other contemporary craftspeople for the period and region (Ruffing 2008, 208). This may reflect the status of professions too poor to have erected funerary monuments, too lowly to be referenced in major laws, or so ignoble that they are referenced demeaningly in literature (Joshel 1992, 1–9). That this was the case for potters is a view perhaps supported by Mayerson (2000), who analyzed the documented payment of potters making jars on Egyptian rural estates.[3] He determined that the payment to these potters was extremely low and supported a general picture of a penurious profession, so much so "that the term 'slave labor' might be appropriate" (Mayerson 2000, 100). Trombley, citing Diocletian's Price Edict, also notes the low wages paid to brickmakers (1987, 20, f. 21). Mees recounts that some potters described in Egyptian sources were cash-strapped to the point that they failed to pay a month's rent (2002, 265–66). What remains unclear, however, is the extent to which these examples of brick and jar manufacturers compare with other ceramicists working in differing contexts (especially urban contexts) and making different wares. Moreover, ancient wage data is inherently difficult to compare across different contexts (see Freu 2015 for discussion). Indeed, Mees notes that Egyptian lease contracts involving potters number approximately forty (out of a corpus of more than 50,000 documents), and these sporadic cases chronologically span a period of more than 1,000 years (2002, 257). The picture that we construct from such textual sources alone is incomplete.

Other references to the social position of potters further reinforce the impression of a laborer profession that was sometimes considered in pejorative terms. Rabbinic sources of the period, for example, describe potting as a dirty

[3] The wages were recorded on three well-known Oxyrhynchus papyri (*P.Oxy.* 3595–97), published by Bowman (1983).

job and reference potters among the "unrefined" people, alongside donkey-drivers, camel-drivers, shepherds, and shopkeepers (Magen and Peleg 2006, 92–93). The status associated with such work was deemed so undesirable that, in one text (B. Qidd. 82a), fathers were advised not to teach their sons the profession because it was a profession of a "robber" (Magen and Peleg 2006, 92–93[4]). Vitto recounts another Rabbinic text involving the son of a man trained in three professions (goldsmithing, glassmaking, and potting) and, when described by an individual who hated him, he was referenced as the "son of a potter," rather than that of a goldsmith or glassmaker (Midrash Numbers Rabbah 2.17, in Vitto 1986, 61). When considered in direct comparison to other craftspeople, again, the references to the status of potters sometimes seem disparaging.

The collective impression derived from these references is that some potters were among the working poor, whose social status was further denigrated through hard, dirty, manual labor. This, alone, makes them a profession of interest for understanding non-elite Roman society, and nuancing the textual record with archaeological data might complicate our understanding of how such a "lowly" profession was experienced in this period. However, status – whether defined through economic standing or social standing – is relative. Ceramic work was considered to involve "strenuous" labor by ancient sources (Midrash Exodus Rabbah 1.27, Vitto 1986, 50–51), but potting was simultaneously recognized as a skilled profession (Ecclesiasticus Ben Sira 38, 29–32; Vitto 1986, 61). It is unlikely that the sorts of views promoted by the likes of Cicero, or the Rabbinic sources, capture the nuance and ambiguity of this profession's status – a profession present in many communities across the eastern Roman provinces and whose products fed very different markets, were widely consumed, and were in constant demand. In fact, potters and ceramicists appear consistently in other (namely papyrological) sources with regular enough frequency to attest to their local importance from the Hellenistic to the Byzantine periods (Ruffing 2008, 80–81).

Funerary contexts offer an alternative view of craftspeople. There are examples of funerary inscriptions commemorating the lives, and the achievements, of many craftspeople and tradespeople from the eastern provinces. Within this larger corpus, references to potters are, again, limited (Freu 2015, 193–95), but there are occasionally rich local examples in an otherwise sparse body of evidence, such as the Late Antique funerary reliefs from the necropolis of Korykos in Cilicia Trachis dated from the fifth and sixth centuries AD (Patlagean 1977; Trombley 1987; Iacomi 2008; Gallimore 2010, 155). Of the 600 funerary reliefs, more than 456 inscriptions provide professional trade titles,

[4] Vitto (1986, 60–61) references this same text according to a different translation that does not include potters.

as well as military, civic, or Church titles. The appearance of so many epigraphic examples referencing modest crafts and trades likely represents a rather unusual regional habit of using professional title in private funerary commemoration within the community (Varinlioğlu 2011),[5] albeit occurring during a period when trade title, in general, is more frequently referenced (Ruffing 2008, 47). Nonetheless, the corpus indicates the active presence of dozens of professional trades in the town (Patlagean 1977, 159–63, tab. 7), and a considerable number (26 cases, or over 5 percent[6]) are described as *potter* (*kerameus* [κεραμεύς]) (Trombley 1987, 20). There are also instances of potters who served in the local Church parish, indicating their public role in local religious institutions (Patlagean 1977, 168, f. 58, inscription no. 643; Varinlioğlu 2011, 178). The frequency and the visibility of potters in this community has been attributed to their role in supporting the flourishing Cilician wine industry of the time and the important status of this industry in supplying Constantinople (Iacomi 2008), although again this was also a period when tradespeople seem to play a more visible civic role generally (Carrié 2002; Sodini 2003; Zanini 2006). Whether this reflects changing social structures in Late Antiquity or simply an unusual economic context, their community roles meant that their burial plots were placed alongside those of civic, military, and Church officials. The Korykos funerary inscriptions stand in contrast to references to the ceramic profession on other media in highlighting both the frequency of potters and their roles within local communities.

THE ARCHAEOLOGY OF POTTERY WORKSHOPS

The textual references to potters are clearly neither consistent nor easily interpreted and surely reflect a more complicated reality than that based on many textual references alone. The limited range of source types about the lives and work of potters places them among the textually "quiet" masses of the Roman world; occasionally appearing in public and private documents but rarely offering much with which to reconstruct biographies or social histories. Of course, many professions might be considered in these terms; based on papyrological sources, Ruffing identified a subset of professions as fundamental to a local village economy; these include baker, weaver, fuller, dyer, tailor, stonecutter, builder, carpenter/joiner, leather worker, blacksmith, goldsmith, barber, as well as potter (2008, 86–87).

Potters and their work, however, differ from these other Roman professions in one major respect: While the written references to potters are relatively

[5] Ruffing (2008, 34) compares the Korykos tradition of including work title to that at Late Antique Tyre.

[6] Gallimore (2010) cites an even higher figure (10 percent) for all ceramicists.

limited (like many other trades), the archaeological record of potters and ceramicists is unusually ubiquitous. In fact, from an archaeological perspective, ceramic work is surely the most widely and best-documented industry of the Roman period. Vestiges of workshop structures, infrastructural features (wheel pits, kilns), material culture used in making pottery (hand tools, molds, wheel bats), traces of raw materials (abandoned clay quarries, charred remains of fuel), as well as many millions of pottery products (both finished and failed) appear extensively, in all regions of the Roman world. Pottery kilns, alone, number in the hundreds across the eastern provinces (Hasaki and Raptis 2016). In contrast to other industries, like carpentry or blacksmithing (thought to have been present in most communities), ceramic workshops tend to be especially conspicuous archaeologically due to the preservation of archaeologically durable heat-transformed materials (kiln fragments, charcoal and ash residues) and the large scale and intrinsic archaeological conspicuousness of dumps with wasters. The specialized use of particular materials (especially clay) and the unique features of updraft pottery kilns (with elevated chamber floor) also make these worksites relatively easy to distinguish from the remains of other pyrotechnological industries.

This paradox – between a highly constrained (and biased) textual record and a prodigiously abundant archaeological record – has been well recognized by the occasional historical treatment of potters in the eastern provinces (Cockle 1981; Vitto 1986; Wilfong 2008; Gallimore 2010). The richness of the archaeological record of potter workshops provides a potential avenue into understanding the experience of lives oriented around craftwork in the Roman East and assessing the internal diversity present therein. A deep and comparative analysis of the archaeological record will show that the social lives and work experiences of potters working across this wide region, manufacturing different products for different consumers, or working in different centuries or within different religious and cultural communities were considerable. Consequently, the following chapters bring current archaeological evidence to bear on the wider discussions concerning the lived experiences of the Roman "working classes" through the occupation of ceramic work. They do so by framing and interpreting the material evidence in ways that draw on current archaeological and social theory in order to vitalize the quotidian experiences of this craft work – working to help, and yet compete with, neighbors in the same profession; working to learn community traditions, sometimes sustained over many generations; working for or within a powerful institution; working and engaging with the material world of the workshop. In these ways, the practices of potters are interpreted in their workplaces to reconstruct the lived experiences, the social contexts, and material entanglements of the Roman potting professions in the eastern provinces.

CERAMIC WORKSHOP STUDIES

In contrast to the potters of Classical Greece, those of the Roman and Late Antique periods have never been seen as artists (Hayes 1997, 12–14) and have never attracted the attention of art historians who long have attempted to understand masters, workshops, and schools making Classical Greek vases (Heilmeyer 2004). This has largely left the study of Roman pottery production in the hands of archaeological ceramologists. Perhaps for this reason, and perhaps in conjunction with the limited historical record regarding potters, many studies of Roman ceramic production have looked for interpretive inspiration in ethnographic studies of modern or historical pottery industries, rather than Renaissance painters. Consequently, the rich ethnographic record of the Mediterranean basin has directed the discussion of these workplaces toward anthropologically inspired social and economic questions (Curtis 1962; Hampe and Winter 1962; Matson 1973; Peacock 1982; Annis 1985, 2007; Nicholson and Patterson 1985a, 1985b; Crane 1988; London 1989; Henein 1997; Hudson 1997; Tekkök 2004; Hasaki 2011). This ethnographic and ethnoarchaeological focus[7] importantly has drawn attention to the people behind the pots and kilns. While comparative historical or ethnographic cases should be used with caution, there are instances in which more modern examples provide fresh perspectives on ancient evidence. As will be discussed, the ability of neighbors to associate products with their makers, the complicated social dynamics of economic competition within a workshop cluster, the "scaffolding" training of apprentices are all widely noted in both ethnographic and historical accounts, and while the specifics of any ethnographic or historical case are not analogous, acknowledging the regular appearance of these social dynamics in contexts of craft production opens opportunities to think through the archaeology of Roman potters.

There has long been an appreciation that these Roman pottery workshops can help to access the experiences of working communities via an understanding the socioeconomic organization of workshops (Peacock 1982; Hasaki 2011), the technologies of the period (Nicholson and Patterson 1985b; Costello 1997; Peña and McCallum 2009; Nicholson 2011), and apprenticeship and training (Hasaki 2012). Most notably, David Peacock's seminal work *Pottery in the Roman World: An Ethnoarchaeological Approach* has had an enduring impact on Roman archaeology. This is in part because of its effectiveness in

[7] Of course, ethnographic and more recent historical data can be overly simplified and analogies can be misused (see Gosselain 2016 for a thoughtful discussion). These are very real concerns; yet, for the study of the Roman past, modern insights into traditional potting work have also importantly helped direct research to the everyday life of non-elite working segments of Roman society.

populating the archaeological remains of workshops with people living according to Roman lifeways and institutions.[8] His interpretation of the archaeological record was consequently and convincingly presented as a means to access both the economic organizations of workshops and the social context of its labor, and it will be revisited in subsequent chapters.

POTTERY STUDIES

While the study of ceramic work and labor has received some attention by Roman archaeologists, the products manufactured in these workshops have attracted far greater interest from archaeologists invested in building local and regional pottery chronologies and typologies. Due to its preservation, frequency, and sensitivity to stylistic change, pottery has proven invaluable to modern archaeological practice. More numerous than coins and cheaper to analyze en masse than radiometric samples, pottery has been almost universally employed within Roman archaeology as a dating tool (for discussion, see Lund et al. 2006a). These typo-chronological studies relying on stylistic trends have additionally demonstrated the diversity of potting traditions and consumer practices maintained by communities across Asia Minor, the Near East, and Egypt, as well as the contours of change within local ceramic industries and their repertoire of wares.

As this foundational literature makes clear, stylistic and formal diversity can be observed even among settlements in the same region, and these local stylistic traditions were sometimes rooted in much earlier traditions that continued and endured in the workshops of the region into and during the Roman period; in some cases, these traditions have been tracked over as many as eight centuries. This is perhaps best documented in the case of tableware, which in the Hellenistic period showed significant variability across the eastern Mediterranean. The very distinctive Nabataean pottery manufactured at Petra is one such case of a distinctive regional tradition with its very thin ("eggshell") walls and its floral and vegetal motifs painted in red or brown paint on a buff fabric (Vickers 1994; Schmid 1995, 1997, 2000, 2007).[9] These wares were first produced in the Hellenistic period and came to influence other production centers. By contrast, the contemporary tableware market of Judaea during the Second Temple period involved locally manufactured plain ware pottery or

[8] The power of Peacock's narrative was its successful integration of social and economic themes, yet its reliance on other theoretical approaches of the 1970s and 1980s (systems modelling, production organization typologies, and neoclassical economics) has perhaps not aged as well.

[9] The pottery styles manufactured at Petra are thought to have inspired technological and stylistic changes at workshops across the wider region, and as far as Aqaba (Gerber 2001), Jerusalem (Perlman et al. 1986), and Taymud in Arabia (Maritan et al. 2017).

limestone carved forms (Magen 2002; Leibner 2010).[10] In Pisidia (Asia Minor), color-coated wares, thought to have been influenced by earlier Achaemenid traditions, were manufactured at Late Hellenistic Sagalassos (van der Enden et al. 2014; Daems and Poblome 2017), while tableware manufactured in other parts of Asia Minor demonstrated stronger influences from the Classical and Hellenistic wares of Greece, particularly through the use of classical Greek mythology and motifs on relief decorated wares. These Greek influences have been particularly well documented with regard to molded relief hemispherical bowl production, bowls which were manufactured at several major Hellenistic production centers in Asia Minor – for example, Pergamon, Kibyra, Ephesos (Rotroff 2006; Ladstätter 2007; Japp 2014). Likewise, Hellenistic black-slipped wares, some with overpainting, were made in the Egyptian delta at Buto (Seton-Williams 1966, 1967; Ballet 2007; Ballet et al. 2007).

By the time that these regions were territorially integrated as Roman provinces, potting communities within them already maintained bustling production centers supporting a rich array of products. Some centers of these "eastern wares" would become major producers of pottery that was shipped across the empire (Eastern Sigillata A [ESA], Eastern Sigillata B [ESB], Eastern Sigillata D [ESD]), influencing and being influenced by other Roman red-slipped tableware traditions (Italian Terra Sigillata [ITS], Gallic Terra Sigillata [GTS], and later African Red Slip [ARS] ware). Tableware industries are perhaps the best-documented examples of heterogeneity, but local workshops making cooking wares across the region display further diversity in typological and stylistic influences related to different culinary traditions at cities like Palmyra, Gerasa, and Petra, and in the Galilee (Adan-Bayewitz 1993; Krogulska 1996, 1985; Gerber 2005, 2010; Kristensen 2017). Likewise, Hellenistic- and Roman-period amphorae present formal distinctions tied to their role as containers for regional agricultural products (Johnson and Stager 1995, 99; Reynolds 2005; Rauh et al. 2013). In the Roman and Late Roman periods, the eastern provinces manufactured very well-known amphora types used to distribute goods throughout the empire. The workshops of Late Roman 1 amphorae from Cilicia and Cyprus (Autret and Rauh 2010; Dodd 2020), Gaza Jars from Palestine (Mayerson 1992; Israel 1995; Johnson and Stager 1995; Oked 2001), Egyptian amphorae from Lake Mareotis (Empereur and Picon 1998; Dixneuf 2011), and Black Sea amphorae from the region of Sinope (Kassab Tezgör 2010) will all be discussed; each is well documented, and they collectively demonstrate different types of production organization, from distributed estate production to urban workshops. The

[10] These patterns have been explained in terms of religious proscriptions or in response to customs duties, with imported tablewares remaining uncommon until the third century AD (Leibner 2010).

landscape of ceramic traditions across the region was both functionally and stylistically diverse already prior to incorporation into the Roman Empire and set an already richly complex stage for subsequent exchanges of ideas and people.

In the eastern provinces, eagerness to reconstruct patterns of supra-regional trade of Roman ceramics, sometimes incited speculation regarding production locations prior to the discovery of associated kilns (for examples of such attributions, see Hayes 1972). The use of pottery as a proxy of trade even instigated regional surveys, with the stated objective to discover ceramic production sites (Empereur and Picon 1986a, 1986b; Mayet and Picon 1986; Empereur et al. 1991; Israel 1993, 1995; for discussion, see Ballet et al. 2019). In these reconstructions, the workshops themselves were seldom of central academic interest but rather were used to set a nodal point from which all distribution paths might emanate. In recent years, the discovery of many more production sites has successfully filled out the manufacturing geography of the eastern Mediterranean and expanded our understanding of economic networks (Bes 2015; Leidwanger 2017). It has also assisted in reconstructing regional economies – perhaps, however, at the expense of more human-scaled geographies and economies. Nevertheless, with a growing recognition that similar wares were sometimes being manufactured at multiple production sites, it is becoming accepted that "wares," like ESA or Late Roman D (LRD) ware, might better be understood as regional products resulting from a shared material culture tradition or "vocabulary," sometimes termed ceramic *koiné* (Reynolds 2005; Leibner 2010; Cau et al. 2011; Poblome and Firat 2011; Versluys 2014; Rotroff et al. 2018).[11] This has implications for how we relate individual workshop sites to one another and to typologically based ceramic fabrics and styles.

This book, by contrast, takes a divergent approach. By focusing on the *workshop* as the starting point, these larger social and economic phenomena, variously described as "ware group" or ceramic *koiné,* can be understood as comprising the cumulative, heterogeneous products of multiple production sites. These macrostructures are necessarily abstracted and simplified categories; uncommon or less popular product types or variants are regularly observed in the repertoire, but later weeded out from the larger ware groups, or vessels are observed as being of variable quality (Jackson et al. 2012; Murphy 2017). However, each of those production areas was typically composed of the products of multiple workshops, which could be further occupied by multiple active potters. In this regard, a deeper analysis of these potters, their workshops, and their communities substantially enriches Roman pottery studies of the

[11] See also the Levantine Ceramic Project (www.levantineceramics.org).

eastern provinces by identifying how large, regional economic processes were articulated with the workings of small-scale, local workshops and industries.

MATERIAL CULTURE STUDIES OF POTTERY

The sorts of typo-chronological and trade analyses that are the backbone of Roman pottery studies rely on changing styles and functions of pottery over time – both to date archaeological contexts and to trace changing market demands. Consequently, there is a (tacit) recognition that ceramic traditions were never static outputs of cultural practices, but they were in part responsive to market forces and changing consumer preferences within the empire. Understanding these changes and their influences has long attracted the attention of scholars concerned with issues of cultural identity and provincial cultural practices. However, social questions concerning pottery have been much more directed at their distribution and consumption than the social context of their making and makers – that is, the locus where decisions concerning particular forms with particular characteristics were taken and actualized. Nonetheless, current interpretations of ceramic consumption and use have moved well beyond equating little red pots with "the Romans" and have come to accommodate ever greater theoretical complexity (Ladstätter 2007; Van Oyen 2015). The shifting cultural influences on local pottery styles have come to be understood as playing a central role in constructing identity, whether theorized in terms of cultural bricolage (Terrenato 1998; Roth 2007), cultural hybridity (Antonaccio 2005), or "glocal" styles (Pitts and Versluys 2015).

The pottery record offers a particularly versatile body of materials with which to ask large-scale questions, as these ceramic goods were widely consumed and are thought to have been affordable to wide swathes of society.[12] Pottery, in this regard, provides a means of differentiating consumer practices between socioeconomic groups and in varied cultural contexts (Greene 2008; Pitts 2008; Dietler 2015). Furthermore, practices involving culinary traditions or commensality were also activities that employed consumer goods beyond pottery, and in this regard, pottery can be seen as part of a larger and richer material world, whether in the dining rooms, kitchens, or *tabernae* of everyday Romans (Vickers and Gill 1994; Cool 2006; Swift 2009, 2017). While these studies of practice, context, and meaning-construction are incorporating the study of pottery into material culture studies in new and exciting ways of thinking, they nonetheless often continue to privilege the users of these items (in contexts of consumption) over their makers (in

[12] The few instances of ceramic vessel prices also offer the impression that pottery was a generally inexpensive household item (Peña 2007, 28–29).

contexts of manufacture). This is unfortunate. As will be demonstrated, knowledge of competing wares made by craft neighbors or made by far-away workshops also influenced the appearance and use of pottery for the period,[13] and a detailed study of workshop contexts can help to reconstruct how, why, and in what circumstances formal and stylistic influences might appear in the repertoire of a potter. After all, every pot that appeared on the Roman table also was once part of a workshop assemblage composed of pottery wheels, molds, tools, kilns, and clay, and decisions affecting form and style could have different meanings and importance within the small-group dynamics of workshops. By foregrounding manufacture over consumption, this book shows how Roman cultural dynamics within the workshop were as much dependent on the social network of production as they were influenced by consumer demand and provincial fashions.

SCOPE: DEFINING CERAMIC INDUSTRIES

Ceramological research on Roman wares is bringing ever greater nuance to the regional traditions of ceramic styles and forms as well as the cultural meanings of such diversity. Appreciating such diversity of product styles and repertoire also complicates how we describe and understand differences among ancient workers of clay. For our present purposes, such an appreciation especially complicates the appropriateness of discussing brickmakers in the same volume as lamp makers, for example. Modern industry is typically defined by the material being processed (clay) or the market sector supplied by the products (building industry, house goods, etc.). Indeed, the material properties of clay make it an extremely adaptive material with which to work and one that was employed in the Roman period for vastly different purposes – from artistic sculpture to cooking pots. This versatility encouraged its use in a wide range of consumption contexts. Pottery, of course, is the most ubiquitous of Roman ceramic artifacts; however, even among ceramic goods, pottery filled a wide range of functions, was manufactured using materials with requisite properties, and was fashioned into shapes with different aesthetic and stylistic characteristics. Excavated workshops are often classified by their wares (e.g., amphorae, lamps, tablewares). We categorize ceramics according to ware type, but it does not always seem that this was a meaningful emic category in terms of how Roman ceramicists defined their industry. With workshops variably specialized in particular types of goods, this leads to various

[13] Pottery has also been seen as an alternative to more expensive, and presumably more desirable, metal plate. That being said, the hierarchy of materials is always difficult to establish with certainty, particularly given the full range of materials (metal, glass, stone, wood) from which vessels were made (Vickers and Gill 1994).

complications in attempting to circumscribe ceramic "industries" in the Roman world. Brick and tile were sometimes produced alongside pottery, and molded lamps were sometimes produced in workshops making wheel-thrown pottery. Categorizing workshops according to simple product groups seems therefore problematic.

These difficulties in defining ceramic industries and workshops are likewise expressed in ancient textual sources, which offer little assistance in clearly bounding our discussion of potters and other ceramicists. This is because there was no single naming system or universal convention for classifying ceramic workshops or ceramicist workers in the Roman world. Some workshops were described as simply a "pottery workshop" (*keramikon ergastērion* [κεραμικὸν ἐργαστήριον]), while others were described more specifically by the products manufactured, for example, "amphora workshop" (*kouphokeramourgion* [κουφοκεραμουργῖον]) (Gallimore 2010, 161). Attempting to understand and define ancient ceramic industries from recorded professional titles is even more problematic (described further in Chapter 3). Indeed, Ruffing (2008, 60–79) notes several ways in which the use of occupational titles in the textual record could be flexible and context-specific.[14] For example, most are described by the general term, "potter" (*kerameus* [κεραμεύς]), although more specific job titles are sometimes also observed referencing the type of product made – for example, fineware potters (*leptokerameis*, [λεπτοκεραμεῖς]) or amphorae potters (*kouphokerameis* [κουφοκεραμεῖς], *kerameis oinikou keramou* [κεραμεῖς οἰνικοῦ κεράμου]) (Gallimore 2010, 161). To further complicate the matter, it has been noted that professional titles become increasingly specialized from the third century AD onwards, with specific reference sometimes given to their products (Ruffing 2008, 83–84). Mees saw this as reflecting a growing horizontal specialization within the ceramic industry, particularly among amphora or jug makers, potters, and brickmakers (2002, 234).

Ruffing (2008), conversely, observed three scales of specialization in clay-working based on professional titles. At the most general level, differences were observed between potter (*kerameus* [κεραμεύς], *keramoplastēs* [κεραμοπλάστης], *keramourgos* [κεραμουργός], *ostrakas* [ὀστρακᾶς]), lamp maker (*lampadiokopos* [λαμπαδιοκόπος], *likhnikarios* [λιχνικάριος]), terracotta maker

[14] Use of job title was subject to changing epigraphic habits, with the frequency of certain titles demonstrating chronological and geographical patterns (Ruffing 2008, 76–83). The use of title also appears to have been flexible, as there are examples of individuals referenced in multiple papyri with different job titles and engaged in activities that were not referenced as their primary profession (Ruffing 2008, 60). Likewise, most references to clay workers derive from the papyrological record of private and legal documents in village or town settings, where there might have been a greater tendency to use a professional title (Ruffing 2008, 61). Martin (2001) notes that use of a professional title may have held legal weight in the Roman world, where – in cases of fault or damage – a tradesperson could be legally liable based on expectations of skill associated with job title.

(*plastēs* [πλάστης]), and brickmaker (*kistiplinthourgos* [κιστιπλινθουργος], *plasteutēs* [πλαστευτής; πλινθευτής], *plinthobolos* [πλινθοβόλος], *plinthopoios* [πλινθοποιός], *plinthoulkos* [πλινθουλκός], *plinthourgos* [πλινθουργός]), with the latter likely referencing the making of mudbricks. These distinctions seem to reflect the sorts of markets that these workers were supplying, for instance, building supplies, household items, ritual items. However, they might also have implications regarding the skills and methods of production involved. Among terracotta makers and potters, more specific product distinctions also could be noted. Among terracotta makers, there were *theopoios* (θεοποιός), *korallioplastēs* (κοραλλιοπλάστης), and *koloplastēs* (κωλοπλάστης). The greatest degree of specialization, however, was described in the work titles of potters including those making large coarse clay vessels (*kouphokerameus* [κουφοκεραμεύς], *kouphokeramourgos* [κουφοκεραμουργός]) with specific types of coarseware sometimes mentioned (*kerameus oinikou keramou* [κεραμεύς οἰνικοῦ κεράμου]). There were also potters making fine, small vessels (*leptokerameus* [λεπτοκεραμεύς]) with specific types of fineware sometimes mentioned (e.g., *ekpōmatopoios* [ἐκπωματοποίος), *kuthrobrokhos* [κυθροβρόχος), *kuthroplastēs* [κυθροπλάστης][15]) (Ruffing 2008, 83–84, 139–40). Ruffing interpreted the ceramics industry as presenting particularly high levels of work title specialization when compared with other crafts industries, and he understood this as a consequence of the wide range of everyday items manufactured in the material, as well as the more frequent appearance of potters in papyrological texts (when compared with references on inscriptions) (2008, 207–8).

If the regional comparative studies present broad yet sometimes ambiguous differences in industry references, then an epigraphic case might offer some insight into contemporary local understanding of ceramic work. The Late Antique funerary record at Korykos once again provides a pertinent dataset of local professional titles. At Korykos, work titles for more than thirty-one ceramicists have been recovered, and the most common professional title used to describe ceramic workers is *kerameus* (κεραμεύς), appearing twenty-nine times (Iacomi 2008, 24). In the corpus, there is little distinction between potters making household pottery and ceramicists making tiles for the building industry (Patlagean 1977, 166). More specific ceramic work titles also appear, although each only once; these terms include a "maker of earthenware vessels" *ostrakarios* (ὀστρακάριος) and a "maker of lekane" *lekaniourgos* (λεκανιουργός) (Iacomi 2008, 24–25). These distinctions fit into the structures and patterns of specialization noted for the wider region and period by Ruffing (2008), in that

[15] Ruffing also includes *lekaniorgos* (λεκανιοργός), *angeirourgos* (ἀγγειρουργός), *kantharopoios* (κανθαροποιός), *katilarios* (κατιλάριος), *keramodetēs* κεραμοδέτης), *lagunarios* (λαγυνάριος), *oinokhopoios* (οἰνοχοποιός) in his table, but they do not appear on the other lists (2008, 83–84, 139–40).

they reference the type of material (i.e., clay) being worked and the sometimes specific product types being manufactured, yet they do not, unsurprisingly, reflect modern typologies of ceramic markets (pottery versus ceramic building materials [CBM]). While there seems to be some variation in title depending on medium and context, the lack of consistency within the Korykos corpus demonstrates a seemingly flexible set of cultural reference points for how differences within ceramic industries might be expressed.

Attempting to reconstruct the structures of, and differences between, ceramic industries from references to individual work titles seems unlikely, but professional titles are nonetheless helpful in identifying some of the ways that occupational differences in ceramic work might have been understood by contemporary society. This is also demonstrated by three lease contracts from Oxyrhynchus (Cockle 1981; Gallimore 2010, 178), which each refer to potters producing the same range of wares (i.e., Oxyrhynchite four-*choes* jars, double *ceramia*, and two-*choes* jars), albeit in variable quantities. One potter was described as simply *kerameus* (κεραμεύς), and a second was described with additional detail as *kerameus oi nikou keramou* (κεραμεύς οἰνικοῦ κεράμου, "a potter who makes earthenware jars") (Cockle 1981, 90; Gallimore 2010, 178). Thus, potters contracted to manufacture similar types of vessels were professionally referenced in slightly different ways, and again, the use of job title was clearly not rigid.

Ultimately, the terminological distinctions according to consumer-defined "industry sectors" (e.g., the building industry, agricultural production and exportation, domestic markets, religious consumption), the repertoire of production (tablewares, cooking wares, amphorae, lamps), or the materials used (e.g., finewares, coarsewares, common wares) find some relation to the specialization of production identified archaeologically with some workshops, although certainly not all and certainly not consistently. Both the archaeological and textual records support a view of flexible job titles and overlapping specializations. For the purposes of the following chapters, these overlapping and sometimes ambiguous references made to individuals working clay are considered to support taking a wide, inclusive view of ceramic industries.

GEOGRAPHIC PARAMETERS

Evidence of pottery production has been found in every province of the Roman Empire and given the distribution of some wares across the breadth of the Mediterranean world (and beyond), it is clear that the economic webs in which these wares were situated rarely respected provincial boundaries and were traded across and beyond the territories of the empire. This book addresses pottery production in the eastern provinces of the Roman Empire in Asia Minor (modern Turkey), the Near East (particularly the areas of modern Israel, Palestine, Jordan, Syria), and Egypt (particularly the delta region) between the late second century BC and the seventh century AD (Figure 1). Within these regions,[16] particular emphasis is on their respective Mediterranean littorals, as home to the largest urban entities and demographic concentrations and as those areas in which most archaeological reconnaissance has been conducted.

Over the last twenty years, the eastern regions of the Roman Empire have yielded a great deal of high-quality published data documenting (in detail) ceramological work. Thus, one reason for the expansive geographic scope of this book is to employ this well-studied and regionally well-published data and to highlight the unique evidence coming from these areas (Figure 1). Additionally, as has been noted, Asia Minor, the Near East, and Egypt supported a number of craft contexts and potting traditions during the period. These were highly varied landscapes occupied by cultural and religious groups with different histories and craft traditions. There is also evidence for differing rates of economic development over time and intensities across these provinces. Consequently, the geographic parameters of the study serve to illustrate the variable social experiences of ceramic work.

Finally, it is perhaps important to mention which regions are (perhaps conspicuously) absent. The book does not, for instance, include Greece or North Africa outside the Nile Valley and Delta. It is impossible to imagine that the workshops of the western coast of Asia Minor were not influenced by the work of crafts in Greece or that the workshops of the Egyptian oases and delta were not more broadly connected to the dynamics of North African production sites. This has been documented. Nonetheless, if this book were to incorporate either Greece with its long-studied Corinthian potters' quarter or Athenian *kerameikos*[17] or North Africa with its regional production of amphorae, cooking wares, or ARS, the sheer quantity and quality of archaeological research already published from those regions would disproportionately skew the discussion. Such is also the case with regions of modern France, Italy, Germany, and Britain[18] where some workshop clusters have been studied for more than a century, such as La Graufesenque and Montans in France or Magdalensberg in Austria. Building on these established traditions of workshop

[16] Here and throughout the text, the term "regional" is used in opposition to "local," with the latter referencing geographic entities at the site or city scale and the former referencing any larger geographic units.

[17] Also, for important recent contributions on the Aegean, see Drogou (2020), and on Cyprus, see Lund (2015).

[18] This includes work at sites such as La Graufesenque, France (Genin 2002, 2007; Schaad 2007), Salles-d'Aude, France (Laubenheimer 2001), Lyon, France (Desbat 2001), Yvelines, France (Dufaÿ et al. 1997), Moorgate, Britain (Seeley and Drummond-Murray 2005), Scoppieto, Italy (Bergamini 2007, 2011), Giancola, Italy (Manacorda and Pallecchi 2012), and El Rinconcillo, Spain (Cacho 1995).

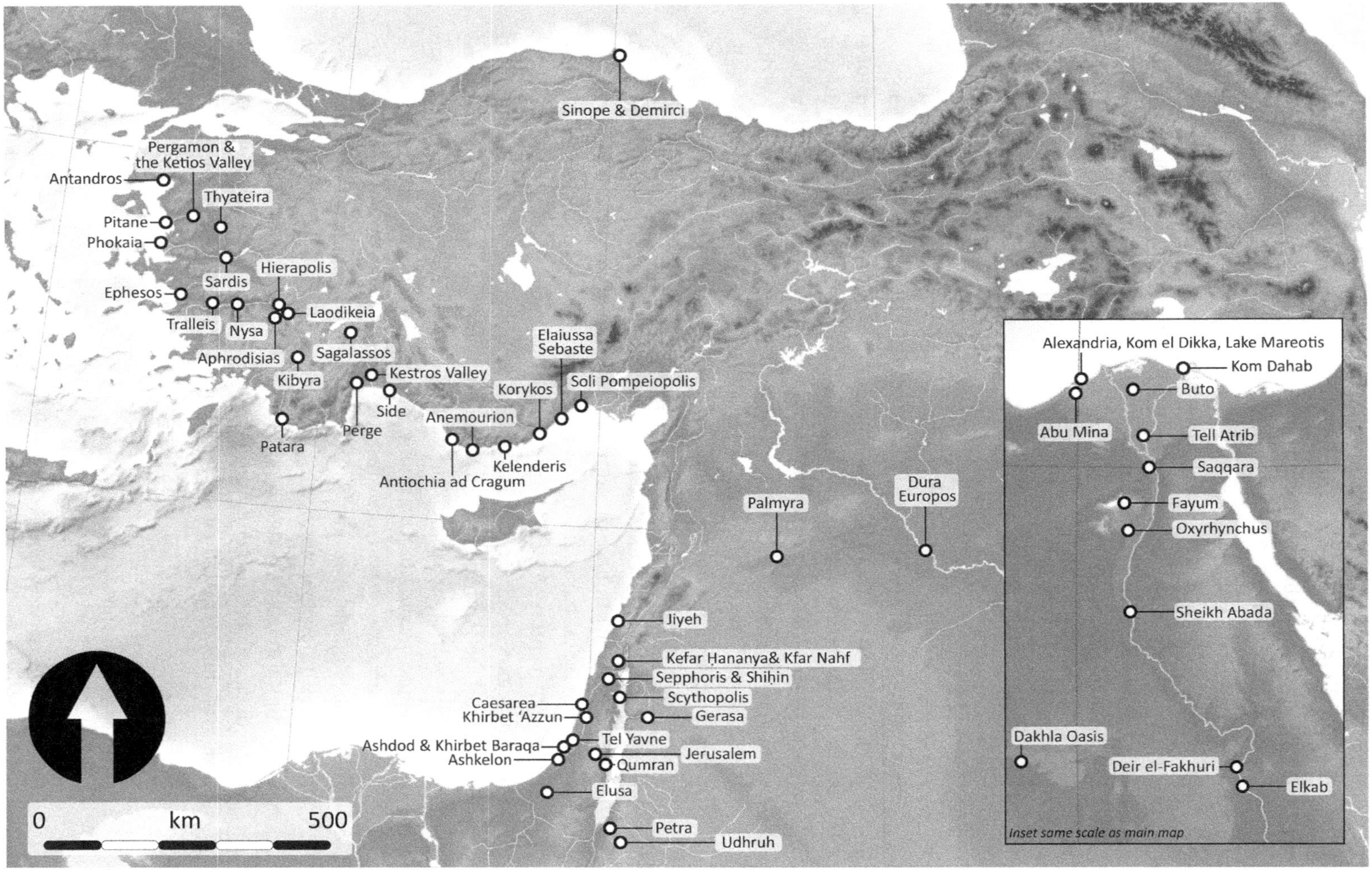

1 Map of sites described in the text.

studies, questions of scale, production organization, and technological know-how – in short, the socioeconomic nature of craft production – have accordingly dominated in those regions of the empire.[19] By contrast, many archaeologists working in the eastern provinces have long been preoccupied by different sorts of questions, particularly relating to urbanism and public building projects. While these research agendas are rapidly expanding to include more information on daily life, there is still much to be done to incorporate the eastern Mediterranean evidence into the systematic and comparative analyses of Roman-period shops and workshops – potteries included. This volume attempts to contribute to those efforts.

CHRONOLOGY

This book is about Roman potters and ceramicists, so the primary aim is to understand ceramic work in the Roman period. However, different regions of the eastern Mediterranean were officially incorporated into Roman territorial domain at different times. This was a gradual process, and – importantly for the study of crafts – there is often clear continuity in the activity of workshops both before and after political horizons (Lund 2005, 241). This is not to say that typologies and styles of pottery remained unchanged; there are well-documented region-wide changes in style (Hawthorne 1997; Hudson 2006; Vroom 2007; Murphy and Poblome 2016); nor is it claimed that political processes might not affect pottery production (Lund 2014; 2016, 839). However, in order to understand the full breadth of these changes, an expansive chronological frame is employed: from the late second century BC into the seventh century AD. This presents some complications, particularly as concerns region-specific periodization and terminology.[20] The transition from Roman to Late Roman or Late Antique phasing also warrants an additional note, as the workshops of the later phases are much better represented in the archaeological record. In fact, many more Late Roman and Late Antique workshop sites are documented from the region than either Late Hellenistic or Roman Imperial periods. This is in part a function of archaeological preservation (the super-positioning of later occupations) and in part due to archaeological research design privileging the excavation of urban centers (as will be discussed in Chapter 8, in the Late Roman period workshops begin to move into cities, where they are found more readily by archaeologists).

[19] It is perhaps for this reason that most archaeological examples used by Peacock (1982) were from the western provinces.

[20] Second Temple period, Hasmonaean, Hellenistic, Roman, Late Antique, Late Roman, East Roman, Early Byzantine, Byzantine, Early Roman, and Early Christian are all terms used to describe some segment of time between of the late second century BC through seventh century AD.

Inclusion of Late Antique workshops warrants other considerations, of course. In Late Antiquity, not only did the styles, motifs, and repertoire of pottery change in relation to changing consumer practices and religious identities (Hudson 2006; Vroom 2007), but also new institutions, particularly the Christian Church, sometimes directly supported these artisans (see Chapter 2). Changing cities and urban society placed trades and craftspeople in new social positions (Sodini 2003; Zanini 2006) alongside a growing role in tax collecting by professional associations (Carrié 2002). Changing regional economies built on agricultural works supported thriving oil and wine industries across much of the eastern Mediterranean, which relied on amphorae for bottling (Wickham 2006; Leidwanger 2017). These changes were experienced differently at different sites, at different times, and in different regions. Nonetheless, several of the local ceramicist communities discussed in the following chapters were continuously active throughout these changes, and, as will be demonstrated, there were continuities in the social practices and working lives of these communities from earlier traditions into the Late Antique period. Thus, this more flexible and wider chronological scope has been adopted to capture long-term sociocultural trends within local communities, rather than reflecting political phases.

CHALLENGES AND BIASES

Ultimately, this book is not intended to be a comprehensive overview of all archaeological workshops or pottery types from the region. There are likely (and inevitably) pottery workshops that are not discussed, and, with the perpetually growing body of published data, there will certainly be other examples that will flesh out the social experience of ceramic work in new ways.

Moreover, there are certain biases within and challenges surrounding the current published data from this region, factors that impact the nature and depth of some discussions and that have guided the selection of case studies described in the following chapters. In terms of workshop excavations, the number of detailed contextual studies that identify the exact findspots of hand tools, molds, and potter's wheels remain relatively limited from the region. Several production sites, by contrast, have been identified only by regional archaeological survey (Empereur and Picon 1986a, 1986b; Israel 1995; Autret and Rauh 2010; Jackson et al. 2012; Vokaer 2013; Ballet et al. 2019), with some projects employing geophysical techniques to supplement surface material (Jackson et al. 2012; Ballet et al. 2019). Therefore, the study of these sites has been conducted using very different methods. Furthermore, tableware, amphorae, and lamp workshops are far better represented than workshops manufacturing cooking wares, everyday kitchen wares, or ceramic building materials,[21] and when a workshop manufactured tablewares, amphorae, or lamps alongside other types of wares, the former types of goods tend to be better published. In spite of these limitations and challenges, the archaeology of workshops recovered and documented from these eastern regions nonetheless presents some extremely important case studies with which to broaden the discussion on potters in the Roman world.

CHAPTER OBJECTIVES AND ORGANIZATION

The following chapters of this volume each focus on different cultural, social, and economic relationships between ancient potters and their craft work. In each section, different sets of relationship (social, material, architectural) are spotlighted via the archaeological record of workshops and their contexts – complex, heterogeneous assemblages of workers, raw materials, products, technologies, workshops, and urban infrastructure. The archaeological evidence is supplemented with insights from social and economic history and modern comparative anthropology.

The structure of the following chapters moves through the archaeological record to highlight different features of social life in these ancient workplaces. Chapter 2, *Workshops: Models versus Practice*, relates the archaeological evidence of pottery workshops from the eastern Mediterranean within several well-established socioeconomic models of production organization. Then, drawing on more recent theoretical approaches, it considers alternative arrangements as reflecting important cultural practices. Chapter 3, *Process, People, and Working Conditions*, focuses specifically on the labor dynamics of these workshops in order to appreciate how the workplace and production process structured the working lives of complex labor groups with different specializations, statuses, and working conditions. Chapter 4, *Cultural Practices and Ritual Lives of Potters in the Workshop*, uses the archaeology of these workplaces to reconstruct daily life in the workshop. More than simply an economic hub of manufacturing, the workshop comes to be seen as a place of social experience and meaning to its occupants. Chapter 5, *Potting Traditions, Craft Learning, and Product Innovation*, investigates traditions in production through intergenerational learning and then considers how product innovations are introduced. Moving beyond models that privilege consumer demand as the primary driver for product change, this chapter balances consumer interests with those of the workshop and long-established local potting traditions. Chapter 6, *Socially Embedded Technologies and Local Technological Styles*, looks at the technologies

[21] Exceptions to this might include the Harbor Bath (*basilica thermarum*) workshop and the Günlük kiln complex at Patara (Dündar 2015) or the legionary kilnworks of Jerusalem (Arubas and Goldfus 2005).

of production, particularly pottery wheels and kilns, in order to contextualize the technological choices and innovations made in the workshops of the eastern provinces.

The subsequent chapters turn to issues beyond the workshop. Chapter 7, *Internal Social Dynamics of Industry Clusters: Cooperation and Competition*, considers the important role of workshop nucleation in creating communities of production, which witnessed complex dynamics of collaboration, as well as competition among workshops. Chapter 8, *Urban Industry, Topographies, and Community Relations*, looks at pottery workshops in urban contexts; often seen as urban outcasts relegated to peri-urban areas, the place of ceramic workshops is instead understood as dynamically placed between a range of push and pull factors that change through time and through the history of cities. Finally, the conclusion reflects upon and draws together the complex social relationships and small-scale community dynamics.

CHAPTER TWO

WORKSHOPS: MODELS VERSUS PRACTICE

Thousands of kilns used to fire ceramic have been excavated across the Roman territories. These kilns thus constitute one of the most abundant bodies of evidence for craft production contexts for the Classical world. Collating, organizing, and interpreting such a large and diverse corpus has resulted in certain approaches and predispositions within the scholarship. In particular, the study of Roman pottery workshops and production sites has been greatly advanced by large and often comparative modelling exercises. Property ownership models have noted instances of workshops operating as independent production units, and there are also instances of leased properties and contracted labor. Site catchment models noted spatial patterning in clay and water resources, as well as trade networks. Such models have, importantly, helped to identify patterns and trends within the diverse and plentiful data from ancient worksites. However, any such models suffer from certain limitations. Most notably, modelling exercises, particularly typological models, are constructed and reliant on variables that are seen to be central to each types and that are shared among individual cases. Models also rely on reconstructions of the archaeological record that often privilege one or another phase in the history of the workshop.

Thus, there are interpretive consequences to the process of modelling and reconstructing production sites in that such processes tend to focus on shared similarities rather than contextualized differences. They often impose a focused (yet static) interpretation of particular phases in the life of a production community, rather than emphasizing dynamic changes over time.

In response, this chapter considers the roles of two important models used to interpret Roman-period production sites: production organization models and resource extraction models. In so doing, we can appreciate the diversity of the evidence from the eastern provinces and begin to appreciate what does not fit – the outliers – in order both to consider alternative experiences of the production process and to see how these reconstructions can be understood as part of a dynamic life of work. Accordingly, this chapter pushes the potential of these models in new directions.

PRODUCTION ORGANIZATION MODELS AND ALTERNATIVE ARRANGEMENTS

Roman pottery workshops were certainly not all the same, and it is important to appreciate the great variability in workshop contexts and in property statuses (e.g., subcontracting, leasing, owning). Moreover, workshops of the Roman world could operate at vastly different scales and organizations of work task, and they could involve very different labor regimes. A range of archaeological production organization models have been developed to identify significant and common variables, to assess patterns in similarities and differences of those variables, and to classify workshops accordingly (van der Leeuw 1977; Peacock 1982; Costin 1991). Issues like scale and intensity of production, investment in technology and infrastructure, and context and density of workshops all have come to be seen as critical to the organization of ancient workshops and their manufacturing (Costin 1991). David Peacock (1982) classified differences specifically among Roman workshops according to his frequently cited "modes of production" model: household industry, individual workshop, nucleated workshops, manufactory, estate production, military and official production. This typological framework represented an important early attempt to interpret the diversity of Roman pottery workshops and to utilize a complex set of variables (e.g., technological investment, workshop scale, work-task specialization, full-time versus part-time work institutional administration) to do so. That model, at its time, was a critical first step in organizing and comparing the growing body of Roman-period workshop evidence from, in particular, the western provinces.

As will be clear in the following pages and outlined in the first sections, the discussed workshops from the Roman East can be categorized in ways that are similar in many respects to Peacock's model and provide important clues as to their property organization and institutional involvement in ceramic production. That evidence provides a structural and institutional background from which to delve deeper into the more localized cultural practices. The chapter then moves on to address evidence that does not quite fit into these models in order to consider alternatives to the ideal types. In so doing, it moves beyond grand narratives of economic models to smaller-scale stories of local practices and working arrangements.

Independent Workshops

Workshops that were independent, self-contained production spaces were, indeed, quite common across the region, and examples have been published from Patara (Özüdoğru and Dökü 2007; Dündar 2015), Tralleis (Yaylalı 2007; Civelek and Atıcı 2014; Akkan et al. 2016), the Ketios Valley outside of Pergamon (Figure 7, Figure 8, and Figure 9; Poblome et al. 2001; Bounegru 2009), Elusa (Bucking and Goldfus 2012), and Elaiussa-Sebaste (Ricci 2007; Borgia and Iacomi 2010; Ferrazzoli and Ricci 2010). These structures appear within a clearly defined property boundary, and there is evidence for all or most of the production cycle (clay preparation, forming, and firing) within the space. This was the case with a workshop in the suburbs of the mountain-side town of Sagalassos in Asia Minor. The East Slope Tableware Workshop was a freestanding building fully equipped with the infrastructure necessary to support wheel-thrown production of tablewares, including a clay preparation area, three pottery wheels, one turntable, a drying and storage space, and two kilns (Figure 2). These workshop remains appear to represent a specialized production space working full-time as an independent property unit without evidence of domestic occupation. This sort of workshop is the easiest to parse in terms of organization and labor.

In contrast, other workshops appear to have accommodated spaces used for a mix of production, commercial, and domestic activities. These tend to be larger than workshops specialized only in production (Table 1). Workshops with domestic space have been proposed at Dura-Europos, where kilns were found in the courtyards of larger building complexes (Figures 3 and 4; Allara 1992), and at Hierapolis, where Late Antique domestic structures located next

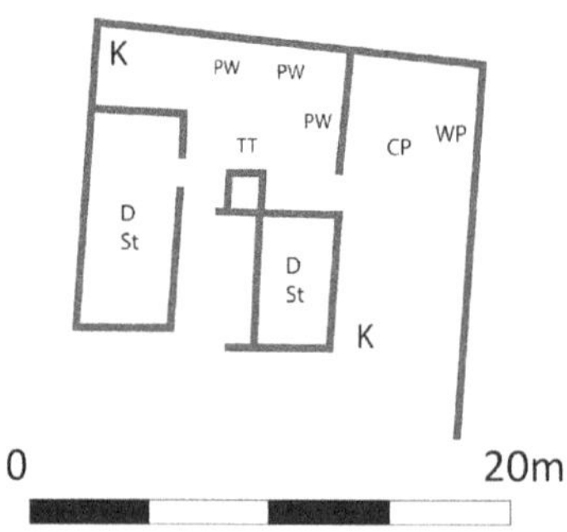

2 Plan of Sagalassos East Slope Tableware Workshop [K: Kiln, PW: Pottery Wheel, TT: Turntable, CP: Clay Preparation, WP: Waterpipe, D: Drying Area, St: Storage]. (Sagalassos Archaeological Research Project)

TABLE 1 *Workshop size estimations (in m^2)*

Specialized Workshop	Overall Area	Interior Space	Exterior Space	Unknown Space	Kiln Area	Clay Prep	Throwing Rooms	Drying / Storage	Unknown Function
Elauissa-Sebaste	315.30	58.40	189.13	67.77	47.06	31.43	43.51	14.89	36.34
Ketios Valley Workshop 1	184.37	54.03	117.34	13.00	68.58	48.76	31.64	5.65*	13.00
Ketios Valley Workshop 2 (North Unit)	90.33	31.64	58.69	n/a	58.69	n/a	31.64	5.65*	n/a
Ketios Valley Workshop 2 (South Unit)	94.04	22.39	58.65	13.00	9.89	48.76	n/a	n/a	13.00
Ketios Valley Workshop 3	249.97	51.67	147.98	50.32	59.00	88.98	23.19	n/a	28.48
Sagalassos ES Workshop	130.44	72.09	20.08	28.89	29.46	28.89	30.62	31.00	10.47
Sagalassos MWWC	113.17	63.47	49.70	n/a	49.70	7.06	36.02	14.99	5.40
Elusa	98.88	98.88	undefined	n/a					
Patara N Slope Tepecik Acropolis Workshop	65.38	30.61	34.77	n/a			n/a	n/a	n/a
Shiḥin	69.75						39.82		
Ephesos Terrace House 2 Workspace	13.35								
Gerasa (single cavea unit)++	34.69								
Gerasa (multiple cavea units)++	85.71								
Domestic Space with Workspace	**Overall Area**	**Interior Space**	**Exterior Space**	**Unknown Space**	**Kiln Area**	**Clay Prep**	**Throwing Rooms**	**Drying / Storage**	**Unknown Function**
Dura-Europos House 1	364.58	122.92	241.66	n/a	208.54				
Dura-Europos House 2	607.22	252.9	354.32	n/a	354.32				
Hierapolis Frontinus Street N House+	224.83	176.97	47.86	n/a					
Hierapolis Frontinus Street S House+	242.79	144.08	98.71	n/a	98.71				
Elkab House F	98.98	98.98							
Elkab House A-B	343.78	343.78							

[ES: East Slope; MWWC: Molded-Wares Workshop Complex].
*Measurements estimated in a space used for both kiln and storage.
+upstairs noted (calculated)
++possible upstairs (not calculated)

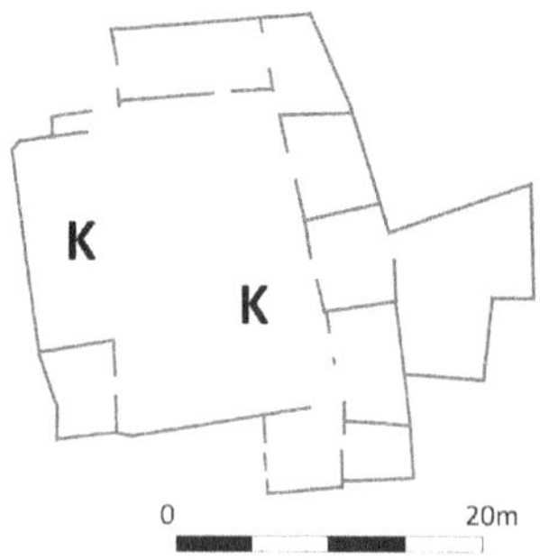

3 Plan of Dura-Europos Workshop 1 [K: Kiln]. (Based on Allara 1992, f. 2)

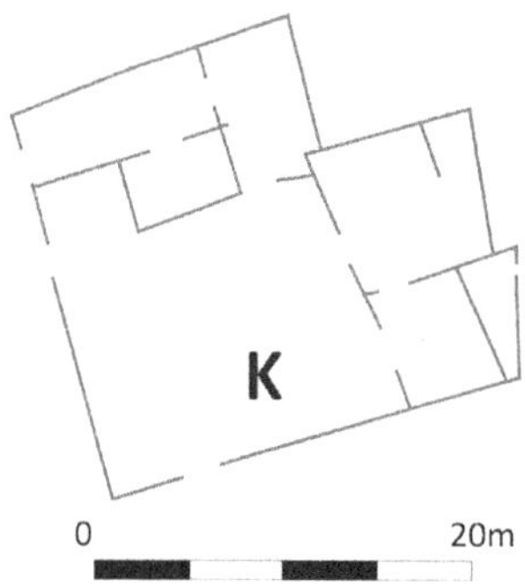

4 Plan of Dura-Europos Workshop 2 [K: Kiln]. (Based on Allara 1992, f. 2)

to very large ceramic kilns were found to contain deposits of clay and kiln furniture (Mastronuzzi and Melissano 2007). Among the clearest evidence for mixed domestic and workspace was at the Egyptian village of Elkab in the second century AD. In particular, House B at Elkab (Figure 6-g) was a large structure composed of nine spaces, with an additional two spaces possibly incorporated through the extension of "House A"[1] (Hendrickx 1998, 1362–69). While accessways could not be reconstructed between the rooms, the distribution of work installations indicates at least two sets of workrooms (Space a and Spaces h–i), with associated domestic space. The smaller work/house unit (Spaces a–c) also seems to have been involved in commercial sales of pottery; in addition to making locally manufactured wares, the occupants appear to have sold imported wares produced in Aswan and Luxor (Hendrickx 1998, 1366).

Extraordinarily, an archive of ostraca was found associated with the House B at Elkab – an archive that in effect describes the presence of multigenerational families living there (Hendrickx 1998, 1358). The ostraca concern the

[1] It is thought that House A and House B were parts of the same property because they shared walls and the use of the two rooms in House A complemented the functions identified in House B (Hendrickx 1998, 1366–69).

family of Psemonchès – who appears to have been the occupying potter – over a period of nearly thirty years, AD 106–132. Two (or possibly three) sons later moved into nearby houses, and another two are thought to have lived in the house until the family moved in AD 132. For a period of that time (AD 118–127), another family (of Niaraus and his son Sisonchis) also may have lived in the building although, based on their tax declarations, these individuals are thought unlikely to have been involved in the potting trade (Hendrickx 1998, 1362–63). While the Elkab production units can be attributed to family groups, the relationship between the family and the ownership of the property is less clear, and either direct ownership or leasing is conceivable. The complex personal histories of the occupants – some tied to ceramic production and others not – living together in these spaces, as well as the absence of kilns, are illustrative of some of the difficulties in trying to disentangle domestic and workshop spaces within the archaeological record.

Whether any of these workshop properties were privately owned or leased is impossible to determine definitively, but there is also reason to suppose that owning workshops could have been within the financial means of at least some potters. It was noted in Chapter 1 that the economic status of potters and ceramicists is thought to have been comparatively modest, even when contextualized among contemporary craftspeople; using wage references, Mayerson even went so far as to claim the income of potters was so low that it equated to "slave labor" (2000, 100). However, one pottery workshop described in a fourth-century sales contract from Oxyrhynchus (*PSI* IV 300) was purchased for just fifteen talents (Rabinowitz 2001, 53). While we do not know the specifications or condition of the property, according to Rabinowitz this was extremely inexpensive, representing a small fraction of the sum documented for annual leases of contemporary houses or linen workshops (2001, 53). At least in this case, it seems that workshop ownership might have been within the reach of some potters.

At massive worksites, such as the amphora kilns around Lake Mareotis, in Egypt, there were certainly workshops tied to larger operations thought in this case to have been part of larger estates. Some of these kiln sites, which encircled the lake, were in the vicinity of wine presses (Empereur and Picon 1992; El-Ashmawi 1998; Rodziewicz 1998, 2011; Babraj and Szymańska 2010; Blue 2010). Nearby docks are thought to have been used to distribute the filled amphorae. Considering this spatial contiguity, these workshops and kilns were presumably part of larger estates or specialized wine packaging sites. The kilns alone at these sites represented major construction works, with some being as large as 13 m in diameter. Given the scale and investment in such estate workshops, it is perhaps not surprising that these types of workshops (manufacturing jars for wine) are most typically referenced in preserved lease contracts from Egypt (Gallimore 2010).

Property Segmentation

In cases where there were multiple units working alongside one another as part of a larger property, it might be easier to claim that these segmented properties may have been rented. Several lease contracts dating between the second and sixth centuries AD from Egypt reference potters renting a fraction of the full property – namely, one-fourteenth, one-third, one-fourth, five-sixths (Mees 2002, 224, t. 75). It is not entirely clear how one-fourteenth of a workshop might have been physically distinguished from the other thirteen-fourteenths of the workshop (e.g., a single workstation, a complete work unit within the building); however, it seems clear that workshop properties could be divided and occupied by different potters working under independent contract.

At Sagalassos, there are examples dated between the fourth and mid sixth centuries AD in which ceramic workshops were part of a larger building complex. At the Molded-Wares Workshop Complex, four (or possibly five[2]) workshops were built on either side of a terrace wall. While at different elevations and accessed via two different streets, these workshop units nonetheless shared structural walls, product repertoire, and occupational phasing, and, as a result, they might be considered to have been neighbors occupying a single property. The units were not connected with doorways, and each was provisioned with the necessary materials, tools, and infrastructure to manufacture a similar repertoire of molded figurines and lamps, multipart (molded and thrown) pilgrim flasks, and stamp-decorated wheel-thrown platters (Murphy and Poblome 2016). The occupation of all units follows a shared chronological sequence (a mid fourth-century-AD construction for ceramic production, an early sixth-century-AD conversion of all units and their kilns to lime burning, and a mid sixth-century final abandonment). In this sense, the units collectively appear to have been managed as a single property and, during their ceramic production phase, they all manufactured a very similar range of products. This arrangement may conceivably be either a modal "manufactory" type of production or a series of leased units manufacturing a contracted repertoire (Peacock 1982; Mees 2002; Murphy and Poblome 2016, 195–96).

Institutional Involvement

While the Sagalassos workshop complex might be understood as a multiunit property complex or even a "modal manufactory," the working community observed at Gerasa (modern Jordan) in the repurposed hippodrome was a much larger and more densely occupied property. Here, individual work units

[2] The entire complex was not excavated, so the estimation of workshop boundaries is based on geophysical survey and changes in the modern surface topography.

were created under the cavea of the earlier structure. For example, during the third and fourth centuries AD, tanning and potting workshops were built within individual cavea chambers. Some units were used as houses, sometimes showing burn marks from a cooking hearth or small fire (Kehrberg and Ostrasz 1997, 169–70). An estimated one-fifth of the 106 cavea units served domestic purposes, including the house of a deacon of the nearby sixth-century church (Gawlikowski and Musa 1986; Ostrasz 1989, 55–59). Many of the other units were used as workshops, however; and, based on the appearance of several human burials (including those of children) associated with individual workshop units, it has been suggested that the potting workshops were family operations (Ostrasz and Kehrberg 2020, 311).

Among the hippodrome workshops, some work units were small, comprising the floor surface area of only a single chamber (ca. 3.6 m by 9.6 m), and some were larger, comprising the floor surface area of multiple chambers that were joined by doorways cut through walls. Beam holes in the walls (8–10 m tall) indicate the construction of an upper floor in some chambers (Kehrberg and Ostrasz 1997, 169). The builders reused materials from the hippodrome (Kehrberg and Ostrasz 1997, 169), and lime kilns found in the area could have supplied raw material for the tanners and lime for building mortar. Some of the workshops were provisioned with infrastructure necessary for tanning, others for potting. In some units, there were ceramic vats or stone basins; large basins also sometimes were dug into the floor, likely used for water storage (Kehrberg and Ostrasz 1997, 170). Lime kilns and pottery kilns were found on the external periphery of the hippodrome, as well as inside units (Units E29, E32, E40) (Kehrberg and Ostrasz 1997, 170). One group of three ceramic kilns was found just outside of a single workshop (Units E36–E38) (Kehrberg and Ostrasz 1997, 170). This variability in industry installations, the reliance on repurposed materials, and the "amateurish" construction techniques used (Kehrberg and Ostrasz 1997, 169–70) collectively illustrate that these renovations and work installations were not coordinated by the centralized property owner, or indeed according to any structuring authority but were rather enacted in an ad hoc fashion by the occupants themselves.

The example of Gerasa's hippodrome demonstrates the transition of an initially public building to ultimately private use[3] (including a short reuse of the northern arena space for public spectacle in the fifth century AD). The

[3] In the third and fourth centuries AD, workshops were implanted in the cavea and accessed from the arena. In the fifth century AD, with the reuse of the northern part of the arena for spectacle, the workshops moved outside of the building to the south end (and no longer occupied the cavea). In the sixth century AD, the spectacle games ceased, and the entire hippodrome was again occupied, but workshops remained outside the building, and the cavea was used to dispose of production waste and as domestic spaces (Kehrberg 2009, 496–97).

nearby placement of a church and a mosaic attesting to the household of a deacon living in some of the cavea spaces also suggests a role of the Church (for phasing, see Kehrberg 2009, 496–97). This process must have involved civic authorities and Church officials at some stage, even if the impact of that authority at Gerasa is hard to discern. This situation is consistent with the type of arrangement described by Saradi (1998; 2006, 186–208) in Late Antique cities, wherein formerly public buildings were sold or rented by civic authorities for private purposes. However, various institutions (e.g., civic, provincial, ecclesiastical, imperial, military) might be invested in more concerted, and potentially conspicuous, ways in ceramic production: as owners, investors, or consumers. Elsewhere, the involvement of these larger institutions has been observed in ceramic production via both the archaeological and textual records. The auctioned rights to set up a second-century-AD brick production and sales business in Kerketheoris, Egypt, demonstrates a role of urban administrations in this regard (Wipszycka 1971, 126–27). Furthermore, it has been suggested that the similarity in construction styles and organization of kilnworks at sites in the region of Ashkelon and Ashdod in the sixth and seventh centuries AD might reflect civic or imperial estate involvement (Safrai 1992, 322; Hirschfeld 1997; Gadot and Tepper 2003, 150–54). Imperial estates presumably also invested in associated ceramic container production, although their presence is less comprehensively documented archaeologically in the region.

Church involvement in production might be implicated elsewhere, using other bodies of evidence (Martorelli 1999). The Late Antique production of ceramic items decorated with religious iconography and small "souvenir" *ampullae* containing oil or water has been tied to early Christian practices, for example (Bangert 2010). However, a more explicit role for Church estates and monasteries in ceramic production has been documented at Korykos, in the form of a funerary inscription referring to a "potter of S. Theoiastros," a potter possibly attached to a monastery (Patlagean 1977, 167, f. 33, inscription no. 737). Several sixth- and seventh-century-AD kilns were also found in the area around the monastery of Saint Jeremia at Saqqara (Ghaly 1992). A coarseware workshop (from sixth to seventh centuries AD) situated only 12 m outside of the monastery wall at Deir el-Fakhuri suggests a close association between the workshop and the religious community, and the local toponym for the site translates as "the monastery of the potter" (Ballet et al. 1991, 140). Thus, religious, as well as civic, authorities frequently had vested interests in the systems of ceramic production.

Perhaps the most impressive archaeological example of institutional investment in ceramic production, however, is the legionary kilnworks found outside ancient Jerusalem and generally dated from the first to third centuries AD (Figure 5; Arubas and Goldfus 1995; 2005). Ceramic kilnworks associated with the legions have been documented in other parts of the empire.[4] They are ubiquitously massive in scale and appear to have been major investments on the part of the legions. These sites manufactured primarily ceramic building materials for military works alongside a range of pottery wares – wares that have sometimes (and problematically) been referred to as "legionary wares" (Ettlinger 1951; for more extensive discussion on history of term see Vamos 2012). It is clear that the Jerusalem legionary production site differs, not only from other production sites across the eastern Mediterranean, but also from its immediate antecedent at the same site: the potters' quarter established in the mid to late first century BC. The earlier workshops published by Rosenthal-Heginbottom (2005),[5] and Levi and Be'eri (2010; 2011; 2017), were modest independent workspaces manufacturing local types of cooking wares. The workshop plans published by Rosenthal-Heginbottom (2005, 230–33, f. 2–4) show workshops of one to four rooms and operating within a dense nucleated community.

Sometime in the first to second centuries AD (after the AD 70 sacking of the Temple), the site took on a very different organization, manufacturing a very different range of products associated with the *Legio X Fretensis*. This is evidenced not least by the appearance of stamped items bearing legionary insignia (Arubas and Goldfus 1995, 104–5). While the chronological specifics of the site are still debated (Magness 2011, 319–21; Levi and Be'eri 2017), there is little disagreement that the occupational history of the production site is connected to the wider events following the destruction of the Jewish Temple by the Roman legions and the establishment of a permanent Roman presence in Jerusalem (Magness 2011, 319–21). This example also highlights the intrusive nature of these Roman imperial activities; the imposition of the military workshop spaces on the site of the earlier local production center appears abruptly in the archaeological record through the intentional clearance of a portion of the earlier potters' quarter. This clearance was achieved by levelling several walls, reusing sections of earlier structures, filling a mitzvah (ritual bath), and constructing an immense battery of kilns (Arubas and Goldfus 1995). In short, the establishment of the military kilnworks represents a rapid and substantive change not only in potting tradition but also in the local industrial

[4] The role of the military in establishing kilnworks has also been identified at Holt in the UK (Grimes 1930) and Holdeurn in the Netherlands (Holwerda and Braat 1946) and has been suggested for Vindonissa at Hunzenschwil-Rupperswil (Schaer 2005; Arnold 1966) and Aquincum (Vamos 2012).

[5] Nearby, additional civilian workshops, which appear to have continued after the legionary production and which may have operated contemporaneously with the legionary kilnworks, were excavated and preliminarily published by Levi and Be'eri (2010; 2011; 2017). These have similar characteristics in terms of size and infrastructure as those published by Rosenthal-Heginbottom (2005).

topography.[6] This worksite moreover presents several unusual features (volume of production, abrupt property transformation, scale of investment in infrastructure, and range of product repertoire) that seem to reflect the role, interests, and capital of the military. While it remains the only military kilnworks found (to date) in the eastern Mediterranean, it also finds parallels with other legionary kilnworks documented from other regions and therefore appears to have been influenced by similar considerations.

COMPLICATING THE MODEL

Interpreting archaeological contexts and structural remains has provided a means to consider the property arrangements and involvement of institutions, as well as the possible statuses of and relations among workers. These observations in many respects parallel the classification types of Peacock's "modes of production" (1982). Nearly all of those modes (i.e., household industry, individual workshops, nucleated workshops, manufactory, estate production, military and official production) can be interpreted in the archaeological record of the region. Yet the variables helping to define these categories are complicated by archaeological evidence of work practice. These outliers are significant in that they provide a means to identify alternative practices and arrangements that challenge our assumptions regarding workshops and their operations. In this sense, Peacock's model is used not as an interpretive outcome but rather as the starting point for deeper sociocultural analysis.

Alternative Spaces and Alternative Organizations

The greatest outlier among the workshops from the region is the military kilnworks situated outside ancient Jerusalem. The unusual size of the site has already been noted, but the organization of production is also unusual. Certain parts of the production process, in particular clay preparation and kiln firing, appear to have occurred in large common areas, while the intermediary forming stages were conducted in sets of smaller rooms located in the southwest areas of the worksite (Figure 5). The pooled infrastructure for clay preparation and kiln firing suggests that the entire organization of labor for these stages was centrally organized in order to support the other stages of production (forming and finishing objects) by specialized workgroups. This relationship of space to task is significant in that it involves not only a centralized organization on a very large scale but also flexibility in labor distribution between highly skilled and less skilled labor demands. This distribution was such that unskilled labor could

[6] It has been suggested that these workshops and the later reestablishment of small-scale production sites approximately 100 m to the south continued in operation alongside the large legionary kilnworks (Levi and Be'eri 2011, f. 1; Cohen-Weinberger et al. 2020).

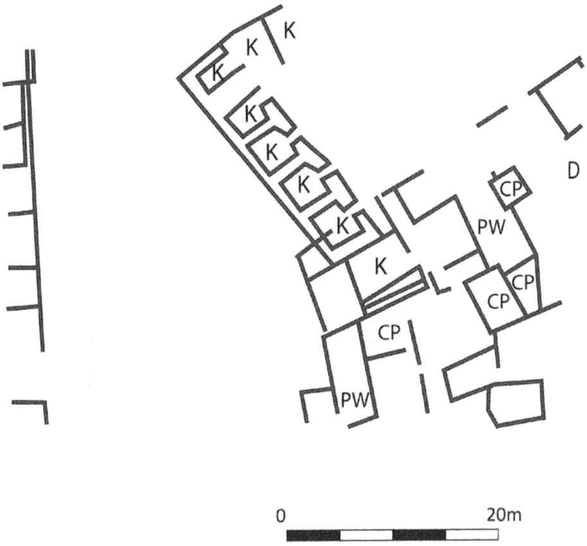

5 Plan of Jerusalem *Legio X Fretensis* Kilnworks [K: Kiln, PW: Pottery Wheel Room, CP: Clay Preparation, D: Drying Area]. (Arubas and Goldfus 2005, 6, f. 1)

be easily rotated into the labor-intensive processing of clay, the preparation of fuel, and the feeding of kilns.

Other alternative arrangements can also be observed at other sites (see Figure 6 and Table 1). For example, not all tasks were necessarily performed within a built structure. Enclosed courtyards or adjacent outside areas are evident at the Patara Northern Slope Tepecik Acropolis Workshop (Figure 6-h; Varkıvanç 2001–2002), the Sagalassos Molded-Wares Workshop Complex (Figure 6-p; Murphy and Poblome 2016), the Ketios Valley Workshop 3 (Figure 6-k; Bounegru 2009, 77–78), the Hierapolis Frontinus Street "houses" (Figure 6-c and Figure 6-d; Mastronuzzi and Melissano 2007), and at Khirbet Baraqa (Gadot and Tepper 2003, 134).[7] While these outside or partially open-air areas were smaller than many modern workshop examples, they nonetheless hosted important work tasks: not only kiln firing but also clay preparation at Ketios Valley Workshop 3 (Figure 6-k; Bounegru 2009, 77–78), vessel drying at Ketios Valley Workshop 4 (Figure 6-m; Bounegru 2009, 77–78), and fuel storage at Elaiussa-Sebaste (Figure 6-i; Borgia and Iacomi 2010, 1037–38). The informal use of nearby community space, even public streets, as extensions of the workshop has been commonly observed ethnographically.[8] This might also have been the case in antiquity, yet these

[7] The low number of workshops represented here is due to the fact that the adjoining outdoor areas of workshops are not typically included in excavation.

[8] Ethnographic examples include workshops at Oristano, Sardinia (Annis 2007, 122, f. 184), and at Udaipuri, India (Kramer 1997, 62–65).

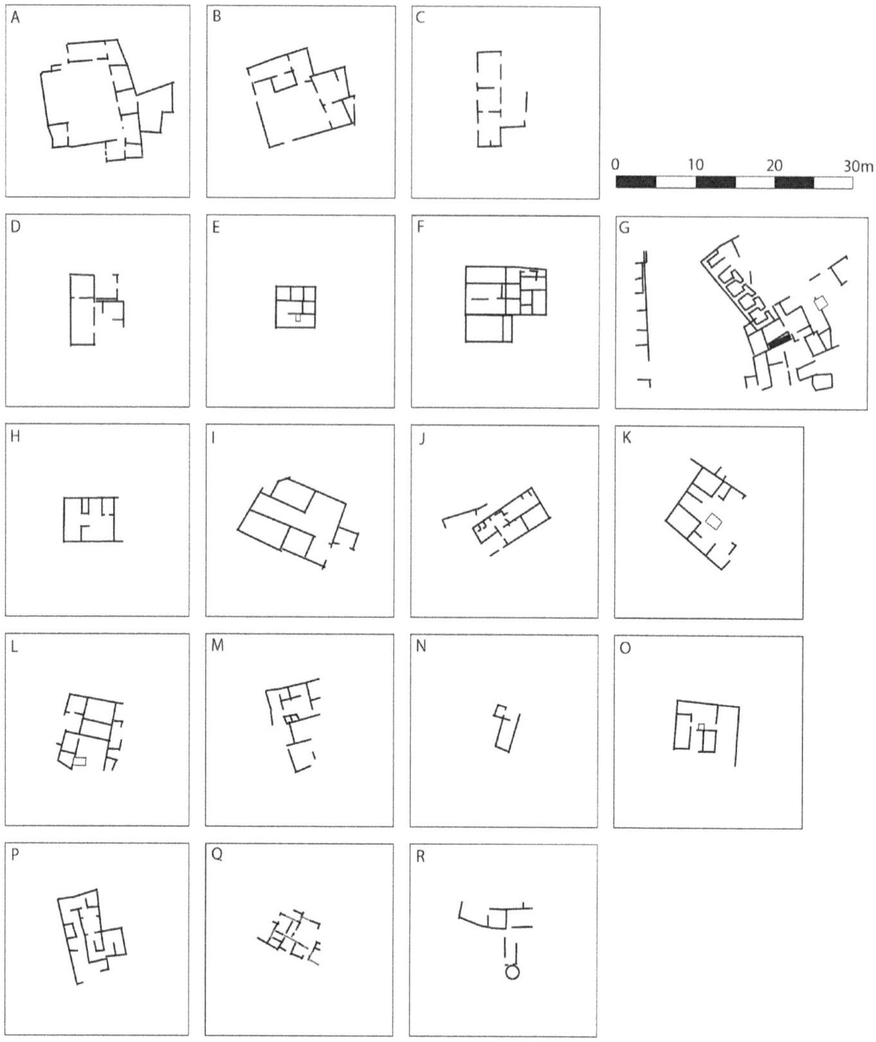

6 Plans of workshops described in the text representing variability in size and spatial organization: Dura-Europos Workshop 1 (a), Workshop 2 (b) [Based on Allara 1992, 105, f. 2]; Hierapolis Frontinus Street North Unit (c), Frontinus Street South Unit (d) [Based on Mastronuzzi and Melissano 2007, 543, f. 2]; Elkab House F (e) [Based on Hendrickx 1998, 1360, f. 2], Elkab House A-B (f) [Based on Hendrickx 1998, 1364, f. 3–4]; Jerusalem *Legio X Fretensis* Kilnworks (g) [Arubas and Goldfus 2005, 6, f. 1]; Patara Northern Slope Tepecik Acropolis Workshop (h) [Based on Varkıvanç 2001–2002, 146, f. 1]; Elaiussa-Sebaste (i) [Based on Borgia and Iacomi 2010, 1031, f. 2]; Elusa (j) [Based on Bucking and Goldfus 2012, 60, f. 9]; Ketios Valley Workshop 3 (k), Workshop 2 (l), Workshop 4 (m) [Based on Bounegru 2009, 89, f. 2], Ephesos Terrace House 2 (n) [Based on Ladstätter 2011, 16, f. 17]; Sagalassos East Slope Tableware Workshop (o) [Sagalassos Archaeological Research Project], Molded-Wares Workshop Complex, SW Unit (p) [Sagalassos Archaeological Research Project]; Shiḥin (q) [Based on Strange and Aviam 2017, 66, f. 3]; Petra (r) [Based on ʻAmr 1991, 314, f. 1]

are intrinsically difficult to detect archaeologically, particularly as these outdoor areas have not always been excavated. However, at Elkab second-century-AD bread ovens were installed in streets in a quarter of the village occupied by potters, suggesting an informal use of community space (Hendrickx 1998, 1356). The existence of outdoor pottery workspaces was also found at the Ketios Valley Workshop 2 (Figure 6-l), which maintained kilns that opened onto yards and alleyways running between workshop buildings (Bounegru 2009, 76–77). At Elusa, workshop activities were documented well beyond the interior walls (Figure 6-j); the excavations found not only an outdoor courtyard space but also kilns built outside of the courtyard (Bucking and Goldfus 2012, 49–50, f. 3).

Elsewhere, there is compelling evidence for a spatially dispersed production cycle, as it appears that some workshops were simply missing critical pieces of infrastructure. This could be a consequence of poor preservation or partial excavation but, in a few instances, it seems more likely that the missing infrastructure reflects an alternative work arrangement. For instance, at Ketios Valley Workshop 2 (Figure 7), there were two architecturally segregated units in the same structure. Each unit (north and south) was of roughly similar size (90 versus 94 m^2) and conducted complementary segments of the production process (Bounegru 2009, 76–77); the south unit possessed large clay basins and fuel storage space, while the north unit was equipped for throwing. While architecturally unconnected in terms of accessways, their proximity and complementary infrastructure suggests they were integrated in terms of workflow patterns (Bounegru 2009, 77). Here, we might support some sort of collaborative work arrangement of material supply between units.

There are also several instances in which kilns are absent from the workshop spaces. At Dura-Europos (Baird 2007, 419–20) and at Caesarea (Sussman 1980), shop spaces were found with molds, but no kilns. It has been assumed that

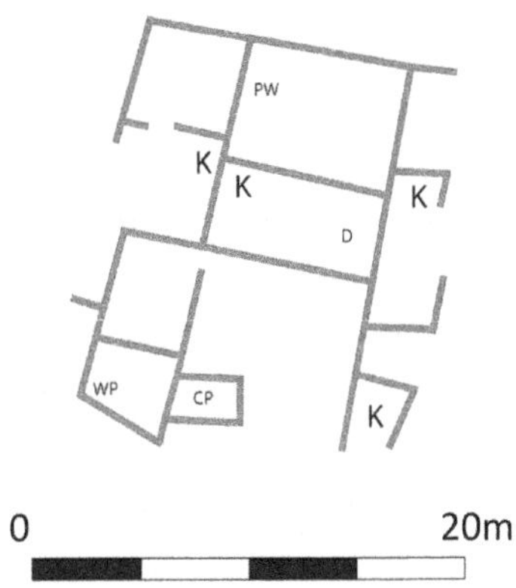

7 Plan of Ketios Valley Workshop 2 [K: Kiln, PW: Pottery Wheel, CP: Clay Preparation, WP: Waterpipe with Pithos, D: Drying Area, St: Storage]. (Based on Bounegru 2009, 89, f. 1)

these workspaces relied on kilns positioned away from the workshop structures, and indeed at Elkab, small ovens were found in the vicinity of the house-workshops, but with only a one-meter diameter they would have been insufficient to fire the workshops' jars in any quantity (Hendrickx 1998, 1359). A more likely candidate for firing the jars was a large kiln with a six-meter diameter found on the northern edge of the village, away from the known workshops. The area was covered with production waste and was thought to contain more such kilns (Hendrickx 1998, 1358). At Buto, a cluster of inwards-facing kilns was considered to be part of a single contemporaneous organization, yet the manufacturing buildings (for forming, drying, and storing) were not found in excavations (Ballet et al. 2019, 61).[9] It was thought that these sets of activities occurred in different sectors of the urban industrial area (Ballet et al. 2019, 288). At Patara's Northern Slope Tepecik Acropolis Workshop, the workshop also lacked a kiln within its immediate property, but it was thought that the workshop might have used a tile kiln located in the nearby necropolis area (Varkıvanç 2001–2002, 138–39, 145). The physical separation of workshops from kilns has been observed at several sites and implies a spatially dispersed *chaîne opératoire*. Again, significant heterogeneity at a granular level is evident.

While separate kilns might be owned by a single workshop, they also might have been organized in ways that are inconsistent with an independent workshop model. At Buto, the two batteries of kilns – five kilns (F3, F4, F5, F6, and F7) to the east and two kilns (F40, F36) to the west – were found in a single excavation area (Area P1) (Ballet et al. 2019, 53–65). The production waste in the surroundings represented a tight chronological phase (second half of the first century AD to early/first half of the second century AD) (Ballet et al. 2019, 130, 132–33), and all the kilns were constructed in the same style. There was no evidence of associated workspaces for forming, drying, or storing vessels. Given the scale of these kiln complexes (and in contrast to other contexts that contained one or two kilns), it has been proposed that this might represent either part of a single large-scale workshop property (with related workspaces situated elsewhere) or a scenario in which the kilns were rented by potters working to order (Ballet et al. 2019, 288). A similar battery of kilns was also noted at Patara, with a complex of five kilns, while most other workshops at that site were supplied with only one or two kilns (Dündar 2015).

This spatially dispersed production process surely has implications in terms of archaeological reconstructions, but there are also implications for the social and economic organization of this production, as well as possible community norms restricting where kilns could be positioned (considered further in

[9] Some of the areas around the kilns were possibly used for storage and dumping (Ballet et al. 2019, 61).

Chapter 8). The precise details of the ownership or management of such kiln complexes are unclear, but perhaps a communal or contractual arrangement might be feasible. Hawkins (2012, 178–82) has suggested that subcontracting of work tasks might have been a feature common to Roman crafts production (particularly in the production of complex luxury items). In an arrangement that he describes as "disintegrated production" he argues, based on evidence of highly specialized job titles and details of contracting, that the movement of semifinished products between worksites may have been a regular practice in the Roman world. Thus, while ceramic production seems far removed from luxury "composite" goods, more complicated production organization arrangements might be reflected in these spatially dispersed workshop infrastructures.

The specialized task of kiln firing is in fact known and better documented at Roman sites from the western provinces, most notably at the GTS production center at La Graufesenque (Marichal 1988, 103–10; Mees 2002). Here, vessels were inscribed *praecottura*, with lists naming potters, types of vessels, and numbers. These kiln dockets are thought to have been an accounting practice whereby individual potters contributed unfired vessels to a large kiln load that was then fired by a specialized kiln operator (Marichal 1988). At La Graufesenque, multiple names also sometimes appeared on a single stamp that was then impressed into wet vessels. These multi-name stamps suggest that potters were working in association, perhaps under a supervisory "foreman" (Hartley 2002). Comparable epigraphic evidence is largely lacking for the eastern provinces, but a list (of seven lines written in Greek) inscribed on the surface of a locally produced vessel was found at the workshops in the Ketios Valley near Pergamon. It has been proposed that this may have been a list of vessel names similar to the kiln dockets of La Graufesenque (Poblome et al. 2001, 156–58, 164–65, f. 19). Another likely kiln load list found on a fragment of papyrus has also been identified from Psabt, Egypt, and roughly dated between the sixth and eight centuries AD (Wilfong 2008). Rather than recording the contributions of vessels to a single kiln load, the Psabt accounts seem to record the number of vessels loaded in multiple firings (i.e., thirteen) conducted over the course of a work season. However, the papyrus is fragmentary and remains an isolated example from the site. While interpreting production organization with such limited evidence is difficult, specialized collaborative work or subcontracted work arrangements might again be conceivable.

The variability in organization and property management of workshops is also evident at the local level, with even neighboring workshops sometimes operating very differently. This is evidenced both archaeologically and textually, and adds further complexity to workshop clusters. Ostraca recovered from two workshop structures at Elkab, for example, demonstrate divergent organizations. One (House F) was an independent workshop and the other (House B) was a workshop with several potters working in neighboring spaces (Hendrickx 1998; Mees 2002, 319). The workshops located in Gerasa's hippodrome also show a substantial size range. Some workshops operated within a very small chamber of approximately 35 m^2, while other workshops in the same complex occupied multiple spaces, resulting in a larger (ca. 86 m^2) workspace (measurements based on plans by Ostrasz and Kehrberg-Ostrasz 2020). These differences may have been related to the different products manufactured in the units; a very wide range of goods was manufactured in the Gerasa Hippodrome. Alternatively, it could be because some workshops placed their kilns inside, while others used their kilns outside the complex (Kehrberg 2009, 495, f. 2).

At Sagalassos, differences in the organization of production have also been noted among contemporary workshop structures. The Library East Workshop was an independent unit manufacturing molded wares provisioned with stamps, molds, kilns (Uleners and Poblome 2014; 2016; Poblome et al. 2015). By contrast, the Molded-Wares Workshop Complex, which seems to have been a sort of "modal manufactory" as described by Peacock (1982), was a large building of at least four units each equipped with the stamps, molds, and kilns necessary to manufacture its wares (Murphy and Poblome 2016). As described previously, the units were likely part of a single property, and there is evidence for the sharing of stamps between units. However, among the three Late Roman workshop buildings of Sagalassos, the individual workshop units show remarkable similarity in size (Table 1). The Library East Workshop, which was part of a larger property and included a ceramic workshop alongside a textile workshop and a house unit, measured 50.7 m^2 (Uleners and Poblome 2014; 2016). Within the Molded-Wares Workshop (a property of 750 m^2 and containing four to five ceramic workshops), the South-East Unit measured 113 m^2. By contrast, the fully independent property unit of the East Slope Tableware Workshop measured 130 m^2. While very different property organizations, the three work units roughly shared similar dimensions.

At the Ketios Valley workshops below Pergamon, four workshops were excavated displaying modest differences in size, ranging between 184 m^2 and 250 m^2 (Bounegru 2009, 85). Yet, among the four workshops, there were strikingly different structural organizations. The largest excavated (Workshop 3) was a fully integrated structure laid out around a central courtyard (Figure 8). Workshop 4, by contrast, appears to have been two independent work units sharing a central storage depot (Figure 9). Workshop 2 (described previously) was also divided into two distinct units (Figure 7), but they were provisioned to support complementary work processes – one dedicated to fuel storage, clay preparation, and some kiln firing, while the other contained wheel-stations and kilns (Bounegru 2009, 85). This is

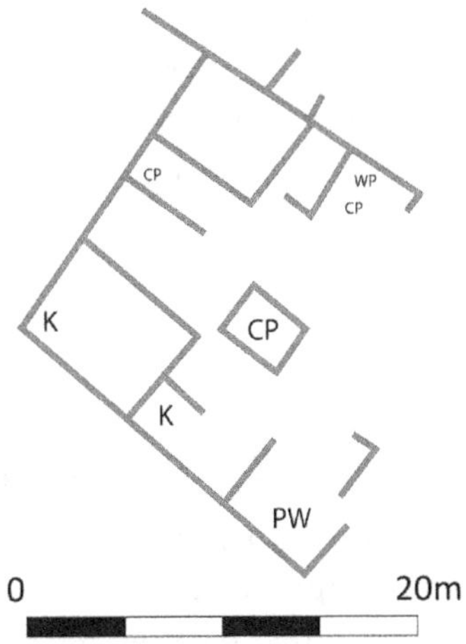

8 Plan of Ketios Valley Workshop 3 [K: Kiln, PW: Pottery Wheel, CP: Clay Preparation, WP: Waterpipe with Pithos]. (Based on Bounegru 2009, 89, f. 2)

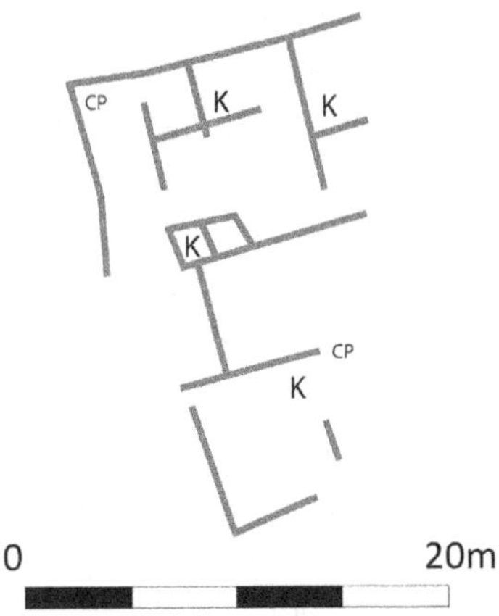

9 Plan of Ketios Valley Workshop 4 [K: Kiln, CP: Clay Preparation]. (Based on Bounegru 2009, 89, f. 2)

described by Bounegru as a "dispersed manufactory" in which the raw material supply and distribution of multiple units was coordinated by an external actor (Stillwell 1948, taf. 51; Bounegru 2009, 85). In this case, the size differences also reflected significant organizational differences.

These differences in the scale and structure of organization of production sometimes occurred among contemporary workshops – and sometimes even among contemporary workshops manufacturing the same items. When considering these workshops as themselves parts of larger clusters of workshops, this might imply associated workgroups that did not operate at similar scales of production and as part of a more heterogeneous community of workshop organizations. There were certainly workshops that functioned as independent businesses, but there were also complexes in which small units were only partially outfitted, requiring higher levels of collaboration with neighbors and sometimes episodic coordination of material and labor. This suggests an unappreciated dimension of difference from workshop to workshop, which exceeds singular variables of size, scale, or repertoire.

Life Histories of Workshops: Changing Structures

Other complications to the workshop typologies arise when tracking the histories of individual workshops. General classifications of the sort outlined by Peacock (1982), van der Leeuw (1977), and Costin (1991) are useful in comparing complex sets of variables between workshops, yet they rely on rather static interpretations of the archaeological remains that typically reflect only a single phase of production, often the final phase prior to abandonment. Papadopoulos (1995), in revisiting one of the modern workshops used by Peacock (1982) to construct his models, noted how significantly that workshop and its operations might change in just a few years, especially from one generation of potters to the next.[10] Life cycles and generational shifts, expressed through professional careers, become imprinted on the material world of workshops in ways that might reinvent a workplace. Rather than as fixed archaeological sites defined by their final abandonment, to the extent possible, these workshops should be seen as dynamic social spaces that framed and directed the daily lives, professional careers, and community histories of local ceramicists.

Workshops across the eastern Mediterranean witnessed generational shifts. Indeed, many ceramic industries of the eastern Mediterranean had deep and persistent roots at a particular locale – from the Hellenistic/Early Imperial period to the Late Roman period at Anemourion, Laodikeia, Sagalassos, Patara, Kibyra, and Buto. At Ephesos, similar clay beds are thought to have been used for local pottery production from the Archaic period through to the Roman and Medieval periods (Vroom 2019, 235). At Phokaia (modern Foça), ceramic production can be documented as persisting from the Hellenistic to the Mid-Byzantine periods (Özyiğit 2017, 125). Here, even individual parcels of land within these workshop clusters document their long-term use by potters. A plot excavated in the Atatürk District of Phokaia was occupied by three successive phases of pottery workshops (mid-late third century AD, mid late fifth century, and sixth century). Successive destructive flood events

[10] Papadopoulos (1995) returned to the modern workshop on the island of Thasos, which Peacock used to illustrate his "individual workshop" type (1982, 31), and Papadopoulos found a very different organization to the workshop fewer than twenty years after Peacock's visit.

covered each of the three workshops in a deep mud layer (Özyiğit 2016, 528; 2017, 116–17), yet the workshops were rebuilt, and the use of the area for potting persisted. By Late Antiquity at Sagalassos, pottery workshops had been present in a specific suburban area for seven or eight centuries – nearly twenty-five generations of potters;[11] Buto's workshops had been active for at least five centuries – more than seventeen generations of potters.

In Egypt, pottery workshop leases typically lasted for one to three years (Cockle 1981; Mees 2002, 254–55). In Judaea, they often covered a period of twelve months when using black clay; when using the scarcer white clay, the contract was valid until the clay supply was exhausted (Vitto 1986, 58; see also Adan-Bayewitz 1993, 25–26). Given these short-term leases and potentially high occupancy turnover, a leased workshop could have hosted many potters over the course of its existence. Even when a workshop was rented, decisions regarding workshop operations and renovation may not have been the sole responsibility of the property owner. Certainly, a leasing potter might offer input into how the workshop was maintained or renovated, and property renovations were sometimes specified in lease contracts, noting that the responsibility of these changes fell on the leaser. For example, a second-century-AD amphora workshop lease (*P. Mert.* 2.76) stipulates that the renting craftsperson would provide a roof for the structure (Gallimore 2010, 162). The renter would then be repaid by the owner for expenses incurred (Gallimore 2010, 162). Based on this text, it seems some workshops may have been leased in poor condition. It also seems that the potters may have had input into – and, in some cases, direct control over – changes made to their workplace, even in cases where they were not the owners.

As noted, the material record of these workshops sometimes extended across centuries of activity. Kilns – as built features hardened through habitual firing – provide good evidence for the changing use of space and infrastructure over time. The duration of a kiln's use depends on a number of factors: for example, materials of construction; duration, regularity, and temperature of firing; maintenance regimes. Once out of commission, shaft kilns were burdensome to remove, leaving a physical testament to the longevity of the workshop's life. To accommodate these ruins, disused kilns came to serve as waste dumps, clay-preparation basins, storage silos, or cisterns. At Demirci, for example, some abandoned kilns were used as rubbish pits (Kassab Tezgör 2010); this was also the case with Kiln I at az-Zurrāba near Petra (Zayadine 1986b, 186), with Kiln 118 at Saqqara (Ghaly 1992, 163), at En Ya'al outside of Jerusalem (Weksler-Bdolah 2016, 109), and at Elkab in Egypt (Hendrickx 1998, 1359). At the kiln site of Khirbet Baraqa, Kiln A was reused for other potting activities, including

[11] Generation here is defined by a period of twenty-five years.

clay-preparation basins for soaking and mixing clays (Gadot and Tepper 2003, 148). Other examples include the reuse of kiln structures as storage silos or (more likely) cisterns; Buto possesses two examples of kiln shafts relined for those purposes (Ballet et al. 2007, 141). The reappropriation of technology speaks both to an attitude toward the history of the workshop structures, and also the perceived opportunities that these features presented for alternative uses.

Kilns, as enclosed and sealed archaeological deposits, can also provide important evidence regarding the final closure of a workshop and the final actions by the occupants before leaving. The purposeful blocking of kiln stoke holes during abandonment has been observed at several sites. The filling and blocking of the stoke hole were among the final actions of the workers that can be archaeologically documented, and the clear intentionality of this action has been noted by excavators. In some cases, this blockage was likely left after the final firing of the kiln. By blocking the stoke hole at the end of the firing, the heat would then slowly and gradually dissipate while preventing any further air draft that might result in thermal shocks to the still hot vessels (Erlich 2017, 199). The closing of the stoke hole in the final stage of firing is certainly documented ethnographically, and archaeological examples of stacks of brick at Khirbet 'Azzun (Erlich 2017, 199), mudbricks (Ashkelon; Israel and Erickson-Gini 2013), dressed stones (Khirbet Baraqa; Gadot and Tepper 2003), or stone walls (Horbat Gelilot; Ayalon and Levy 2011), and a single stone slab at Horvat 'Uza (Getzov 2019, 7) might represent such practices. Thus, it is conceivable that the remains found archaeologically simply reflect the kiln blockage(s) left in place after the final firing of the kiln.

In other examples, however, the filling of the stoke hole may reflect a practice more directly tied to the formal abandonment and "closing" of the workshop. At Sagalassos' East Slope Tableware Workshop, a stack of vessels was placed inside the stoke hole, but the interior of the kiln's chamber was devoid of ash and charcoal, suggesting the vessels had been placed there after the kiln was cleaned. The cleaning of kilns may reflect the sort of abandonment practices outlined in a third-century pottery workshop lease contract from Oxyrhynchus. This document records that the potter will leave the workshop at the end of the lease term "free from ash and sherds" (Cockle 1981, 90; J. Poblome, pers. comm.), and in so doing, it attests to the expected final actions leaving a workshop that had been constructed more than a century prior.

The robusticity of a kiln also means that it often endured long after potters moved on and in this way, become a lasting trace – a sort of postscript of the workshop – that was later employed in innovative ways by subsequent inhabitants. These kilns could therefore have "lives" well beyond that of their associated workshop. On the southwest shore of Lake Mareotis,[12] an especially large Roman amphora kiln (8 m in diameter) was used as the foundation for a later church apse (Babraj and Szymańska 2010, 82–83), with the kiln's elevated floor found immediately under the Christian burials. In other cases, the workshop and its infrastructure might be reemployed for other industry uses. At the workshops at Saqqara at the Monastery of Jeramia in the sixth–seventh centuries AD, a kiln (Kiln 117) with lime across the chamber floor was identified, arguably representing a pottery kiln renovated for burning lime (Ghaly 1992, 162–63). The renovation of a pottery kiln for lime was also speculated with the "Axial Channel" kilns at Buto in the second–fourth centuries AD (Area P4, Kilns F2 and F3; Ballet et al. 2007, 142–43; Ballet et al. 2019, 150–58).

Sagalassos presents an example of a highly organized industry reappropriation. Here, eight kilns were found with lime residue across their combustion chamber floors. These represented refashioned pottery kilns from the earlier Molded-Wares Workshop Complex (Murphy and Poblome 2016; 2021). In the best preserved example, it was possible to reconstruct how this conversion was accomplished (Figure 10); the raised floor and central column were pulled out of the kiln creating an uninterrupted vertical shaft, leaving only the remains of a slight ledge where the elevated floor had been (Murphy and Poblome 2016; 2021). In the inner rooms of one workshop, piles of rubblerock had been found on the final phase of the floor levels and may have been the stock for lime burning. The conversion of all the kilns to lime seems to occur in the same phase, indicating a centralized change across the entire complex from ceramic to lime production in the mid to late sixth century AD. Each pottery kiln was relatively small (all had interior diameters of less than 1.3 m), so the use of pottery kilns would have yielded small lime charges (Murphy and Poblome 2016; 2021). In this case, kiln structures linked the industrial histories of the community.

MODELLING RESOURCE PROCUREMENT

Production organization models and property management models are not the only models to have been applied to Roman ceramic production. Resource procurement and site catchment models have also successfully related spatial data to economic exploitation. Yet these reconstructions too can offer useful starting points for alternative cultural interpretations.

In building a predictive map of Roman pottery kiln installations, the Service Régional de l'Archéologie (SRA) of the Lorraine region (northeast France)

[12] The site's identification is contested, but it has been proposed as ancient Marea (for discussion, see Babraj and Szymańska 2010, 77–78).

10 Photo of repurposed pottery kiln used for lime burning. Traces of the (removed) upper firing chamber floor are visible on the wall, as well as deposits of lime on the lower combustion chamber floor. (Sagalassos Archaeological Research Project)

designed a model of locational factors with which to identify and protect ancient kiln sites from modern development projects (Verhagen and Gazenbeek 2006). The critical factor that the project saw as determining Roman workshop location was vicinity to water and clay sources, variables which incidentally often co-occurred in valleys and around spring sites. In the SRA model, proximity to ancient fuel, particularly firewood, was deemed too difficult to reconstruct across the region for antiquity, and accessibility to roadways was considered of secondary importance, as products could more easily be transported to market than the bulky raw materials transported to the worksite (Verhagen and Gazenbeek 2006, 452). When tested by ground survey, the model showed some success in identifying kiln sites. It also suggested a locational preference for a particular type of clay (*sables vert*) found only in certain parts of the region (Verhagen and Gazenbeek 2006, 452). The results of the SRA model confirmed how resource catchment – particularly of clays – might be critical in determining where Roman workshops in the region developed. Such resource catchments have been observed ethnographically as well, with clay, again, being seen as especially important. Arnold (1985, 38–51), for example, noted clay-exploitation distance thresholds within which modern potters might travel (without the aid of modern vehicles) to retrieve their primary clays. Most documented ethnographic cases (84 percent) were under 7 km from the primary clay source, and one-third was within 1 km (Arnold 1985, 50; 2006). The establishment of pottery industries in proximity to these bulk raw materials is and was both efficient and pragmatic.

In the eastern Mediterranean, the natural distribution of clay and water resources, as well as a locational preference for particular types of clay, had implications for geographies of production at a regional scale that perhaps parallel the SRA model for Lorraine. In Egypt, for example, concentrations of workshops have been found primarily in relation to major water systems, which not only supplied water but also deposits of clay. Workshop clusters have been found in the Delta region (Ballet et al. 2019), around Lake Mareotis (Blue 2010), along the Nile, in the oases, and in the littoral Marmarica region of Libya and Egypt (Rieger and Moeller 2011). Elsewhere, regional production geographies are not so clearly defined, but we still can observe that many workshop sites were situated next to rivers. This is the case with the workshop at Elusa (Naḥal Besor), Dura-Europos (Euphrates), Gerasa / Jerash (Wadi Jerash), near Pergamon (Ketios Valley), the Late Roman D workshops near the Kestros River, or at coastal sites such as at Pitane (modern Çandarlı) (Loeschcke 1912). Even at these sites, the water supply might be supplemented with wells, such as those at Dura-Europos (Allara 1992, 108) or with *pithoi* collection points, such as those fed through waterpipes at the Ketios Valley workshops (Bounegru 2009, 87–88). Thus, clay access was perhaps a greater locational determinant than water alone.

Fuel supply might also rely on networks that extended well beyond the workshop and into wider forest lands in ways that had lasting impact. That massive quantities of fuel might be consumed by a local pottery industry is evidenced at Demirci, where the charcoal remains from kilns demonstrate a preference for hardwoods, particularly oak (Emery-Barbier 2010, 39). The quantities of fuel consumed at Demirci were so great that they are thought to have had environmental impact, with an accelerated loss of the slow-growing hardwood forests and replacement by pine and other conifers. In the Sharon Plain (modern Israel), the consumption of fuel by Late Roman industry also has been attributed to the reduction of oak forests (Erlich 2017, 202). Clearly, over generational time, routinized *taskscapes* involving wood collection might instigate broader environmental and landscape changes.

At Buto, in the Egyptian delta, it was assumed that the workshops employed reeds, straw, and branch clippings as kiln fuel – resulting in sustainable firing but at relatively low temperatures (Ballet et al. 2019, 287). This local solution to supplying fuel in marginal environments relied on a wide range of ecological zones. The use of a range of fuel types is also observed at Aqaba, where agricultural by-products, especially olive pomace but also date palm and tamarisk, have been noted (Parker 2000, 378), while at Udhruh brushy pistachio sources were used (Killick 1990, 249–52). It was proposed that brushwood and straw were used at the kiln site of Deir el-Haggar, in the Dakhla Oasis (Egypt), due to the composition of ash and charcoal remains (Hope 1978, 199). Vitto (1986, 54) describes ancient Rabbinic references to wood and olive press cakes (pomace) used as fuel in the region for long firings (Mishnah Shabbath 3.2) and a more specific reference to fruit shells as fuel in relation to pottery kilns (in this case prohibiting the use of fruit shells in the first three years of production, but with the assumption that it was allowed in the fourth year). At az-Zurrāba (near Petra), ash layers within area A12 included no charcoal or large plant remains, but earlier seasons of excavation (in area A10) noted an "abundance of olive stones" ('Amr 1991, 321), likely from fuel use and possibly from later olive processing. Here, the excavators also proposed the use of wild bushes for kiln fuel ('Amr 1991, 321), although these represented a notably poor fuel source for long kiln firings. Kiln use of hardwoods appears quite rare in the archaeology of these regions, giving the impression that fuel selection was determined more by availability than by particular firing properties. These agricultural geographies were of course tied to seasonal pruning, and the preparation and drying of olive press waste set other seasonal work rhythms.

While adaptation to the environmental conditions is clear, the environment might also be reworked to accommodate the potter. At Qumran, from the mid first century BC until AD 68,[13] the pottery workshops situated in the Judaean Desert utilized complex channeling systems to transport rain-fed water that was first collected into reservoirs and then into settling basins near the workshops (Magen and Peleg 2006). As reconstructed by Magen and Peleg (2006), this system served to not only transport the sediment but also levigate and refine the clay for potting use.[14] The quantities involved were impressive, with just one reservoir (Locus 71) discovered still containing three tons of prepared potting clay – enough to manufacture many thousands of vessels (Magen and Peleg 2006, 110–11). These water systems required the adaptation of earlier water systems as well as a deep understanding of the local topography and hydrology.

In some urbanized contexts of the Roman eastern provinces, catchment models also prove less helpful in interpreting how workshops acquired

[13] The date of the pottery workshops is contested. Magness (2002, 64) sees the kilns as possibly already in operation by the Iron Age, although she admits the evidence is limited.

[14] For a critical review of the clay in the reservoirs having been used for pottery production, see Gunneweg and Balla 2010.

materials. This is, in part, because workshop clusters in closer proximity to urban areas sometimes needed to attain their raw materials from more distant sources; clays might not be just outside the potters' doors, or even down the road, and these workshops needed to be actively provisioned from around or beyond the urbanized zone. The clays used in Gerasa's long-running production were found all around the city, but they still would have required transport from extraction point to workshop (Möller 2017, 63). At Ephesos, local producers are thought to have used (in part) micaceous clays from the Kaystros Valley (Ladstätter and Sauer 2005, 152–53). At Sagalassos, two different clays (one for the slip and one for the body) were employed by the tableware workshops of the city yet, contrary to the SRA model, these were extracted from sources separated by several kilometers (Degryse and Poblome 2008). The clay used for slip was widely available, including in the immediate vicinity of the workshops, from where in the earlier centuries it had, in fact, been quarried. The more distant clay used for the ceramic body, however, was extracted from beds 8 km from the city in the Çanaklı Valley (Poblome et al. 2002; Degryse and Poblome 2008).

In unusual examples in which clays were transported many kilometers, the quarrying and transport may have involved specialists. Leases of rural (estate) workshops sometimes stipulated that the clays and fuel used by the potter were provisioned by the property owner leaving the potter little choice in selecting materials. There is an example of a late (eighth century AD) professional association of potters in Egypt paying tax on a property that is thought by Mees to perhaps refer to a shared clay quarry (*P.Lond.* 4.1419; as per Mees 2002, 220). Another document regarding brickmakers refers to what may be a first-century-BC dispute over a clay quarry and suggests competing claims to the property (*P.Tempeleide* 29; Mees 2002, 234, 386). Thus, while it is difficult to specify the actors involved, knowledge of these clay resources was clearly maintained over many generations, and in the Roman world particular clay quarries often were mined for centuries by local ceramicists.[15] While pottery styles changed, the resources continued to be utilized over decades, if not centuries, and the transmission of this knowledge about local clays at these centers must have been embedded in a deeper craft history maintained into the Roman and Late Antique periods.

[15] For example, this is the case from the Iron Age through Late Antiquity at Sagalassos (Braekmans et al. 2011), from the Iron Age through Roman periods at Jerusalem (Goren 2005), from the Roman period to Late Antiquity at Anemourion (Russell 2002, 225), from the Hellenistic through Late Antique periods at Patara (Dündar 2015, 203), from the Iron Age through Late Antiquity at Laodikeia (Şimşek and Bilgin 2018); and from the Archaic period through the Middle Ages at Ephesos (Vroom 2019, 235).

COMPLICATING THE MODEL: CULTURAL *TASKSCAPES*

As the SRA clay catchment model noted preferences for certain types of clay, comparable preferences for particular materials have also been observed in the eastern provinces. In these cases, it is also constructive to begin to assess how these differences and selections were made based on culturally embedded knowledge of landscapes and materials. The artisans of any workshop were dependent on raw materials, with their respective and variable properties and affordances. Numerous natural materials besides clay were brought into the potting process (e.g., organic fuels, tempers). Gosselain has described these work geographies of potters as *spaces of experience* (1992; 2008; 2010). Alternatively, Ingold has highlighted the lived experience of a productive landscape, what he calls a "dwelling experience" (1993) whereby the temporal rhythms experienced through the performance of daily and seasonal cycles of work helps to create *taskscapes*, mediated by the routinization of activities that are intimately intertwined with the natural environment (for archaeological application, see Rajala and Mills 2017).

The social relationships maintaining ancient *taskscapes* are difficult to reconstruct archaeologically, but at the regional scale some of these patterns of movement might be traced through the use of particular raw materials. Selection of clays, for example, are influenced not only by availability, costs of procurement, technical properties of the raw materials, but also the social understanding of local geographies (Ingold 1993; Sillar 1997; Albero Santacreu 2017). Albero Santacreu (2017, 509) has described these conjoining physical and social factors as *clayscapes*, as locations of procurement and routinized paths of travel and social encounters, which can be maintained over the long-term by communities of potters. In some cases, the experiential *taskscapes* of Roman potters appear varied and expansive. At Sagalassos, such clayscapes can be reconstructed through the material culture and raw materials of the workplace: clay from the Çanaklı clay beds in the lower valley systems 8 km from the city; polishing tools made from river pebbles retrieved from the river systems of the lower valleys; hand tools fashioned from hairpins and metal plating retrieved from the city (Murphy and Poblome 2012, 207–8). Such assemblages of materials help to reconstruct the work geographies of these potters within their wider urban and rural worlds.

In spite of selective procurement, naturally deposited clays are not internally uniform. Different beds of clay at the same location might have significantly different geological composition depending on when and how they were formed; different areas may be more or less mixed with sands or organic particulates; and the mineralogical composition of the clays may result in different colors and sintering / vitrification temperatures. However, the cultural understanding of these materials and geographies of extraction almost certainly differed from the ways that we, as archaeologists, discuss them. Ancient potters would not have articulated these preferences and differences in clay by the terms described today in archaeometric literature – for instance, according to kaolinite, smectite, and illite mineral classifications (Rice 2015, 35–60). Indeed, even modern potters describe clays according to embodied cultural categories of color, feel (plasticity), taste (some potters describe their ideal clays as "salty"), or by their response to production processes (if they crack when dry) (Nicklin 1979, 439). In modern Egypt, color is still used by professional ceramic industries to distinguish the (red and white) clays of Aswan (Mahmoud 1992, 183).

In antiquity, cultural understandings of materials and their properties were also often framed in terms of color and feel. A mid third-century workshop contract from Oxyrhynchus described the provisioning of "friable earth, the sandy and the black earths" thought to reference the natural mix of desert marl, sand temper, and Nile alluvial clay know to have been used for pottery production in Egypt (Cockle 1981, 90–93). A later (tenth century AD) compilation of earlier sources, the *Geoponica,* describes the use of different colored clays (yellow and white) that could be mixed (*Geoponica* VI 3, 1; Giannopoulou 2010, 49). Rabbinic literature described two types of soil, earth, or dust (Hb. *'afar*), here seemingly referring to clay – black clay and white clay (Tosefta Baba Metzia 6.3, 8.27; Jerusalem Talmud, Baba Metzia 8.8; Babylonian Talmud, Baba Metzia 74a; as per Vitto 1986, 51–52). The black variety was more widely available and is thought to refer to secondary clays enriched with impurities (Vitto 1986, 51–52). These different clays not only had different properties, but their use also had implications for the duration of lease contracts, with leases for potters using the more abundant black clay lasting twelve months, and those using white clay lasting until the exhaustion of its deposit (Vitto 1986, 51).

These references to color as a means of distinguishing the types of clay may reflect one means of knowing local materials. At Sagalassos, the two raw clays used in production are strikingly different in color, with the raw ophiolitic clays (which were bright red in color) used for slip, and the raw Çanaklı clays (which were distinctively blue-green in color) used for the body. Modern exploitations of the Çanaklı clay beds demonstrate that this type of blue-green clay was so distinctive that it stands out from the other deposits in the same quarry, which were not exploited for pottery in antiquity (Figure 11). A similar situation has been observed with the 'Ain at-Tinah (Arabic for "spring of clay") near Petra (Mason and 'Amr 1990, 288–89; 'Amr 1986; 1987). These 15-m-thick clay beds were exploited for over 700 years by the ceramic workshops of az-Zurrāba (Gerber 2010, 891–93). The natural deposits are complicated beds comprising clays with varying properties. Included among these layers were clays of different colors, with the green clays suitable for pottery and

11 Photo of modern exploitation of Çanaklı clay beds demonstrating the multiple layers of clay deposit, each with different properties and only one of which presented properties similar to the clays used to manufacture Roman-period Sagalassos Red Slip wares. (Photo taken by the author)

yellow and red clays unsuitable (Mason and 'Amr 1990, 288–89; Gerber 2005; 2010). There is some reason to suspect that these clays were purposely mixed, cleaned, and tempers were added, as the chemical compositions of those clay beds do not completely match any of those from ceramic samples (Gerber 2010). Over many centuries of use, there is also evidence to suggest that changes were made to the clay recipe at specific periods of time, particularly during the early first century AD and also in the third century AD – periods in which the production repertoire of the site also changed (Gerber 2005, 729).

Ingold's *taskscape* has come to be utilized as a means of understanding cultural perceptions of time and place as experienced through routines of work and daily life. The specification of the ceramicist's *taskscape* through the acquisition of clays and other materials further draws on cultural understandings of materials, their properties, and where they are found. In particular, the references to clays were experiential in terms of color and texture, and highly specific exploitation of certain deposits at certain locations evidence a shared knowledge of these resources. In these respects, catchment models become socialized *taskscapes* appreciated and understood through routinized experience.

CONCLUSION

Archaeological evidence for pottery workshops has been found across the territories of the Roman Empire, comprising a complex and diverse corpus with which to evaluate the organization of ceramic production. Modelling has provided an important means to grapple with such datasets, and the modelling exercises developed for Roman ceramic production have supplied some of the most important contributions to characterizing the industry of the period according to different "modes of production" and according to economically rational spatial patterning. These ways of describing and interpreting workshop organization have become fundamental to nearly any discussion of Roman ceramic workshops. This chapter began with such models in order to demonstrate that the widespread patterns observed in other regions of the Roman Empire can also be observed in the eastern provinces. Indeed, household workshops, independent workshops, nucleated workshops, and estate and military kilnworks all can be observed in the evidence from the eastern Mediterranean. Property segmentation and leased spaces are also present. While those exercises serve to establish important baselines and criteria, not infrequently there are examples that fail to easily fit into the parameters. As such, these models provide structures by which to identify alternative arrangements and to evaluate how workshops might change and be altered over the course of their "lives." Importantly, these alternative narratives allow us to consider local work practices, innovative ways to arrange workshops, and changes over time that otherwise can be lost in larger narratives and modelling exercises.

CHAPTER THREE

PROCESS, PEOPLE, AND WORKING CONDITIONS

The essential work process of preparing clay and then forming, drying, and firing vessels can be reconstructed for most Roman pottery workshops, and it is similar in many respects to the process still followed by many "traditional" potters today (Rice 1987, 113–67). However, while these processes may parallel one another, culturally specific understandings of work tasks can differ and in ways that reflect variances in specialized labor.[1] For example, most modern professional potters – and ethnographers – describe six stages in the production process: clay acquisition, clay preparation, forming, finishing, drying, firing. By contrast, Rabbinic sources described five points in the production process: forming, drying, filling the kiln, firing, and removing vessels from the kiln – a sequence of actions more focused on the kiln and less on clay quarrying and preparation (Babylonian Talmud, Baba Metzia 74a; Vitto 1986, 51). Cultural understandings of the work process vary.

These cultural framings of the technical process find some parallel in the work of Pierre Lemonnier (1986), who viewed variations in production techniques as a consequence of local cultural technological choices. Lemonnier distinguished between strategic tasks, which are indispensable to

[1] In the earlier Greek context, Hasaki (2021, 19) notes that depictions of pottery making by Athenian potters and Corinthian potters emphasized different stages of production (throwing versus firing, respectively). She understood this as reflecting stages deemed more critical to their pottery styles.

producing a type of object, and technical variants, in which variable technological choices can be applied (1986, 155). All culturally embedded production processes reflect a combination of both strategic tasks and technological choices. Considering evidence from the Roman East in this chapter, there is local variation in the production processes that seems to reflect local technological choices. This can be seen when analyzing the techniques used by different potters to manufacture similar vessels, and it can be seen when comparing workshop infrastructure used to execute particular strategic tasks. Moreover, as with Chapter 2 (which evaluated well-established models and then supplemented them with deeper social interpretations), this chapter will further analyze these processes in terms of lived experience in order to demonstrate how different working conditions, tasks, and responsibilities affected well-being in the workplace.

SIMILAR GOODS, DIVERGENT LOCAL PROCESSES

All ceramics manufacturing requires some sort of clay collection and preparation, object forming, finishing and decorating, and drying and firing. The execution of these production steps can be achieved through innumerable combinations of techniques, to various degrees of elaboration, and using a multiplicity of technologies (Rice 1987, 113–67). Even similar vessel types can be made using varying techniques, and this variability has implications for the overall organization of production (e.g., investments in production infrastructure, use of specialized workers, timing of production steps). The interpretive implications of disentangling product types from production process are perhaps best illustrated with an example published by Ballet and Mahmoud (1987). They documented how similar products were manufactured contemporaneously at two locations by different groups of potters. By comparing the techniques of the two centers, the ceramic workshops at Abu Mina (located near Alexandria) and those at Elephantine (located near Aswan), it is possible to appreciate two local potting traditions that achieved similar goods in terms of function and style, but which did so using different techniques and process. Both production centers manufactured a range of molded wares from the fifth through seventh centuries AD. The product repertoires included a range of lamps, figurines, and pilgrims' flasks (*ampullae*, *oinophoroi*), and – based on the use of Christian iconography and inscriptions naming saints, bishops, and archbishops (Ballet and Mahmoud 1987, 56) – both production centers are also thought to have been supplying a similar consumer Christian market. The products from both sites used two-part molds, into which clay was pressed and then joined together to form the completed object.

In spite of these categorical similarities, however, the two production centers followed notably different production sequences in the forming of these items, particularly the *ampullae*. The Elephantine workshops employed molds into which the body, neck, and rim of the vessel might be impressed; after molding, the only vessel parts that needed to be added were the handles. By contrast, the Abu Mina production employed two-part molds that lacked the vessel neck and rim entirely (Ballet and Mahmoud 1987, 58). This upper section of the Abu Mina vessels would therefore have been made separately and then joined. Subsequent to these joins, the handles made at the respective sites would have been either pulled or rolled and then attached. At Abu Mina, this multipart process – pieces made by using different forming techniques (throwing, handmaking) – is also evident in the production of figurines of horsemen, animals, or standing women (either with hands to breast or holding a child). This process involved the molding of heads and bodies of the figures and the later application of hand-modelled arms and decorative details, such as hairstyles (Ballet and Mahmoud 1987, 60). These differing approaches to forming complex molded objects seem to reflect different local ceramic technical traditions with comparably equifinal products, underscoring just how many ways there are to make ostensibly comparable ceramic objects.

While we do not have the physical remains of the workshops making these ceramics, this seemingly minor distinction between similar molded wares nonetheless must have had significant implications for the workshop production process. These differing operational sequences or *chaînes opératoires* would have variably impacted the timing and phasing of production steps. If we lay out the operational sequences of forming these vessels (Table 2), it is clear that the Abu Mina process was not only much more involved, requiring several points of partial drying and reworking of the object, but it also would have increased the production time invested in each product. Moreover, the workshops at Abu Mina required investment in a pottery wheel and the skilled work of a thrower to form the non-molded neck and rim sections, therefore

TABLE 2 *Variable operational sequences of similar molded vessels manufactured at different Egyptian production sites, based on description by Ballet and Mahmoud (1987).*

Abu Mina *ampullae*	Elephantine *ampullae*
Pressing of clay into each of the molds	Pressing of clay into each of the molds
Partial drying	Joining two halves
Throwing of neck and rim on wheel	Partial drying
Partial drying	Pulling of handles
Joining neck and two molded sides	Attachment of handles
Partial drying	Full drying
Pulling of handles	
Attachment of handles	
Full drying	

also involving a different set of technologies and techniques. These contrasting production sequences are all the more surprising because the wares being compared were molded, a forming technique that inherently results in quite standardized products and offers fewer opportunities for formal innovation – at least when compared with hand building or wheel throwing, which are more improvisational forming processes. Therefore, in spite of the fact that these two contemporary production sites were down the Nile River from one another, that they manufactured a similar repertoire of functional items intended for similar Christian consumer markets, and that they employed two-part molds to do so – the resulting products were of notably different local ceramic traditions that must have relied on distinctive workshop organizations.

CONTEXTUALIZING WORK PROCESS

The foregoing example demonstrates the potential diversity in techniques and organization in producing similar goods, but there is of course much more evidence from workshops from across the eastern provinces that further demonstrates enormous variability in alternative work processes. In the dozens of pottery workshops from the eastern provinces, where architecture, materials, tools, and products have been successfully contextualized, daily work cycles, operational sequences, and human practice have become richly apparent.

These interdependent connections between work rhythms, operational regularity, and practice are most easily tracked in the case of permanent workshop infrastructure. Such infrastructure and equipment were embedded in the workshop's physical space; Egyptian lease contracts, for example, specified basins, wheels, kilns, water sources, storerooms, and other fixtures, demonstrating that they were understood as critical components of ceramic workshops (Gallimore 2010, 162–63). Infrastructure therefore should be viewed as intrinsic to the larger workshop structure, and any built structure ineluctably mediates the activities of its inhabitants, either by facilitating (through the construction of doors, stairways, and corridors) or by restricting (through the construction of enclosed spaces, partitioning walls, or blocked doorways) the movement of people and materials.

With regard to how space constrains, directs, and facilitates the movement of bodies and things, access points for movement and intervisibility can be identified from the workshop structures. Built structures encourage or discourage movement and communication between specific spaces by setting them at a greater or lesser distance from well-trafficked areas. These basic factors (accessibility, visibility, and proximity) affect the use of any space. Workshops, however, represent a particular type of space. This is due to highly regularized movement and action associated with the production cycle and its infrastructure, the allocation of space being contingent upon workers performing certain actions in sequence and at specific points of time in relation to the changing properties of the clay material (drying, firing). In addition, workshops are also spaces occupied by workgroups that could carry professional distinctions (rank, age, specialized task). Accordingly, the way production actions are spatially distributed also reflects a variety of choices concerning worker responsibilities, and as intrinsically social environments, workshops reinforce different types of relations among co-workers.

Given certain shared needs to support strategic production tasks, it is perhaps surprising then that, in terms of overall plan, there is so little uniformity in how workshop spaces in the Roman East were arranged. Rather, each workshop followed a decidedly unique plan (Figure 6). Even at large production centers composed of multiple workshops, contemporaneous workspaces were designed and used in very different ways that speak to the diversity of organizations and processes within a local industry, as well as to the existence of disparate specialized labor structures.[2] Some workshops were composed of just two spaces, such as Sagalassos Library East Workshop (Uleners and Poblome 2014; 2016; Poblome et al. 2015), Ephesos Terrace House 2 workshop (Ladstätter 2011, 14, f. 17), Gerasa Hippodrome workshop (Ostrasz and Kehrberg-Ostrasz 2020, 425, f. 209), Patara Northern Slope Tepecik Acropolis Workshop (Varkıvanç 2001–2002, 146, f. 1). Others, meanwhile, had five spaces at Elusa (Bucking and Goldfus 2012, 49–50, f. 3) and Sagalassos Molded-Wares Workshop, SW Unit (Figure 12; Murphy and Poblome 2016), the Sagalassos East Slope Tableware Workshop (Figure 2; Poblome et al. 2001), while there were seven spaces at Elaiussa-Sebaste (Borgia and Iacomi 2010, 1030, f. 2). The size of the workshops, both in terms of total area and number of rooms, reflects both the size of the products being manufactured and the scale of production output (Table 1). Some layouts encircled open courtyards, for instance, Ketios Valley Workshop 3 (Figure 8; Bounegru 2009, 77–78) and the Dura-Europos workshops (Figure 3 and Figure 4; Allara 1992; 1994); workshops with courtyards also tended to be larger properties. Others, such as the Sagalassos East Slope Tableware Workshop, had a linear organization, with rooms leading back into a series of connected work tasks occurring in the back of the building, which must have been only partially roofed.

Assuming that the spaces containing kilns were uncovered (otherwise posing an intolerably high fire risk), many key workrooms appear to have been situated next to open spaces and thus could be provisioned with light through doorways and windows. By contrast, storage and drying spaces were typically tucked into corner rooms. Some storage spaces could be very large, reflecting

[2] The workshops used in this discussion include the more fully excavated examples for which room function has been attributed and which were constructed specifically as workshops in their first phase of occupation.

the size of products and probably also the regularity of sales or distribution. At Elkab, House B (with the extension of House A) was estimated to have a storage capacity of 1,000 vessels (Hendrickx 1998, 1368–69), and House F was estimated to have a storage capacity of more than 950 jars (Hendrickx 1998, 1365). The drying space of the molded wares workshop at Sagalassos, by contrast, was a small (6.74 m^2), windowless corner space providing a dark environment with cool, still air – conditions critical for drying multipart products with appliqué.

Clay Preparation

The first work task – in terms of the ceramic production sequence – that can be regularly documented in the archaeological record is clay preparation. Rarely was clay used in its raw state, and at most workshop sites some method of cleaning, preparing, or altering the clay would have been used. In this sense, the clay used by the potter on the wheel or in the mold was not an unaltered material but rather already a manufactured product in its own right, and the composition prepared was a manipulated recipe that nonetheless had some unavoidable variation between prepared batches. Likewise, clays might be mixed together to control for certain properties (Cockle 1981, 93). In Rabbinic literature, the prepared portions of clay, ready for forming, were described as "eggs" (*betsim*), perhaps a reference to their shape as well as their transformative potential (Vitto 1983–1984, 52).

Preparing the clays could involve any number of techniques, requiring variable investments in labor, time, and infrastructure. At Elkab, Gerasa, Pergamon, and Shiḥin, vats and basins were used to soak and "levigate" the clay by means of water. In this process, water was added to bring the clay into suspension; the coarse fraction was settled out, leaving clay-rich water (often suitable for slip) and the clay body. Once drained, the remaining clay could then be trodden in the basin (Hendrickx 1998, 1357). Other features, such as *pithoi,* might also be used to levigate the clay. At Khirbet Baraqa (Gadot and Tepper 2003, 148), an abandoned and partially filled kiln was reused as a large soaking vat for clay. At Sagalassos, simple disused quarry pits outside the workshop were thought to have been used for weathering, rotting, or soaking the clays to increase the plasticity of the clay.

Other techniques of preparing the clay were more labor intensive and could involve kneading the clay with the feet or hands. That the latter technique was employed in the ancient world was mentioned by Herodotus, who described the unusual Egyptian practice of wedging mud with the hands and kneading bread with the feet (Her. II, 36, 78; Neuburger 1930). The accuracy of his statements regarding Egyptian workers may be doubted, but his assumption that the opposite scenario (i.e., hand-kneading bread and foot-treading earth) was

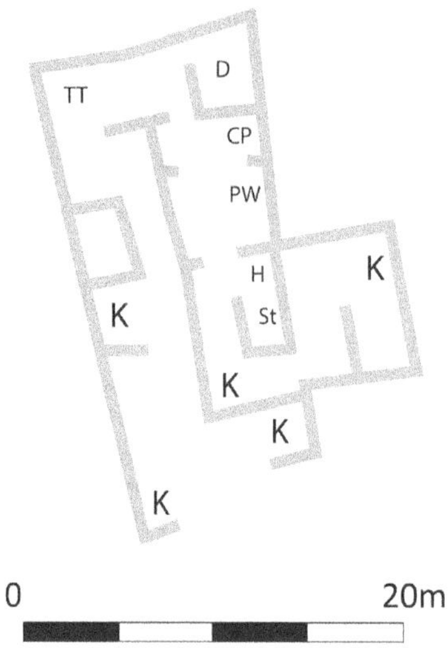

12 Plan of Sagalassos Molded-Wares Workshop Complex, SW Unit [K: Kiln, PW: Pottery Wheel, TT: Turntable, CP: Clay Preparation, D: Drying Area, St: Storage, H: Cooking Hearth]. (Sagalassos Archaeological Research Project)

somehow the "correct" way of doing things may be more telling. In fact, there is evidence in Egypt for hand-wedging clay; in House F at Elkab, a smoothed stone, found in proximity to the levigation tanks and the pottery wheel-station(s), offered a surface on which to wedge the clay by hand before it was put on the wheel (Hendrickx 1998, 1357). There is also evidence for foot-treading clay; at Sagalassos, an approximately 30-cm-thick deposit of prepared clay was found along the wall of the SW Workshop in the Molded-Wares Workshop Complex (Figure 12; Murphy and Poblome 2016, 192). Upright stones on the edge of this deposit seem to have helped support wooden planks in forming a low partition wall. This deposit was almost certainly trodden with the feet, and water contained in the basin in the corner of the deposit would have been incorporated into the mixture to increase the workability of the clay. Tiles found over the clay and near the door may have provided a walking surface over the deposit. This Sagalassos archaeological context presents a similar arrangement to that painted on an earlier Corinthian *pinax* dated to the sixth century BC. According to the reconstruction of that image by Hasaki (2021, 86–88, f. 4.2), a worker is shown treading a pile of clay on the floor. Like hand-wedging, treading of clay, as a means of incorporating water and adjusting the clay recipes, thus appears at some of the archaeologically documented workshops.

Within workshops, enormous quantities of clay would have been consumed, even when manufacturing relatively small objects. To provide a sense of the quantities involved in making basic forms, Rye and Evans noted that 2.5 kg of clay was needed to throw a single, medium-sized dish (diameter of 35 cm) in modern Shadiwal Village, Pakistan (1976, 60–61). Sustaining the preparation of such quantities at a rate necessary to continually feed the next stage in the production cycle could fully occupy some of the workshop's labor (Rye and Evans 1976, 61). With estimates of ancient kiln loads sometimes reaching the thousands of vessels, significant volumes of clay must have been moving through full-time workshops. Spatial organizations that facilitated and eased the movement of these large quantities of clay may therefore have been preferred, and this might explain why clay preparation and forming are often found in very close proximity, either in the same or adjacent rooms of a workshop.[3] At Sagalassos Molded-Wares Workshop (SW Workshop), the clay was trodden in the same room as the pottery wheels were located (Figure 12; Murphy and Poblome 2016); at the House F workshop of Elkab, the basins and wheel installations were also in the same room. The large sunken basins were 2–3 m in length, and some were provisioned with drainpipes. These basins not only served as decanters but also tanks in which the clay could be trodden by foot (Hendrickx 1998, 1357–58). Just before being put onto the wheel, the clay received a final wedging (by hand) on top of a nearby flat stone (Hendrickx 1998, 1357). By contrast, at the legionary kilnworks of Jerusalem, primary large-scale clay preparation appears to have taken place in a central area of the site. Smaller pit installations (ranging in area approximately between 1.46 and 6.8 m^2)[4] in the immediate vicinity of potter's wheels were likely for the short-term storage of and final refinement of clay for the potters at work. Notably, the main clay preparation area was not immediately accessible from the throwing rooms (Arubas and Goldfus 1995, 100–2, f. 6).

A wide range of techniques and features associated with this stage of production has been documented across the region. The level of investment of labor and infrastructure needed for these different steps reflected the qualities and properties of the clays, and differing levels of modification reflecting the different uses of respective clays (the pertinent technological traditions and knowledge are discussed in greater detail in Chapter 5). The arrangement of these activities would have had implications for the individuals performing these tasks, with clay preparation and wheel throwing typically occurring within a few steps of each other, thereby not only enhancing the efficiency of transporting clay to the wheel but also providing a ready supply of help to assist potters at the wheel. Moreover, this proximity would also allow the clay preparation process to be closely overseen by skilled potters working at the wheel.

[3] This is the case at Shiḥin, Sagalassos Mold-Made Wares Complex SW Unit (Murphy and Poblome 2016), Sagalassos East Slope Tableware Workshop, Patara Northern Slope Tepecik Acropolis Workshop (Varkıvanç 2001–2002), Ketios Valley Workshop 3 (Bounegru 2009, 77–78); Elkab (Hendrickx 1998, 1357).

[4] These areas were calculated from published plans of the site.

Forming

Vessels were formed using a number of techniques – hand forming (pinching, coiling, slab building), molding (pressing, casting), and throwing (free-throwing, mold throwing, throwing in parts) – any of which could be used in combination, even for a single vessel. Throwing vessels inside of a mold (in a so-called jolly arrangement) or finishing hand-built vessels on the wheel are both documented for the region. At Gerasa, locally made basin vessels were sometimes formed using a combination of coiling and wheel-forming techniques (Möller 2024), and clays of different composition and tempering were employed when adding sections to the same vessel (Möller 2024). A few vessels from the Roman eastern provinces were also formed entirely by hand, such as large *pithoi*, although their production sites remain elusive (Giannopoulou 2010, 49–50). Nevertheless, most of the archaeologically documented forming techniques were reliant on either molds or some sort of rotational platform – the most common being a potter's wheel.

In the eastern Mediterranean, certain parts of a potter's wheel – in particular the axle and wheel heads – were frequently made from organic materials and thus rarely preserved, and with so many critical parts missing, reconstructing the wheel design is challenging. For instance, at the amphora workshops of Demirci, an otherwise enigmatic large stone ring likely represents the lower socket receptacle of a wheel (Kassab Tezgör 2010, 97, f. 1). At Sagalassos, pits are thought each to have accommodated a sunken top-mounted wheel with a thin axle (Murphy and Poblome 2012; 2016). The few stone rotational heads that are preserved (mostly from Judaea/Syria-Palaestina) are all under 50 cm in diameter, and all were positioned in such a manner that the (now missing) wheel head would have been set close to the ground (Israel 1995). Several wheel features were also accompanied by a low bench or seat (Sagalassos [Murphy and Poblome 2012; 2016], Jerusalem [Murphy et al. 2018], Ketios Valley / Pergamon [Bounegru 2009], Demirci [Kassab Tezgör 2010, 97, f. 1], Mefalsim [Amiran and Shenhav 1984]). The general impression that can be garnered from the archaeological examples found in workshop contexts is that, where wheel parts have been definitively identified, there is substantial variation in their design and materials.

These common features of the wheels are consistent with the few preserved depictions of Roman-period potters at their wheels (Dufaÿ et al. 1997, 70–79).[5] Well-known examples include an appliqué on an African Red Slip ware bowl (Mackensen 1993, 65, f. 12) and the Pompeian wall fresco showing

[5] More images of potters exist from Classical Greece, and they are all also consistent with rod, foot, or hand-propelled types (Hasaki 2002). Foot-turned examples appear in early Egyptian figural reliefs (Rieth 1960, 48–49), and there is a Rabbinic reference to a potter turning his wheel by foot (*Ecclesiasticus Ben Sirah* 38, 29–30; Vitto 1983–1984, 21).

a work scene of *putti*-potters in the House of the *Vettii* (Peña and McCallum 2009, 68, f. 4). Such examples show potters seated on short stools, working at wheels of variable diameter and utilizing rods to propel them. These Roman depictions have certain similarities with rod-propelled wheels still used today in parts of Pakistan and India (Peña and McCallum 2009, 59–62, f. 5–6; Rye and Evans 1976, 87, f. 22; Kramer 1997, 62). As the examples of wheels found archaeologically were all sunken types and many had accompanying low stools, these were unlikely to have been "kick wheels," whereby a large lower wheel was kicked into motion (Loebert 1984).[6]

The means of propelling the wheel affects the speed at which it rotates, the time over which the wheel maintains its rotation and the consistency and regularity of the rotation (Rye 1981; Loebert 1984; Dufaÿ et al. 1997). These may have had organizational consequences in workshops with two different rotational wheel technologies of both fast- and slow-turning varieties – one for throwing vessels and another for trimming vessels in their "leather hard" state or for applying decorations. At workshops like those at Sagalassos, which manufactured molded wares with thrown parts and objects with both incised and appliqué decorations, a specialized turntable workstation may have been especially efficient, and the spatial separation of the two technologies presumably represented specialized work tasks. The two wheel types were moreover different in design and use. The fast-turning wheel had a thin vertical axle (likely in wood or metal) that spun on a small, receiving socket stone embedded at the bottom of a shallow pit. The wheel head was likely made of wood and attached by a copper-alloy flange (Murphy and Poblome 2012, 201). The small pits found in several workshops were accompanied by a flat stone (presumably used as a low seat).[7] The second rotational technology is evidenced by vertical, column-shaped drums embedded in the dirt floors of the workshops[8] with a second flat stone (likely a seat) positioned a short (approx. 30–40 cm) distance away (Murphy and Poblome 2016, 193).[9] On the upper face of the column support, a shallow dimple (ca. 10 cm diameter) with a highly polished surface received the bossing of a turning wheel. Incapable of

[6] With the "spindle" or "kick" wheel, the momentum of the smaller, upper throwing wheel is maintained by kicking a large lower wheel into motion.

[7] These components and the appearance of small pits with nearby seats are all consistent with the type of wheel found in situ at a Roman-period workshop at Herforst-Speicher in Germany (Rieth 1960, 50–53).

[8] Examples have been found in a workshop east of the city's Neon Library and dated from the late fifth to early sixth centuries AD (Uleners and Poblome 2014; 2016), at the Molded-Wares Workshop Complex dated from the mid fourth to early sixth centuries AD, and the Tableware Workshop in the Eastern Suburbium dated from the third to fifth centuries AD (Murphy and Poblome 2016).

[9] One such seat was made from a spoliated column base (Murphy and Poblome 2016, 193).

sustaining a high speed, it seems likely that these supports are the remains of turntables or slow-turning "tour-toupie" (as described by Dufaÿ et al. 1997; for ethnographic examples, see Rye and Evans 1976, 87, f. 22).

Multiple wheel-stations of the same type suggest that several potters might simultaneously perform the same or similar tasks in the workshop, as they do in modern examples at Thasos, Greece (four wheels, Papadopoulos 1995, 597), Kangan, Iran (three wheels, Whitehouse 1977, 42), and the Dakhla Oasis, Egypt (Henein 1997, 185–88). The Sagalassos Tableware Workshop contained three wheel-stations and a turntable in one of its rooms (Figure 2). In the Sagalassos Molded-Wares Workshop Complex (SW workshop unit), one wheel, one molding place, and one turntable were found (Figure 12). In the legionary kilnworks outside of Jerusalem, the workrooms hosted even more pottery wheels (Murphy et al. 2018); at least nine wheel-pits were discovered across four rooms, with one room provisioned with five potter's wheels,[10] and each potter was supplied clay from a nearby vat (Figure 5). In this latter space, with four wheels occupied at the same time, the working conditions here would have been tight (an average distance of approximately 1.4 m, as measured from the center of the wheel-sockets[11]).

The identification of individual wheel workstations in the same room also demonstrates how differently work was socio-spatially experienced in different workshops – both in terms of the number of workers and the proximity of their workstations. To demonstrate, the allocation of space for workstations as spatially discrete throwing areas has been calculated from published plans, when possible, and in contrast to the 1.4-m-spaced wheels of the legionary kilnworks at Jerusalem, the private workshops at Sagalassos and Pergamon seem to have provided greater space for potters in the throwing space. Sagalassos East Slope Tableware Workshop offers evidence for four workstations (three fast-turning wheels, one turntable), and these were separated on average by approximately 3 m.[12] In Pergamon's Workshop 2 (North Unit, Room C), a throwing room (of 35.28-m^2 floor area) was identified with two stone platforms. One of the platforms (approx. 2.9 m by 1.6 m) was found in association with a perforated ceramic disk, and the other measured 1.3 m in width and ran the length (approx. 5 m) of the room. These give the impression

[10] Clear evidence of four wheel-stations was preserved archaeologically, but given the regularity in the spacing of those preserved wheels, it is clear that one is missing.

[11] These distances were calculated from published plans (Arubas and Goldfus 2005, f. 1) and yielded distances ranging from 1.26 m to 1.48 m (as measured from the center of the wheel-socket to the center of wheel-socket).

[12] These distances were calculated from excavation plans and yielded distances ranging from 2.57 m to 3.44 m (as measured from the estimated center of wheel-socket to the estimated center of wheel-socket).

of similarly spaced workstations and may reflect local expectations of working conditions in the throwing room.[13]

While many workshops appear to have multiple wheel-stations often in the same room, an Oxyrhynchus papyrus (*P.Oxy.* 3595), with its references to a potter (*kerameus*) and a hired "modeler" (*plastēs*), is a reminder that similar work conditions and performance of similar tasks still might not reflect equal status or responsibility in other regards. The same contract also mentions that the workshop employed "assistants" to perform supporting tasks. Mees likewise has suggested that in larger workshops, efforts would have been made to avoid using potting specialists to perform mundane and unskilled tasks (2002, 237). These less skilled tasks conceivably involved preparing and bringing clay, removing the formed objects to the drying space, and preparing fuel for the kiln, thus minimizing the potters' time away from their wheels. Similar arrangements are known from ethnographic sources of potters. At Bailen, Spain, young apprentices were charged with applying handles to jugs drying in the courtyard (Curtis 1962, 501), and at Kangan (Whitehouse 1977, 42) and modern Dakhla (Henein 1997, 187–88), assistants prepared clay and brought it to the potters at work on their wheels. In these cases, young apprentices and assistants were typically allocated different tasks from older, full-time potters, although over time they would assume work tasks with increasing responsibility. While requiring less skill, the activities of young workers were critical to the functioning of the workshop as a whole; they are nonetheless some of the most difficult to see in the archaeological record, appearing rarely to have been provisioned with permanent workstations.

Such tasks are typically undertaken by younger workers (at least in the ethnographic record) but specifically by apprentices learning the trade. Indeed, in antiquity, multiple apprentices might be employed in a craft workshop at a time, a group of workers with their own internal hierarchies (Bergamasco 1995, 126). Some apprenticeship contracts outline a gradual increase in the scale of compensation with each year of experience (Bergamasco 1995, 145, n. 28, 31, 32, 35, 36).[14] These apprentices might also have fundamentally different statuses, as freemen, freedmen, or slaves. As to whether apprentices worked under formal apprenticeship structure, as more casual family workers, or as wage labor is clearly hard to establish from the archaeological record alone. However, children were certainly working in such shops; fingerprints of children have been noted on pottery and lamps from the region (Vitto et al. 1980; Vitto 1983–1984, 60; Dzierzykray-Rogalski

13 These numbers are closer to those seen in the throwing "galleries" at Roman-period sites in other regions (e.g., Scoppieto in Italy, Rozier in France).

14 Curtis (1962, 488–90) documented modern workshops where, as assistants and apprentices acquire more skill, they receive higher rates of pay and increased status.

and Grzeszyk 1991). Otherwise, the presence of assistants and apprentices, who might not have held responsibility for a single work task or over a single workstation, remains frustratingly elusive archaeologically. However, as discussed in greater detail in Chapter 5, these were learning environments both for skills training and the broader cultural literacy of the profession.

Kiln Firing

The technologies of potting and ceramic work necessarily involve a range of built infrastructure (basins, water tanks, wheels), as well as smaller portable items (hand tools, molds). Yet the physical appearance of associated pyrotechnologies, red scorched earth and blackened kiln slag, is hugely conspicuous in the archaeological record and, consequently, such features tend to receive disproportionate attention in excavation reports. The exposure of raw clay to heat, however, does not need to occur in a kiln, or even in a formal structure, to result in viable ceramic. Bonfires, pit fires, clamp kilns, and single-chambered kilns are among the many means of firing ceramics; all have been well documented ethnographically and have been suggested to have been used in the Roman world (Peacock 1982; Darvill and McWhirr 1984, 254). Nonetheless, the use of purposely constructed kilns is overwhelmingly represented in the archaeological record of the Roman East (Table 3).

Essentially all kilns recorded for the period and region were (or are reasonably assumed to have been) updraft kilns. In this kiln type, the fire is stoked in a combustion chamber situated beneath a firing chamber filled with vessels. The chamber could be oval, circular, or rectangular in plan. In this arrangement, the draft draws the air upward to heat the vessels in the upper chamber. A variety of flue systems and floor support types have been observed in the eastern Mediterranean (Table 3). Due to the generally poor state of preservation, it is seldom possible to determine whether an individual kiln originally had a closed roof (which is simply no longer preserved); or whether it was designed so that the top would be closed with a nonpermanent roof that was dismantled after each firing; or whether the kiln was open and received a temporary covering (e.g., of tiles or wasters). Using the latter kiln design, it is more difficult to control the firing temperature, but such light coverings often allow the introduction of oxygen into the chamber, which could have been desirable for some wares (Hines 2012). In terms of construction material, across the region, kilns constructed in various combinations of stone, fired brick, mudbrick, mud mortar, and pressed clay have all been documented.

There are few discernible large-scale trends in changing kiln technologies in the dataset, either spatially or temporally. Different kiln designs and construction materials were used throughout the Roman and Late Roman periods, with implications for work practice associated with that variability. In terms of

TABLE 3 *Listing of kiln attributes represented in eastern Mediterranean workshops.*

Kiln Draft	Construction Materials (often used in combination)	Plan Shape	Number of Flues	Elevated Floor Support Structure	Superstructure
Simple Updraft: Ground Level	Mudbrick	Oval, Circular, Rounded, Pear-Shaped, Keyhole-shaped*	Single Stokehole	Transverse Arches	Open-Topped
Simple Updraft: Sunken Foundation	Fired Brick	Rectangular, Square	Double Stokehole	Central Pedestal/Column with Radiating Arches	Closed Vault
Simple Updraft: Rock-Cut Foundation	Stone		Side-Wall Vent Shaft into Combustion Chamber (Buto)	Central Pedestal/Column with Bars	Closed Vault with *Tubuli* (pipes)
	Reused Amphorae, Cut Tiles, *Pilae*		Lower-Floor Channel Shaft into Combustion Chamber (Buto)	"Tongue" Support Projecting from Rear Wall	
	Mudplaster			Pilasters Projecting from Side Walls	
				Internal Ledge along Wall	
				Internal Corbels along Wall	

*Oval versus circular distinctions are often ambiguous, and variations on a rounded form often appear at the same site.

daily operations of the workshop, kiln firing was a critical stage in production, not least as delays in firing had the potential to create bottlenecks in the production process and complicate storage and, ultimately, distribution. For example, Yannai (2012, 98) estimates that filling, firing, cooling, and unloading a large amphora kiln near Tel Yavne would take five days. Ethnographically, Hankey (1968, 30) describes a large kiln at Beit Shebab (Lebanon) fired for eight days and left to cool on the ninth. Workshops with only a single kiln necessitated fully cooling and then slowly reheating the kiln, which could take considerable time. Perhaps not surprisingly, among the archaeological examples considered in this book, many workshops were equipped with multiple kilns of similar size and design. With some workshops maintaining as many as four kilns – for example, Ketios Valley Workshop 4 (Figure 9), Workshop 2 (Figure 7) (Bounegru 2009, 76–79), Sagalassos Molded-Wares Workshop SW Unit (Figure 12) – it is hard to imagine that this would not have consumed the attention of several workers.

Variability in kiln size, in part, reflects variability in vessel size and ware type, and disparate use of kilns certainly affected work organization. At a workshop at Elaiussa-Sebaste, two kilns of a similar (rectangular) design and constructed of the same type of bricks were uncovered – one of 35.0 m^2 and the other of 1.05 m^2 (interior floor area calculated from measurements provided by Borgia and Iacomi 2010). The smaller kiln is thought to have been used for lamps, while the larger kiln fired amphorae and other larger common wares (Borgia and Iacomi 2010, 1048). At az-Zurrāba, two kilns associated with a single workshop had chamber floor surface areas of 7.44 m^2 and 0.64 m^2 (interior floor surface area calculated from measurements provided by Zayadine 1981, 351). In terms of work organization, the specialized use of kilns for different products also suggests that different products made in the same workshop might follow different production and firing schedules. At the legionary kiln-works outside Jerusalem, the scale of the kiln battery was notable (Figure 23), and – as with other features of the production organization of the site – the arrangement of its furnaces reflects a highly (likely task-specific) specialization on the part of the labor force working there (Figure 5). The excavators note different types of wares associated with different kilns (Arubas and Goldfus 1995, 104). Nonetheless, kilns of variable size (and even design) were positioned with their flues oriented in the same direction, resulting in a linear or U-shaped configuration by its final phase, an orientation that would have facilitated the management of the firings by a single workgroup.

The presence of multiple kilns at any site would necessitate more complex timing and labor rotations, and the spatial segregation of firing areas from other parts of the work process observed at so many of the workshops echoes the specialized title noted in the Oxyrhynchus papyrus – that is, the *hupokaustēs*, the "one who burns [things] up" (Freu 2015, 167). Given the long hours (even running into and over the night) required to fire a kiln to high temperatures and given the substantial quantities of fuel required, the kiln stokers may have been allocated additional, segregated space. The separation of kilns from other activities in the workshop could also reflect community cultural norms regarding furnaces (described in greater detail in Chapter 5). Yet the experience of the kiln firing could also be very different between potters working at different sites and according to different traditions, even in cases when kiln design was similar. Many kilns, particularly from Asia Minor, were either slightly below or at ground level and in well-ventilated contexts like courtyards. Other kiln designs are also known, particularly those in the Near East, which demonstrate especially deeply positioned stoke holes. This would have imposed different working conditions and bodily dynamics on workers whose tasks may, initially, seem similar.

PUTTING LABOR TO PRODUCTION TASK

These differences in the corporeal experience of kiln loading, firing, and unloading are only one dimension in which potters might experience work differently across the industry and profession; there were also other perceptible differences within the workplace. In discussing industry definitions in Chapter 5, it was shown that specializations among ancient potters and ceramicists were described in textual sources according to varied criteria, notably product type and industry supplied. Yet other textual sources also describe worker specialization according to work task. For example, a third-century-AD papyrus from Oxyrhynchus (*P.Oxy.* 3595), describing the lease of a pottery workshop on a rural estate (Cockle 1981; Freu 2015, 167), references professional differences among and between workshop colleagues. Several terms are used to describe specialized roles within the workshop. The text stipulates that although the lease is held in the name of a single potter, described as a *kerameus*, it uses alternative terms to describe additional positions that could be filled by other workers – "modeler" (*plastēs*), "assistant" (*hupourgos*), and "kiln stoker" or literally "one who burns [things] up" (*hupokaustēs*) (Freu 2015, 167). According to the distinctions made in this lease, there appears to have been some differentiation between craftspeople involved in different stages of the production and according to different levels of responsibility, skill, or experience. This is what Mees (2002) has described as *horizontal specialization*. He considers the use of the term *kerameus* as specifically referencing a trained professional potter, a term that is reserved for the leasing potter and possibly differentiating him as a sort of "master potter" (Mees 2002, 236–37). Moreover, plural terms used for each of the other three specializations suggest multiple individuals performing those manufacturing roles in the shop.

The differentiation among workers assigned to different tasks described in the Oxyrhynchus papyrus echoes the spatial layout of many ancient workshop structures. Within workshops, different tasks were separated into different spaces or rooms according to the ceramic production sequence (*chaîne opératoire*) – clay preparation, forming, drying, finishing, firing. The location of features (vats / basins, wheels, kilns) helped to anchor certain production activities within the workshop in ways that reflect the labor allocations of tasks and responsibilities (i.e., division of labor). The spatial reconstruction of the work process can then be related to other variables, such as individual work-stations, repetitious infrastructure, and segregated work tasks.

Working Conditions and Well-Being

The modern anthropologist of work, Vis, saw such spatially segregated tasks as translating the practicalities of work activities into labor relations inherent within the workgroup (Vis 2009). One means to begin to confront the implications of labor difference in and among workplaces is through different working conditions and the different physical working experience among specialized co-workers.

The artificially sunken kilns at az-Zurrāba (near Petra), and those across Judaea/Syria-Palaestina associated with Gaza Jar production, represent what must have been especially challenging working environments. The az-Zurrāba kilns are approximately 1.5 m below their contemporary ground level, while the Gaza Jar production centers[15] were dug to a depth of 5–6 m below the ancient ground level (Figure 13). The latter complexes, each with multiple kilns, were accessed via stone-walled passageways. The abandoned oil lamps found in one such passageway at Khirbet Baraqa attest to just how dark and challenging these working conditions would have been for the kiln operators. Confined to such a narrow, restricted subterranean corridor space, those working the kiln would have been exposed to very high temperatures with minimal ventilation. Local variations to the design may evidence that this was the case because, at a site near Tel Yavne, stone-lined windows cut into the roof of the access corridors provide light and ventilation from above, much like modern skylights (Yannai 2012, 96). While the depth of these kilns likely assisted in refracting additional heat (making them more fuel efficient[16]), these sunken kiln arrangements would have created constricted working conditions of extreme heat, darkness, and smoke for the individuals stoking the fire.

[15] These include kiln complexes at Khirbet Baraqa (Gadot and Tepper 2003), Giv'ati Junction (Baumgarten 1997), Khirbet Irza (Israel 1997), Ashkelon (Israel 1993, 1995), and Tel Yavne (Yannai 2012).

[16] The appearance of sunken kilns in the Levant has also been noted by Krogulska (1985, 65–66).

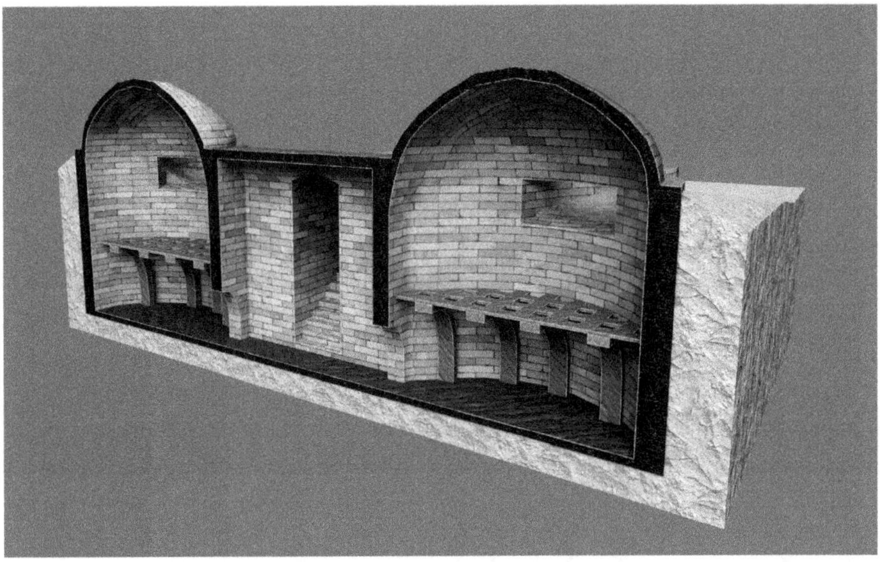

13 Gaza Jar kiln complex reconstruction conveying the depth of the combustion chambers and narrow stairway to the workstation. (Based on the reconstruction of kilns at Khirbet Baraqa by Gadot and Tepper 2003, 140, f. 12)

Such working conditions had the potential to impact worker health. Several Roman authors describe occupation-related illnesses and ailments of workers. Some ailments were attributed to the risk and dangers of physical labor, while others seemingly related to their specific working environments. Lucretius describes a particular illness of gold miners (Lucretius *De Rerum Natura,* VI. 808–812); Juvenal describes one of blacksmiths; Martial describes those of sulfur workers (Rosen 1958, 45–46). Galen, in his visits to a Cyprus copper-sulfate mine, describes the dangers of acidic fumes for miners' health and the destructive effects of the acid mists on clothing, effects that motivated the miners to work naked (Felton 1963, 9). Concern over airborne dust motivated the use of face masks fashioned from animal bladders or cloth (Pliny the Elder; Julius Pollus, referenced in Rosen 1958, 44–46). Working conditions in antiquity could, evidently then, be quite toxic, and the textual record is supported by bioarchaeological evidence. Skeletal analysis of individuals (from Lucus Feroniae, Italy) has identified occupational stress markers, including degenerative skeletal diseases, changes in muscle and ligament attachments due to repeated movements, and traumas, which are associated with sustained heavy labor of agricultural workers, particularly the male skeletons (Sperduti 1997). The skeletal evidence from Early Byzantine mining communities in Jordan demonstrates not only osteological disorders associated with hard labor but also high levels of bioaccumulation of heavy metals from environmental pollutants (Pyatt et al. 2005).

While ceramic workers are not specifically referenced by ancient authors, according to modern health and safety conventions (Princeton University

Environmental Health and Safety 2022), work in pottery and ceramic production is recognized as having specific risks and associated ailments. Some of these reflect the physical labor involved with repetitive actions (e.g., many hours sitting hunched over a low wheel). Others reflect environmental working conditions, particularly relating to dust and smoke, certainly problematic in ancient, as well as modern, potting shops. Dry-working clay can introduce silica particles to the air, and inhaling such dust over the long term can induce a respiratory disease known colloquially as "potters' rot" (silicosis). Inhaling such particles would have been unavoidable in the working environment generally, but exposure to them was likely more substantial for those preparing dry clay. There is also modern evidence to support ceramic-specific occupational illnesses caused by working conditions at the kiln. Several recent studies of workers in ceramic industries utilizing wood-fired kilns in Bangladesh (Biswas et al. 2018), India (Tandon et al. 2017), Pakistan (Shaikh et al. 2012), Croatia (Zuskin et al. 1998), and Nepal (Joshi and Dudani 2008) have documented other chronic health conditions attributed to the conditions of ceramic work environments. These include highly elevated frequencies of musculoskeletal and respiratory illnesses (chronic cough and phlegm, asthma, bronchitis) among kiln-firing specialists, elevated even when compared with other workers in the same ceramic workshops, such as carriage drivers and loaders (Shaikh et al. 2012). It is notable that, while these diseases became more pronounced with age, symptoms were exhibited already in young kiln operators.[17]

These studies highlight ailments associated with specific work tasks in modern workshops, with particular health risks attributed to the conditions of clay preparation and kiln firing. Moreover, young workers were not unaffected by these ailments. We can reasonably assume that at least some of these conditions were similar in the Roman world. The sometimes close proximity of kilns to workrooms, and the lenses and piles of clay on floors near workstations, would have placed Roman-period potters in contexts known to have health impacts. Yet some workshops with more constricted working conditions or linearly arranged rooms (with less ventilation) may have been particularly dire. Working dry clay versus working wet clay may have had an impact. Kilns with covered stoke holes may have protected operators from bad weather and sun, but in so doing put them at greater risk of smoke inhalation. Thus, we might begin to consider differences, not only in the daily working conditions of ancient ceramicists laboring in different parts of the workshop but also in terms of health consequences for these specialized workers. While we lack specific skeletal evidence for ancient ceramicists, similar occupational respiratory health risks have been suggested regarding

[17] Another study (from Nepal) demonstrated, however, that such industries could also have damaging effects on respiratory systems of children residing nearby (Joshi and Dudani 2008).

Roman and Early Byzantine glassworkers at Sepphoris (Fischer 2007). While the evidence remains fragmentary, there is reason to suggest that some of these specialized work roles observed among ceramic workers may have exposed them to occupational health risks and that such ailments might have disproportionately affected those who performed certain tasks in the production cycle, particularly clay preparation and kiln firing.

In tracing the evidence of ceramic production in the Roman East through its major sequences of operations (clay preparation, forming, and firing), the great variability of workshop organization is striking. The archaeological analysis also finds points of agreement with the textual record that some workers were likely specialized in task-specific work, albeit others, such as assistants (also referenced in textual sources), remain difficult to identify archaeologically. In this regard, the differences in roles, skills, and responsibilities that can be interpreted within workshops would have important impacts on the comparative working conditions and potential health hazards experienced differently among co-workers. While specialized workers are well documented in the textual record, it is necessary to stress that such specialization did not only imply difference in professional status and pay rates. There also might be critical differences in working conditions, and associated likelihood and severity of physical harm, in performing certain tasks.

SEASONALITY

The production cycle of any workshop is tied to the stages of material transformation: raw clay to prepared clay to formed object to finished object to fired object. Those sequences drive any workshop and impose particular temporalities on the lives of its workers. Yet production cycles are connected to other social and natural temporalities (Ingold 1993; 2007). Seasonal changes must, for example, have impacted production. The seasonal changes that might affect a workshop seem to be referenced in a description of a potter's dwelling provided in Talmudic sources (Babylonian Talmud, Sukkah 8b; Babylonian Talmud, Mezuzah 63a; Vitto 1983–1984, 58–59). The discussion documented in these sources concerns the placement of a mezuzah on the doorpost of a potter's property. The typical potter's property is described as being composed of two structures, translated as "huts" or "booths" (sukkah), implying that these were modest buildings (Vitto 1983–1984, 58–59). The discussion focused on whether the structures had a year-round or only a seasonal occupation, with the outer structure (thought to display wares) seemingly used on a more seasonal basis (Vitto 1983–1984, 58–59).

It is unlikely that at mountainous sites, such as Sagalassos or Kibyra (both in the Taurus Mountains and at altitudes over 1,000 m above sea level [MASL]), potting was conducted year-round or at the same intensity throughout the year. Winter drying and firing times would have been uneconomically long in those locations, and resources (fuel, clay) would have been difficult to acquire. At some Roman workshops in the other provinces of the Empire, drying rooms with hypocaust-style heating systems have been documented archaeologically (Harizanov 2016). This would have presumably helped to expedite drying of both fuel and vessels in cold, wet climates. At Scoppieto (Italy), hearths within the workshop, situated near wheel throwing stations, would have helped potters working wet clay with bare hands to maintain year-round production (Bergamini 2007, 62, 67, f. 5, 12). In the eastern provinces, however, no such infrastructure has been observed. In fact, some workshops appear to have been constructed with work areas partially open to the elements. This is the case at Patara's Northern Slope Tepecik Acropolis Workshop (Varkıvanç 2001–2002, 144–45) and at Sagalassos' East Slope Tableware Workshop. These conditions would have made year-round manufacturing extremely unlikely. At sites in arid regions with hot summers (e.g., at Petra, Gerasa, Elusa), the drying time and conditions for drying vessels were also likely adjusted to avoid shrinkage cracks before firing.

The seasonal cycles would also have affected the composition and configuration of workgroups. Some of these workshops must have been vacant at certain times of the year or populated by changing numbers of seasonal workers through the annual calendar. While outside the study region, at La Graufesenque (Marichal 1988, 106–7, 226–27; graffito no. 169), a graffito describes the workshop use of rented slaves as assistants in the workshop for a period of one month (Marichal 1988, 106–7, 226–27). The use of temporary workers of different legal status is not yet identified in the workshops of the eastern provinces, but itinerant potters do appear in the Zenon Archive in Egypt (Gallimore 2010, 159), and seasonal work cycles might result in changing compositions and numbers of workers and also workers of different statuses. Potting consequently might not have been a full-time job for everyone. Among the Korykos funerary records, epitaphs sometimes describe individuals with multiple occupations, including a potter who was also a manufacturer of goat-hair cloth (Patlagean 1977, 167, f. 51, inscription no. 470) and a potter who was also a lessor of work (Patlagean 1977, 167, f. 50, inscription no. 627, 678). What is of some interest with regard to these inscriptions is that the two work titles held by potters seem rather unrelated, with few transferrable skills; potters could clearly occupy multiple roles in a community.[18]

[18] While outside of the study region, an even less formal work arrangement is documented among the texts preserved from pottery workshops of La Graufesenque (France), where a contract describes the rental of slaves for a one-month period to assist with various tasks (Marichal 1988, 106–7, 226–27; graffito no. 169).

Modern potters who divide their time between agricultural work and specialized potting are well documented ethnographically (e.g., Hampe and Winter 1962, 37; Arnold 1985, 18–19) and, for the Roman world, Erdkamp (2001; 2016) has also modelled seasonal migrations of urban labor in response to agricultural harvests. In the context of brick manufacture, Pliny (*Nat. Hist.* 25.49) describes spring production, and Vitruvius (*De Arch.* 2.3.2) describes spring and autumn as ideal for production (Börker 1978, 194). As regards Roman potting, there is not much evidence for urban potters directly engaging in agricultural activity; however, it is clear from workshop lease contracts that container production (amphorae, *pithoi*) was tied to the farm cycle, and the agricultural harvest set deadlines by when containers needed to be ready for filling (Cockle 1981, 93; Gallimore 2010, 169–70). This is likewise supported by the stamps on the Rhodian amphora (third through mid first century BC), which often record both the year and month of production. Variable representations of certain months demonstrate periods of increased and reduced production related to the wet winter season (Börker 1978, 193–94; see also Badoud 2015). A reference to a potter participating in irrigation works might also indicate that potters could be pulled into work projects in the off-season (*P.Oxy.* 16.1913.16–23, Gallimore 2010, 170). This, presumably, partly necessitated a varied and fluctuating workforce.

CONCLUSION

This chapter has considered the built environment of ceramic workshops from the region, as well as the diversity of work processes and, by extension, the lived experiences of the laborers of workshops. It has made clear that the techniques and production processes of potters and ceramicists across the Roman eastern Mediterranean workshops varied significantly and that even similar goods might be manufactured using very different techniques and following different processes. These variances are important, as they impacted the rhythms of making ceramic goods and the investment in different types of infrastructure. They also have implications for the division of task responsibility among workers. By tracking differences at similar stages of the work cycle, it is possible to tease out contrasts in the spatial distribution of specialized labor tasks, as well as the architectural separation of work tasks and workstations, in ways that sometimes align with textual descriptions of ceramic workers. Consequently, the valuable role of otherwise invisible assistants can be conjectured, and alternative labor organizations might be represented through the further physical separation of certain types of infrastructure, particularly kilns. These archaeological elements help to populate a workshop with multiple actors working together as a small collective body, presumably with its own social structures. However, even beyond differences in work skill, status, and remuneration, differences in work responsibility potentially had substantive physical implications, via working conditions, for the health of specialist workers within the workgroup.

CHAPTER FOUR

CULTURAL PRACTICES AND RITUAL LIVES OF POTTERS IN THE WORKSHOP

Workgroups develop their own ways of doing things. Spending long hours together, working on shared tasks, and being reliant on the efforts of colleagues, family, or hired hands build and reinforce a sense of community. In one sense, Roman workshops were undeniably economic spaces, as they were structures and properties facilitating the manufacture of goods. Yet, to the extent they were occupied by work groups, they were also fundamentally social and cultural places. The previous chapters have already shown how economic organization and work process might intersect with cultural perceptions of landscape, as well as changing social contexts. To see a workshop in purely economic terms – as simply a static shelter to the production process – fails to appreciate the workplace as a *place*, one populated by workers with social roles and cultural practices. Wenger has described such contexts as communities of practice, wherein "The repertoire of a community of practice includes routines, words, tools, ways of doing things, stories, gestures, symbols, genres, actions, or concepts that the community has produced or adopted in the course of its existence, and which have become part of its practice" (Wenger 1998, 83).

This chapter delves deeper into the cultural lives of ceramicist workgroups. By reconstructing the everyday practices that occurred alongside the work process, it is possible to better appreciate who these ceramicists were in terms of status, religion, and literacy and to understand how the material culture of their working lives helped constitute their individual roles in the workplace and reflected their experiences beyond the workshop walls. First, the chapter attempts to better understand cultural practices in the workshop, exploring the materiality of those practices to see how potters brought their wider material worlds into the workplace and into their work process. Second, appreciating the cultural place of the workshop in daily life, it then further investigates evidence for ritual and funerary practices.

CERAMICIST WORKGROUPS

As we have seen in Chapter 2, some workshops hosted domestic and commercial activities alongside manufacture, and textual documents, such as the Elkab ostraca, describe multiple generations of potters within the same family as active in the same potting community. The examples from Elkab and Gerasa highlight the interweaving of family and professional lives within local household workshops, but other examples of mixed domestic and work space also have been documented in the region at Hierapolis and – possibly –at Dura-Europos.[1] At Hierapolis, two houses situated on Frontinus Street dated to the fifth through seventh centuries AD appear to have been involved in potting activity (Mastronuzzi and Melissano 2007). They were positioned immediately next to two large kilns, and clay and kiln supports were found in one of the houses. These two-storey structures, built of reused materials and partially incorporating the ruins of the earlier commercial agora, were modest in dimension but included rather substantial cooking facilities. The artifacts found in the houses are likewise mostly common ceramic goods. These were simple structures filled with (relatively) low-cost everyday items.

In these cases, work and living space were well integrated, but reconstructing the well-being and status of these potters without further evidence of domestic activity is more challenging. That is not to say, however, that the everyday social experiences of these craftspeople are inaccessible, and in this respect, we might consider current scholarship in household archaeology as potentially "good to think with" particularly about the range of activities associated with a category of building. Viewing the Roman house as more than simply a place for human habitation, such approaches to Roman domestic structures emphasize that a house might shelter many other categories of human activity – economic work, ritual activity, and political and social performance (Wallace-Hadrill 1996; Allison 2006; Dardenay and Laubry 2020). In much the same way that Roman house studies increasingly utilize

[1] The Library East excavations at Sagalassos uncovered a domestic space near a textile workshop and a small pottery workshop, although it is unclear if the domestic unit was associated with one or the other workshop (Uleners and Poblome 2014). At Dura-Europos, kilns were found in the courtyards of houses, but the phasing and dating of the kilns and buildings is problematic (Figures 3 and 4; Allara 1992, 1994).

living contexts and material culture assemblages of households to understand domestic practices, social status, and identity, so the abandonment contexts and associated waste deposits of workshops offer critical evidence for the social lives of artisans and the culture of workgroups (Murphy 2016).

Some of the material evidence from these workshops is illustrative of the daily life of laborers. For instance, in one workshop at Sagalassos (the SW Workshop in the Molded-Wares Workshop Complex), several reconstructable cooking vessels were found in the workshop, including a spouted jug and jar. These coarsewares were not manufactured in the workshop itself but rather would have been made by other potters, acquired, and brought into the workspace – highlighting the role of the potters of this workshop as consumers, as well as producers, of local pottery. These vessels presumably would have been used over the cooking oven or hearth that was observed in the corner of a small outdoor space of the workshop (Figure 12). Constructed of stacked tile and brick, this small oven (dimensions: length ca. 51 cm, width ca. 60 cm, preserved height ca. 30 cm) would have offered two side-by-side heating features (Murphy and Poblome 2016, 193). This type of oven (Figure 14) finds

14 Photo of cooking hearth found in the corner of the Sagalassos Molded-Wares Workshop Complex, SW Unit, and thought to have been used during the phase of ceramic production. (Sagalassos Archaeological Research Project)

15 Photo of the stack of bowls found in the Sagalassos East Slope Tableware Workshop. These display use-wear and are thought to have been used by the workers there. (Sagalassos Archaeological Research Project)

parallels with examples observed in contemporary domestic contexts in the city (Poblome 2012, 90, f. 5), and similar examples have been found in houses at Elaiussa-Sebaste (Iacomi 2019, 314, f. 4). In another Sagalassos workshop (East Slope Tableware Workshop), a stack of seven bowls was found stored in one of the workrooms (Figure 15). The vessels, all of a single type (Sagalassos Red Slip Ware 1B200), were likely manufactured in the workshop, but surface wear patterns suggest that the stack of tableware vessels was actually used, likely by the potters, for eating.

At Sinope, material culture associated with the daily lives of the workers manufacturing amphorae has also been identified. In this case, examples of fishing net weights (fashioned from the workshop's clays) were likely employed by the workers of this coastal kiln site (Kassab Tezgör 2010, 97–98). Cooking pots and kettles with use-wear and sooting were also found in the workshop contexts, along with lamps displaying sooting (Kassab Tezgör 2010, 97). Not a for-sale product made in the workshop, the lamps are thought to have been manufactured for the workshop's needs, as evidenced by the fabric composition and appearance of lamp molds recovered from the site (Kassab Tezgör 2010, 97).

Neither of the two Sagalassos workshops nor the Demirci workshop structures included domestic spaces. However, the number of consecutive hours spent in the workshop by the potters must have been considerable, as evidenced by the need for lighting implements and cooking installations. Kiln firings, which are known ethnographically to last many hours, if not days, would have especially demanded long hours spent at the workshop. Overnight tending of the kiln must also have been relatively common, a supposition supported by a reference in Rabbinic sources to pottery kiln firings being watched through the night (Mishnah Parah 5.1; Tosefta Parah 5.1 per Vitto 1986, 54). The installation of cooking hearths speaks to an investment in the workplace for those extended hours. That potters might have eaten meals in their place of work is perhaps not all that revelatory a conclusion, yet recognizing that cooking and consumption occurred in workshops prompts further reflections about commensal preparation and consumption; in short, the nature and sociability of eating at work. Chapter 3 showed how the layout of infrastructure in a workshop provides both evidence for multi-person workgroups at many workshops and evidence for specialized roles and tasks in the workplace. However, the professional and work-based distinctions within the workgroup are only one axis along which it is possible to consider the potters in the workplace. The preparation and consumption of meals within the workshop gives other evidence of shared practices and experiences among those workers.

WHO WERE THESE POTTERS?

While it is always difficult to "see" individuals in the archaeological record of ancient pottery production (Crown 2007), occasional evidence is preserved related to the presence and activities of individual workers in the workshop, and, sometimes, the names of those individuals have been preserved archaeologically or epigraphically. We should of course err toward reticence in making assumptions about the status and identity of ancient individuals based entirely on personal names, but names stamped into vessels at the very least provide a means of associating individuals with workshops. The question persists, of course, as to whom a given name refers; it is not clear whether it is necessarily the maker of the vessel, the owner of a workshop, or some other individual associated with the management of work (Zoroğlu 1989, 573; Slane 1997, 334; Mees 2002; Lund 2016, 839). At the Ketios Valley workshops near Pergamon, the names (written in the genitive case) of Late Hellenistic/Early Roman potters are stamped on some of the tablewares manufactured at the site. These include HEPOΔO, MENEAXOY, ΛEYKOY, MOΣXOY, NOΣTOY (Bounegru 2014, 27). These, like all of the names associated with the production of ESA and Eastern Sigillata C, are attributed to men (Lund 2009). Late Hellenistic to Early Roman ESA ware was also sometimes stamped with personal names in the genitive;[2] many of the names are Greek, but some are

[2] It should be recognized that examples of ESA stamped with personal names (in the genitive form) represent a minority of stamp impressions, and both motto and anepigraphic stamps were more common (Lund 2016, 838).

Latin names written in Greek letters. Lund (2016, 839) has suggested that the appearance of Latin names on stamped tableware types, inspired by Italian sigillata, may have enhanced the marketability of "Italian"-style wares for an eastern Mediterranean consumer. In these major production centers with multiple potters, some may have moved from other parts of the Roman world, yet how one presented oneself on products might also reflect a savvy marketing strategy.[3]

Given the difficulties in associating names stamped on vessels to potters in the workshop, we consequently seek other means of accessing individuals at work. Textual references to named potters in legal documents, or names inscribed onto tools and work-related artifacts, might be more directly related to ceramists on the workshop floor. The ostraca found in the house-workshops of Elkab were inscribed with both Greek and Demotic script, suggesting the potters were living and working in a multilingual environment (Hendrickx 1998, 1360–62). The Greek texts indicate that the occupants of the houses (like Psemonchès) often had (traditional) Egyptian names.[4] Nearly all references to potting and pottery in the ostraca appear on the Demotic ostraca, so much so that the excavator suggested that potting might have been considered among the traditional Egyptian professions that largely fell outside of Roman oversight (Hendrickx 1998, 1369). Yet this must have been a fluid linguistic context, whereby even references to vessel types (*lkjnws* or *lgjnws*) in the Demotic texts used words related to Greek terms. For instance, λάγυνος is typically translated as "flagon" or "flask"; however, the term at Elkab seems to reference the locally manufactured amphorae (Hendrickx 1998, 1369–71).

At Gerasa in the first- and second-century-AD Cave Workshop, a lamp was stamped with the name Stephanos (ϛτεφανο) (Iliffe 1945, 2). In Asia Minor, nearly all the names inscribed on tools and materials of the workshops are Greek and written in Greek script. At Demirci, the Greek names Yiorgos (Γεώρ[γος]), Eudoros or Eudorides (Εὔδωρ[ος] or Εὔδωρ[ίδης]), and Herakleios (Ἡράκλειος) appear inscribed on a vessel stands (Kassab Tezgör and Tatlıcan 1998, 429, f. 10; Kassab Tezgör 2010, 99, f. 5). At Sagalassos, a scraper tool made in clay was also inscribed (σoλy-) made prior to firing; while broken, it may have read (the name) *Solymos* (Figure 16).[5] The names of potters in these sources are again all male, and the one reference to a seven-year-old female potter (κεραμεύς) dated to the Hellenistic period (*SB* I 31) is thought to have

[3] Use of name stamps has been variously interpreted for the western Roman production centers, including as a means of offering quality assurances and for workshop accounting (Mees 2002, 261).

[4] This onomastic diversity is consistent with other Egyptian records listing apprentices with names of Egyptian, Latin, or Greek origin (Bergamasco 1995, 108).

[5] Special thanks to Jim Sickinger, who identified the inscribed name and who suggested that the script is likely Hellenistic or later in date due to the use of a lunate *sigma* (pers. comm.).

16 Photo of a potter's rib (scraper tool) with part of an inscribed name found in the workshop areas of Sagalassos. (Sagalassos Archaeological Research Project)

been a typographical error referencing her father (Worp 2011, 80, 86; see also Lund 2009).

Yet the workshop need not have been an exclusively gendered space. In fact, it would seem surprising that women would not, at least informally, take part in the production process, particularly in workshops associated with domestic spaces (and conceivably involving the wider household).[6] Moreover, Egyptian leases (*P.Cair.Masp.* 1.671.10; *P.BL* VII 34) have named women as workshop property owners (Cockle 1981; Rowlandson 1998, 262–63). The presence of children, working as assistants or apprentices, is also documented in these pottery workshops (and is discussed in greater detail in Chapter 5). The composition of ceramicist workgroups therefore could be quite diverse, and this is also reflected in the legal statuses of labor. The question of the scale, organization, and professional roles of slave labor involved in the pottery industries of the western provinces has been much debated.[7] Nevertheless, both slaves and freedmen were certainly active at some major production sites – like Arezzo, where approximately 630 slaves or freedmen are attested in the epigraphic record (Prachner 1980; Verboven 2011b, 93). For the Roman

[6] This phenomenon has been recorded ethnographically, where men are the only household members described as professional "potters," yet the entire family is observed performing work tasks (Kramer 1997, 49–51; Kelly and Arden 2016, 8–9).

[7] More generally, Bodel (2011) observed that free work was not necessarily differentiated from slave work, and this may be reflected in the observation by Paulus that it was difficult to distinguish between a slave and a free man (*Dig.* 18.1.5).

East, where we have far fewer names of potters stamped onto vessels, the evidence is even more difficult to interpret. Nonetheless, it is clear that slaves were involved in ceramic industries there as well. For instance, Mayerson (2000, 100) observes that in two of the Oxyrhynchus contracts, the potters were described as slaves (ἴδιοι) (*P. Oxy.* L 3596.3 and 3597.2, n. 15; see also Cockle 1981). Mees also notes the ambiguity in the use of titles, legal statuses, and labor dependencies but suggests that slave labor, while extant in the sources, was not predominant (Mees 2002, 212–13).

The appearance of written names on so many different workshop items suggests a willingness to autograph things the potters likely owned. Many of these scripts were not intended for consumers but rather were meant to be read by the occupants of the workshop. Among the production waste at the Hippodrome workshops of Gerasa, a text (possibly a contract) was written in red dye on a broken sherd (Kehrberg 2020, 3556–57). At Elusa, the literary practices may be even more elaborate. Here, two ostraca found on the floor of a fifth-century workshop, and thirteen more mixed into a production waste dump just outside the workshop, are interpreted as letter and number writing exercises, and examples of what are thought to be Christian date formulae were inscribed on sherds of the jars being made at the workshop (Bucking and Goldfus 2012). Such writing exercises performed in the production context would have prepared workers to compose the sort of texts found on professional jar labels (Bucking and Goldfus 2012, 59–61). This not only potentially situates literate workers within the workplace but establishes the workshop as a place of learning.

More casual uses of script are also observed in workshops across the region. Numbering systems or other coded use of Greek letters appear in contexts for work purposes. At Sagalassos, Greek letters (i.e., Π, Δ, β, θ, φ, λ) inscribed on the outer faces of lamp and *oinophoroi* molds seem to mark mold sets. At the fifth–seventh centuries-AD workshops of Elephantine, the outer faces of lamp and *oinophoroi* molds also were incised with combinations of Greek letters (ΡΝΓ, Πβ, ΚΖ) (Ballet and Mahmoud 1987), while in Gerasa, at the first- and second-centuries-AD Cave Workshop, lamps display Greek letters inscribed and stamped into their bases (Iliffe 1945, 2). These, like the inscribed alignment markings on the sides of the molds, were probably used as internal systems to demarcate sets of molds in the workshop and products by individuals.

The assumptions that can be made about an individual from a name, or the levels of literacy from the occasional instance of writing, must be handled cautiously. However, the intersection of work occupation with other aspects of social identity has implications for one's place in the workshop and one's place in society. The dearth of women's names, particularly on vessel stamps, while perhaps not reflecting the realities of women in the workplace, does perhaps speak to the public face of professional identity and gender conventions. We have also seen multilingual work contexts. The appearance of writing in workshops gives the impression that some workers were at least semiliterate and that writing might be deployed for marketing wares. In tracing some of this evidence, it is clear that these workgroups were composed of individuals with different social and educational statuses, suggesting that a monolithic approach to "potters" as a meaningful Roman social category elides a considerable degree of difference, not only in skill and training, but also gender, education, literacy, and resulting subtle gradations in status.

INDIVIDUALS AND THEIR PROFESSION: MAKERS AND THEIR TOOLS

While some artifacts found in the workshops offer glimpses into the literacy levels and linguistic contexts of potters, this type of evidence remains rather uncommon. The tools of these workshops can alternatively, and arguably more effectively, be used to reconstruct the material culture that tied workers to their tasks and to their profession. Few items are as closely associated with working professions as hand tools (Sennett 2008, 194–213). Some professions are nearly impossible to disassociate from the instruments of work (Ulrich 2007, 13–58; Humphreys 2018); what was a blacksmith without a hammer and anvil or a carpenter without a chisel? In Asia Minor, even on funerary reliefs that offer no figural image of the deceased, sickles and scythes signaled the professional status of the farmer, and swords and armor that of the soldier (Waelkens 1977, 1986; Zimmer 1985). There was a long tradition of depicting tools on funerary reliefs in many regions of the Roman world that reflects these associations between tools and profession. Representations of tools in two-dimensional form were used as a shorthand for professional identity, economic industry, and community status. In some cases, individuals were interred with their professional instruments for the afterlife, such as the grave of a Late Antique dentist that contained an entire kit of medical tools (dental forceps, pincers, spoons, spatulas), as well as small stone palettes and glass vials for medications (Künzl and Weber 1990).[8]

Potters, while rarely, if ever, eternalized on funerary monuments (by either title or image), nonetheless had very particular sets of professional tools that were composed of a wide range of materials, including ceramic, metal, worked bone, and stone. In most cases, these objects (or the raw materials used to fashion them) appear to have been locally acquired. The tableware production site of Sagalassos has provided the richest corpus of potting tools from the region, with more than seventy individual tools found in the potting workshops and associated production waste deposits (Murphy and Poblome 2012).

[8] Stacking rings for pottery appear as grave goods in Athens in earlier contexts (Kunze-Götte 1999, 103; Steinmann 2020, 107).

The range of items found within a single production center is striking: potters' ribs (used for scraping and forming), point tools like styluses and hairpins (used for incising, trimming, and puncturing), metal fettling knives (used for cutting), combs and roulette wheels (for incising decoration), and grinding stones and palettes (for crushing small quantities of clay). River pebbles were even transported from the valley system below the site and brought to the workshop for use as polishers (Murphy and Poblome 2012, 206, f. 3). The toolkit of the Sagalassian potters was specialized and richly varied in its material.

While there was great diversity in the range of tool classes found at these workshops, few would have been manufactured as specialized potting instruments. Instead, they reflect the appropriation of materials originally intended for other uses and incorporated into the production process. This repurposing is not unique to Sagalassos, and the practice appears at many other production sites. A metal knife and spatula have been found at Udhruh (Killick 1987, 8), and worked bone styluses and a spoon were interpreted as tools used in terracotta figurine production at Troy (Miller 1991, 56–57, f. 35). Several worked bone styluses, hairpins, and punches were found in the excavations at Buto[9] (Ballet et al. 2019, 282–84, pl. 57). A thin bronze rod with twisted handle was found inside a kiln at az-Zurrāba near Petra and was interpreted as a tool to gauge the wall thickness of vessels ('Amr and al-Momani 1999, 180, f. 8), and a bronze spatula and an iron knife were found in the Late Antique house-workshops of Hierapolis (Mastronuzzi and Melissano 2007, 576, f. 49–50). At the legionary kilnworks at Jerusalem, a worked bone modelling tool and fragments of point tools (pins and hairpins) were recovered, as was a piece of copper-alloy sheeting that was recut for use as rib scraper tool (Murphy et al. 2018, f. 7). At Sagalassos, a scrap of copper-alloy sheeting that once formed part of a dedicatory inscription was recut for use as a scraper (Murphy and Poblome 2012, 203, f. 2). Worked pebbles, likely polishers and ribs for scraping, were found with surface remains of production material at Tschandarlı (Loeschcke 1912, 353, f. 4.3, 4.9). The appropriation of artifacts for ceramic work reflects the sorts of objects available in the wider material environments in which potters were working and an apparent enthusiasm for recycling tools in novel contexts, both through wholesale appropriation and modification. Indeed, several of these objects must have acquired complex biographies, in part involving the potting process.

At many ceramic workshop sites, potting tools were also fashioned from materials available in the workplace. At Sagalassos, a funnel used in the Molded-Wares Workshop Complex was almost certainly made by the potters there, as the unusual shape of the funnel's mouth was the same form as that of

[9] The attribution of these pins as potting tools was not stated by the excavators.

the *oinophoroi* manufactured (as a product) in the workshop, representing a transfer in formal knowledge (Murphy and Poblome 2012, t. 1). The production of tools in the workshops is also evident in the reworking of discarded pottery sherds at several sites. At Panskoye on the Black Sea, broken amphora handles and toes were used as polishers, and a fragment of an amphora neck was used as a cutting board (Handberg 2011). At Buto, several amphora toes were repurposed as polishing tools (Ballet et al. 2019, 274–75), while at Gerasa and at az-Zurrāba near Petra, another approach to reusing material was observed. In the Gerasa Hippodrome workshops, pottery sherds were cut and broken for use as tools in potting. That these were designed tools is evident in the charcoal guidelines drawn on the sherd surface to trace the contour of the tool's edge before cutting ('Amr 1991, 319–20; Kehrberg 2016, 2020). Specific types of ceramic sherds were also preferentially selected for different types of tools used for particular functions; coarseware pottery sherds were used for polishing and grinding, while finewares were used for point tools and scrapers (Kehrberg 2020, 421). Sagalassos likewise presents several cut-sherd tools that were used as rib scrapers, and others were fashioned (from scratch) using the workshop's clay. Making the latter types was an involved process, involving designing, cutting, refining the shape by secondary working in a partial dry state, and then firing to a hardened state. Glass shards have been observed that had been repurposed as cutting and scraping tools by using a flaking technique more commonly employed for chipped stone ('Amr 1991, 319–20; Kehrberg 2016, 2020). Kehrberg (2020) has identified similar objects in regional surveys and suggests that these cutting tools associated with pottery production and tanning in the Hippodrome of Gerasa may be a small part of a wider tradition of Roman-period flaked tool production in the region.

That these tools were made in the workshop from workshop materials suggests that they were designed, made, and used by the potters themselves and therefore embody craft skill in working clay, but for totally different purposes than vessel construction. Thus, a sort of technical "translation" is evidenced by the two-dimensional modelling of the scrapers' edges and secondary working of the leather-hard surface. These could be highly specialized tools, and the range of contour shapes observed in the corpus from Sagalassos includes squared, elongated, rounded, and angled edges. In some cases, they were even made for specific pottery forms. At Sagalassos, the contoured edge of one such potters' rib corresponds to a distinctive inturned platter form (1C170) (Murphy and Poblome 2012, 207, f. 4). The examples of scraper tools from the workshops of the Hippodrome of Gerasa (third through seventh centuries AD) show similar variability in form that likely also relates to the range of forms (Kehrberg 2020). Kehrberg also highlights a more specialized association between a tool type fashioned from pottery handles that was specifically used to incise the ribbing on jars (Kehrberg 2020, 421). Similarly, the stone scraper/polishing tools from Tschandarlı display a slight depression on the long side of the tool, which was thought to have been used specifically to smooth the rims of vessels (Loeschcke 1912, 353). Molds and stamps are also sometimes made in clay materials available within the workshop. Decorative stamps have been found at Pergamon, Sagalassos, Jerusalem (Binyanei Ha'uma), and Tralleis (Civelek and Atıcı 2014, 429–31, f. 8), and they were used to make appliqué molds, to decorate lamp and vessel molds, and to impress directly into vessels.

The attention paid and the significance given to their self-fashioned tools by potters may be inferred from the appearance of reworked sherd tools with drill holes (Panskoye, Gerasa), presumably so the tool could be hung and kept on a string for easy access (Handberg 2011, f. 3c; Kerhberg 2020, f. 4.1). Examples of hand tools with inscribed names appear at Sagalassos and Demirci, indicating personal possessions within a workplace presumably populated by multiple potters. Mees has suggested that, in contrast to items referenced in leases of pottery workshops, such as wheels (described as "accessories"), items with the potter's name (such as molds and stamps) should better be understood as personal property, which could be taken with the potter at the end of the lease (2002, 264). Some of these items are clearly claimed by a named individual, accentuating the association between a potter and their product through the mediation of a toolkit.

Acquired in their lived "spaces of experience," these tools manifest a creative reworking of the material world. In constructing their toolkits, potters reused and adapted materials and goods to construct similar functional types common to the profession, yet each tool uniquely reflected the material worlds in which these craftspeople circulated. These tools, in their individual creation and specialized use, became a critical component in the link between the potter, their craft, and their wares. The patterns of tool acquisition and tool making reflect the cultural practices and professional material culture of potters in the workshop.

RITUALIZED CRAFT, RITUAL SPACES?

Many craft activities, even today, are described by their practitioners in performatively ritualized terms. These have received ethnographical attention in a wide range of cultural contexts (Rye and Evans 1976; Krause 1985; Henein 1997; Schmidt 2009). In these instances, the successful completion of the product is understood as contingent on the quasi-ritualized acts of production (Henein 1997, 198–99); prayers might be made at particular points in the production cycle (Rye and Evans 1976, 191–92), or the description of kilns or materials might be personified or spiritually embodied (Krause 1985). Success or failure is framed in these ritualized or supernaturally influenced terms.

Sometimes described as "superstitions," these belief systems might perhaps be better understood as simply a different way of knowing and understanding the world of work. In antiquity, the world of the workshop might be inhabited by spirits, saints, or *daemion* – which might influence everyday craftwork.

In the study of classical antiquity, there also has been interest in the intersection of ritual, magic, and craft production (Gager 1992; Faraone 2001; Blakely 2006; Rotroff 2013; Steinmann 2020, 107; Hasaki 2021, 192–93). In Athens, the appearance of ritual offerings (so-called saucer pyres) under workshop and shop floors has been interpreted as a ritual act by craftspeople and tradespeople in response to, or in attempted avoidance of, various stresses and concerns. Workplaces were certainly places of risk, both financial and bodily; the professional risks associated with setting up a new workshop, and the physical risks of work-related accidents or even death, were real (Rotroff 2013, 80–85). Curses enacted by malicious spirits were also threats, and Pliny (*Nat. Hist.* 28.4.19) reports that pottery was thought to be particularly susceptible to the effects of curses (Gager 1992, 153–54). The well-known Pseudo-Herodotean poem dedicated to the *daemion* of the kiln is often cited as evidence for superstition and magic associated with the ceramic production process (Gager 1992, 153–54; Faraone 2001; Hasaki 2021, 214–18).[10] Faraone (2001) argues that the poem referred to as *Kaminos* ("The Kiln")[11] or "the Potters' Hymn" is, based on syntax and language, composed from three different kiln curses, with later editions dated to the Hellenistic-Early Roman periods; and Gager proposes that such curses would have been made by competing potters (1992, 153–54). The poem describes "demons" or "gremlins" of the kiln, with names translated as terms akin to "Smasher," "Cracker," "Shake-to-Pieces," and "Conqueror of the Unbaked," and apparently references individual abilities in breaking vessels during the firing. Yet the spirits of the kiln could be impelled to enact blessings instead of curses on the potter, with benefactions of pottery firing to a "good black" (presumably a consistently dark reduction), being "well fired" (fully sintered), and fetching "the price asked" on the market (Faraone 2001, 436–37).

Thus, the pottery kiln represents a particular type of feature within the pottery workshop – charged both ritually and pragmatically with risks and costs that differed from other types of potting technology. At any other stage prior to kiln firing, clay can be recovered from the formed vessel, and the fact that the clay was sometimes recovered is actually evidenced by formed (but unfired) pottery found in a clay washing basin at Elkab, where it had been

[10] This view is supported by Gager (1992, 153–54).

[11] The poem has been attributed to the sixth–fifth centuries BC but with Hellenistic/Early Roman alterations (Faraone 2001).

set to soak and recuperate its clay (Hendrickx 1998, 1357). However, once exposed to heat, the clay (and time and labor effort) invested in a ceramic vessel could not be recovered. Once the kiln was filled, sealed, and lit, the potter was to some extent at the mercy of the firing, which could not be quickly stopped without major loss of the load. If problems began to appear, it was difficult to drastically alter the overall process; adjusting temperature must be done incrementally, and changes to the atmosphere must be introduced gradually to prevent quick changes in temperature. The powerlessness of experiencing a kiln misfiring might be enhanced by the popping sounds of vessels breaking inside.

Archaeological examples of these catastrophes are known. For example, at Kom Dahab (Egypt), a fully loaded collapsed kiln shows where the dome of a Late Antique amphora kiln collapsed onto a loaded kiln (Coulson and Wilkie 1986, 68). Evidence of major kiln failure has also been found at other production sites – for instance, a group of twenty-one overfired and melted vessels found in Kiln I of az-Zurrāba near Petra (Zayadine 1986b, 188). At Faras, the elevated floor of a kiln collapsed during firing (Adams 1986, 33), while at a workshop in the Ketios Valley below Pergamon, much of a third-century-AD load, comprising more than twenty jugs, was discovered still in the kiln (Kiln 14; Bounegru 2009, 79; 2014, 28). At the Hippodrome workshops of Gerasa, thousands of unfired/underfired vessel fragments found in a single production dump were assumed to represent the loss of a complete kiln load (Kehrberg 2020, 351). With amphora kiln loads comprising anywhere from a few dozen to several hundred vessels, and with tableware kiln load estimates ranging from several hundred to several thousand tableware vessels,[12] the destruction of a full kiln load represented a major loss of work, time, and materials. These losses were all the more acute because, in addition to the production costs (especially the costs associated with the expenditure of fuel for firing over many hours or even days[13]), they reflected the loss of critical infrastructure that, as will be demonstrated, required specialized technical skill to build and repair.

The collapse of the kiln while firing represents an extreme accident, but no potter was immune to rejects. Some degree of vessel loss is always expected, even by modern professional potters; Nicholson and Patterson (1989, 80) describe a typical waster (loss) rate of 5–10 percent in an ethnographic

[12] Amphora kiln load estimates included 60 amphorae at Khirbet Baraqa (Gadot and Tepper 2003, 149), 450 amphorae at Tel Yavne (Yannai 2012, 98), and 247–330 amphorae at Elaiussa-Sebaste (Borgia and Iacomi 2010, 1047). Tableware kiln load estimates from Sagalassos include 1,500–2,000 vessels in the second century AD and 350–450 vessels in the sixth century AD (Murphy and Poblome 2017, 81).

[13] Yannai (2012, 98) estimates that filling, firing, cooling, and unloading a large amphora kiln near Tel Yavne would take five days.

context using simple updraft kilns in Egypt, while Hankey (1968, 29–30) estimates a much lower damage rate of 50 vessels per 1,500 fired. Archaeologically, the waste dumps found at most production sites attest to some regularity of misfires. Artificial hills and mounds composed of waster heaps were documented at Burg el-Arab (El-Ashmawi 1998, 57–58, f. 2); over a dozen mounds of 5–10 m height have been found in the area around Ashkelon (Johnson and Stager 1995, 100); a 4-m-tall mound discovered outside Soli-Pompeiopolis (Autret et al. 2010, 204); a mound 50–60 m across was found at Tell el-Haraby (Majcherek and el-Shennawi 1991, 4); and a 60-m^2 area of wasters was noted at Anemourion (Russell 2002, 225). To relate these mounds to vessels, a production dump at Kefar Ḥananya contained an estimated 9,500–13,000 vessels (Adan-Bayewitz 1991, 187), and nearly 5,700 sherds were recovered with the workshop excavation of Naḥf (Vitto 1983–1984, 21). Near Petra, the excavation of a single trench among the potter workshops at az-Zurrāba generated 250,000 sherds (ʻAmr 1991, 321), and hundreds of thousands of wasters were estimated in the workshop dumps near Tel Yavne (Yannai 2012, 101). Sometimes it was even possible to differentiate types of misfires between dumps – presumably a result of sorted waste disposal. In a survey of the Marmarica, dozens of kiln sites were identified primarily from surface waste heaps as tall as 6 m (at Bir Helua), and color variations were found to reflect different relative frequencies of sherds to slag (Rieger and Möller 2011, 148).

While most wasters seem to have been discarded, some of these wasters were recovered and recycled by the workshop (for a more extensive discussion of recycled ceramics, see Peña 2007). Examples of tools made from reworked sherds have already been considered; at Elkab and at Demirci, however, amphora necks and toes were used to construct water conduits (Hendrickx 1998, 1359; Billot et al. 2010, 114). It was proposed that, at mid first-century-BC/mid first-century-AD Qumran, such production rejects were used by the community as rubbish containers for cooked animal bones, in order to avoid attracting wild animals (Magen and Peleg 2006, 94–96). In other cases, vessels with production flaws still had some consumer value. Rabbinic sources described the purchase of production-damaged pottery for use by children, suggesting a market for "seconds" (Babylonian Talmud, Yoma 78b; Vitto 1986, 55). While such reuse practices were quite common at workshops, it is still difficult to imagine that these repurposed vessels and purchases of "seconds" significantly offset the regular quantities of production rejects – particularly in cases of catastrophic misheating or structural failings of the kiln.

It was to appease and protect against such damaging actions, understood to be at least partly a function of malevolence on behalf of spirits, that we might understand the appearance of ritualized actions focused on or around kilns.

Examples have been discussed from Classical Greece,[14] but instances from later periods may also be noted. One is at Naḥf in Galilee; at "Naḥf, the humerus of a young person was found, embedded into a groove specially cut into the threshold of one of the kilns. This discovery can apparently be explained as a foundation rite, which was carried out to assuage the natural forces ruling on a firing." (Vitto 1983–1984, 22). While difficult to ascertain the supernatural meaning of such kiln remains, it nonetheless suggests that the kiln might become a locus of particular types of ritual action that are not easily accounted in functionalist terms.

With the adoption of Christianity in the Late Roman period, some of these workshop concerns seem to have been expressed through changing ritual practices. At the amphora production site of Demirci, several crosses were inscribed (pre-firing) on vessel supports, probably suggesting religious affinities among the potters working there (Kassab Tezör 2010, 98). In the Molded-Wares Workshop Complex at Sagalassos, there is also evidence of early Christian symbols on tools. A funnel that was found on a workshop floor has what appears to be a cross and palmette inscribed (post-firing) on the outer surface, and a scraper tool (Figure 17) also displays a Chi-Rho and a cross (Poblome 2014, 19). In Late Antique Antioch on the Orontes, textual sources describe images of Saint Simeon the Stylite placed as protection outside of craft workshops (Frankfurter 2017, 148). Use of Christian symbols, such as crosses on kiln furniture (e.g., a vessel stand at Demirci), might be seen in these apotropaic terms as they are in other craft contexts (see Frankfurter 2017, 145–83). Inscribed Christian symbols on molds and on other tools at Sagalassos and Demirci may reflect the religious identity of potters, but they might likewise be understood as "activated" in ritualized terms. Inscriptions of Christian symbols on objects have been documented and interpreted as active agents in other Late Antique domestic and funerary contexts (Russell 1995; Cline 2019). Crosses were described in an ancient homily as being "found everywhere, among rulers, among subjects, among women and slaves and freedmen" (trans. Dauterman Maguire et al. 1989, 18–19) and as explicitly performing a protective role in everyday life. Given the central place that the workshop played in the lives of potters, it is perhaps unsurprising that such ritual practices should appear there as well.

In the Jewish tradition, other features of ritualized activity described in texts can be observed within pottery workshops. These actions more directly concern the ritual status (especially the ritual purity) of the vessels intended for sale, as pottery was seen as being vulnerable to pollution, notably via breakage or exposure of the interior to impurities (Bran 1953; Vitto

[14] The use of apotropaic figurines placed on or around metal furnaces and pottery kilns in Classical Greece is well documented (Blakely 2006, 33; see also Rotroff 2013, 80–85).

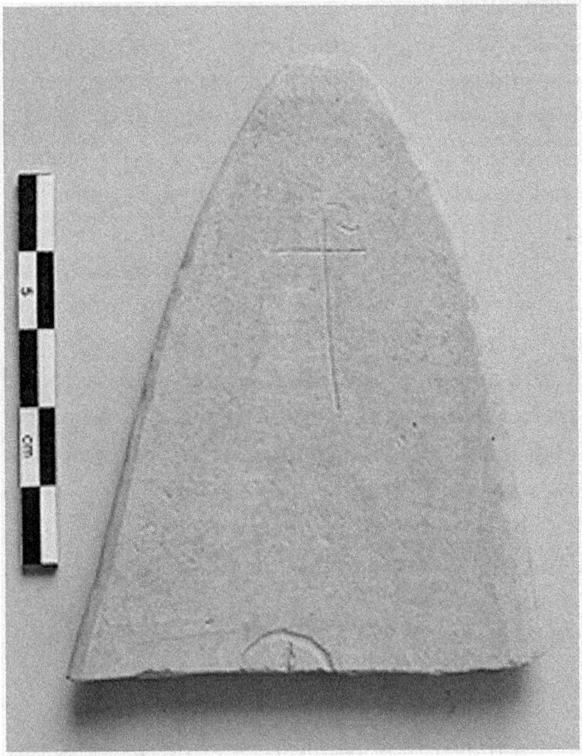

17 Photo of a potter's rib (scraper tool) inscribed with Christian symbols and found in the workshop areas of Sagalassos. (Sagalassos Archeological Research Project)

1983–1984, 54–55; Magen and Peleg 2006, 92–93). The risk of contamination occurred following kiln firing and, if there was contact with any surface of impurity, it was advised that the vessel should be broken and discarded. The use of vessels in ritual acts and as offerings was of even greater concern. To ensure that these vessels were of requisite cleanliness, it was advised that they be attended during firing and that they should even be extracted from the kiln by the consumer purchasing them for dedication (Mishnah Parah 5.1; Tosefta Parah 5.1; Vitto 1983–1984, 54). Unusual techniques of making lidded cooking pots have been understood according to these concerns and are referenced in Talmudic sources (Zevulun and Olenik 1979, 33–35; van den Brink et al. 2016, 7–8). In making these cooking pots, the lid was thrown as part of the wall of the pot (with a hole at the top of the handle to allow steam to escape). Reattached after cutting, the lid and vessel were then fired together, allowing the consumer to break off the lid to ensure the vessel's interior was not touched and polluted (Zevulun and Olenik 1979, 33–35). Efforts to preserve the state of the vessels may have reflected the material properties of fired clay, as well as the conditions of the workshop. Because potters were listed among the "unrefined" people described by Rabbinic sources, concern was expressed regarding their personal state of cleanliness, lest they pollute the vessels prior to use (B. Qidd. 82a; Magen and Peleg 2006, 92–93). The provisioning of ritual baths (mikveh) at and around Hasmonaean period pottery workshops at Qumran (Locus 138, Magen and Peleg 2006, 92–93) and (Binyanei Ha'uma) Jerusalem (Rosenthal-Heginbottom 2005) is thought to result from the need of potters and other laborers to maintain standards of necessary cleanliness.

These examples demonstrate that, while workshops were undeniably economic spaces, they were also places of everyday dwelling, where ritual practices and religious beliefs might intersect with the work process. In addition to reflecting the stresses, concerns, and worries of potters (and their perceived means of mitigating risk), these images, deposits, and symbols also speak to a different understanding of craft knowledge. Couched in ritualized terms, craft knowledge was more than simply physical labor and skill applied to passive materials and their properties. There were other, sometimes even supernatural, factors also at play, and there is some evidence that the potters attempted to engage directly with those forces.

THE AFTERLIVES OF WORKSHOPS: PLACES OF BURIAL

It has already been proposed that the workshops of the eastern Roman Empire were complex social contexts, in which workshop culture was fostered and sustained by daily life practices. It has also been demonstrated that work practices and ritualized actions might be incorporated into the everyday happenings of a workshop. Yet the meaning and significance of the workplace in constructing one's view of both social and ritual relationships is perhaps more intimately expressed through the association of workshops with human burials.

Many active pottery workshops across the eastern provinces were situated in proximity to human burials. Consequently, the ancient association between pottery works and human interments is not unique, even in the eastern provinces. Burials cutting into the remains of earlier workshops, or workshops placed over burial monuments, are attested at numerous sites – for example at Sagalassos (Poblome et al. 2001, 159), Ketios Valley/Pergamon (Bounegru 2009, 83), Patara (Varkıvanç 2001–2002, 137), Tel Abila (de Vreis and Bikai 1993, 491), Buto (Seton-Williams 1967, 152; Ballet and von der Way 1993; Ballet et al. 2019, 67), and Naḥf (Vitto 1983–1984, 22). The cultural norms and urban dynamics that drove these activities are the subject of Chapter 8. However, here, it is worth stressing that the proximity of workshops and necropoleis was very common, and it is in this context that workshops occasionally became a locus for the dead. Human burials have been documented at other ceramic production sites from the Roman world, predominately in the northwestern provinces,[15] yet there are also occasional examples from the eastern Mediterranean. For example, at the hippodrome workshops of Gerasa, an infant was interred under the threshold of an active workshop (Kehrberg and Ostrasz 2020, 309). In other workshops in the Hippodrome, multiple individuals were buried in the rooms of abandoned workshops. At this time, the workshops were part of a larger community that included domestic structures, and it was suggested that these may have been family interments for the craft workers (Ostrasz and Kehrberg 2020, 310–11).[16]

We have seen the unique role of kilns in the production process – often kept at a distance from the main workshop or operated by specialized workers. We have also seen how the transformative and risky process of firing the kiln might consequently attract a ritualized focus. When it comes to funerary activity, the special role and status of the kiln is again evident. At the production site of Buto, in early excavations conducted in the 1960s and 1970s, a second-century-BC kiln was found that had been renovated (but not fired) and then abandoned (Seton-Williams 1967, 152; Charlesworth 1972, 46). It lacked an elevated floor and was large enough to be entered. In twelve wedge-shaped niches cut into the inner wall of the kiln, twelve disarticulated skulls had been found crushed into the vent holes (c. 26–36 cm wide), creating what the excavators described as a "family mausoleum" (Charlesworth 1967, 152; 1972, 46).[17] This kiln "mausoleum" was maintained while nearby kilns continued to be used for ceramic production. As at Gerasa, we can view the workplace as a collective final resting place.

While the number of cases of funerary interments or ritual practices in the eastern Mediterranean remains limited, there does seem to be a growing body of evidence for ritual practices that took place within the workshops of potters. However, the workshops were not just passive actors in these rituals: they were not just places where ritual activity took place. The production process was lived out in the workplace, informed by a world view influenced as much by the technical know-how of clays and kilns as by the presence of spirits and the

[15] At the production site of Amphoralis (Salles-d'Aude, France), infants were found buried under the floors of active workshops (Coulon 1994, 141–42, 160–62). At La Graufesenque (France), an infant was found under the door lintel of a tableware workshop (Schaad and Vernhet 2007, 155; for a summary, see Murphy 2016, 143–45). At Haltern, skeletal remains of at least twenty-four individuals were found in Kiln 10 after production ceased at the site (Borchardt-Ott 2001, 187–248).

[16] Frankfurter notes that, with Egyptian binding spells, reference to workshops used similar terms as those used for domestic spaces, perhaps reflecting similar ritual associations (Frankfurter 2017, 153).

[17] The excavators speculated that the kiln may have been a sort of family mausoleum, even relating it to a Ptolemaic massacre described by Juvenal (Charlesworth 1972, 46–47).

remains of the dead. The kiln especially was a precarious entity susceptible to the influence of spirits. The workrooms were, at least on occasion, the resting places of the dead. In this sense, workshops could be places of significance, intimately weaving ritual and ceramic work through everyday acts of dwelling.

CONCLUSION

This chapter has spotlighted fragmentary evidence that has been too often presented as footnotes or asides in the excavation reports of workshops that are otherwise preoccupied by the technical and economic aspects of pottery production. However, pottery production is also a type of craftwork that can involve immensely long hours. It is often seasonal (or influenced by changes in seasons), meaning that production needs to be maximized in certain months. Firing a kiln can last many hours, even days, depending on the furnace size and design and the types of products inside, and there are a few ancient texts that describe kiln firings running overnight. In such contexts, it is perhaps not surprising that the workplace might take on added significance for the work-group and might become a focal point of daily life. Evidence of cooking and other such daily life activities can be documented within the workshops, and there is evidence of personal names and by extension literacy (and, indeed, a sense of ownership and investment in the material of the workplace) on the part of potters. Items might be collected elsewhere and adapted as tools for pottery work. The appearance of ritual activities and religious symbols, as well as the association of some workshops with funerary activities, reinforces the image of a workshop that might become a meaningful focal point of social life. These sorts of details help to reconstruct a workplace that was more than just an economic unit, and one that was experienced daily through social relationships and work cultures.

CHAPTER FIVE

POTTING TRADITIONS, CRAFT LEARNING, AND PRODUCT INNOVATION

The relationship between potter and pot is neither easily nor universally characterized. The decision-making process informing what a potter intends to make and how such a pot is perceived in relation to consumers and other craft producers can vary in different social contexts. The quintessential triad of economic relationships between consumer, producer, and distributor has often been the framework within which (what are assumed to be market-driven) product innovations are socially interpreted (Temin 2013; Brughmans and Poblome 2016). In accordance with this view, new products and styles of pottery – as identified from consumption contexts or post-consumption discard – were inextricably entwined with and generative of local cultural food and dining practices, while simultaneously reflecting the highly diverse culinary and dining traditions across different areas and different social strata within the empire (Cool 2006; Roth 2007; Greene 2008; Pitts 2008; van Oyen 2012; Pitts and Versluys 2015; Willet 2018). As generally understood, novelties in vessel style and vessel use have been seen as driven, ultimately, by consumer preferences and practices.

While widespread changes in pottery and ceramic wares can certainly be interpreted in this way, a perspective that is wholly focused on the consumer as the causal force also serves to relegate the workshop and its potters a passive role in the development of their products. Alternatively, the changing styles of pottery might also be seen *in the context of making* (Auer 2018; Sutton 2020; Borgers et al. 2021). In the workshop, decisions concerning product types and styles might be influenced by additional and wide-ranging local factors – traditional ways of making, certainly, but also new ideas inspired by other craft neighbors, changes in visual arts of public building, and imported objects seen in the marketplace. In this sense, traditions of craft knowledge and know-how, as evidenced by the resulting ceramic vessels, become localized within the workplace and by the hand of the maker. Roux's phrasing is insightful and illuminating: "In the heated debate on the equation stating that 'pots equal people', which is a rather fuzzy reference to assumed relationships between (mostly) ethnic groups and pottery, technology enables us to propose with conviction the equation 'pots equal potters'" (Roux 2019, 316). Pots and products should be understood as manifestations of the culture of a particular work community.

If both style and repertoire are the outcomes of communities of practice instantiated by workshops and craft communities, then both sustained tradition and processes of craft innovation involved agentive potters, the cultural *habitus* of craft making, as well as complex networks of social relationships embedded in a rich material world. In more fully appreciating the context of making and the role of the maker, both innovating production and sustaining a traditional repertoire required active choices. These dynamics – by which Roman potting communities sustained production tradition, introduced innovations, and translated new ideas through the established manufacturing process – are the central issues addressed over the following pages. This chapter investigates these dynamics by considering the experiences of intergenerational craft learning that maintained craft traditions in the Roman East, both by contextualizing documented product innovations within the repertoire of local craft communities, and by considering the adaptation costs incurred by adopting new ideas.

SOCIALLY UNDERSTANDING TRADITIONS

All traditions are maintained and reenacted through shared everyday practices and norms (Bourdieu 1977; de Certeau 1984). In a pottery workshop, these work cultures are maintained contemporaneously among peers of potters, but also over time, through intergenerational learning. In the context of craftwork, learning involves embodied training of technique and know-how, development of formal and aesthetic cognition, and the achievement of collectively recognized professional skill (Stark 1998). Acquiring skill necessitates iterative physical training in working and manipulating materials and working with tools and technologies (Leroi-Gourhan 1993; Loney 2007; Apel 2008; Bender Jøgensen 2012). Through hands-on training, embodied means of knowing materials and their properties, and cognitive understanding of pot forms and characteristics, skill within craft traditions is developed (Wendrich 2006; Ferguson 2008; Ingold 2010; Bentz Høgseth 2012). In learning a craft tradition, such a tradition can either be actively maintained, or it can offer a framework through which new ideas on pottery form and style come to be interpreted (Wendrich 2012).

Such craft training, as documented ethnographically and historically, can occur in any number of social environments, although rarely are those formal learning environments (Herzfeld 2004; Wendrich 2012; Gandon and Roux 2019). Historical and ethnographic studies of work communities also highlight that intergenerational training involves learning business practices, as well as in developing personal relationships and professional standing (Sorenson and Audia 2000, 442–44; Hite and Hesterly 2001). In this sense, training is conceived as being a process of socialization within such small-scale communities (Ortiz 2002; Herzfeld 2004; Wendrich 2012). Therefore, the learning of product types and styles is only a constituent part of a larger socialization within a local work culture. Given the multi-century longevity of some workshops in the Roman East, some vessel forms, and some potting traditions, coming to terms with the dynamics of tradition (as well as innovation) are central to understanding the long-term social relations between generations of potters and the tradition of their craftwork.

Identifying contexts of pottery learning and the presence of craft novices from or within the archaeological record is challenging (see Smith 2006; Crown 2007; Apel 2008; Wendrich 2012). Osteological and textual evidence indicates that physical labor by children was common throughout antiquity and that the beginning of professional training in a trade began at a young age (Laes 2008). The presence of children in Roman ceramic workshops can be documented by the occasional child-sized footprints on tile and brick. At Brigetio, Pannonia, a tile was observed with a small hobnailed shoe impression derived from the bottom of a low-quality shoe of a child estimated to be eight to ten years of age (Dobosi 2016). At Naḥf, the small size of fingerprints observed in pressmarks made when joining the handles to jars have been used to suggest the activity of children learning the trade (Vitto et al. 1980; Vitto 1986, 60). The involvement of children in ceramic work is even more strongly supported, however, by evidence from the site of Kôm el-Dikka (Egypt), where a molded lamp dated to the sixth century AD has been identified as bearing interior fingerprint impressions (Dzierzykray-Rogalski and Grzeszyk 1991; see also Murphy 2017, 106). Analyzing the age-based papillary line on a fingerprint impression has verified the ceramic work of a youth between ten and fourteen years of age (Dzierzykray-Rogalski and Grzeszyk 1991).[1] The use of small fingers to press clay into a

[1] For other archaeological examples of fingerprints used to identify child ceramicists, see Kamp et al. (1999).

small mold is perhaps not surprising, especially given the relatively limited skill necessary to do so.

The appearance of children in these workshop settings and involvement in simple tasks also finds parallels in ethnographic accounts, in which the youngest workers were given tasks requiring minimal skill (e.g., digging clay, moving vessels, hauling fuel) that nonetheless allowed them to build familiarity with the production process.[2] Ethnographic studies have documented that the time necessary to develop motor skills required for different types of ceramic production techniques (coiling, throwing, molding, etc.) varies between two and ten years of training (Gandon and Roux 2019, 229), with wheel throwing taking longer to learn than other techniques (Roux and Corbetta 1989). Over time, apprentices take on ever more skilled duties – from simple (e.g., handle pulling and attaching, simple decorative treatments) to more complex tasks (e.g., wheel throwing, turning, and finishing) (Curtis 1962, 488–89; Henein 1997, 186–87). This guided task-specific learning is described by Crown as "scaffolding," whereby simple, achievable tasks performed by a learner are collaboratively worked into the larger production process (2007, 680). Such simple tasks are also in keeping with cognitive development studies, which demonstrate that children can reproduce highly complex designs only by the age of seven to nine years (Crown 2007, 683).

Considering evidence from other industries of the Roman world, an important social institution in professional training generally was likely the family (Vitto 1986, 60). Indeed, in the Roman period, children are thought to have received much professional education within the household (Bradley 1985, 313). Saller has suggested that the family might be considered as the fundamental economic unit of the Roman world (2011, 117)[3] and that instruction regarding professional crafts and farming, in addition to domestic tasks, was conducted by family members (2011, 124). Membership lists of professional associations of trades certainly seem to suggest that association membership (and conceivably, by extension, profession) was often maintained within families (Venticinque 2010, 278–79). The epitaphs in the Late Roman necropolis of Korykos indicate that the profession was maintained within potting families, with an example of a father and two sons, and another example of three brothers, all potters (Patlagean 1977, 168, f. 74, 79, inscription no. 702, 726).[4]

[2] This was also noted by Vitto (1986, 60).

[3] Others disagree, seeing the firm as a key form of organization (Hawkins 2012).

[4] This need not always have been the case, however, as there was also an example of a potter who was the son of a construction worker (Varinlioğlu 2011, 178), and children were not always exchanged in marriage among families in the same profession, as evidenced by an example of a daughter of a fisherman who married a potter (Patlagean 1977, 168, f. 81, inscription no. 411a).

Such family-based learning may be proposed for the ceramic workshops at Dura-Europos, where workspaces were sometimes built into courtyard houses (Figures 3 and 4; Allara 1992; 1994), or in the case of Hierapolis, where it is difficult to disentangle domestic and workspaces inside the Frontinus Street houses (Mastronuzzi and Melissano 2007). At Elkab, an ostrakon found in one of the potters' houses mentions two brothers who were raised in one of the house-workshops, with each settling in their own houses in the community, and it is thought that they may have worked as potters in the paternal house-workshop (Hendrickx 1998, 1358). Beyond the limited number of workshops with domestic spaces, however, the role of the family in training new potters is difficult to pin down. As informal household training was not legally contracted, we lack textual evidence concerning its organization. Moreover, as ceramic workshops in the region tended to be separated from domestic spaces, attempts to link these workplaces to specific social (particularly household) groups remain tenuous (for further discussion on workplaces, see Chapter 2; see also Auer 2014 and 2018 for discussion on the archaeological identification of household pottery production in Noricum).

Alternatively, it is feasible that the child-ceramicist of Kôm el-Dikka was working according to a more formal apprenticeship arrangement. As of yet, apprenticeship contracts specifically for potters have not yet been recovered in the Roman East (Mees 2002, 214), yet a reference to a potter and male apprentice does appear in a Talmudic source, in which an act of theft of clay by the apprentice from his master is described (Midrash Leviticus Rabbah 23.12; Vitto 1986, 60). Ample evidence for apprentices and master craftsmen can be found in Roman textual sources for many other crafts and, while most contracts concern textile work, a wider variety of trades is also represented (e.g., weaving, wool carding, coppersmithing, nailmaking, bricklaying). It is conceivable that these arrangements also might involve training potters (Westermann 1914a; Bradley 1985; Bergamasco 1995; Freu 2016; for discussion on ceramic apprenticeship in Classical Greece, see Hasaki 2012). As legal contracts, these documents outline arrangements in which a youth is instructed in a craft or trade, and they address issues of board, food and clothing provisions, holidays, taxes, and contract violations (Bergamasco 1995, 99). Based on this information, it seems that (at least in Roman Egypt) freed boys, slave boys, and slave girls would typically be apprenticed between the ages of ten and fifteen. In the case of craft production, apprenticeships lasted from six months to five years (depending on the trade), and, at the end of that period, it was expected that the apprentice was proficiently skilled in that occupation (Westermann 1914a; 1914b). Several of the contracts specify that the master craftsman would teach the apprentice the trade "as he himself knows it" (Bergamasco 1995, 117; Freu 2016, 187), thereby not only instilling a sense of professional competence but also sustaining the tradition in which he works and not withholding trade secrets.

Such training arrangements – both those documented specifically for potters and those known for other craftwork – have implications for understanding work communities. In Egyptian archives, it is clear that a single industry, such as weaving, could be organized either according to family (especially father-to-son) training or according to apprenticeship contracts (Bergamasco 1995, 154–55) and that both could co-occur. Some masters exerted particularly pronounced influence in establishing new generations of craft professionals by training multiple apprentices at a time (Bergamasco 1995, 126). Moreover, while there are examples of apprentices moving some distance to be trained by a particularly renowned master (Freu 2016, 185–86), such apprenticeships could be much more locally situated in communities, where the role of family networks and apprenticeship arrangements might be tightly enmeshed. Among individuals living in the same town or city, these apprenticeship arrangements might reflect and sustain deeper, more personal ties between the family of the apprentices and the master craftsperson (Bergamasco 1995, 107, 159–61); for example, Bergamasco describes an apprentice contract in which a trainee is entrusted to an uncle (1995, 104, 115). Venticinque (2010, 288–92) and Liu (2017, 217–24), by tracing personal relationships recorded on Egyptian contracts, similarly note the important role that contracting arrangements played within some local craft communities. In the case of the local community of weavers of Oxyrhynchus, their children were sometimes exchanged for apprenticeship. Apprenticeship has been thought by some to have provided children more disciplined instruction and a means of acquiring specialized skills unknown to the craft family (Bergamasco 1995, 150). Some of these exchanges were made among local guild members, thereby serving to strengthen the social ties within these local institutions, as well as supporting the economic well-being of professional peers and community members (Liu 2017, 217–19; also see Venticinque 2010, 277, 288–92).

These family and training arrangements might overlap with local professional associations, institutions that generated trust networks among craft families, by reinforcing collective cooperation and potentially restricting access to the trade (Liu 2017). While no association statute lists are preserved for potters' associations (Mees 2002, 214), associations of potters (*kerameis*, κεραμεῖς) are nonetheless known from epigraphic sources from across the eastern Mediterranean. They appear at Gerasa (SEG VII, 879; Vitto 1986, 60), Ephesos (Outschar 1991, 319), Thyateira in Lydia (Arnaoutoglou 2011, 270; see also Lydian example TAM 5.2 914 in Mees 2002, 229, tab. 53), and possibly at Korykos in Cilicia (Trombley 1987; for a contrary interpretation, see Patlagean 1977, 169). Papyrological references to associations of potters are also known from the first through sixth centuries AD in Egypt in Oxyrhynchites (*P. Oxy.* 54.3766; *P. Oxy.* 31.2570), Arsinoites (*SB* 01.05175; *SPP* 04, S.70) and Hermonthites (*P. Lips.* 97) (Cockle 1981, 91; Mees 2002,

228–29, tab. 53).[5] While guilds may not have been a common feature to all local industries (particularly those outside of cities) and the roles and activities of local guilds appear to have varied depending on the needs of members (Arnaoutoglou 2011), these sources nonetheless highlight the sorts of institutional collectives of professional potters that could exist and that further could intensify and regularize professional relationships over generations.

Family learning, apprenticeship arrangements, and participation in professional associations are all documented ways in which socio-professional networks might influence and direct work practices. Instilling ideas about how work and business should be conducted, as well as how products should look and be made, these training arrangements supported cross-generational transmission of skill sets and sustained craft traditions in manufacturing techniques and product styles. Rather than encouraging trade secrets or monopolies of knowledge among peers (known from other historical contexts), such trust networks instead supported the training of new generations of artisans in techniques, technologies, and perceptions of form and aesthetics. In extreme cases, however, these trust networks might also conceivably stifle new ideas and innovations by preventing an influx of perspectives from outside the community. As Liu (2017) has also noted, guild actions might serve to close off trade communities by restricting access to the profession by outsiders[6] and thus restricting local industry's exposure to and receptiveness toward new ideas over time. This process is described in modern literature on industry clusters as innovation "lock-in" (Boschma 2005, 163–64). However, it was also in this institutional context that practices and traditions changed, and professional networks also could encourage innovation, particularly innovation "spillovers" between workgroups within a production cluster (Jaffe et al. 1993; Saxenian 1994). The success of new ideas associated with one potter or workgroup could be quickly appreciated, and the innovations learned and adopted by others in the social network. These professional networks, therefore, could reinforce traditions of craft making within a community (maintaining conservativeness in product appearance and type), but they also could stimulate the adoption and facilitate the spread of new ideas.

TRACKING INNOVATION

Social and professional networks are the matrix through which traditions are sustained and through which innovative ideas move, and this recognition raises further questions, not least: *Where do these new ideas come from, and how are they*

[5] Examples (*O.Bodl.* 2.2143.4 and *SB* 10.10258) are also known from Egypt, without more specific geographical information (Mees 2002, 228–29, tab. 53).

[6] This is likewise echoed by Venticinque (2010).

interpreted through cultural understandings of craftwork? The movement of potters, trained in a distinct tradition, into new environments is certainly one means to introduce new ideas on form, technique, and technology (Gauß et al. 2015). Such movement, which has been documented in other parts of the empire (Johnston 1985), is more difficult to establish for these eastern regions, given the limited number of textual sources and the fact that, in many industries, the potters of the region did not stamp their tablewares with maker marks. Occasional evidence, however, demonstrates that potters did sometimes move from large production centers to new locations. Outschar (1991, 318) describes an earlier example of two Attic potters, Kittos and Bakchios (presumably trained in the widely popular black-gloss tableware tradition of the fourth through first centuries BC), who were granted citizenship by the people and council of Ephesos so as to settle and work in the city. It has also been noted that first-century-BC/first-century-AD vessels stamped with the name *C. Sentius* derived from multiple industry centers in both the western provinces (at Arezzo, Padana, Lyon) as well as an eastern provinces (ESB) (Outschar 1991; Zabehlicky-Scheffenegger 2003; Rotroff et al. 2018, 133–34). The Italian examples stamped with *C. Sentius* (thought to be the workshop owner) sometimes included a second name (possibly a worker in the workshop).[7] The name of *Q. Pompeius Serenus* (a potter known to be associated with the industry at Puteoli) also has appeared on an ESB vessel (Wrabetz 1977; Zabehlicky-Scheffenegger 2003; Rotroff et al. 2018, 133–34). The development of ESB as an eastern tableware, and its early production of forms influenced by ITS, has led some to propose that this production may have been initiated by potters from Italy in the mid-Augustan period (Hayes 1985), with the workshop of *C. Sentius* perhaps being among its early entrepreneurs (Zabehlicky-Scheffenegger 2003; for contrary interpretation, see Kenrick 2000, 48).

The movement of potters might not necessarily imply the establishment of new workshops, however. Lamps stamped with the name *Faustus* have been found at sites in Israel, Lebanon, Jordan, Libya, Egypt, and Cyprus (Bailey 1988; Oziol 1993; Lynch 1995; Mikati 2003), and the remains have been variably interpreted. The products appear in several fabrics, in some cases that match the clay compositions used in local pottery production (Lynch 1995, 115). Similar stamp impressions and particularities in the signatures observed on lamps of different fabrics at different sites are further suggestive of a potter who moved several times over the course of his career (Bailey 1988, 97), who was involved in the establishment of branch workshops across the eastern Mediterranean (Oziol 1993, 34–36), or who operated as an itinerant potter

[7] Kenrick (2000, 48) disagrees with this branch workshop model, particularly in the case of *C. Sestius*, and provides some alternative interpretations.

using the same tools and producing in different locales using local clays (Lynch 1995). In any such scenario, ceramicists, such as *Faustus*, would have been moving considerable distances around the eastern Mediterranean and potentially influencing local consumer markets as they introduced their wares.

These examples highlight the roles that individual potters and businessmen might have in establishing and developing tableware industries across provinces, possibly through the establishment of "branch workshops" (Outschar 1991, 318; Zabehlicky-Scheffenegger 2003) or through itinerant producers (Lynch 1995).[8] Such examples suggest that at least some innovations regarding pottery style involved the movement and migration of trained potters, bringing new ideas about pottery that were then enacted using local materials. Movement by potters might also not be unidirectional. Citing evidence of graffiti written in Greek script on wares from Arezzo, Lund has proposed the possibility that, in the mid first century BC, potters from the eastern Mediterranean (including those working in the ESA industry) may have been involved in the early establishment of Italian sigillata production centers (Lund 2005, 243).[9] Also, movements of potters might occur across smaller geographic scales through movement among different workshops. Mees, in reconstructing the co-occurrence of stamped names on vessels, showed that a single potter's name might appear alongside as many as eight or nine other names (presumed to be workshop managers) (2002, 289–90). He also argued that, among the Italian workshops, a potter might average ten years of employment in the same workshop before moving to a new workplace (2002, 299). If his reconstructions are accurate, this would mean that potters moved both between workshops and between production centers, presumably picking up new ideas and techniques along the way.

Innovations in pottery need not involve the relocation of potters, of course, and there are examples in which certain vessels or attributes within a larger local potting repertoire were partially changed, suggesting the selective adoption of new ideas rather than a movement of people.[10] That such a change in production may not require the arrival of new potters can be observed with the Ketios Valley workshops (third–first centuries BC), for example, where

[8] Outschar (1991, 318) notes that, with 174 ESB vessels stamped with *C. Sestius* and discovered in the Lower Agora of Ephesos, the workshop may have been in or near the city.

[9] Mees has observed the appearance of Greek names in these industries (alongside Latin names) and suggests that they may have played a dependent role (2002, 279–80).

[10] Similar situations have been observed elsewhere in the Roman world. In Early Roman Campania, Roth interprets black-gloss tableware produced in fabric VI as representing a "hybrid product" (2007, 143). Blending local clays and shapes with a foreign surface treatment (i.e., black gloss), the fabric VI pottery products represented "competitive emulation," whereby certain features of more costly, elite-associated goods were imitated in order to convey a higher social status. As such, Roth describes the hybridity of the ceramic style as a reflection of "cultural bricolage."

production transitioned from black-gloss to red-slip tableware. At this site, vessels were recovered with manufacturer stamp marks – a feature that is not always common across the eastern provinces but that offers important evidence concerning potters and stylistic change.[11] Here, the appearance of a single name (*Menemachos*) has been documented on vessels of red-slip, black-gloss, and a brown-red finish (Bounegru 2014, 27). This variation in surface color (which results from different kiln firing conditions) follows the growing popularity of red-slipped wares at this time (Hayes 1972; Vickers 1994), with the brown-red coloration thought to represent a phase of experimentation (Bounegru 2014, 27). This sequence therefore highlights the versatility of potters and their ability to adapt their work to new economic influences. It also demonstrates that some of these changes could take place quite quickly, even within the career of a single potter.

The previous example highlights the interplay between pottery industries that drew on wider regional trends to inspire changes in local production, but Vickers (1994) has also suggested that such changes (particularly this transition from black gloss to red slip) could also reflect changing consumer preferences concerning forms, surface treatments, and decorative elements in other materials (especially silver plate and other metal wares). Of course, much literature has addressed such *skeuomorphism*, where "the manufacture of vessels in one material intended to evoke the appearance of vessels regularly made in another" (Vickers and Gill 1994, 106; also used in Knappett 2002, 108–9; see also Frieman 2013; Blitz 2015). There was certainly a large and heterogeneous market of table settings during the period – many of which we know we are largely missing from the archaeological record (baskets, most metal, glass, wooden, and stone vessels) – and attempting to pin down directionality and origins of influential ideas between media is consequently a challenge.

In some cases, the crossover between metal wares and ceramics, however, can be archaeologically traced in the workshops. A mold for a hemispherical bowl discovered at Sardis, for example, presented pressmarks on the exterior and raised/recessed details on the interior of the mold, suggesting that it was pressed directly from a metal vessel (Rotroff and Oliver 2003, 96).[12] Such relief wares manufactured in ceramic have long been assumed to have been influenced by examples in metal (for discussion, see Rotroff 2006), but the mold demonstrates an even closer encounter between a potter and metal vessels. Glass wares were part of the wider tableware milieu of the period.

[11] For a similar exercise for Sardis Eastern Sigillata production, see Rotroff et al. (2018).

[12] Rotroff and Oliver note that the irregular exterior of the mold would have made it difficult to mount on a wheel, and therefore other craft uses (e.g., metalworking) should be considered.

At Sagalassos, there is evidence of some industry interaction between the local glass and pottery industries. In this case, a type of pontil rod (a mandril) used in the manufacture of glass rings and beads was identified composed of the same clay used for the local pottery tablewares (Lauwers et al. 2007), evidencing glassworkers drawing on raw materials typically provisioned to the potters. At Khirbet 'Azzun, a village in the area of modern Israel, ceramic kilns dated to the third and fourth centuries AD and associated with the production of jars were found alongside glass waste (Erlich 2017, 193). The nature, intensity, and regularity of these encounters is difficult to ascertain, but reconstructing such business interactions places local craftspeople working in different media nonetheless in some degree of proximity and mutual awareness, perhaps facilitating the transmission of ideas and concepts concerning craft techniques, materials, and products.

The sources of inspiration about product trends might also have resulted from far more mundane encounters, via traded pottery. For example, at Anemourion in the Late Roman period, the Small Baths were employed for housing, commercial trade, and production purposes, whereby neighbors appear to have engaged in both pottery manufacture and commercial trade (Russell 2002, 226–27). A dump deposit of production waste was identified just outside the northern service areas of the Small Baths – where a kiln has been identified – and the composition of the dump demonstrated a workshop manufacturing a range of locally produced common and cooking wares ("Piecrust Rim" ware) (Russell 2002, 226–27). Additionally, several tableware bowl and plate forms were manufactured by the workshop in the same local coarse fabric. Those coarse tableware forms appear to follow the shapes and profiles of imported Cypriot Red Slip (CRS) and ARS wares being sold in some quantity by the traders in the other areas of the same bath complex (Russell 2002, 226–27). Thus, it seems that this local workshop, making pottery in local coarse clay, offered a line of tablewares for local consumption (presumably that were more affordable), but that drew inspiration from the finer imported types being sold next door. A similar situation may also have occurred at Elkab, where a structure thought to have been used by a potter also may have been involved in the sale of pottery. The pottery being sold included both locally manufactured wares as well as imported types brought from Aswan and Luxor (Hendrickx 1998, 1366). In these cases, the spread of ideas about form and style could be received through traded pots, rather than any direct social encounters.

Moreover, while the general shape or color of a vessel might follow large-scale trends of "ware groups," the particular decorative motifs of a vessel might be selected to catch the eye of local consumers. For example, the second-century-AD Sagalassos Red Slip ware (SRSW) platter is a shape commonly produced at Sagalassos (Figure 18). These platters often included

18 Photo of Dionysos statue found in the Upper Agora of Sagalassos (a) and relief decoration with a similar image on Sagalassos Red Slip ware platter manufactured in the city's workshops (b). (Sagalassos Archaeological Research Project)

decorative medallions depicting figures or scenes in relief and around the rim. The vessel itself is clearly from a tradition that referenced metal plate, with incised rim decoration and raised central relief appliqué decoration (Talloen and Poblome 2019, f. 2, 3). However, the decorative feature of the central medallion showed an image of Dionysos, which was a clear reference to a particular type of statue found locally in the city. Two marble statues with Dionysos leaning on a smaller satyr have been found at Sagalassos, one of which was recovered in the Antonine Nymphaeum, where it was likely relocated in Late Antiquity (although the original placement of the statues is not known). The appearance of this specific image on a ceramic platter manufactured in one of the city's workshops reflects a potter familiar with the statue type (so much so that they were able to reproduce it in clay). The use of visual references, utilizing motifs that derive from local urban spaces to decorate ceramics, has also been observed at Gerasa. In this case, a molded head of a bearded Dionysos framed with vines showed striking similarity to contemporary images from the same site; specifically, from mosaics that decorated the floors of local churches (Kehrberg 2009, 502; see also Watson 1989, 242–45; Csitneki 2017, 102). While manufacturing items that fit into a common typology, the specifics are translated through points of cultural reference associated with specific public monuments and visual arts familiar from everyday life in the city. Such urban references may have even been selling points for local consumers.

These examples demonstrate some of the ways that potters might encounter new product ideas about form, style, and decorative motifs from outside of a craft tradition. Rather than production simply or only following abstracted consumer demand, they serve to demonstrate the actual lived circumstances by which potters could be exposed to new ideas. Embedded in complex social and material webs (potter-potter, potter-other-artisans, potter-distributors, potter-consumers, and potter-material culture) these examples also highlight the creative milieu of craft relationships in the Roman world.

Adaptation Costs

At this point, this chapter has considered how traditions are maintained through professional networks and institutions of craft learning, and it has demonstrated from where innovative ideas might derive. At issue now is how these different influences – embodied skill, technical knowledge, product traditions, and innovative ideas – come together in the process of making. Here, it is useful to turn to the recent cognitive experimental work conducted by Gandon and Roux (2019), whose study sheds some light on the workshop and workgroup dynamics of vessel innovations by modern potters in India. In this experiment, the potters were shown a drawing of a vessel form and asked to reproduce it on the wheel. The study had results that are of interest for this discussion.

Most notably, Gandon and Roux (2019) offer some perspective on how we observe innovative ideas being brought into a tradition. They noted that their modern potters were not only able to throw the unfamiliar form from an abstracted drawing, but also each threw the shape using a unique combination of gestures, primarily based on the hand gestures that were familiar to them. One-half to two-thirds of their hand gestures and motor skills were "transferred" in making the unfamiliar forms. The professional training of each potter seems to have provided them with a toolkit of gestures (in these examples, approximately thirty hand positions per potter) that could be deployed to experiment with new forms (Gandon and Roux 2019, 237). Such improvised innovation that relies upon embodied skill and familiar techniques can be observed archaeologically. The study also noted that the ability of a potter to efficiently adapt their motor skills to make a new form was most significantly influenced by the expertise and skill of the individual potter (Gandon and Roux 2019, 237); the more experienced and more highly skilled potters had a larger toolkit involving a wider range of gestures with which to successfully experiment and only required a slight modification of their skills to reproduce and standardize the new shapes. Potters skilled in manufacturing fewer forms or small, open forms (which require only a few hand positions) therefore had higher adaptation costs in making new shapes, in that they required a longer period of training (possibly as much as two years) to acquire the motor skills necessary for such new shapes (Gandon and Roux 2019, 237). In this regard, not all potters were equally positioned in their career to easily adopt new styles, and, within a workshop, there might be differences in terms of the skill level, experience, and economic standing of a given potter.

The process of transferring skills, techniques, and understandings of form in order to make these new types has been long recognized by archaeologists. While these changes can rarely be related archaeologically to the hand of an individual potter (see Crown 2007 for discussion), they have been observed in larger corpora of material, accounting for repertoire changes over periods on the scale of the half- or quarter-century. Once referred to as "imitations,"[13] in more recent material culture studies, these changing styles have been referred to as object "hybrids" (Antonaccio 2005), evidence of "cultural bricolage" (Terrenato 1998; Roth 2007), or "glocal" styles (Hodos 2009; Pitts and Versluys 2015). This terminology reflects an attempt to capture the process in which stylistic features of wares associated with other groups become adopted, while certain characteristics of local traditions of material culture were maintained. In reinterpreting those new ideas through tradition and embodied *habitus*, pottery innovations become tradition, and "imitations" of foreign wares become local products. Such innovations, therefore, very much become local stories; and the local specificities of such processes that balance tradition and innovation are, over time, well demonstrated in the following examples from the tableware industry at Sagalassos. Each example appears to have followed widespread changes in larger and more widely distributed production centers in ways that might be described as "imitations," yet they were very much transferred through established traditions. These examples also highlight some of the constellations of factors (traditional and innovative) that influenced the final form and appearance of locally manufactured vessels.

Local Stories of Innovation: Sagalassos' Tableware Industry

Three published examples, taken from the repertoire of a long-running pottery industry, provide evidence of how potters working in a local tradition took on innovative ideas from divergent sources, with varying degrees of consumer success, and varying degrees of adaptation cost. Some innovations proved highly successful, while others were commercial failures. Importantly,

[13] The term "imitation" has been rightly criticized for its allusions to inferior quality and design and for its assumptions of cultural dominance and emulation.

in particular periods in the history of this local industry, different influences on the local choices of products can be observed.

The area around Sagalassos had long supported ceramic production, since at least the Iron Age. Within the urban area, however, the earliest evidence for pottery manufacture (of color-coated wares) is dated to the Hellenistic period (Braekmans 2011; Braekmans et al. 2011; van der Enden et al. 2014; Kelepeshi et al. 2024). By the late first century BC/early first century AD, the workshops of the city seem to have moved to the eastern suburbs, where they began to manufacture tablewares with a glossy red-orange slip, designated SRSW. In experimenting with new techniques and styles, they followed wider trends in eastern sigillata and Italian sigillata, while also sustaining local vessel shapes – like the so-called *mastos* cup type, which was already popular in the Hellenistic period (Poblome 1999, 311; Waelkens and Poblome 2011, 64–65; Poblome et al. 2013, 180–281; van der Enden et al. 2014, 91–93). Thus, at the time in which local potters began manufacturing Roman-period red-slipped wares, the industry was already blending these new ideas within the framework of established potting traditions.

Another significant change in the production tradition appeared substantially later in the industry's history. Beginning in the fourth century AD, the Sagalassos workshops began to manufacture a repertoire comprising mostly large open forms (plates, large bowls, and platters). Inspiration for the new SRSW forms has been related (either directly or indirectly) to wider trends in pottery production sites in North Africa, as well as in the metal plate industries of the period (Poblome 1999, 24–26; Talloen and Poblome 2005; Poblome and Firat 2011). These vessels are thought to be formally related to changes in Late Antique dining practices, particularly the use of larger open forms of platters, bowls, and basins likely used in communal dining (Hawthorne 1997; Hudson 2006; Vroom 2007; Murphy and Poblome 2016).[14] Again, these ideas were transferred through earlier techniques and styles known to the potter. Thus, while some forms closely resemble vessels of ARS and LRD, other forms are adapted from the extant local repertoire. For example, the small cups (SRSW form 1F150) typical of the high imperial period, while retaining their proportions and shape, were made much larger in the later periods (changing from an average diameter of 8 cm to 32 cm). Therefore, a vessel shape that might, in the second century, have been used as a small cup or bowl may, in the fourth century, be better understood as a basin (Figure 19). The form was reinterpreted by the potter for a new

[14] Sagalassos Red Slip ware vessels dated to the first and second centuries AD tended to be approximately 15 cm in diameter and were predominately under 25 cm in diameter, while the SRSW dated to the late fifth and early sixth centuries tended to be approximately 27 cm in diameter and were typically less than 35 cm in diameter (Murphy and Poblome 2016, 64).

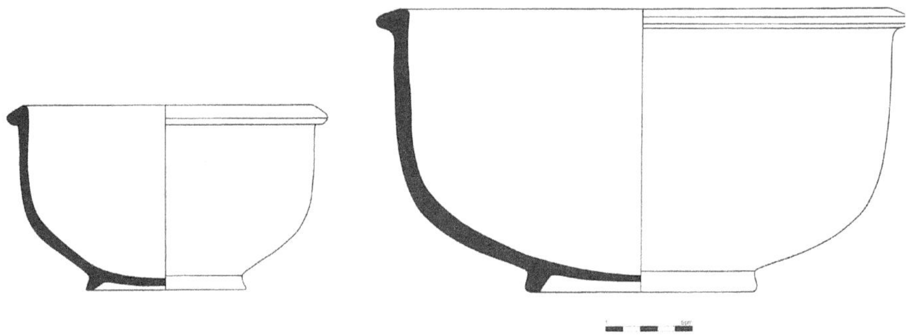

19 Sagalassos Red Slip ware form 1F150 demonstrating change in size over the time, from a small cup to a large basin. (Based on Poblome 1999, 421–42, f. 79)

consumer – conceivably one that took their meals from large, shared bowls and plates while dining at a U-shaped table.[15]

Such changes in repertoire involved "tuning" traditional techniques and gestures to create the traditional rim form and wall curvature, thus lowering the costs associated with learning the new form. The cited earlier ethnographic study by Gandon and Roux (2019) considered the relative adaptation costs of innovation. These major shifts in the repertoire of Sagalassos potters would have had broader economic consequences, however. The production of larger vessels presented particular production challenges (Murphy 2017). They also had implications for the economics of workshops; bigger vessels required larger quantities of clay, took longer to dry, consumed more space in a kiln, and required longer fuel-expending firings (Murphy and Poblome 2017); and these factors affected the overall vessel output of their kilns (Murphy and Poblome 2017, 81, f. 12). Thus, what may seem to be a simple scaling-up of a vessel shape to meet changing consumer demand would have had substantial impacts on the everyday work practices and economics of potting. Innovations, thus, could have offset the increased production costs with lower adaptation costs.

In the seven centuries of production at the workshops of Sagalassos, many more stories of potters drawing influences from wider Mediterranean trends could be constructed, demonstrating "hybrid" production practices that blended wider pottery trends with local work practice (Hodos 2009; Van Oyen 2012; Pitts and Versluys 2015). Reconstructing the constellations of ideas, materials, and craft know-how that come together in the process of making often focuses on these types of stories: complex "globalized" networks

[15] A case of local consumer tastes influencing the product choices of local potters has similarly been interpreted at the Late Hellenistic workshops of Kibyra, where Japp (2009, 104) observes that several common Eastern Sigillata forms (i.e., "dishes with profiled rims," "hemispherical bows with collars") were absent from the local repertoire.

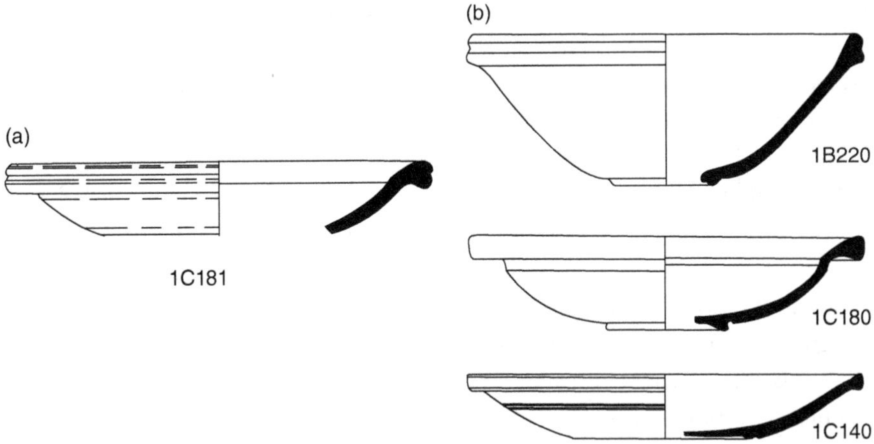

20 Sagalassos Red Slip ware (SRSW) form 1C181 shape (a) alongside 1B220, 1C180, 1C140 (b). The experimental 1C181 form demonstrates influences from existing popular SRSW vessel types. (Based on Murphy 2017, 111–12, f. 8.2)

that link a potter in Asia Minor to ideas pulled from a pot or potter in Italy or Gaul or Syria. These networks demonstrate that these potters on a Pisidian mountain were not working in isolation, but rather were tapped into a larger world of producers and consumers. In the Roman Empire, even modest craftspeople were interconnected in a "globalized" world.

While external influences, particularly from the major ceramic wares of a period, are relatively easy to identify in the formal and stylistic characteristics of pottery, it is also possible to identify instances in which the inspiration for new product ideas can be seen as deriving entirely from *within* the production tradition, mixing and matching ideas from well-known product types already made within the community. The published example of an SRSW 1C181 offers a helpful example (Murphy 2017, where it is noted as 1CXXX). This dish is consistent in finish with other vessels manufactured at the site, but it is in its profile that the patterns of innovation can be seen. The shape seems to be a composite shape, made up of elements characteristic of other common forms. For instance, its grooved rim seems to reference that of a known bowl shape (SRSW form 1B220); the low angle of the wall is similar to a known dish (SRSW form 1C180); and the inner groove of its wall is distinct to a particular dish (SRSW form 1C140) (Murphy 2017, 111–12, f. 8.2). Each of these other three vessel shapes (Figure 20) was common and long-produced at Sagalassos. These forms were produced since the first half of the fourth century AD (Poblome 1999, 304–10). This 1C181 vessel type never gained great popularity. Nonetheless, it embodied a reinterpreted tradition, drawing inspiration from within the production tradition itself.

While many of the innovations and changes made in the product repertoire of Sagalassos' potters can be traced to wider consumer phenomena also observed in other parts of the Roman world, these exotic introductions are only one part of the story, and there is a real danger in privileging these international connections over a more balanced reading of the repertoire of local producers. Focusing on the external influences runs the risk of first overlooking changing patterns in innovation. Indeed, over the course of a production center's history, it might undergo different phases of innovation, inspired at different times by different sources – sometimes from outside the community and sometimes from within. No pottery tradition or industry is ever static, although it need not look far afield to find inspiration. The example of the 1C181 vessel also highlights the fact that a degree of ongoing "background noise" of experimentation might always be taking place at a production site.

The examples of the *mastos* cup, the adapted cup-basin forms, and the composite dish are just a few from the ceramic industry of Sagalassos, and many local histories of other industries could be told that likewise reflect innovations within a long tradition of ceramic work. Even in long-running industries, there were innovations and changes that appear in the potting repertoire demonstrating that traditions are not some sort of reflexive default, but rather required sustained cultural transmission and shared practices. The influences identified might be drawn from diverse sources – global wares and local forms. They might recombine ideas concerning form, function, and finish in different ways. They might also balance new economic costs by mitigating adaptation costs via "tuning" known techniques. Local examples of innovation, in isolation, demonstrate the creativity and ingenuity of potters and workshops to take ideas from a range of sources and recombine them in new ways. However, by considering these individual cases of innovation within the longer history of the industry serves to highlight the resilience and adaptability of a local community to balance the dangers of the stagnating effects of innovative lock-in by training new generations in craft trades "as he himself knows it," and accepting innovations reinterpreted through established tradition.

CONCLUSION

The eastern provinces of the Roman Empire had long-established traditions of pottery production. With some industries active for many centuries, they would have relied on intergenerational patterns of learning. Evidence for apprentices and young individuals in pottery workshops highlights their important role in maintaining learned craft traditions and sustaining the professional community. However, in all local industries, new influences and repertoire changes can be observed, with much attention given to the influence of "international" styles. These changes show notably different local responses to changing fashions; some changes appear to draw on a wider network that reaches outside of the local community or beyond industry lines, while others demonstrate networks that seem more locally bound within the production center itself. In either of these cases, while certain features (surface treatment, firing atmosphere, size of vessels) or individual vessel forms are incorporated into the established repertoire, they come to be interpreted through and in relation to the already established tradition of potting and can be assessed according to adaptation costs. Thus, this chapter has attempted to demonstrate how, in social terms, these traditions were maintained, the ways in which innovation might be introduced, and how that innovation might be translated through established production *habitus*.

CHAPTER SIX

SOCIALLY EMBEDDED TECHNOLOGIES AND LOCAL TECHNOLOGICAL STYLES

Everyday arts and crafts witnessed several important technological developments during the Roman period. Among the ceramic industries of the period, the best known and most complex innovations concern some of the large-scale tableware industries of Italy, Gaul, and North Africa, which utilized molds positioned atop a potter's wheel in a "jolly" arrangement and large kilns with a tubular design or saggar use that fired the vessels in a protected, oxidized environment. In functionalist terms, such "advanced" specialized technologies encouraged economic efficiency and contributed to increased production output (Bailey 1997; Hayes 1997, 220–21). However, the technological histories of the period also have been understood in more social terms, whereby the diffusion of pottery technologies, particularly the pottery wheel and updraft kiln in the northern provinces, has been seen as a selective adoption by local potters as well as the arrival of new artisans (Auer 2014; Sutton 2020; Borgers et al. 2021). Such technological histories have been understood in the context of "Romanization" debates.

The histories of pottery technologies in the eastern Mediterranean, however, are different (both in social and economic terms) than those better-known examples from other provinces, at least in part because potters working in these eastern regions had long employed complex industrial technologies. By the Roman period, pottery wheels had been used in the eastern Mediterranean (particularly in the Levant and Egypt) for millennia (Amiran 1956, 48; Hope 1982; Amiran and Shenhav 1984; Israel 1995; Spencer 1997;

Roux and de Miroschedji 2009; Doherty 2015) and, since the later Neolithic and Chalcolithic periods, both single-chambered and two-chambered updraft kilns had been used (Hansen Streily 2000). Consequently, the ceramic industries of this region exhibit both long-maintained technical traditions as well as a significant local diversity in technological innovation that likewise represents local and regional variants. In some cases, these spatial and temporal patterns constitute what Lechtman has called technological styles, which manifest as ingrained traditions of technological choice (Lechtman 1977; Lechtman and Steinberg 1979). According to Lemonnier (1992), community choices in technology use and innovation can only be understood when contextually situated within culturally constructed conceptions of need, function, design, and style. In this respect, local decisions concerning technology design and use represent cultural practices, and technological traditions provide a means to distinguish locally embedded technological decision-making and to better appreciate the diversity of work cultures and industry challenges.

This chapter will focus on two key infrastructural technologies that have received some attention in academic literature: firing technologies (kilns) and rotational technologies (pottery wheels and turntables). Reconstructing the design and use of these features highlights local developments in craft technology and helps to situate the technological choices within changing economic and social contexts. In contrast to the local styles of wares and products (discussed in Chapter 5), however, in the case of choices and styles pertaining to technologies of making, the builders and users of these technologies might not always have been the same individuals. This has implications for how we understand the decision-making of technological changes, the adaptability of ceramicists to available technological styles, and the embeddedness of ceramic workshops in wider networks of tradespeople.

KILN DESIGN VARIABILITY ACROSS THE REGION

Kilns represent the largest and most varied dataset with which to analyze technological choices made by pottery workshops. They also provide rich evidence to link technological choices by individual workshops to wider trends associated with communities across the region and period. Fundamentally, kilns are effective means of firing ceramics as long as they have "(1) a simple rectangular or cylindrical shape, (2) ample fireboxes and room for combustion to take place, (3) good circulation, (4) adequate flue, and (5) a sufficiently large and tall chimney" (Rhodes 1968, 118).[1] Beyond these

[1] Several modern technical treatises have been written on pottery production (e.g., Leach 1949; Rhodes 1968; Zamek 1999). There are also historical treatises, such as the sixteenth-century example by Piccolpasso (1934).

basic constraints, naturally, there is remarkable diversity. Kiln compendia and typologies have proven useful in tracking variability in kiln design in the classical world.[2] Such compendia have identified variations in size, plan, construction material, and mechanisms for the dispersion of heat/flame/smoke – variables that affect the performance of the kiln but that also reflect different traditions in kiln design (for a listing of kiln attributes documented for the region, see Table 3).

Attempts to relate kiln characteristics to meaningful chronological and functional patterns across the wider eastern provinces have been less successful than elsewhere in the Roman world. If we consider rectangular plans in other parts of the empire, for example, it has been proposed that they were specifically used for the firing of brick and tile (Martin 1965; Orlandos 1966; Hasaki 2002, 166; 2006),[3] and in Pannonia and the Rhineland, their appearance in the first century AD has been attributed to the arrival of the Roman army (Swan 1984, 83–85). In her diachronic study of ancient kilns in Greece, Hasaki (2006, 224) noted a minor regional preference for circular types, with rectangular kilns more often associated with tile kilns of the Classical period (particularly at Corinth and Nemea). However, by contrast, in Asia Minor, the Levant, and Egypt, rectangular kilns are associated with nearly all types of products, from amphorae to tablewares (e.g., at Elaiussa-Sebaste, Palmyra, Pergamon, Sagalassos). Thus, interpretations of kiln design and use do not fit very well with the examples documented across the eastern provinces during the Roman period, perhaps due to the great diversity in kiln technologies already developed across the large region over so many millennia of use.

Community-Based Technological Styles

In the eastern provinces, kiln design seems to have been influenced by more local and regional factors than by wider influences. For example, Erlich (2017) has noted patterns in the design and construction of kilns from the area of

[2] Multiple kiln typologies have been developed for different regions in this manner: for Roman Britain by Swan (1984, 2021), for Italy and other regions of Europe by Cuomo Di Caprio (1982, 1992, 2007), for Greece by Hasaki (2002) and Seifert (1993), for the Levant by Delcroix and Huot (1972), and for Hungary by Vamos (2010). Some such compendia are also available online (https://atlasgreekkilns.arizona.edu and https://romankilns.net). These typologies have attracted some criticism regarding their emphasis on morphology (rather than technical performance or social context) and on evolutionarily relating chronological changes in kiln technology to complexity of production organization (Hansen Streily 2000, 70).

[3] Rectangular kilns with transverse arches are thought to have been better suited to hold heavy rectangular loads, although they were more difficult to sustain even firing. Relatedly, there is a notable underrepresentation of tile and brick workshops in the corpus. This may be due to either research bias or due to preservation issues with temporary "Clamp Kilns" (Peacock 1982; Darvill and McWhirr 1984, 254).

modern Israel as being influenced by regional, chronological, and geological contexts, as well as the organization of production (scale of operations and private versus public ownership of the kilnworks). This complex set of variables is difficult to disentangle (Erlich 2017, 200–2). Likewise, local concerns over fuel availability and heat retention might also be expressed in the design of sunken kilns (typically less than a meter below the surface) that would better refract the heat and sustain a longer firing. This is the case at Deir el-Haggar (Dakhla Oasis), Kefar Ḥananya, Khirbet 'Azzun, Buto, Demirci, Palmyra, Saqqara, and Ein Ya'al. At az-Zurrāba (near Petra), several kilns were sunk as much as 1.5 m below ground (Zayadine 1982, 380–82), and one was accessed by way of steps and stone-built corridors. Even on agricultural estates, where some agricultural waste may have been available, kilns were deeply sunken (such as those at Burg el-Arab, Khirbet Baraqa, Giv'ati Junction, Khirbet Irza). This may be related to viticulture, which provides limited, but high-quality,[4] agricultural trimmings for fuel (Matson 1966; Forbes 1996, 84; Foxhall 1998, 37). Thus, even in contexts where design features are thought to be influenced by fuel selection, it is difficult to distinguish or classify these preferences as either environmental or cultural preference.

Occasionally, production centers demonstrated variability in contemporary kiln design that is tied to specialized product needs. This has been shown already with very large, and very small, kilns appearing in the same workshop at Elaiussa-Sebaste. This variability is likewise the case at the Ketios Valley workshops, where multiple kiln designs (circular and rectangular, different combinations of building materials, different pillar versus tongue floor supports) were in use – not only across the wider community but even within a single workshop (Workshop 2, Bounegru 2009, 76). Bounegru suggests that the workshops might have used some kilns for specialized oxygen-rich firings and others for oxygen-starved firings. This would be consistent with pottery evidence from the site that shows both black-gloss and red-gloss vessels manufactured by the same potter (Bounegru 2009, 87). Among the Ketios Valley workshops, the diversity of kiln types might be understood as capturing a period of production innovation among potters.

The evidence from across the eastern provinces is highly varied, but the choices that can be observed tend to manifest within local communities, rather than at larger scales. These technical practices were neither static nor monolithic; rather, as circumstances changed, the technological choices made within communities changed as well. Therefore, it is worthwhile to take a closer look at some of the local influences on kiln designs and design changes over time.

[4] Ethnographically, vine trimmings are often preferred for kiln fuel because they burn hot.

Technological Innovations

In most cases, at sites where multiple workshops were situated in proximity to one another, kilns were often of the same design and constructed of the same materials. In the case of az-Zurrāba, near Petra, enduring local traditions in kiln construction are exhibited over a period of five centuries (i.e., something in the order of twenty generations of potters). Kilns are deeply sunken, constructed in mudbrick, and circular/oval in plan, with traverse arches supporting the oven floor and a domed superstructure. Yet even here the technological traditions were not static, and over time the proportions changed from deeper and narrower kilns to shallower and slightly wider kilns ('Amr 1991, 321). Most of these changes might best be described as tweaks to or gradual shifts in an existing technological practice, rather than a clear break with tradition. Such cultural patterns constitute what Lechtman has called "technological styles" and are manifested as ingrained traditions of technological habit (Lechtman 1977; Lechtman and Steinberg 1979). In a region with hundreds of documented kilns, technologies were constructed according to complex, culturally informed decision-making, rather than strict expectations of economic efficiency or introductions of new technological ideas (Lechtman 1977; Lechtman and Steinberg 1979; Lemonnier 1986, 1992; Pfaffenberger 1992).

This variability in kiln design places the potting community in a key position in both sustaining and innovating local kiln-building traditions. With some of the well-documented and long-running production centers, it becomes possible to trace out the local history of these technological styles. Through these micro-histories of local technology, phases of greater or lesser innovation can be observed across the many centuries of local production. What will be shown is that these kiln changes can often be related to other changes in the history of these working communities – changes in product styles, changes in local building traditions, changes in other local crafts, etc. Providing evidence from three production centers gives a sense of how these local kiln traditions might change over time and how they might tap into local knowledge networks to do so. These three micro-histories are especially useful to juxtapose, as each community appears to have responded to Mediterranean-wide shifts in pottery style by making unique sets of technological choices.

Sagalassos, Southwest Turkey

The kilns at Sagalassos show how technological innovations were introduced and developed through time. In general, several shifts in both kiln design and kiln construction can be observed in Sagalassos' tableware industry through the seven centuries of production in the city. From the Late Hellenistic to Early Imperial periods, four kilns have been identified. The earliest of these kilns, found beneath the Roman Odeion, was rounded in plan and composed of baked earth and used to manufacture a color-coated Late Hellenistic tableware common to the region (Braekmans 2011; Braekmans et al. 2011; Poblome et al. 2013; van der Enden et al. 2014). From the late first century BC to early first century AD, red-slipped tableware became the primary style of tableware manufactured in the city (Poblome 1999). A pottery kiln destroyed in the Augustan period and thought to have been associated with the early phases of the red-slipped ware production was found in the eastern suburbs of the city; it was rectangular in shape and constructed of mudbrick (Poblome et al. 2001, 161). All subsequent kilns found in the city and dated over the next six centuries were round in plan and composed of fired brick with mud lining. At Sagalassos, kiln design became more regularized over time, regularization that accompanies the growth of the local industry.

Even once the local industry was well established and rounded kiln plans became the dominant tradition, there were still changes made to their construction – particularly with the adoption of new building materials. Poblome (1999) has observed that, after the late second century AD, all pottery kilns at Sagalassos were constructed of fired brick and tile; prior to this, the kilns were made entirely of clay or mudbrick. He notes that this transition correlates with the new use of fired brick in major building projects in the city, particularly works on public baths. These bricks were not manufactured in the suburban tableware workshops. Rather, the ceramic building material industry worked with different clays from the city's lower hinterland and, thus, the tableware workshops acquired the tile and brick as consumers. The bricks themselves were often secondarily cut to build the kiln and were not made to order. Moreover, as the tableware workshop buildings themselves continued to be built of mudbrick, the use of fired brick and tile for kilns appears to have been highly specific, likely reflecting a recognition of the benefits and fire-resistant properties of ceramic building material.[5]

Another major change in the tradition of kiln technology at Sagalassos occurred in the Late Roman period. Beginning in the fourth century AD, and as discussed previously, the workshops began to manufacture a repertoire consisting primarily of larger open forms (Poblome 1999, 304–13). These forms were in keeping with tableware trends set by ARS and other major "international" ware groups and probably represent local supplies for changing dining practices of the period (Hawthorne 1997; Hudson 2006; Vroom 2007; Murphy and Poblome 2016; 2017; see also Chapter 1). These larger, open forms set new production demands. Yet the workshops did not adapt the size of their kilns to accommodate these vessels but rather continued to build kilns approximately 1.0–1.5 m in diameter. Instead, where significant changes can

[5] As Rhodes (1968, 83) notes, "Once clay has been fired it becomes very stable and may be reheated again and again with little change occurring."

21 Photo of Sagalassos saggar reconstruction with a coarse ware basin containing table wares that would have been stacked inside. (Sagalassos Archaeological Research Project)

be observed is in the types of kiln furniture employed at this time, including the adoption of saggar-like vessels into which stacks of tableware (SRSW) vessels were placed for firing (Figure 21). The use of these saggars would have affected changes in the kiln loading and firing process. There were also related changes in the use of other types of kiln furniture (e.g., clay spacers and wedges), likely reflecting these new kiln-loading techniques.

The reason for these changes may have also been related to changing reliance on fuel types, as palynological analyses from the region suggest contemporary changes in landscape use (Vermoere et al. 2003; Murphy and Poblome 2017, 76). The use of these saggars might also reflect the greater investment made on the part of potters in their wares. It has been demonstrated that, for the Sagalassos potters, these changes to the loading system would have drastically affected the number of vessels fired in each kiln load. In fact, sixth-century-AD kiln loads using saggars are thought to have reduced the number of vessels by more than two-thirds[6] when compared with the firing of earlier styles of smaller vessels (Murphy and Poblome 2017, 81). There is also reason to suspect that the use of saggars had side effects, resulting in darker surface color and discolorations – thus also affecting the overall

[6] The reconstructions resulted in 1,500–2,000 vessels per second-century-AD kiln load and 350–450 vessels per sixth-century-AD kiln load (Murphy and Poblome 2017, 81).

appearance of the tablewares. In order to more efficiently prepare the kiln loads, the loads seem to have been formed, dried, and slipped as batches, indicated by a lightly incised line running down vessel stacks (Murphy and Poblome 2017, 78). In these Late Roman phases, despite these changes, what is striking is that the kilns at Sagalassos continued to be made and maintained according to many centuries of tradition, while the entire technological system related to loading and stacking the kiln was altered and adapted.

Although composed from a different clay fabric, the saggars themselves could have been manufactured in the workshops, and the rim morphology of these coarseware vessels finds parallels in some of the red-slipped tableware lekane forms popular at the time.[7] The production of saggars was therefore likely local or regional, while the inspiration for their use in firing at Sagalassos may have come from outside the community. One possibility for the introduction of saggar use is from North African production centers manufacturing ARS from the third through seventh centuries AD (Peacock 1990; Mackensen 1993; Bonifay 2004). The North African saggars were uniquely designed for stacking, by contrast to the more multifunctional Sagalassos examples. Moreover, Bonifay has suggested that the development of saggar technologies in North Africa may have been inspired by faience production or the tubular terra sigillata kilns (Bonifay 2004, 60–61; Nenna and Nicholson 2013). The appearance of these container forms also corresponds to a growing repertoire of ARS-related forms at Sagalassos and other Asia Minor production sites by the fourth century AD. However, there is no particular reason to assume technological transfers followed pottery styles. Alternatively, it is worth noting that saggars were also used in glazed ware and faience production, as it prevented glaze from fusing between adjacent vessels and, indeed, glazed ware production has been documented much closer to Sagalassos at Tarsus (Goldmann 1950), Perge (Atik 1995), and even Dura-Europos (Toll 1943).

The Sagalassos example highlights the interplay of a complex set of variables that seems to have influenced changes in local technological choices. Consumer trends and preferences, availability of fuel sources, introductions of building materials, and new trends in the pyrotechnologies of other crafts, all appear to have influenced the development and use of pottery technologies. Moreover, the kiln furnace was just one part of a larger technological system and, even if furnace design itself might not change, important introductions in the accessories (i.e., kiln furniture) of the technological process might have major impacts on the practices of work.

7 The wall contours and rim shapes are very similar to red-slipped lekane forms – particularly SRSW 1F160 and SRSW 1F140.

Buto, Egypt

It is helpful to contrast the local technological traditions and innovations of Sagalassos with trends observed at the site of Buto, as the latter site offers an opportunity for the most detailed technological study of pottery kilns from a single production center in the study region. A range of variation in kiln design has been documented here from the Hellenistic through Late Roman periods (Ballet et al. 2006; 2007; 2019). Buto also provides another example of how local kiln technology might be adapted to achieve new pottery styles.

Tableware production at Buto began in the Hellenistic period (second–first century BC), with evidence for the production of black-gloss tablewares. Buto represents a rare example of an Egyptian potting site manufacturing black gloss with overpaint (Ballet 2011). Ballet suggests that the stylistic inspiration for these products was mediated through Alexandria from the wider Mediterranean (particularly from production in Italy, Greece, and Asia Minor) (Ballet 2011; Ballet et al. 2019, 287). The Hellenistic-period kilns were primarily round in plan, constructed of mudbrick, and designed with closed superstructures (Charlesworth 1972). Such "beehive" kilns would have helped to induce a darkened slip by closing the upper firing chamber and starving it of oxygen. Such enclosed oven designs also offer advantages in that they more effectively retain heat, driving greater fuel efficiency (Rhodes 1968, 116–17); probably related to fuel needs and perceived efficiency, Ballet has noted that low firing was a common production problem at the site (2019, 287).

While the earlier kilns at Buto were primarily composed of mudbrick with mud mortar, a change to fired brick with mud mortar appeared in the second century AD (Ballet et al. 2006; 2019, 290). This change did not impact the general design of the kiln but rather reflects the Roman-period kiln builders employing newly available building materials. Similarly to the situation at Sagalassos – at Buto, contemporary with the conversion of a nearby Greek/Hellenistic? tholos bath into a bath with a hypocaust system (Ballet et al. 2019, 290), kiln builders also began to employ fired brick. At least one of the kilns (Kiln 7) even used the bath-specific, round *pilae* tiles in construction (Ballet et al. 2019, pl. 32–33). Ballet has questioned whether this adaptation of the baths might be part of a wider set of technological influences introduced from outside the community (2019, 290) because, by the second half of the first century AD, red-slipped tablewares also began to appear in the Buto repertoire. These styles should be contextualized within the growing popularity of other wares (i.e., ESA, ESC, and ITS) across the eastern Mediterranean (Ballet 2007, 19; Ballet et al. 2007, 135). To achieve the production of these new red-slipped pottery styles, there were also noted changes in the local kiln design, including the appearance of a small conduit made of reused amphora necks and terracotta pipes (Figure 22). These channels either ran under the stoke hole or

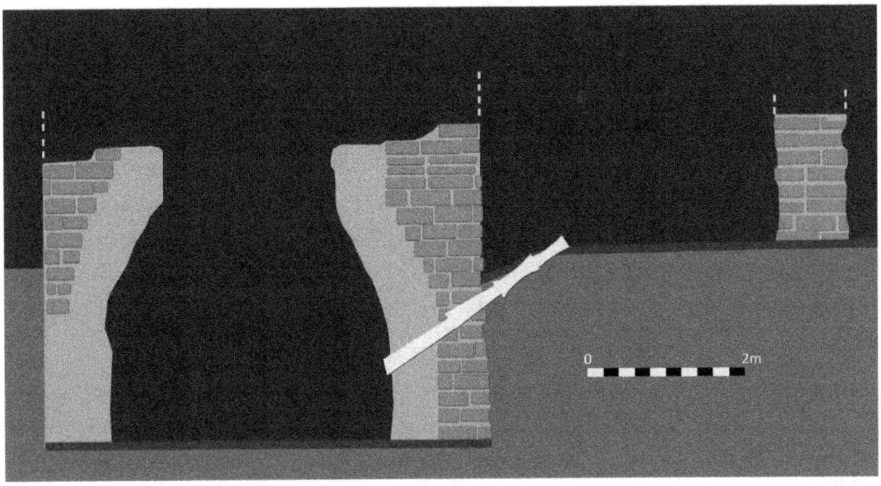

22 Reconstruction of a kiln found at Buto (Egypt) with the side flue. (Based on Ballet et al. 2006, 21, f. 4)

cut through the kiln wall and into the firing chamber (Hartung et al. 2007, 131–33). The conduit of one such kiln (F40) was found blocked by an amphora toe, suggesting that the vent could be opened and closed (Béguin et al. 2019, 63, pl. 14b). The closed dome structures, which had been so critical for the production of earlier black gloss, were maintained, however. The insertion of these conduits into the firing chamber has been explained by the excavators as a means to rush the chamber with oxygen using bellows (Ballet et al. 2006, 21, f. 4; Schmitt 2019, 188–89). This air-intake valve would have helped to induce a red (oxidized) coloration of the ware while maintaining heat retention at other stages of the firing (Ballet et al. 2006).

These tweaks to kiln design are thought to reflect ideas transmitted through wider knowledge networks connecting potters and other craftspeople in the region, although the social mechanism directing this process remains unclear (Ballet et al. 2019, 290). One possible inspiration for this ventilation feature in kiln design could be contemporary sigillata industries in Gaul, Italy, and Syria that used "tubular" kiln designs (Ballet et al. 2019, 289). In this sense, the influences of production technology would follow the influences of product style. However, at another Egyptian production site at Tell Atrib (approximately 150 km from Buto), a kiln associated with another late Ptolemaic, red-slipped ware production site has been discovered, and it was also observed to have small conduits lined with amphora sherds running into the chamber (Scholl 1995, 423). It is not clear what function the conduit had, but its appearance may be suggestive of a more widespread technological feature in the delta region.

Another source of inspiration for these ventilation shafts might be found in the furnace traditions of other local industries. Two kilns (interior diameters of

0.93 m and 1.2 m) with the remains of lime residue were found in Area P4, *Four* 2 and *Four* 3 (Lecuyot and Schmitt 2019, 157–58, f. 53–54). These were unusual furnaces, contrasting with the other pottery kilns excavated (Schmitt 2019, 187, pl. 34–35). They were cut into an earlier mudbrick wall and exhibit an unusual draft feature: a channel of fired bricks running horizontally along the length of the chamber (Schmitt 2019, 187, t. 36, pl. 34–35). It was proposed by Schmitt (2019, 187) that these might be lime kilns or pottery kilns converted for lime burning, but for our immediate purposes they importantly demonstrate a common concern with draft and the channeling of air. It may be indicative of cross-industry sharing of pyrotechnological knowledge. In addition to lime burning and pottery production, Buto is also thought to have hosted metal-working and faience production, according to excavators working in the 1960s (Seton-Williams 1967). Those early excavations found two very small furnaces (internal diameters of 0.32 m and 0.48 m) with tuyères that they associated with metalworking (Seton-Williams 1967, 152).[8] Faience vessel production was also reported by the early excavations, with remains of a rectangular faience kiln and stacking furniture found at the site (Charlesworth 1972, 45–46). Although in a poor state of preservation, it was nonetheless clear that the dimensions of that faience kiln (1.6 m by 7.0 m) differed from those associated with most of the contemporary pottery kilns. Faience kilns found at Roman-period Memphis also employed vent holes thought to accommodate bellows shafts (Nicholson and Peltenburg 2000, 186; Nicholson 2013, 62), and Nicholson (2013, 62) even proposed that this use of tuyères may have been related to the pottery kilns used at Buto. While a somewhat speculative observation, such features found across contemporary Egyptian industries may provide local contexts for the innovations in pottery kiln design.

At Buto, like at Sagalassos, changing product trends, fuel conservation, the pyrotechnologies of other local industries, and local building projects influenced the choices made in new kiln design and use. While the specifics of how and why choices are made are decidedly local in expression, they illustrate the dynamic nature of technological choices and shared technological styles.

Legionary Kilnworks, Jerusalem

The kilnworks attributed to *Legio X Fretensis* found outside of ancient Jerusalem present a more abrupt series of technological changes in kiln design. Prior to the establishment of the military site, the area was already occupied by pottery workshops dated to the Second Temple period from the first century BC (Berlin 2005; Rosenthal-Heginbottom 2005; Arubas and Goldfus 2008b;

[8] Significant quantities of metal slag were also reported in the area (Charlesworth 1972, 46), although some of the larger kilns with tuyères might be better understood as pottery kilns in light of more recent excavations (Charlesworth 1972, 45–46).

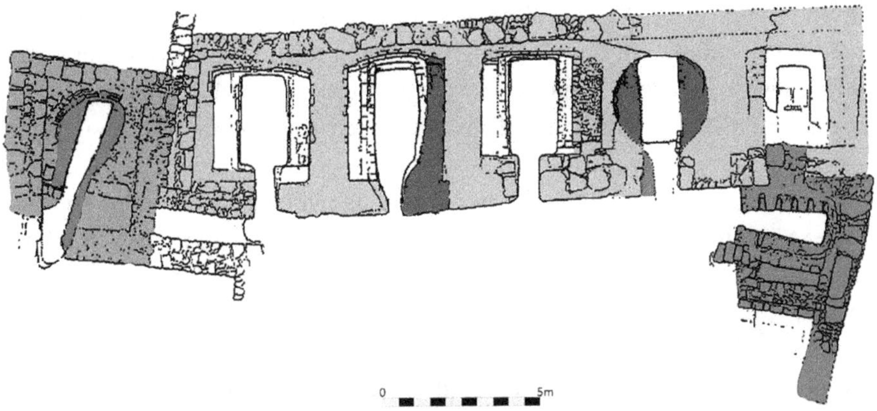

23 Plan of legionary kiln battery in Jerusalem (Israel) showing the scale of the complex and the multiple phases of kiln construction. (Based on Arubas and Goldfus 1995, 101, f. 6)

Levi and Be'eri 2010; 2011; 2017). These workshops possessed simple updraft kilns with a circular plan shape built in stone and mudbrick, with a central round pilaster supporting the oven floor (Arubas and Goldfus 2005; 2008; Levi and Be'eri 2011, f. 7). These civilian kilns were much smaller than most of those associated with the later legionary production.[9] There is some consistency in the design and construction of the kilns across the site in this earlier phase, and they appear to have been associated with individual workshops.

By contrast, the kilns associated with the legionary production (first/second–third centuries AD) display multiple subphases of construction and renovation (Murphy et al. 2018, 458), as well as a greater range of construction and design styles (Figure 23). The earliest installation of the legionary kilns – at least five kilns linearly arranged and built together with shared partitioning walls – clearly was conceived as a single complex from initial planning. By the final phase of production, the workshop sustained an enlarged battery of at least eight kilns (Arubas and Goldfus 1995, 102; 2005; Murphy et al. 2018). The earliest phases of the legionary kilns were composed of cut bedrock, mudbrick, and stone; however, by the later phases of kiln construction, the CBM being manufactured on-site was used for new kiln construction (for a detailed discussion on the phasing, design, and construction of the kilns, see Arubas and Goldfus 2005; Murphy et al. 2018). The extent to which the structural supports for the elevated chamber floor differed between these types is unclear, as kilns were regularly renovated and as some "keyhole" kilns were converted to rectangular plans in later phases. Throughout the duration of production, multiple kiln designs were employed at the site: some were keyhole in plan (with a circular combustion chamber), while others were

[9] A published example by Levi and Be'eri (2011, f. 7–8) measured 1.40 m in diameter.

rectangular in plan. What is clear in outlining these differences, however, is that the site exhibits an unusually high degree of technological variability over only a few generations of potters at the legionary site (Magness 2005; 2011, 319–21). This represents a rapid change in terms of both kiln design and construction materials.

The wares attributed to the kilnworks are likewise notable in their regional context. Alongside CBM, tableware of different finishes and forms, cooking pots, and kitchen wares – including *mortaria* – were all manufactured at the site. This diversity prompts a question: To what extent were these changes in kiln technology made in order to manufacture more efficiently a wide range of products? While it is not possible to tightly correlate smaller shifts in repertoire to technological choices about kiln design at the site, the preserved evidence gives the impression that the legionary technologies offered some degree of flexibility in meeting the production needs of such a diverse product repertoire. The co-occurrence of different kiln types and the changes in the number and size of kilns through time suggest a much more adaptable production tradition, in terms of firing different ceramic goods (product type vis-à-vis kiln size and design), as well as different quantities of ceramics (number and size of kilns vis-à-vis the scale of output).

While both the scale and organization of the legionary kilns outside of Jerusalem were unusual for the region, military production sites from other regions of the empire provide some clear correspondences with the Jerusalem case. The closest parallel can be found at Holt (Wales) (Arubas and Goldfus 1995, 102), a site that supplied the fort at Chester in the first and second centuries AD (Grimes 1930; Swan 1984, 92–95; 2021; Murphy et al. 2018). However, additional sites situated in the northern frontier regions also provide further parallels (Murphy et al. 2018). At Holdeurn, in the Netherlands, a similar kilnworks dated to the first century AD supplied the nearby fort of Nijmegen (Holwerda and Braat 1946; Murphy et al. 2018), while at Hunzenschwil and Rupperswil in Switzerland several kilns were discovered possibly supplying Vindonissa, although this site was only partially excavated in function of a modern building project (Arnold 1966; Schauer 2005). In addition, at Kaiseraugst, also in Switzerland, brick kilns of the *Legio I Martia* have been uncovered (Tomasevic-Buck 1982; Maggetti and Galetti 1993). The similarities between these worksites include very large spaces dedicated to production, integrated kilnworks arranged in a battery (identified at Holdeurn, Holt, and Jerusalem), smaller throwing rooms (identified at Holt and Jerusalem), and a barracks block (identified at Holt and Jerusalem).

Considering its association with the historically documented Roman military occupation of Jerusalem, the establishment of the legionary kilnworks accompanied major social and political changes. Indeed, the destruction of extant walls, which underly the legionary worksite, may suggest that the abrupt technological introductions involved new management and possibly even new labor regimes. Be'eri and Levi (2011; 2012) have proposed that the local potters continued to work in parts of the earlier industrial quarter, making the juxtaposition of the legionary kilnworks with smaller-scale private workshops all the more striking. There is reason to suspect that labor itself changed at the site, and we can assume some degree of new technical expertise either following along with or composed within the legionary ranks. Thus, the unprecedented introduction of new pottery technologies to the region should perhaps be understood as one that likely directly involved an influx of new craftspeople.

Discussion: Embedded Technologies Production Practices and Kiln Design

The cases of technological change at Buto, Sagalassos, and Jerusalem, while involving very different industries in different contexts, nonetheless demonstrate similar processes of innovation, whereby a local industry supported a long-running technological tradition that nonetheless was repurposed to make novel pottery styles – in some cases introduced from elsewhere. However, this production was uniquely translated through local production knowledge and technological styles. That is, rather than wholesale transfers of stylistic "packages" of both pottery styles and technological styles, these examples better reflect a local appropriation of pottery styles by experienced potters working in their own technological traditions. The Buto case (and possibly also other sites in the region) demonstrates a particular interest in control of the air intake of the furnaces. With the potting industry, adapting the beehive kiln design (a highly fuel-efficient design) to accommodate an air vent may demonstrate a local response to changing product repertoire that drew on knowledge networks sustained either by other potters (near or far) or by other local craft professionals. At Sagalassos, after an early period of experimentation, the overall design of pottery kilns seems to have been highly conservative and curated within the potting community, and when changes to the product repertoire were pursued, it was not the kiln that underwent innovation, but the loading system. At the legionary kilnworks outside of Jerusalem, the appearance of new kiln technologies appears even more abrupt and dramatic. Disentangling the particular direction and origins of influences on these design innovations is difficult; any or all of the proposed influences could be implicated. Nonetheless, what these developments in kiln design demonstrate is that technological styles were not static; they were embedded in local knowledge networks and, when economic circumstances changed, those heterogeneous networks of materials, craftspeople, and ideas could be drawn upon to adapt technological traditions and innovate the production process.

IDENTIFYING TECHNOLOGICAL DESIGNERS

Having established how changing technological styles and contexts might reflect local community choices, it may also be possible to investigate the role of different actors in this process as well, particularly through the evidence of kilns and wheels. Kilns were an infrastructural technology that required specialized and skilled knowledge both to build and use. As discussed in Chapter 4, kilns held heightened significance in the production process, as kiln firing was typically the riskiest stage in ceramic manufacturing. The existence of failed kilns, such as the example from Khirbet ‘Azzun, which was used only a few times before it collapsed (Erlich 2017, 202), evidences the destructive implications for poor kiln construction. Updraft kilns were complex structures, sometimes involving arch constructions, and composed of a combination of materials (e.g., mudbrick, ashlars, rubblestone, compressed clay, mud mortar, and/or fired brick). Moreover, an efficient design needed to evenly distribute heat through flue and draft structures. Updraft kiln construction would have been a serious undertaking and a considerable investment of skilled labor and technical knowledge. While it is generally difficult to identify individuals or groups of kiln builders archaeologically, it is nonetheless important to attempt to do so, as these complex combinations of actors contributed to the diversity of ever adapting technological styles that are observed through local case studies.

Ancient terminology offers only limited help in understanding pottery kilns in relation to other industrial furnaces. That pottery kilns were recognized as a specialized type of furnace (and possibly requiring specialized knowledge in construction) is reflected in ancient terminology. Kiln (κάμινος) is the general term used in Greek to describe any pyrotechnological installation (Hasaki 2006, 222), including bathhouse furnaces and plaster kilns (Saliou 2012, 44, tab. 1); however, more specific references to the pottery kiln (φοῦρνος κεραμικός) are also known (Saliou 2012, 44, tab. 1). In Latin legal terms, distinctions were made between the domestic oven or hearth (*focus*) and the industrial furnace (*furnus*) (Saliou 2012, 41). From a functional perspective, there would be good reason to distinguish pottery kilns from other types of industrial ovens and furnaces. Unlike many smelting, smithing, glassworking, or lime-burning furnaces, pottery kilns did not require charcoal to reach necessary temperatures. Also, the separation of the vessel load from the burning fuel by means of elevated floors supported by pillars, crossbars, or arches was a defining design feature, making pottery kilns more complicated to build than many other types of furnaces.

The amphora production site of Burg el-Arab in the Mareotis region of Egypt provides further evidence to suppose that pottery kilns were conceived as being different in design from other types of ovens. Here, an oven that was thought to have had a domestic function (1.6 m diameter / 2.0 m^2 interior surface area) was found in the general vicinity of a massive Dressel 2-4 amphora kiln (7.4 m interior diameter / 43.0 m^2 interior surface area, 12.0 m exterior diameter). The smaller circular oven (likely a cooking oven) was constructed of thin walls composed of a single line of fired brick, while the neighboring amphora kiln was constructed of thick (1.0–2.8 m) walls of mudbrick, with an elevated floor supported by pillars perforated by reused amphorae necks (El-Ashmawi 1998, 58). While situated less than 5 m from one another, these two ovens were categorically different in terms of size and construction techniques, and they required different techniques to make and use. By contrast, the workshop of Elaiussa-Sebaste had multiple kilns of different dimensions (the smaller kiln thought to have been used for lamps, the larger kiln for amphorae and other common wares). While different sizes, the kilns were constructed of the same type of mudbricks and were designed according to similar plans, suggesting a common builder (Borgia and Iacomi 2010, 1048). Here, the shared design, but smaller size, distinguished specialized pottery use.

Identifying Kiln Makers

The amphora kilns of the Mareotis region and those at Elaiussa-Sebaste provide other examples, as these were massive constructions that would have required substantial investment and builder knowledge. In such circumstances, the responsibility of kiln construction might fall to individuals who did not use the kiln (i.e., specialists). The lease contract for a pottery workshop on an estate near the village of Senepta, in Egypt, for example, described a scenario in which the infrastructure of production (pottery wheel, storerooms, and kiln) was entirely provided for the potter by the property owner (Cockle 1981; Mees 2002, 247). In such cases, the provisioned kilns would have been designed and constructed before the potter came to work at the site.

One possibility is that specialized kiln builders were itinerant, travelling to workshops to build kilns for potters. Such a scenario seems to be implied by Gadot and Tepper (2003) for the region around Ashkelon, where multiple kiln complexes associated with estates and situated across the countryside display striking similarities in workshop plan and layout. These "double kilns" were circular, sunken kilns associated with the manufacture of a type of transport vessel known as the Gaza Jar (Erlich 2017, 198). Double kilns have been excavated at Khirbet Baraqa (Gadot and Tepper 2003), Giv'ati Junction (Baumgarten 1997), Khirbet Irza (Israel 1997), and Ashkelon (Israel 1993, 1995). Near Tel Yavne, two sets of three kilns were excavated (Yannai 2012). With such double kilns, the floors of the lower combustion chambers could be as deep as 5 or 6 m below the associated outdoor walking surface. The stoke holes of multiple kilns were accessed via stone-built vaulted stairways (with seventeen–eighteen steps) and subterranean corridors. These kiln features do not appear in other regions of the Levant, and Erlich (2017), Israel (1997), and Gadot and Tepper (2003) have all seen this as a regionally circumscribed type of kiln complex related to a particular type of estate product. The high-quality construction work used in their building suggests a major investment in these facilities – so much so that the workshops might have been designed by an architect or group who travelled to different estates (Gadot and Tepper 2003, 151–52). Such regional patterns of closely shared kiln design might be understood as the product of itinerant builders.

For many small-scale or isolated workshops, it is difficult to envision that the local demand for kiln construction could have sustained a full-time specialized builder of kilns or attracted itinerant builders. A fourth-century-AD invoice from Kellis (Egypt) appears to document payment to a potter for building a bread oven (*P.Kell.* 4.96; Mees 2002, 238, 369). Importantly, this suggests that some potters seem to have had the technical knowledge and skills to construct pyrotechnological installations. However, it also suggests that furnace design knowledge and construction skills might exist within local communities, to the extent that tradespeople of one industry might be contracted to build ovens for other industries. Moreover, the duration of kiln use-life also means that, if properly maintained (and depending on the rates of use), a single kiln might only need to be replaced once or twice in the career of a potter. There are some examples of the replacement of a kiln by a workshop. Replacement of older kilns has been observed at Ashkelon, Khirbet Baraqa, and Horbat Gelilot (Erlich 2017, 202). Aviam observed the same phenomenon at Yodefat in the courtyard of a workshop, where two phases of kilns were constructed (one over the other), and according to the same orientation (Aviam 2014, 140). The second kiln was built shortly after the first kiln had been destroyed, but it was ultimately never used.

The appearance of tweaks or changes made to a kiln after its construction suggest either a sustained presence of kiln builders, or that the later operators also must have had some technical understanding of the kiln design and construction. At Kfar Naḥf, a ramp of fieldstones was placed at the back of the combustion chamber and was thought to have helped to more evenly distribute heat in an already operational kiln (Vitto et al. 1980). At Buto, a bench of mudbrick was added subsequent to construction to reinforce and support the kiln's combustion chamber walls (Area P1 East, Kiln 5; Ballet et al. 2019, 58). There may have been a wider design or construction flaw to the design, as another slightly later kiln of the same design and construction (Area P1 East, Kiln 7) and located in the same area, displayed a second ring of mudbricks thought to have acted as a buttress for the combustion chamber. These types of ad hoc modifications give the impression that the kilns were receiving regular maintenance and were subjected to alteration during their use-life. Once constructed, kilns also required basic maintenance, such as replastering of their walls. If properly maintained in this fashion, they could last for decades. There is evidence for this sort of general maintenance at Elaiussa-Sebaste, where a kiln displayed three phases of floor pavements on the combustion chamber (Borgia and Iacomi 2010, 1045); at Palmyra, Kiln 2 displays at least three phases and Kiln 3 at least two phases of perforated floor renovation (Krogulska 1985, 56–62, 67). These examples demonstrate an ongoing investment in active kilns.

In nearly all cases, local materials were employed in the construction of kilns, implying a knowledge of local materials and their properties. In the Levant, Erlich has noted that regional differences in kiln materials reflect local geology, with kilns of the western Galilee built nearly entirely of the local hard limestone, while those in the Sharon Plain were cut into the *hamra* and alluvial soils and were composed entirely of mudbricks and mortar (2017, 200–1). On a gross conceptual scale, the geology and pedology of an area presented locally available materials that could be exploited for kiln construction. However, and significantly, the choice of materials used in kiln construction did not always correspond to the construction material used for the workshop building, reinforcing the supposition that the construction techniques and material were based on highly specialized construction knowledge of kilns that differed from that involved with everyday building industries. For example, at Sagalassos and Demirci (Kassab Tezgör 2010), most of the kilns thus far excavated were constructed of fired ceramic building materials with a mudplaster mortar and lining, while the workshop buildings were constructed of mudbrick on a stone socle. At Khirbet Baraqa, the kilns were constructed of mudbrick, but the access corridor and stairway were entirely of plastered *kurkar* stone, while the workshop itself was composed of mortared stone with an intersecting barrel-vault ceiling (Gadot and Tepper 2003, 133–34). At az-Zurrāba, the workshop buildings were primarily constructed in stone, while the kilns were fashioned from fired brick ('Amr and al-Momani 1999). Taken in sum, it appears that kilns were designed and constructed with specific materials in mind, rather than following local trends in vernacular construction techniques. While these examples were constructed in affordable, local materials, they were often carefully selected for their properties, particularly (and not surprisingly) their heat resistance and durability.

Such materials need not be costly or involve specialized supply lines. While certain types of material were clearly selected for kiln construction, seldom do the building components used in kilns appear to have been commissioned especially for the kiln construction. Some components were probably made by the builders, such as mud/clay bars and mudbricks. By contrast, the thick circular bricks of the central pillar in the kiln at Shiḥin are described as being specially made to purpose (Strange and Aviam 2017, 67). However, materials were also sometimes recycled; reused tile and reused clay bars from earlier kilns were used to support the raised floor at Demirci (Kassab Tezgör 2010). Reused amphora parts were commonly employed for the perforations of the elevated floors (Burg el-Arab, Kiln 121 at Saqqara (Ghaly 1992, 163) or for vents (Area P3 Kiln 7 and Area P1 Kiln 5) at Buto (Ballet et al. 2019, 32–33, pl. 9), or to build dome roofs at Demirci (Kassab Tezgör 2010).[10] In the case of Buto, the amphorae used in kiln construction were not even produced at the site and instead were reused consumer goods.

Pottery technologies were highly specialized. Kilns were not a common construction project, either by the standards of the workshop building or by the designs of other types of ovens. Identifying the makers and maintainers of these technologies is difficult. However, once in operation, the continued engagement with these technologies and the continued modification of their design and components suggests that some degree of maintenance was performed by active workshops. Thus, technological choices regarding the kiln construction were ongoing, and, over the course of a kiln's life, these decisions could be made by a number of actors.

Wheel Makers and Wheel Users

As was the case with the kilns, there is evidence that the making of pottery wheels might also have involved wider networks of craftspeople. The physical action of throwing a vessel on a pottery wheel involves a complex interaction of "brain, body, wheel, and clay" (Malafouris 2008, 19; see also Ingold 2010; Malafouris 2013, 207–26). It relies on an embodied know-how on the part of the potter working in dynamic response to the properties of the materials in motion. Too much force applied at the wrong time, at the wrong angle, or at the wrong circulating speed and the beginnings of a vessel can transform into a handful of clay or lumps on the floor. In this assemblage, the wheel plays a central role, and an unwieldy wheel size, or friction slowing the rate of turning, or regularity and smoothness of rotation (and even a slight wobble), affects the action and success of throwing. Controlling these factors relies on the technical knowledge of the wheel design and construction. Thus, understanding the dynamic between wheel, material, and maker relies on an appreciation not only of its use when manipulating clay into form by the potter but also of the design and construction of the wheel by its maker.

Given the potter's intimate know-how of throwing, it might seem surprising that, in the Roman world, pottery wheels may not have always been the property of a potter (see also Chapter 3). Importantly, the fact that the pottery

[10] By contrast, Erlich observed that the use of reused amphorae in kiln construction was not common in the coastal plain of modern Israel (2017, 200).

maker and the wheel maker might not be the same individual introduces additional complexity in how we understand technological choices for the period. In leased workshops, Mees considers wheels and turntables to have been part of the workshop inventory listed among "accessories" and, therefore, not the property of the potter but rather tied to the workshop (2002, 247).[11] This conceivably could establish a circumstance in which some potters would need to become familiar with and adapt to different wheels over the course of a career. As wheels might already exist on a workshop inventory at the arrival of a leasing potter, this then raises the question of who the makers of pottery wheels might have been. Textual sources are not helpful here. However, reconstructions of wheels (as composed of multiple parts and of multiple specially crafted materials) suggest that the manufacture and design of such a technology may have been reliant on craftspeople from other trades.

The fast-turning wheels from Sagalassos are thought to have been composed of a (presumed) wooden wheel head, attached with a metal axle and copper-alloy flange, with a small socket stone (Figure 24; see also Murphy and Poblome 2012). By contrast, the slow-turning turntables at the same site were made of reused stone drums with a dimpled depression on one end (Figure 24; see also Murphy and Poblome 2012), and at Shiḥin a reused column drum with a hollowed-out depression on one end was also thought to have been a slow-rotating wheel (Strange 2019). Unlike the hand tools (described in Chapter 5), which display complex patterns of appropriation and self-production by potters, parts or all of these wheels likely would have needed to be commissioned from skilled tradespeople outside the pottery workshop, requiring some degree of cross-industry engagement. They, like the lease contract evidence, also demonstrate that the user and maker of these technologies were not always the same individuals, and that potters in many circumstances were reliant on other people for the design and specificities of their key infrastructural technologies.

The reliance by ceramicists on other tradespeople in the design and making of their technologies is also evidenced elsewhere. In the Levant, preserved wheel parts dated to the Roman and Late Antique periods were commonly made in limestone.[12] During the Roman and Late Antique periods, limestone wheel heads had a platform on a cone-shaped boss fitted into a limestone socket stone. At the legionary kilnworks outside of Jerusalem, these pieces were found with the lower stone embedded in the floor. Here, the upper face of the top stone was flat, but its surface was roughened, suggesting that it

[11] A sixth-century-AD Egyptian papyrus similarly describes a textile loom being let between guild members (*SB* XVI 12282; van Minnen 1986, 57).

[12] In the Bronze and Iron Ages, most wheels were composed of two stones of basalt or andesite (an upper rotating head and a lower fixed socket) – both with rounded faces. By the Roman and Late Antique periods, limestone wheels display a heavier bottom stone, and the socket was much deeper (presumably for greater stability and momentum).

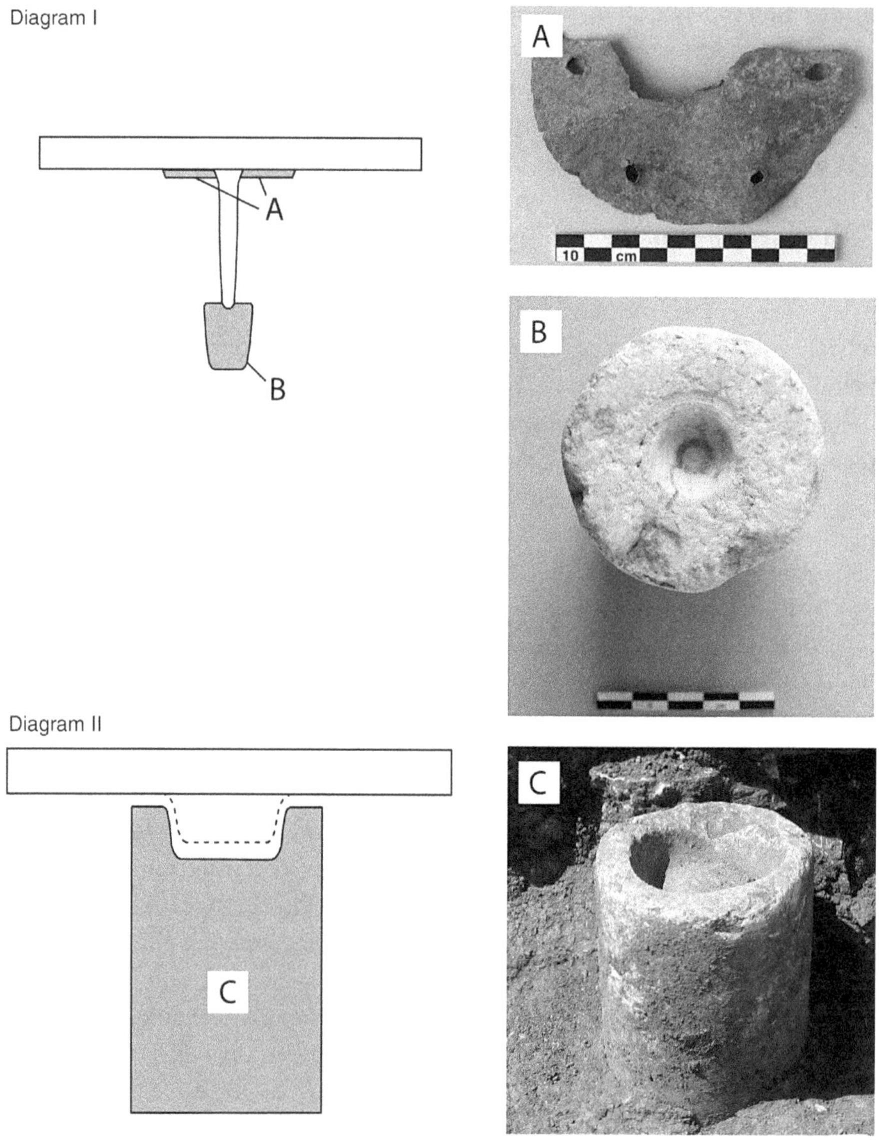

24 Sagalassos fast-turning wheel components and reconstruction (Diagram I) and slow-turning wheel components and reconstruction (Diagram II). (Sagalassos Archaeological Research Project)

required the addition of a wooden or ceramic disk (Murphy et al. 2018, 449). A Late Roman example of a similar type from the site of Mefalsim presents the remains of rust assumed to have derived from an encircling iron belt (Amiran and Shenhav 1984, 108). This belt is thought to have encircled the stone head and offered a flange to which a larger wooden wheel head could have been affixed (Amiran and Shenhav 1984, 108). If we consider these examples together, the making of this wheel type involved composite construction work using stone, iron, and wood. Given the skill necessary to prepare these materials, particularly the stone and iron components, the involvement of at least a stone cutter, stone turner, and blacksmith might be surmised. Technological choices and details of design are thereby distributed across an extensive network of tradespeople.

Evidence at other sites also suggests a close relationship between craftspeople working in different materials, all involved in the development of potting technology. Wheels might not be the only limestone objects found in ceramic workshops in this region. In fact, the appearance of lamp molds in the region, manufactured from the wasters of limestone lathe-working, further links these two industries (Strange 2019, f. 8). The use of limestone molds, particularly for lamp production, has been noted at several sites, including Dura-Europos (Baird 2007, 419), and there seems to have been a particularly strong tradition of using soft, chalky limestone molds in the region of Judaea/Syria-Palaestina (Leibner 2010, 270). These molds have been observed at the sites of Sepphoris (Adan-Bayewitz 1995), Caesarea (Strange and Aviam 2017, 71–78), Beit She'an/Scythopolis (Strange and Aviam 2017, 71–78), and Beit Natif (Lichtenberger 2016). Acquiring such stone molds involved a significant investment in their production, but they would have had certain technical advantage as their surfaces were comparatively resilient to wear.

The level of investment involved in acquiring these tools from other industries is well demonstrated at Shiḥin (located 2 km northwest of Sepphoris), where coroplasts employed soft limestone for molds (Strange 2019). The Shiḥin molds demonstrate a clear link between local potters and the nearby stone quarries that manufactured vessels in soft chalky limestone, as the lamp molds here were produced from leftover stone cores that had been discarded from the lathe (Strange 2019, f. 8). These blanks were cut in half, the (negative) form of the lamp carved into each face, and the halves were then used as two-part molds. Surveys in the area of the stone quarries demonstrate that, in addition to supplying the ceramic industry, the quarries also appear to have been provisioning material for loom weights. This cross-craft relationship between multiple industries, employing the waste of one industry as a raw material of another, is notable, as are the local networks of crafts working in different media. Again, the involvement of other tradespeople potentially introduces additional actors in the making of technological choices in the workshop. It is unclear if the lamp shape carved into the stone was rendered by the stonemason or the potter. However, according to Sussman (1980), the production of limestone lamp molds at Caesarea required the use of specialized tools and carving techniques in their making: Drills were likely used to carve out the hollow; a compass and sharp tool used to shape and define the lamp features (nozzle, fill hole, base); and then designs and decorations were carved by hand, suggesting that it was made by a stone carver (Sussman 1980).

The precise nature and circumstances of interaction between ceramic and stone workers are unclear. The lamp molds (like the limestone wheels) demonstrate the local ceramicists were tied into a wider world of craftspeople and a wider economic community where trades were more or less prevalent and established. However, the carving and lathe work used to manufacture these wheel parts and molds seems to reflect the growing importance and growth of local limestone industries, beginning in the Hellenistic period (Magen 2002). These stoneworkers manufactured a range of products, including ossuaries, tables, and – importantly – vessels (Magen 2002). While using traditional stone cutting and carving skills, the detailing of the molds reflects knowledge regarding popular forms and styles of ceramic lamps and may perhaps reflect some collaboration between local industries. Indeed, such similarities also appear between pottery vessels and limestone tablewares (Leibner 2020).

While specialist trades were almost certainly involved in the initial making of pottery wheels, tweaks and adjustments might have been subsequently made by the potters themselves. For instance, maintaining rotational momentum has been a problem documented by experimental studies of ancient wheel designs but could be addressed by employing lubricants and also by affixing a larger wheel head (Amiran and Shenhav 1984, 108). Adaptations might then be made to the wheel heads; these do not typically survive from the region but, in Italy, a ceramic disk dated to the Roman period near Arezzo was thought to have been part of a wheel head, with lead fixed along the outer side to add weight and increase overall momentum (Rieth 1960, 52).

The addition of components could help to adapt the wheel without making major or lasting changes to the wheel itself, and as such it is difficult to imagine that potters were not somehow involved or consulted regarding such adjustments to the design of wheels. In fact, a ceramic disk mold used atop a fast-turning wheel has been found at Buto in Egypt (Ballet et al. 2019, 73). According to the reconstruction provided by the excavators, this mold displayed a ridge incised on the upper surface that is thought to have impressed a shallow ("false") base for large platters. A similar use of a "jolly" has been proposed for the production of ESA (Hayes 1997, 220–21; Meyza 2000, 237–39). Essentially, the disk functioned as a mold in which the vessel was thrown and in this way presents a sort of hybrid forming technique between throwing and molding (Ballet et al. 2019, 196–98). Examples of Megarian bowls at Pergamon (Rotroff 2006; Rogl 2014) and molded *oinophoroi* at Sagalassos (Murphy and Poblome 2012, 211) were also sometimes formed in a mold mounted on a wheel. Wheels might also be mounted with ceramic disks, called bats, which were removable. Bats have been documented at several sites with either fast-turning wheels or turntables. They were likely affixed with a simple coil of clay to the wheel head, as they show no means of clamping. Bats found at the workshops of the Ketios Valley (Bounegru 2009,

95, f. 6.1a–b), Jerusalem (Murphy et al. 2018, 449), and Sagalassos display concentric circles incised into the upper face, likely used as diameter measures for the vessels being thrown on them.

The technological evidence of wheels and turntables offers several points of discussion that help to reframe our discussion on craftspeople and the technologies of their trades in the following manner. While the techniques and embodied know-how of forming vessels on a wheel certainly informed how wheels were designed, in this region and period there is evidence that potters were sometimes reliant on others to help build and supply their key technologies. This necessitated adaptability and negotiation on the part of the potter (see Shimada 2007 for a comparative discussion of cross-craft relations). These dependencies on property owners and on other crafts professions embedded the potters in wider networks of crafts and trades. As observed in Chapter 5 when analyzing the influences of other crafts on stylistic choices of ceramics, the development and use of ceramic technologies likewise highlights an inter-industry reliance and community of tradespeople. Moreover, interventions could be made by the user, and examples demonstrate manipulations of the wheel, providing an ongoing negotiation between potter and wheel.

CONCLUSION

This chapter has approached potting technologies in ways that move beyond simple technological specifications and economic efficiencies in order to see them as cultural features. The eastern Mediterranean had a long-established history of using complex pottery wheel and kiln technologies, and across the region, there was much local variability in technological design, construction, and use. Local micro-histories of potting technology help to reconstruct how changing work environments and economic contexts might encourage curation or innovation in technological styles and how new ideas might be understood through those existing traditions and in relation to other local industries. In this context, the potting and craft communities might curate technological styles, and contemporary workshops at a production center might follow a similar kiln design. Micro-histories of kiln designs also, however, highlight the locally embedded nature of innovation and technological choices. Additionally, technical knowledge of building and using pottery technologies could be distributed across a range of actors. Some of those actors were within the workshop, but others must also have been brought in as craftspeople working in other trades who possessed specialized skills and methods. In the case of these major technologies, the "knowledge networks" necessary to build them could extend well beyond the workshop.

CHAPTER SEVEN

INTERNAL SOCIAL DYNAMICS OF INDUSTRY CLUSTERS: COOPERATION AND COMPETITION

Chapter 5 demonstrated how, in long-established industries, craft traditions were learned intergenerationally through everyday work practices. Such traditions relied on curated knowledge of raw material extraction, embodied ways of understanding materials, and a common appreciation of style and form. We have also seen how craft training might draw on professional and social networks, so-called trust networks, of peers. Repeatedly, the role of a craft community has been demonstrated to be important in sustaining traditions, inviting innovations, and developing local work cultures. Among clustered workshops where potters were also neighbors, such social relationships might be all the more intense, with physical proximity of workplaces encouraging regular interaction. In fact, such collaborative work practices among nucleated workshops have been seen as foundational (Peacock 1982).

In light of the shared experiences among such workshops, this chapter delves more deeply into the social dynamics within industry nucleation – identifying socioeconomic interactions between and within these collectives, considering how these relationships might affect producers at work, and analyzing the role of products as agents in negotiating social dynamics between potters. By more closely considering, via the historical and archaeological records, the interrelationships of these artisanal communities and the types of social bonds curated among neighboring craftspeople, nucleated workshops are seen as more than simply spatially defined entities and instead as small communities. Moreover, definitions of nucleated industries have emphasized the collaborative benefits of working in a larger craft community. However, such contexts must have also been competitive economic environments.[1] In this chapter, we investigate this tension between economic competition and social collaboration within workshop clusters.

NUCLEATED WORKSHOPS IN THE EASTERN PROVINCES

Clusters of workshops are well known both ethnographically and in preindustrial historical contexts (van der Leeuw 1977, 73), and as such, there is a substantial diversity in what can be classified as a "cluster." Costin, for example, distinguished between "Community specialization: autonomous individual or household-based production units, aggregated within a single community, producing for unrestricted regional consumption" and "Nucleated workshops: larger workshops aggregated within a single community, producing for unrestricted regional consumption" (1991, 8). Clusters of workshops seem to have been relatively common for the Roman world, so much so that industry nucleation has been seen as one of the key "modes of production" used to characterize ceramic manufacturing of the period (Peacock 1982). Peacock's definition of workshop nucleation similarly distinguished between "urban nucleated workshops" and "nucleated industries in the countryside" (1982, 99–113).

While Peacock mostly focused on Roman workshops in the western provinces, Roman-period workshop clusters have also been identified in both urban and rural contexts in the eastern Mediterranean. Such highly specialized rural industries are challenging to identify archaeologically. Most rural workshop clusters (seemingly unrelated to estate production of amphorae) have been identified only through pedestrian surveys, and very few have been excavated, so we lack a sense of the internal organization and scale of the workshops. One example that was successfully studied is at the cooking ware production site of Kefar Ḥananya in Israel (Adan-Bayewitz 1993). Fabric studies first identified the site as one of two major centers of cooking ware production in the Galilee, and the association of the site with pottery manufacture was further established by references in several historical sources (Adan-Bayewitz 1991; 1993).[2] Given the regional status and the major output of production from this site, it might be considered as a highly specialized "village industry" economy, of the type described by van der Leeuw (1977).

[1] While Peacock's description of nucleated industries is most commonly cited by Mediterranean archaeologists (1982, 99–113), a similar classificatory scheme was proposed by van der Leeuw (1977). These were later elaborated by Costin (1991) in her "spectrum of workshop concentration."

[2] Small-scale excavations were conducted at Kefar Ḥananya and brought to light kilns and clay processing features dated from the Early to Late Roman periods (Adan-Bayewitz 1991).

Another challenge concerning potting industries in rural villages is assessing their proportional contribution to the local economy – especially the extent to which a surveyed site represented either a single pottery workshop in a rural village or a community of potters with a collective rural presence. While, in ethnographic examples, as many as one in ten of the inhabitants could be involved in the pottery business (van der Leeuw 1977, 71–73), this is more difficult to determine archaeologically. For example, workshops at the rural settlement of Porphyreon (modern Jiyeh, Lebanon), 14 km outside of Sidon and dated from the Hellenistic to the Byzantine periods, give a mixed picture (Waliszewski and Gwiazda 2015, 331; Wicenciak 2016, 31–35). Based on the excavated kiln and waste material, the workshops appear to have been manufacturing a wide range of products, including amphorae, commonware, coarseware, and plain wares (Wicenciak 2016). While potting may have been a long-running industry in the community, glassworking and wine production were also noted, suggesting a mixed economy based on agriculture and craft production (Waliszewski and Gwiazda 2015, 340–41, 346). In the Sharon Plain of modern Israel, there is likewise evidence for mixed industry (Erlich 2017, 202). At Khirbet ʻAzzun, workshops documented in an industrial zone on the edge of the settlement involved the manufacture of pottery (storage jars) and glass (Erlich 2017, 202). With these clusters, it is unclear to what degree potting might have defined the economic activity of these settlements, at least to the extent deemed significant by van der Leeuw (1977).[3]

By contrast, the evidence for urban clusters (i.e., Peacock's urban nucleated workshops) is more robust for the eastern provinces, and clusters of pottery workshops have been identified and excavated in the peripheries of many cities. Several of these examples have already been discussed in previous chapters; however, they are worth quickly revisiting here. Sagalassos' suburbs east of the city's theater hosted workshops in an area of eight hectares, probably about half of which was occupied by workshops (Martens et al. 2012, 87, f. 9.3; Claeys and Poblome 2019, 138, f. 2), and more than one hundred kilns have been identified in a magnetometer survey recording the upper 1.5 m of deposit.[4] Kibyra's fineware workshops (identified through an urban survey) were similarly situated upslope and nearing the outskirts of the city, to the northwest of the theater and *odeion* / bouleuterion (Özüdoğru and Dündar 2007; Japp 2009). At Anemourion, the Roman-period urban potters' quarter was located near clay beds at the northern edge of the city,[5] as evidenced by a

[3] The Hellenistic-Roman tableware production site at Asar Tepe in the Kibyratis (Turkey) might also be understood in this way, although it is difficult to estimate (from the reported surface material alone) the number of workshops (Kugler 2018, 487).

[4] With some areas yielding archaeological deposits at depths of more than 4 m, it is assumed that these kiln counts are low.

[5] This was prior to the sixth-century-AD movement of pottery workshops into the city.

mound of production waste (Russell 2002, 225). In the case of Patara's industry, seven kilns and one workshop have been identified dating between the Late Hellenistic and Late Roman periods in the general northern regions of the city, particularly around the Tepecik Acropolis (Özüdoğru and Dökü 2007, 399–400; Dündar 2015, 204–5). In the third century AD at Gerasa, part of the city's hippodrome was converted into an industrial quarter with tanning and potting workshops (Ostrasz and Kehrberg 2020). At Buto, the excavations of the 1960s uncovered at least nineteen pottery kilns (Charlesworth 1969, 29[6]), and subsequent work since the 1990s has resulted in the excavation of more than nine kilns (Schmitt 2019, 188). Based on geophysical prospections across the area, more than fifty magnetic anomalies (in the upper 1.5 m of deposit) were detected across an area of three hectares (Ballet and Schmitt 2019, 51), with particular concentrations in one hectare of Buto's northernmost mound (Kôm A) (Ballet 2011, 190). While the kilns and production dumps are numerous, as yet, the recent excavations have focused on kilns and adjacent work surfaces, leaving the forming and drying workspaces yet to be uncovered (Ballet et al. 2019, 61). These examples demonstrate that nucleated ceramic industries were common, and they have been well documented around towns and cities in the Roman East.

Outside these village industries and urban peripheral work zones, there is further variability that can be noted among nucleated workshops. Some examples of workshop clusters are more difficult to fit into Peacock's distinction between urban (or, more accurately, peri-urban) and rural. These workshops, while not part of the contiguous urban built space, seem more closely bound to the urban sphere than the rural countryside. Pergamon's Ketios Valley cluster, located just east of and below the city's citadel, perhaps might be understood as a village industry but one not far from the urban zone (Bounegru and Erdemgil 1998; Poblome et al. 2001). The potters' village of Jerusalem (active already prior to the installation of the legionary kilnworks in the first century AD) offers another such example (Arubas and Goldfus 2008b, 1828; Levi and Be'eri 2010; 2011; 2017; Be'eri and Levi 2011). It was situated about 2.2 km to the west of the Old City along a route toward the coastal plain "at the start of the descent for those leaving the old city of Jerusalem" (Arubas and Goldfus 2005, 11). The production site at az-Zurrāba near Petra, with ten kilns and one workshop excavated, is estimated to have been approximately 0.5 km^2 in area based on the surface scatter of production waste dating from the first until the sixth century AD uninterrupted ('Amr 1991, 320–21). Like

[6] It is unclear if this tally includes the nine pottery kilns excavated in 1966 (Seton-Williams 1966, 164) or if the identification of metal furnaces (with tuyères) were, in fact, examples of the tubular pottery kilns later identified by Ballet et al. (2019). See Chapter 6 for further discussion.

Jerusalem's cluster, that at az-Zurrāba was situated on a major road (a sacred way in the Roman period) leading from Petra to Wadi Musa (Zayadine 1982, 393). Some workshop clusters were, then, clearly in a slightly ambiguous position – closely tied to urban markets only a few kilometers down the road, yet placed beyond the contiguous urban built space.

The density or concentration of workshops in an area might also challenge the definition of what we consider a nucleated industry. Jackson and colleagues (2012, 112) suggested that the seven production sites found near the Kestros River (modern Aksu Çayı) in the vicinity of Gebiz (SW Turkey), all manufacturing LRD tablewares, should be understood as a nucleated rural industry, as defined by Peacock (1982). Based on surface survey and geophysical prospection, each production site appears to have been limited in size and scale. Surface scatters were documented ranging from 40 m to 45 m in diameter (at Kömbeci Mevkii and Budaklar Mevkiisi) to one hectare in surface area (at Camii Yıkığı), while the magnetometry survey seems to have identified multiple, sometimes large, kilns (ca. 3 m in diameter) at several of these sites (Jackson et al. 2012, 91–96).[7] These each likely represent the remains of one or two workshops, yet the seven discrete sites were spread across an area of 5 by 7 km along the river that ultimately connected to the city of Perge (Jackson et al. 2012, 91). With the river acting as a transportation conduit, the travel time separating workshops might have been reduced, but it is nonetheless challenging to see this organization as anything other than very loosely integrated nucleation. Moreover, a structure at one of these sites has been interpreted as domestic in character (Kadirgürü Mevkiisi), suggesting these pottery workshops were related to household groups, while at another (Hacıahmet Kırı), olive press stones were found indicating agricultural activity (Jackson et al. 2012, 91). Accepting the poor chronological resolution of surface features from survey alone, there is good reason to suspect that these workshops were related to these domestic and agricultural structures.

Clearly, the examples that can be classified as nucleated workshops are varied, with that variation being expressed in different ways (i.e., spatial density, relation to markets). Nonetheless, what these examples have in common is a sense on the part of the relevant researchers that the collective presence and activity of these workshops helped to define not only the local economy but also the local craft tradition. Site-by-site variation notwithstanding, it seems to be the case that clusters like these represent particular types of craft collectives. The effects such collective organization would have had on labor, production, and accompanying social experience require further interrogation.

[7] Three or more kilns and several more anomalies seem to appear on the magnetometry plan of Kadirgürü Mevkiisi (Jackson et al. 2012, 97, f. 8).

Life in Nucleated Workshops

If one of the defining characteristics shared by these diverse examples of nucleated workshops is that they are all spatially concentrated in ways that were socially and economically meaningful, then it is important to understand how such a nucleated industry might appear archaeologically at the local level and to reconstruct the intensity of interaction experienced therein. To do so, we can turn to a particularly well-published and illustrative example. In the Ketios Valley (situated below Pergamon and east of the city), a cluster of pottery workshops was unearthed in the 1970s and 1980s. In an area of approximately 1,700 m^2, twenty-four kilns and four workshops were exposed, although more workshops certainly remained unexcavated (Bounegru 2014, 24). The workshops shared outside courtyard areas, and small streets and alleyways wove around the work structures (Bounegru 2003, 138). With doorways only a few meters apart from one another, it is hard to imagine that these potters were not well aware of the daily happenings in the other workshops, of the comings and goings of their neighbors, as well as of visits by potential customers or middlemen traders (*negotiatores*). This was a small working community, defined by a common profession and a shared reliance on clays, fuel, and water from the neighboring river. This community of potters making tableware was active for more than two centuries (approximately eight generations).[8] In the earliest phases of production, these workshops tended to manufacture molded relief bowls; later ceramics with appliqué; and then, the wheel-thrown tableware, referred to as ESC (Meyer-Schlichtmann 1988; Bounegru 2009; Japp 2014).

Some of the pottery found at this site included a relatively uncommon corpus for an eastern Mediterranean tableware production site – eighty-eight vessels stamped with names in the genitive form (impressed by thirty-three different stamps).[9] Several names, including Theogenes, Menemachos, Herodos, Leikos, Moschos, Nostos, Satyros, and Caius, could be identified (Bounegru and Erdemgil 1998; Poblome et al. 2001, 156; Bounegru 2014, 27). It is difficult to determine to whom the names of these stamps refer (workshop owner, hired potter, master potter, overseer, etc.) (Zoroğlu 1989; Slane 1997; Lund 2016; Rotroff et al. 2018, 139). The spatial distribution of names on stamped vessels did not correlate with individual workshops and was thought to possibly reflect either mixed deposits or some collaborative or contracted

[8] A Late Roman community of potters manufacturing common wares and table wares later came to reoccupy the site in the mid third century AD, but only a kiln and associated production waste was excavated (Bounegru 2009, 79–80).

[9] Stamping Eastern Sigillata tableware was uncommon after the second century AD, perhaps because the practice is thought to have been influenced by trends in stamped western sigillata (Poblome et al. 2001, 158).

organization of production among the workshops (Poblome et al. 2001, 156–58) – particularly between Workshop 2 and Workshop 3 – which shared a courtyard space and where there was a higher concentration of stamped sigillata (Bounegru 2009, 84). Stamped vessels recovered from nearby Pergamon (a major consumer of these products) offered additional forms and names that could be attributed to the Ketios Valley workshops.

From these contexts, vessel types, and stamp impressions, it was possible to outline a rough chronology of the names (Bounegru and Erdemgil 1998, 265). Among these stamped vessels, several named an individual, Menemachos, who was associated with one of the earlier workshops in the cluster that manufactured sigillata. Menemachos appears to have been working contemporaneously (sometime in the third quarter of the second century BC to the mid first century) with potters (or workshops) associated with Caius and Satyros (Bounegru and Erdemgil 1998, 265). Menemachos (or his workshop) made some of the same forms as those stamped with another later name, Herodos, active at some time between 75 and 25 BC (Bounegru and Erdemgil 1998, 265). This same Herodos (or his workshop) was making vessel forms similar to those stamped with the name Leukos. Both Herodos and Leukos were active at the same time as Pothos and Moschos (Bounegru and Erdemgil 1998, 265). Creating a network of names, dates, and forms, these relationships attest to the overlapping professional careers, or at least overlapping workshops, within the cluster. In fact, in the period between 75 and 25 BC, all eleven names attributed to the Ketios Valley workshops appear on the products from the site (Bounegru and Erdemgil 1998, 265).

These reconstructions hardly equate to the biographies of potters, but they nevertheless demonstrate that these workshops were active over the course of only a few generations as part of a tightly integrated potting community. Sometimes ideas appear to have been exchanged, with similar vessel forms and techniques of production identified with different names. Beyond this cluster of workshops, at least one other community of potters was also manufacturing tablewares within a 40-km radius of Pergamon. The workshops at Pitane (Çandarlı), along the coast to the west of Pergamon, also manufactured ESC, although with greatest intensity of production slightly later than those in the Ketios Valley (in the second and third centuries AD). Some of the same vessel forms were made by both communities (Loeschcke 1912; Domżalski 2014, 154; Japp 2014). Thus, the bustling workshops of the Ketios Valley, while forming a densely clustered set of professional neighbors with their own internal dynamics, were only one constituent community in a larger, dynamic economic landscape.

The workshops of the Ketios Valley neatly fall into the category of production organization described as "workshop nucleation" or "industry clustering," defined by a spatial concentration of workshops manufacturing similar goods

(Costin 1991, 8, 13–15). Contexts of nucleated workshops are particularly effective places to consider the social lives of potters because, as we have seen in the Ketios Valley, the spatial proximity of clustered ceramic workshops – sometimes with doors just meters apart – presupposes some degree of sustained inter-workshop contact that is often evidenced by shared supply networks and product repertoire.

IDENTIFYING COLLABORATIVE PRACTICES WITHIN NUCLEATED WORKSHOPS

Proximity between workers, such as that observed at the Ketios Valley workshops, raises a set of questions concerning the nature of the implied relationships. One of the associated key assumptions about nucleated workshops is that these environments involved collaborative groups. Peacock argues that "Nucleated industries benefit from the natural development of ancillary services, in fuel supply, transport, material supply or kiln building. In addition, cooperation rather than competition seems to be the rule and mutual aid is commonplace." (Peacock 1982, 43). The archaeological definitions of nucleated industries, emphasizing collective benefits and mutual assistance drew on economic theory of the 1970s and 1980s (van der Leeuw 1977; Peacock 1982); at the time, the driving motivation for clustering was explained as a collective economic advantage – sharing of local raw materials, and (once established) common access to supporting industries, consumer networks, and a skilled labor pool. Indeed, in the western provinces, Goodman (2013, 123–26) noted that a significant number of terra sigillata production centers developed in areas that already supported ceramic works, perhaps suggesting that the existence of a potting community might attract other ceramicists. These are, essentially, what economists have described as "locational factor endowments" in nucleation (Feldman 2003, 383–86 for recent discussion; Weber 1928).

At a workshop level, a specific example of how workshops might collaborate in their everyday activities can be observed at Sagalassos (Murphy and Poblome 2016). Here, a building complex comprising at least four discrete workshops formed a single property unit, sharing walls and likely also a roof structure. In the complex, each workshop specialized in making pilgrim's flasks, figurines, face-pots, and lamps – many of which were formed using handmade or wheel-thrown mold "blanks" decorated with stamps. In addition to producing similar wares and using (more or less) similar mold, wheel, and kiln technologies, there are some hints that this small set of workshops was not only in tight spatial proximity but was engaging in some degree of cooperative work relationship. This is apparent, for example, in mapping stamps and matching them with stamp impressions on molds and molded objects. Many examples indicate the sharing of individual stamps between otherwise

25 Photo of stamp and matching stamp impression on mold found in the Molded-Wares Workshop Complex at Sagalassos. (Sagalassos Archaeological Research Project)

independent working units (Figure 25; see also Murphy and Poblome 2016, 191; Murphy 2017, 116–19). These hand tools were among the most specialized tools (in terms of time and skill) in the workshops, with each individually hand carved or sculpted in the potting clay (Murphy 2017, 116–19). In his model of workshop lease organizations, Mees (2002, 299–300) suggested that some materials, like decorative stamps and molds, might have been considered part of the workshop property, which was used (but not owned) by the occupying potter. If this was the case for the Molded-Wares Workshop Complex, these minor acts of sharing might reflect shared workshop inventory. Nonetheless, these were also tools that gave distinctive decorative details to otherwise similar wares. These workshops were sharing unique tools, including one of the more "costly" tools needed in this manufacturing.

At a wider community scale, there is also reason to suspect collective interests and coordination operating within these workshop clusters, both in terms of their supply of materials and their collective waste disposal. In most industry clusters, workshops relied on one or two clay sources prepared according to similar enough recipes that products today can be attributed to the center through their fabric characteristics (see the Levantine Ceramic Group for such fabric descriptions of ware groups); and as discussed in Chapter 1, these clay beds could be exploited for many centuries. In some cases, it can be further assumed that the exploitation of clays involved an organized operation at a scale beyond the activities of a single workshop or workgroup. A documented dispute among first-century-BC brickworkers concerning rights and access to a clay quarry gives the impression that the exploitation of quarries might have resulted in disputes and thereby required arrangements between workshops (*P. Tempeleide* 29; Mees 2002, 234, 386).

That clay exploitation was organized at the community scale might also be supported archaeologically. For example, Sagalassos' potters used, for more than 700 years, clays quarried from the Çanaklı Valley beds that were located 8 km from (and 300 m below) the workshops (Poblome et al. 2002; Degryse and Poblome 2008), and the SRSW production, when established in the first century BC, drew on the same clay beds that already had been continually exploited in the region for at least 400 years (Kelepeshi et al. 2024). At Qumran, the elaborate water systems of the settlement used settling basins to capture sediments; collected among these sediments were clays that were "quarried" by the potters (Magen and Peleg 2006, 100). The maintenance of the water channels and basins indicates an organized system that likely required labor investment and management by (as well as access points implicating) more than one workshop. This suggests that some activities in these clusters were coordinated either collaboratively or through centralized administration.

Production waste dumps occasionally offer additional evidence for coordination among multiple workshops. Sometimes spilling from a scarp or scattered across the ground surface, waste dumps are often one of the first features identifying a production site. If the Ballas Pottery Project's estimation of a 5- to 10-percent waster rate per firing is representative, the quantities of wasters could quickly accumulate (Nicholson and Patterson 1989, 80). The majority of waste found in the general vicinity of workshops demonstrates repetitive and organized waste disposal practices at many sites.[10] As discussed in Chapter 4, these dumps might be large (likely community-based) waste areas. For example, the two mounds associated with pottery workshops manufacturing Late Antique amphorae, tablewares, and cooking pots were identified at Sheikh Abada in Middle Egypt; one of these deposits was nearly 30 m high (Ballet et al. 1991, 134–36). At Ashmunein in Egypt, the workshop dumps were identified as mounds confined to a particular area of the site, reaching as tall as 4–5 m in height (Ballet et al. 1991, 137–38). At Qumran, the production waste of the local potters was largely confined to the eastern refuse dump and the smaller dump northwest of the site (Magen and Peleg 2006). At Anemourion, the waste heaps comprised a mound covering an area of 60 m^2 (Russell 2002, 225). Given their large size and limited number, these were likely locations of communal dumping. Collective and coordinated waste removal presents one way in which workshops might have shared interests.

At Gerasa, both individual workshop and community-wide waste disposal patterns have been noted. The production waste of more than three centuries of ceramic work was substantial and accumulated over time around the outskirts of the hippodrome building (Kehrberg 2020, 414, t. 1). The dumps

10 See Dufaÿ et al. (1997) for archaeological reconstruction of production waste patterns in Gaul.

outside the hippodrome were so substantial that they were partially dug out in antiquity to give access to the workshops (Kehrberg 2007, 33). By contrast, the central arena of the hippodrome, from which the northern cavae units were entered, functioned as a sort of central courtyard and was kept clean of production waste throughout the many centuries of workshop activity (Kehrberg and Ostrasz 1997, 170). In addition to the outer waste dumps, which accumulated waste such that they were several meters tall, by the sixth and early seventh centuries AD, abandoned workshops inside the cavea of the hippodrome at Gerasa also began to be used for waste disposal, with some dumps standing more than 3 m tall and blocking doorways[11] (Kehrberg 2007, 33; 2009, 493; 2020, 414, t. 1). These interior deposits appear to be associated with the waste of individual workshops or workshop groups operating outside of the hippodrome by this time (Kehrberg and Ostrasz 1997, 171). These shifting patterns of waste disposal, with workshops first built inside the cavea units and dumping on the perimeter, followed by workshops situated outside and dumping inside the cavea units (all while keeping the arena clear), give the impression of a self-run but organized arrangement among the workshops. Again, at Gerasa, we see cooperative works among clustered workshops.

The separation of waste from the active workshops, and the discrete boundaries of these dumps at many workshop clusters, suggests that there was some sort of normalized understanding among workshops as to these garbage habits, understandings which at the very least must have involved shared expectations of removal and placement.

Textual Evidence for Collaborative or Supportive Craft Practices

The archaeological evidence of supply chains and waste disposal demonstrates coordinated (and potentially cooperative) work organization, and the workshop complex at Sagalassos reveals intense daily life interactions among workshops in the same building complex. As will be discussed in the following section, the textual record of craft production describes other practices that helped to maintain professional communities, particularly practices that might sustain social cohesion and goodwill through sharing, collaboration, and cooperative action. Some papyri from Egypt dated to the Roman and Late Antique periods describe the activities of small-group social networks in local work communities and demonstrate the way in which familial, social, and professional activities often intersected in the context of the associations. As is typically the case, only a few historical texts for the period specifically describe

[11] In the fifth century AD, the northern end of the building was used again (for a short period) for public spectacle, and the workshops abandoned the cavae units.

the activities of potters, although professional associations of potters are known from the study region.[12]

Some of these cooperative actions might explicitly exclude outsiders. A tax list of professions from the Apolloniou Parembole district of Arsinoe [*SPP* IV, p. 70–71 Coll. VII, IX, X] notes that four potters were working there and that, as long as they continued to work, it was expected that no additional potters would establish a business there (Wipszycka 1971, 126–27). However, other documented activities offer insights into intragroup relations. One such cooperative activity (as discussed in Chapter 5) involved exchanging children in apprenticeship relationships. From a social perspective, this meant taking a child into the workplace for one or two years; from a professional perspective, this was a means of exchanging trade and business knowledge among families (Venticinque 2016, 84–85). In addition to apprenticeships, Venticinque (2010; 2016; see also van Minnen 1986, 50; Liu 2005, 287–91; 2017), working with archive data, has been able to trace relationships and business interactions among guild members – for example, sharing information on prices and markets, and sharing labor for large commissions or projects. Members seem to have privileged one another in partnerships, in the sale of properties, and when offering interest-free loans (Venticinque 2010; 2016, 78–80). Such relationships were sometimes family affairs, with business dealings maintained between association members across generations of families (Venticinque 2010, 278–79). Documenting the activities of first-century-AD weavers at Oxyrhynchus, Liu (2017) was able to reconstruct local social networks in the weaving community, and at least one of her social networks could be related to local geography, with members living in the same quarter of the town (Liu 2017, 217–19).

The sorts of collaborative work practices recorded in contracts and guild charters, which Liu and Venticinque see as building "trust networks," are very much in keeping with the sorts of activities reconstructed archaeologically among the potters' workshops. Everyday acts of sharing tools, coordinating waste disposal, demarcating community areas for particularly dirty jobs, and controlling access to supply chains of raw materials can be witnessed archaeologically and then interpreted in terms of the sort of collaboration envisaged by Venticinque and Liu. These practices indicate means by which workshop clusters could work together to pursue common interests in both formal contract arrangements, as well as more mundane and informal interactions.

12 Professional associations of potters have been documented at Gerasa (*SEG* VII, 879; Vitto 1986, 60), at Ephesos (Outschar 1991, 319), at Thyateira in Lydia (Arnaoutoglou 2011, 270), possibly at Korykos in Cilicia, although this is contested (Patlagean 1977; Trombley 1987), and more generally in third/fourth-century Egypt (Gallimore 2010, 161; *O.Bodl.* 2.2143.4 and *P. Lips.* 97).

However, by emphasizing these collaborative efforts, other competition-driven interactions are perhaps not fully appreciated.

CONFLICT AND COMPETITION

While supportive cooperation and mutual interests have long been seen as defining the socioeconomic dynamics within nucleated workshops, more recent historical and economic research since the 1980s nuances the picture of professional interactions in industry clusters.[13] Variously described in modern contexts as "aggregate industry," "industry agglomeration," or "innovation clusters," these production contexts have received extensive treatment that has highlighted the complex motivations and interactions that might play out within these work communities. Historical studies of nineteenth- and twentieth-century industries have demonstrated, for instance, that concentrations of industry manufacturing similar products create a highly competitive economic environment. While useful in terms of professional networking and knowledge "spillovers" (Jaffe et al. 1993; Boschma 2005), these were particularly challenging environments in which to establish new businesses. In some documented cases, failure rates of new manufacturing businesses were as many as three times higher than in contemporary nonnucleated contexts (Sorenson and Audia 2000, 440).[14] If an arriving craftsperson was without established professional networks, such clusters could be hostile environments for new businesses.

Some of these (modern) observations might help explain the ancient evidence. The importance of social networking in establishing a professional reputation has been well understood for antiquity (Verboven 2002; 2011a); conversely, it can be assumed that there were real challenges to becoming professionally established in an existing industry cluster without those networks. Apprenticeship under an established craftsperson might offer one avenue into such networks (Freu 2016, 189–93), and there were certainly craftspeople in some professions who were highly regarded for their professional skill, so much so that they were sought after by apprentices (Freu 2016, 185–89). Among apprentices themselves, there might also be those who were favored over others, either on account of their skill or personal relationships (Freu 2016, 191). Underlying competitive relationships might be what Pliny the Elder is alluding to in his description of Erythraean potters, when he writes:

[13] My intention in introducing these discussions from modern economics is not to make a direct analogy with the ancient world, but rather because they offer some new perspectives on nucleated industry based on updated economic theory.

[14] The cited failure rate reflects twentieth-century US footwear industries (Sorenson and Audia 2000).

> In a temple at Erythrae even today are on view two wine-jars which were dedicated on account of their fine material, owing to a competition between a master potter and his apprentice as to which would make thinner earthenware. (Pliny, *Nat. Hist.* 35.161, trans. Rackham 1952, 378–81)

Contests of skill were certainly a feature of Greek athletic and artistic culture, but this example was set in an artisanal context between a master and apprentice, with trade-specific challenges of wheel throwing and thin-walled vessels set as a standard of excellence.[15] One might wonder if this reflects broader, underlying competitive dynamics within craft trades.[16]

That clustering of workshops might exacerbate competition between workshops in the Roman world has been noted by Ruffing (2016). Outside the Roman world, nonindustrial workshop clusters of small-scale producers certainly could be highly competitive environments, and underlying tensions were seen to threaten community cohesion. After all, in these small communities, potters are not only neighbors but also professional competitors. Annis describes modern potters working in nucleated workshops in Sardinia, and the inherent and underlying tensions among competing neighbors:

> I think that when we speak of solidarity when dealing with a concentration of workshops (Goudineau 1968; Peacock 1982, 43), we must draw a distinction. It seems that this co-operation will only bear upon the *technical* aspects of the craft and will do nothing to stop the potter's "envy" which remains a threatening destructive force. In general, if it is opportunely defended, the equilibrium between the centrifugal and the centripetal forces will persist as long as the socio-economic structure in which the production is developing is not disturbed. (1985, 244)

Annis here highlights the sensitive nature of these relationships between professional peers, as well as the delicate balance between individual and community interests. There are other ethnographic accounts (i.e., at Salvatiera de los Barros in Spain) in which such tensions proved so disruptive that potters ultimately left an established community to live and work elsewhere with less competition (Vossen 1984, 346). Among certain communities, competition could assume many forms: political competition between settlements, control over clay beds, and accessibility to consumers and other producers.

15 This competitive ethos is likewise echoed on a late sixth-century-BC Attic ware amphora painted by Euthymides, which included a disparaging message to Euphronios (presumably a rival painter) (www.beazley.ox.ac.uk/carc/resources/Introduction-to-Greek-Pottery/Keypieces/redfigure/euthymides).

16 The trope of an apprentice surpassing the master in skill appears with other trades as well (Tran 2016, 259).

Moreover, the potter's envy described by Annis seems to echo a sentiment observed by Ruffing for the ancient world, wherein competition between fellow craftspeople was expressed through petty curse tablets (2016, 120–21). The appearance of curse tablets in Classical Athens indicates that rivalries among competing potters existed in antiquity (*SGD* 44; Gager 1992, 162–63). The poem "The Kiln" (*Kaminos*) (already described in Chapter 4) is thought to have been composed from curses dated sometime in the sixth–fourth centuries BC; yet, elements of the composition seem Hellenistic or Roman in date, indicating a continued transmission history (Faraone 2001). The poem (and the curses) specifically describes inciting spirits in the kiln to destroy and break the vessels when firing. That such curses might have still resonated with Roman-period potters is suggested by a statement of Pliny (*Nat. Hist.* 28.4.19) referring to the effectiveness of curses on the products of a potter's shop (Gager 1992, 153–54). That tensions might also flare within workshops may also be evidenced by a recorded dispute involving brickworkers and quarry property rights (P. Tempeleide 29; Mees 2002, 234, 386).

Hesiod – at the start of *Works and Days* – describes such jealousy as being a powerful (and productive) motivation for potters and as driving the otherwise lazy workers to toil (lines 20–25; Gager 1992, 151–52).[17] Such competitive forces could certainly be powerful stimuli yet, as the ethnographic studies demonstrate, they were also potentially corrosive to social relations. Thus, regardless of the context of the industry – whether in modern industry clusters or ancient craft communities – there seem to be inherent challenges involved in balancing even moderate levels of competition with the cooperative benefits of nucleation. Thus, rather than focusing exclusively on the cooperative works of clustering and assuming universal benefits, it is perhaps better to consider actions (both collaborative and competitive in nature) as inherent to such contexts.

MEDIATION MEASURES

Accepting that workshop clusters create a situation in which both cooperative and competitive drives might be fostered for both positive and negative economic gain, how were such potentially corrosive social dynamics curbed?

Ancient historical sources on professional associations (with membership typically between ten and twenty-five individuals) might offer some ideas, in that these documents provide a helpful corpus of material in which concern is expressed regarding craftsmen acting selfishly or failing to meet social

[17] Ruffing saw ancient competitive markets as encouraging specialization and economic niches (2016, 118–23).

responsibilities among professional peers (Venticinque 2010, 278). Professional association charters (*nomoi*) sometimes outline rules of conduct, which often concerned inappropriate behavior between members and provisions for mutual assistance either in the form of financial and legal help for members (Boak 1937, 216–18; Venticinque 2010, 277–78). Such statutes are not preserved for any potters' associations (Mees 2002, 214), but those that do for other professions seem to recognize that shirking of expected social obligations (e.g., offering financial support to other members in need, helping to coordinate tax collection, paying of dues, celebrating family events) occurred with enough regularity that they required specific handling. The charters also specified financial penalties for such bad behavior – thereby also controlling and standardizing the levelling of punishment by the association. Both the naming of transgressions and the formalization of penalties represent attempts to discourage behavior that might damage the reputation or standing of the association and its members (Venticinque 2010, 286), as well as to prevent abuses of power on the part of the officials of the association when levelling judgement.

While it is not possible to equate professional associations (which were institutions among professional peers with formalized etiquette) with nucleated workshops (which represented a more neighborly form of professional community), the sorts of behaviors outlined in the charters nonetheless indicate potential types of social tension and professional disagreement that could threaten collective interests. The example of association charters not only highlights the likely occurrence of deviant behaviors within a professional collective but also measures to mediate and discourage such behaviors. They highlight how social groups required the active curation of sociability (van Nijf 2002).

Organizations within a Cluster

Other ways that potters might mediate the tensions present within competitive clusters of workshops can be garnered from other sources. For instance, it is clear from ethnographic studies of pottery clusters that there are many ways that potters curate social networks and alleviate tensions, and these conscious decisions can be expressed in a number of ways in the workshop – for instance, by pooling workers to achieve labor-intensive seasonal tasks (Dietler and Herbich 1989, 155; Henein 1997, 192–93), administrating equal pay rates among workers (Winslow 2009, 267–69), or sharing expensive equipment between workshops (Winslow 2009, 267–69). Heinen (1997), for instance, describes professional potting families within workshop clusters in the Dakhla Oasis of Egypt offering open kiln space to be filled with the vessels of neighbors (Henein 1997, 192–93), and larger potting families offering help to the workshops of families with fewer members (Heinen 1997, 192–93). In these casual ways, social debts accrue such that ties of mutual obligation are the result. Cooperative work and sociability practices serve not only as evidence of successful community bonds within work communities but also by performing these collaborative work practices, those community bonds were iteratively maintained and curated (Ortiz 2002, 893).

Product Specialization

As already discussed, social relations *within* workshop clusters have been overwhelmingly interpreted as collaborative in nature, despite evidence for more complex competitive and collaborative actions. The relationship *between* clusters, by contrast, has been much more commonly characterized by economic competition, and from a long-term, large-scale perspective, such competitive, market-driven models probably fit the evidence. Bes (2015) has successfully outlined the shifting patterns and frequencies in consumption between major Hellenistic and Roman tablewares across the eastern provinces through time, patterns that have been seen as market driven (Brughmans and Poblome 2016). Even at a small scale, Late Antique lamp production in the Levant shows changing structures of competition and supply, with a market-driven explosion of small-scale producers in the fourth through sixth centuries AD (da Costa 2010, 86).

Likewise, if we return to the example of the Ketios Valley workshops (discussed earlier in the chapter), the shifting fortunes of the Pergamon workshop clusters have been seen as reflecting competition between local production centers (Bounegru 2009; Domżalski 2014). The interior Ketios Valley workshops thrived from the third century BC but, in the first century AD, with the growth of the harbor and the decline in the export of ESB, the coastal Pitane (Çandarlı) workshops seem to have flourished in the second and third centuries AD. This occurs around the time that the Ketios Valley workshops were abandoned (Bounegru 2009, 83; Domżalski 2014, 154).[18] However, by the Late Roman period, another production center came to dominate the regional market; beginning in the fourth century AD, Phokaia, located just down the coast, began producing Late Roman C (i.e., Phocaean red-slipped tablewares) (Mayet and Picon 1986; Domżalski 2014, 159). These shifting industry geographies, in which centers of production are overtaken by new centers, assumes high levels of sustained competition among production centers in a region over the long term, with shifting fortunes attributed to

[18] The establishment of ESB production at Tralleis also has been seen as contributing to the demise of the workshops of Ephesos, which were reliant on poorer quality raw materials (Ladstätter 2007, 209–10).

various factors including exogenous factors (e.g., changing economic geographies) and endogenous factors (e.g., innovations in product line).

These sorts of long-term regional economic histories are founded on assumptions regarding economic competition among major production centers manufacturing similar goods, assumptions that fit well with macro-patterns in the data. However, on a smaller (more social) scale, these economic terms are not the ones expressed in most ethnographic sources. Instead, ethnographic accounts often discuss conscious attempts to mitigate direct competition between regional potting communities. Arnold describes such a situation between potting communities:

> Although they undoubtedly make this ware for their own use, little, if any, of this pottery from Quinua is found in the markets of the valley... In order to avoid competition with these communities, potters concentrated on making strictly the decorated ware which is distinct from pottery made elsewhere in the valley. (1972, 864)

Importantly, these potters seem to frame the discussion of competition in social terms that relate market-oriented pots to social relations with other potting communities, with deliberate choices in product repertoire made to avoid direct competition. In this regard, pots serve as a means of negotiating one community's place in a wider production landscape. Obviously identifying the motivation behind such choices is not possible in most archaeological cases. Yet, in comparing the repertoire of some well-published workshop sites from the region, it is clear that there was no single model by which nucleated clusters might specialize. Some clusters manufactured all the pottery needs of a market (tablewares, cooking and common wares, lamps, etc.). Gerasa's Late Antique workshops operating in the hippodrome appear to have supplied a tremendous range of products to the city (Möller 2017), so much so that 99 percent of the more than 600,000 sherds recovered from the Northwest Quarter excavations of the city were locally produced, with particularly high frequencies of local plainwares represented (Romanowska et al. 2021). By contrast, other clusters specialized in very particular functional categories that were distributed across a wider region. For example, some workshop clusters manufactured a limited number of vessel types; the workshops at Kefar Ḥananya specialized in only seven functional types (Adan-Bayewitz 1991; 1993). These patterns might be understood as production centers and workshop clusters filling economic niches at different scales but, in social terms, these might also mediate competition between centers in mutually beneficial ways and maintain positive professional relations.

The role of pots as social mediators of competition is perhaps even more pronounced within workshop clusters, where particular pottery styles are attributed to individual artisans. This begins with the simple observation that potters regularly claim to be able to identify the work of other potters within their community. In one ethnoarchaeological study, Nicholson and Patterson (1985b, 234–35) tested claims made by modern Egyptian potters and confirmed that potters could distinguish slight differences in rim shape, such that "pots are like people, each alike yet different from others" (Nicholson and Patterson 1985b, 234–35). Patterns in these slight differences are what Dietler and Herbich (1989) describe as "micro-styles" and what Gandon and colleagues (2020a; 2020b) see as resulting from an individual's vessel "morphogenesis." Such identifying characteristics might include subtle differences in neck curvature, rim shape, or patterns of incised decoration (London 1989; 2000[19]). As Dietler and Herbich describe:

> While preferences in decorative motifs employed or their arrangement in the decorative field are sometimes also indicative of individual potters... Although they may not be able to explicitly articulate the diagnostic attributes, potters can also usually distinguish their own and other potters' work quite easily even when decoration and form are virtually identical. This sense of individual "style" is known [...] ("this is the hand of Anyango") [...] and is expressed differently from recognition of the "style" of a given potter community [...] ("this is the Boro way of making") [...] all potters are able to recognize alien pots as not being of their own local style. (1989, 153–54)

In such scenarios, in which pots can be so closely associated with individuals, it is easy to understand how decisions regarding repertoire could be conspicuous to others working in the community and how the choice of pots manufactured is not necessarily so much about direct competition and economic advantage, as it is grounds for social negotiation – a negotiation in which individual artisans and workshops position themselves within the larger community based on skill sets, personal histories of craft learning, and networks of distribution. In such situations, pots become, in some sense, mediators or agents in social relations. Individualized product specialization among workshops then is seen as a means of diffusing competition within a community, by distributing high-demand product types between potters at a production site.

Occasionally such micro-styles have been observed archaeologically, mostly in the context of jar or amphorae production in which there is already a very narrow range of forms being manufactured by multiple hands. For example, workshops producing barrel jars in the Zevulun Valley and western Galilee regions of Israel have noted nine different rim and neck shape variations across four different workshops at Aḥihud, Yodefat, Yavor, and 'Uza (Avshalom-Gorni and Shapiro 2015, 87–97, f. 10; see also Vitto 1983–1984, 19). Among

19 London (1989; 2000) working with traditional potters in Cyprus likewise observed individual potter styles.

the production waste at Gerasa's hippodrome, such micro-styles have been identified in the production of molded lamps with figurine heads; produced from the same mold, the heads display a slight tilt to the left, seemingly a result of the individual gesture of the potter's hand when applying pressure (Kehrberg 2009, 502–4). Typological variants have also been noted at Gerasa that do not easily fit into established typological classifications (Kehrberg and Ostrasz 1997, 171); they see these as being "unintentional" variations, but these variations might also be understood as personal styles or experimentation by individual potters. Archaeologically, these variants are often attributed to a workshop, rather than an individual potter, largely due to the difficulties in identifying individuals in the archaeological record (Crown 2007; see also Heilmeyer 2004 on attributing workshops from pottery alone).

Comparing Repertoire

If we can begin to identify the presence of micro-styles in the archaeological record, this also has implications for the recognition of products among contemporary potters. Archaeologically it is easier to attribute repertoire and products to a workshop rather than individual potters, and there are cases where multiple workshops have been excavated and vessel repertoire was attributed to individual workshops in ways that may reflect similar socially negotiated production specializations. Among the Ketios Valley workshops, the distribution of pottery types around individual workshops showed varying frequencies: Workshop 1 was associated with higher frequencies of matrices for Megarian bowls, Workshop 2 and Workshop 3 were associated with greater numbers of sigillata vessels with maker stamps, and Workshop 4 was associated with higher frequencies of appliqué-decorated wares (Bounegru 2009, 184). While there must be a chronological dimension to these production specializations, these differing distributions give the impression that techniques of production (molding, throwing, throwing with appliqué) may have helped defined the repertoire of the different workshops.

At Petra's az-Zurrāba workshops, the workshop and kiln areas are littered with the production waste of many types of products – painted tablewares, molded figurines and lamps, common wares including bowls, jars, jugs, and cooking pots. However, conspicuously missing from the waster heaps were local products known from urban domestic consumption contexts, including unguentaria and tablewares that drew inspiration from sigillata and red-slipped wares ('Amr 1991, 321). This absence may suggest a product specialization by other workshops.

At Buto, areas of workshop debris attest to local products from different phases of the center's production. The seven kilns from excavation Area P1 provided evidence for red-slipped ware production from the first and early second centuries AD. The repertoire associated with the workshop(s) of this area encompassed sixteen major type groups, including a range of bowls, cups and goblets, plates, large open forms, jugs, flasks, miniature amphorae, and lamps. Many of these groups were further composed of subtypes and type variants (Ballet et al. 2019, 72–73). This range of tableware types, all manufactured as red-slipped tableware, demonstrates a large spectrum of forms and functions, with several typological variants comprising less than 1 percent of the represented corpus – for example, Type 3.4, *Bol à double collerette* and Type 5.4 *Petits "craters" a col haut* (Ballet et al. 2019, 79, f. 21.9, 82, f. 6.8). Whether these uncommon products represent failed experiments or forms made by fewer potters is difficult to say. Another area of the site (Area P3) offers evidence for the repertoire of Late Roman workshop(s) manufacturing a much wider range of ceramic wares in the late second and early third centuries AD (Lecuyot and Schmitt 2019, 155). These included table or presentation wares (cups, bowls, dishes), pitchers, jars, and bottles with strainer spout, cooking pots, and storage containers; some of the wares were painted with white slip decorations. In this later phase of production at Buto, the center appears to have been less specialized in its ceramic production.

Accepting this variability, and given the appearance of micro-styles, it is fruitful to look at a few other archaeological examples of intra-industry specialization from a small number of nucleated production centers where we have repertoire attributed to individual workshops, in order to attempt to establish if any of these repertoires might be understood through a lens of community social negotiation.

Kestros River LRD Workshops (Southwest Turkey)

Among the rural nucleated workshops found along the Kestros River and manufacturing LRD tableware, seven production sites were identified through surface survey by the Pisidia Survey Project (Jackson et al. 2012). Intensive (5 m by 5 m gridded) collection of the surface material was performed at three of the seven production sites (Kadirgürü Mevkiisi, Kömbeci Mevkii, and Camii Yıkığı). The diagnostic (mostly rim) sherds were then quantified to assess the comparative repertoire between roughly contemporaneous production sites located in the 5 km by 7 km area (Jackson et al. 2012, 91). As this was surface material, these are unlikely to be representative of all periods of production at the site, but the assemblages should offer some general contours within and ratios of the repertoire in the final phase of production. Only the Estimated Vessel Equivalent results of the sherd assemblages have been reproduced in Figure 26, but rim counts and sherd weights from the sites mostly follow similar trends (Jackson et al. 2012, 110–11, t. 1, 2, 3). From these statistics, a few comments can be made in reference to the relationships between workshop clusters, individual production units, and their products.

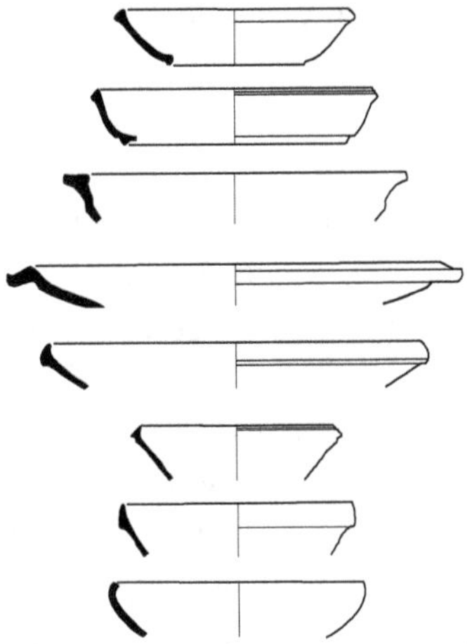

	Relative Frequency of EVE			EVE		
	Kadirgürü Mevkiisi	Kömbeci Mevkii	Camii Yıkığı	Kadirgürü Mevkiisi	Kömbeci Mevkii	Camii Yıkığı
Hayes Form 1	<5	<5	10.09			648
Hayes Form 2	**10.89**	**25.66**	**34.39**	2497	1252	2208
Hayes Form 7	5.46	<5	**15.28**	1253		981
Hayes Form 8	**14.02**	<5	8.8	3216		565
Hayes Form 9B	**28.84**	**16.77**	**12.38**	6614	818	795
Hayes Form 10	7.34	4.04	<5	1683	197	
Meyza Form K5.2	7.69	6.27	<5	1764	306	
Meyza Form 6	**13.88**	6.76	<5	3184	330	
Other Forms <5% Represented	11.88	**31.53**	9.05	2722	1538	581
Cooking	<5	6.72	<5		328	
Amphora	<5	2.25	<5		110	
Large Basin	<5	<5	6.49			417
Dolium	<5	<5	3.52			226

26 Product repertoire and the frequencies of tableware forms thought to have been manufactured at different production sites near the Kestros River (Turkey) [EVE: estimated vessel equivalent] (Based on Jackson et al. 2012, tables 1–3, 110–11).

First, it is clear that each of the three workshops produced a unique repertoire. These were not "cookie cutter" production units all producing the same LRD products for the same market. So the LRD ware or *koiné*, as archaeologists define it, is composed and categorized from the heterogenous contributions of products from multiple workshops. Because of the heterogenous types and quality of production from these sites, some of these products, when found in consumption contexts, are likely being misidentified as "imitations" (Jackson et al. 2012, 110). Second, the ratios of different types of vessels varied between production sites. Even when manufacturing similar items to one another, they often did so with notably different intensities of production. For example, a wide bowl form (Hayes Form 7) appears at two of the sites (Kadirgürü Mevkiisi and Camii Yıkığı) but in notably different relative frequencies (5 percent and 15 percent, respectively). These workshops seem to have invested in this product at different levels.

When comparing the vessel forms manufactured, it is also clear that there were some forms (Hayes Form 2 and Hayes Form 9B) that were produced in considerable quantity at each site (Figure 26). The representation of these shared shapes varied between 11 percent and 34 percent among each site's surface assemblages, so these two shapes were important products at all three production sites (Jackson et al. 2012, 99–100, f. 10–11; 105, f. 16). However, besides these commonly manufactured products, some forms seem to have been made at one site and not the others, or appear in decidedly greater or lesser frequency at the different sites. For example, Hayes Form 1 (a dish) only appeared at Camii Yıkığı, where it represented more than 10 percent of the surface assemblage. This is suggestive that the form was manufactured in perhaps only a limited number of workshops but, in those in which it was produced, it could be a significant product of the workshop. Additionally, all sites had forms that were represented in small quantities (less than 5 percent of the total surface assemblage), but at Kömbeci Mevkii, this category (of different forms produced in small quantities) comprised almost one-third of the surface assemblage found at the site. Seemingly some sites might have been more invested in producing a wider range of forms yet in smaller numbers.

The general impression from the three Kestros River workshop sites is that there were some forms shared by all the production sites and manufactured as key products in the community-wide repertoire. Other forms, however, were either produced only at some workshops or at multiple workshops with notably different levels of investment. Some workshops might have even adopted a diversification approach, manufacturing smaller quantities of lesser-made vessel types. Rather than specialization in particular functional classes or techniques of production, there seem to have been a range of economic strategies at play within the cluster.

Sagalassos

The workshop cluster at Sagalassos manufactured, throughout most of its history, red-slipped tablewares, figurines, lamps, and small household items. There is little evidence for the manufacture of the common wares, cooking wares, or ceramic building materials nonetheless identified in the immediate area of the city. Instead, such items are believed, based on the compositions of their fabrics, to have been manufactured in the hinterland of the city (Neyt et al. 2012). Consequently, there was a clear specialization among ceramicist communities across the city's environs that reflected differing specialized production based on function and clay quarries between ceramicists.

Within the cluster at Sagalassos, other distinctions in the product repertoire can be observed. Nearly all products manufactured at the site from the first century AD, including the tablewares, lamps, and figurines, were manufactured using the same two clays, one of which was used to fashion a slip, fired to a red color. Here we see the defining specialization factor as finish and fabric. If we consider, however, the nature of organization within this urban community, there are several features that suggest differences among ceramicists working in the red-slipped ware tradition. Evidence for the Late Antique phases of production is the clearest, with three production areas having been excavated, the occupational dates of which overlap. Among these workshop sites, the first distinction in the repertoire of these workshops is a technical distinction in the forming stage of production. Two workshop sites (the Molded-Wares Workshop Complex and the Library East Workshop) manufactured molded items with thrown parts from the fourth through sixth centuries AD (Uleners and Poblome 2014; 2016; Murphy and Poblome 2016) and one (the East Slope Tableware Workshop) manufactured wheel-thrown tablewares in the fourth and fifth centuries AD (Poblome et al. 2001, 159–64).

The so-called East Slope Tableware Workshop has been associated with manufacturing only seven open forms in a range of functionally diverse types (Figure 27), including a cup (SRSW form 1A140-3), several bowls and dishes (SRSW forms 1B210, 1B220, 1B130, 1C180-3, and 1C140), and a mixing container (SRSW form 1F160).[20] This range effectively would have supplied the full functional suite of tablewares typically used at the time, excluding closed forms (such as jugs and jars). Yet when compared to the wider product line coming from the center at this time, this single workshop repertoire represents less than one-third of all SRSW open forms (Poblome 1999; Murphy and Poblome 2017). The workshop's repertoire included some of the most common forms of the period (e.g., SRSW forms 1B220, 1C140, 1F160), but it also included some less common, but very distinctive, variants and subtypes (e.g., 1C180-3). Thus, rather than being specialized in the full range of a vessel type (for instance, all variants of 1A140 cups or all variants of 1C180 dishes), instead the potters manufactured variants based on particular formal and decorative details.

This mixed repertoire of a workshop manufacturing both very popular forms alongside more "niche" types may reflect wider strategies in the local industry. Willet, for example, has noted that for much of the history of Sagalassos' workshops only ten forms comprised 64 percent of consumed SRSW (Willet 2018), while dozens of individual forms have been classified at the site (Poblome 1999). Some of the forms manufactured in the East Slope Tableware Workshop were very specific versions of vessel types and recall the sort of "micro-styles" described previously by ethnographers (Nicholson and Patterson 1985b, 234–35; Dietler and Herbich 1989; London 1989; 2000; Gandon et al. 2020a, 2020b). This selection of repertoire seems similar to the case of the LRD Kestros River workshops, which balanced largely consumed vessel types with more specialized types.

[20] For typological description of SRSW, see Poblome 1999. Special thanks to Jeroen Poblome for providing the product repertoire associated with the East Slope Tableware Workshop (pers. comm.).

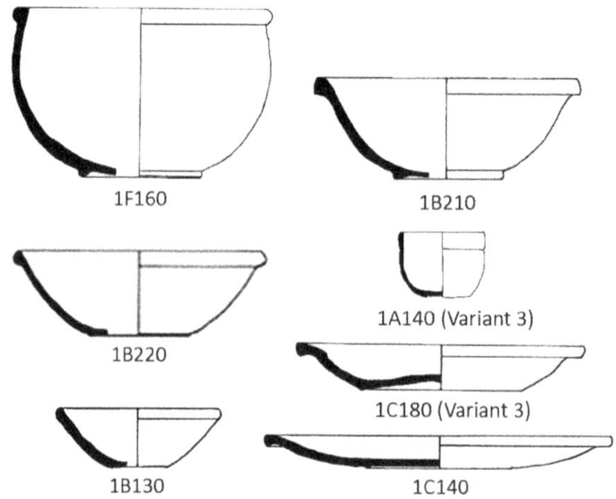

27 Repertoire of the East Slope Tableware Workshop at Sagalassos demonstrating the specific form variants manufactured there.

The selective repertoire of the wheel-thrown vessels, however, contrasts with the situation at the two contemporary molded-wares workshop sites at Sagalassos – the Molded-Wares Workshop Complex active from the mid fourth to sixth century AD (Murphy and Poblome 2016) and the Library East Workshop dated to the second half of the fifth and early sixth century AD (Uleners and Poblome 2014; 2016, 90). These two workshop sites seem to have been in direct competition with one another, as they were both manufacturing essentially the same functional classes of molded wares (pilgrim's flasks, figurines, and lamps) although the Library East Workshop may have been more focused on lamps, as most molds found in the workshop were for lamps (Uleners and Poblome 2016, 91). The iconography and some of the motifs used to decorate the products were also in some cases similar. While the products manufactured were very similar, they were organized at very different scales of production and coordinated different sets of work units, with one a single workshop unit and the other a multi-workshop complex.

In contrast to the case of the Kestros River workshops, the workshop repertoire within the Sagalassos cluster was influenced, in part, by different production techniques, particularly those using molds. Among the workshops making wheel-thrown wares, there seems to be a degree of generalization covering a range of functional classes, but with particular subvariants possibly reflecting highly personalized micro-styles.

Patara

The ceramic production center at the city of Patara presents another picture of a local urban production center. The workshops, mostly concentrated in the northern outskirts of town around the Tepecik Acropolis and Necropolis, were active from the Late Hellenistic period through Late Antiquity, but most were active in the Late Roman period (between the third and sixth centuries AD). A large complex in the northeast of the city (the Günlük kilns), with five kilns operating from the third through the sixth centuries AD, was documented as producing a wide range of goods, including small amphorae, ceramic pots, roof tiles and bricks. A workshop on the north slope of the Tepecik Acropolis, active from the fifth and sixth centuries AD, appears to have manufactured lamps (Varkıvanç 2001–2002; Dündar 2015, 204–5), while another kiln on the acropolis manufactured Patara red-slip ware, jugs, amphorae, and lekanai (Dündar 2015, 205). Another workshop was found in the *basilica thermarum* of the Harbor Baths, dated to the fifth and sixth centuries AD and manufacturing large ceramics, amphorae, bricks, and roof tiles (Dündar 2015, 205; Erkoç 2019, 203). It seems that product specialization at Patara may have been less rigidly defined, with pottery manufactured alongside ceramic building materials. Some pottery workshops could be highly specialized in manufacturing lamps, while other potters were making lamps, alongside tablewares and amphorae.

Gerasa

An even less specialized product repertoire can be seen among the workshops of the hippodrome of Gerasa. Here, as we have seen, the cavea of the hippodrome began to be occupied by workshops beginning in the third century AD. Three waste dumps from the general area have been recovered. Each of these was attributed to a single workshop, the assemblages contained a striking range of functional and stylistic types, including cooking pots, casseroles, slipped tablewares (open and closed forms), molded lamps, face-pots, and CBM. All were manufactured in the same clay using the same recipe. While it is difficult to directly attribute such production dumps to single workshops, what is nonetheless striking is that, within this spatially restricted ceramic workshop cluster, so many different functional classes, forms, and styles were being produced alongside one another in shared fabrics. Essentially, these workshops (or perhaps, more likely, this concentrated group of potters) appear to have supplied the entire ceramic needs of the city (Möller 2017; Romanowska et al. 2021). As an unspecialized nucleated industry, the Gerasa case presents a different way of defining a concentrated craft community and its repertoire.

One deposit of production waste found in a dump in cavea units W2 and W3 was thought to represent the discarded remains of a failed kiln load dated to the sixth century AD (Kehrberg 2009, 497–500). These fragments of unfired, finished wares included a wide range of functional groups similar to the fired wares found in other sections of the deposit. In addition to the remarkable preservation of this firing mistake, the wares represented are noteworthy. The unfired contents included cooking pots, bowls, jars, casseroles, lids, as well as figurines, molded lamps, and decorated finewares (including painted Jerash bowls); in addition to the pottery, unfired tiles and pipes were found in the deposit (Kehrberg 2009, 497–500). If this deposit represents the products from a single workshop, it would suggest that the workshops or at least the kiln firings were unspecialized in their product repertoire – both in terms of production technique and functional class. Pottery was fired with ceramic building material; painted wares were fired with plain wares; molded objects were fired with wheel-thrown wares; and cooking pots were fired with tablewares and lamps.

Unlike the more specialized local nucleated industries observed within the tableware industries of Sagalassos and Kestros River, these workshops supplied a much wider range of wares, in terms of functional categories and in terms of fabric groups. The evidence for workshop specialization within this local ceramicist community appears, likewise, to have been relatively unspecialized, covering a range of ware groups and production methods. This represents an alternative set of arrangements, based on a diversified repertoire.

Considering Workshop Specialization

In each of these examples, we can infer very different strategies in the development of repertoire – at both the cluster and individual workshop scales. These potting workshops were not all churning out the same sets of wares, nor were they highly specialized according to production method or functional class. Instead, each seems to have occupied a unique place within their local economic environment. There was no single response to specialization, and the repertoire appears not to have been driven exclusively by efficiency or method. Workshops at Patara and Gerasa seem to have maintained an extremely diverse repertoire in terms of consumer markets – building industries, transport vessels, household pottery, and household implements (e.g., lamps). From an economic perspective, however, it is surprising that so many wares might be produced in a single context, as these products required different tools and infrastructure and were manufactured on different schedules of production. In these respects, these workshops are notably diverse in their repertoire. Perhaps this was a response, in the case of Gerasa, to minimal competition, as the city was clearly consuming the products of its workshops in massive quantities, with more than 99 percent of its consumed ceramics from the local workshops (Romanowska et al. 2021).

At the Kestros River workshops and the Sagalassos tableware workshops, there seems to have been a tendency for workshops to specialize in only a portion of all the wares being manufactured at the time. Workshops do not appear to have simply made all the most popular wares, despite having the skill and means to do so. This is perhaps not surprising, as there are potential economic benefits for specializing within a cluster. Larger clusters draw customers, and by filling a particular niche market within that wider selection of goods a workshop can create a specialized place therein (Ruffing 2016, 121–22). Likewise, contrary to an efficiency-based model, these were not exclusively "cup workshops" or specialized "plate workshops," nor did these workshops specialize in a particular shape and then offer variations on that shape. Yet, at the workshop scale, the potters seem to have balanced their repertoires, making both very popular forms as well as more specialized types. Each workshop offered a unique range of shapes and invested in those shapes to different degrees. These nuances to product specialization might suggest the delicate way that potters positioned themselves within a larger professional community, particularly one with an already specialized (i.e., tableware) market. In these archaeological contexts, in helping mitigate tensions between individual economic ambitions and community cohesion, the pots themselves may have played a unique role. That being said, even within the community, there might be workshops operating to varying degrees of direct competition and at variable scales, such as the molded-wares production sites of Sagalassos.

It is clear from outlining the workshop product specializations found within these communities that the product repertoire of workshops could be extremely variable. This may seem surprising for the Roman world, where specialization and standardization have almost come to be assumed (Bailey 1997); yet workshop specialization, in all these cases (from highly diversified repertoire to highly specialized repertoire), fails to meet efficiency-driven or market-driven expectations, and pushes us to look for more flexible and contextual interpretations. In these cases, we might begin to, in part, see these product decisions as social responses to the particular circumstances in which one's neighbor was also one's competitor.

CONCLUSION

Workshop nucleation has been viewed as a common form of production organization for the Roman world. Much literature on these clustered industries has focused on the benefits of collaboration and shared resource networks, and there is, indeed, good reason to suspect that everyday cooperative work was a feature of these working communities. However, clusters of workshops producing similar wares for market are also inherently competitive environments, and those competitive features of the economic context also introduce potentially destructive social dynamics among neighbors, dynamics that necessitated mediation. Some of these mediation measures are evident in the organization of the workshop activities; others, such as the choice of repertoire, are less clear and warrant closer inspection. What is evident is that production dynamics in such contexts are not simple outcomes of supply and demand, but they also represent a means of mediation in the tensions within communities of potters. While neighborly cooperative action and avoidance of direct competition were certainly important for the success and stability of a tight-knit professional community, comparative historical and ethnographic studies demonstrate that such efforts also served to balance individual economic interests. It is by understanding these dynamics in concert that it is possible to access not only why workshop communities might come together, but also how they might be sustained over the long term.

CHAPTER EIGHT

URBAN INDUSTRY, TOPOGRAPHIES, AND COMMUNITY RELATIONS

Throughout this book, we have seen how the location of production framed different sets of relationships both between professional ceramicists and with their environment. Chapter 2 demonstrated how catchment models, tracking the availability of raw materials across a landscape, proved effective in capturing general trends in workshop distribution across large regions. In those models, the choice of workshop location was related to efficiently extracting clay and water for production. Approaching the lived experience of these workplaces through an understanding of *taskscapes* helped to draw together the rhythms of work and the physical landscape. Chapter 2 considered how spatial concentrations of workshops might encourage both collaboration and economic competition. At smaller social scales, however, modern ethnographic examples have been used to show that local cultural, social, and political issues also – and more particularly – influence the specific sites where potters work (Nicklin 1979; Gosselain 2008). In this regard the placement of workshops in relation to the wider community reflects the status and position of ceramic work within society more generally.

This chapter examines local cultural factors that might have influenced industry geographies in the eastern Roman world. It does so primarily in urban environments where industrial encounters with a local population would have been both intense and regular, and particularly where multiple workshops created an archaeologically detectable collective presence.[1] Understanding these dynamics is central in placing industry, physically and socially, within the wider urban community. Through time, the location of workshops within a cityscape might shift; they could be displaced by other activities, relegated to the outskirts of town, or moved into abandoned buildings. These practices reflected the changing relationship between craftspeople, the city environment, and their neighboring townspeople. They also reflected changing expectations of urban life and the place of potentially noxious craftwork therein. Tracking these changes through time highlights differences, not only in the negotiated place of pottery industries within cities but also demonstrates potters and ceramicists to be important actors, contributing to larger trends in urban change.

NAMING CONVENTIONS AND LOCAL INDUSTRY TOPOGRAPHIES

Toponyms offer some insights into how these industrial elements were seen in the city and how workshops were conceived in relation to broader social geographies. In smaller towns, like Oxyrhynchus (Alston 2001, 262–69), personal names (accompanied by professional title) referenced physical locations in the listings (*P.Oxy.* I 43 *verso*) of early fourth-century guard stations (e.g., "opposite the house of Epimachus, wax maker," "towards the house of Ammonios, bean seller," "the street at the house of the fuller" (Alston 2001, 263–65). The toponyms of Oxyrhynchus are characteristic of the socioeconomic geographies of a small community; however, in larger urban contexts, artisanal workshops might be identified within the experience of built space. Workshops, particularly clusters of workshops, were sometimes described as landmarks in ancient cities. At Herakleopolis, there is a reference to a "street of the bag-bearers" (Rabinowitz 2001, 56), and at Antioch on the Orontes, fullers are described as being located along a particular canal (Feissel 1985; Saliou 2012, 40–41). At Apameia in Phrygia a *plateia* was named after shoemakers, and at Sattai in Lydia a *plateia* was named after linen-makers and shoemakers (Wipszycka 1971, 117; Barry 1993, 84–86; Mayer 2012, 79–82). These cases demonstrate an association between work and urban topographies, wherein the act of place naming reflects the significance of collective artisanal presence.

The lasting associations with these industries might also continue long after the area acquired a different function – as seen most famously with Athens'

[1] That industries, like ceramic production, were situated outside of the city center means that at many cities these peripheral (and sometimes suburban) industry installations remain unidentified and unexcavated. Nonetheless, at some sites, it has been possible to identify the locations of urban industrial spaces from high concentrations of surface production waste.

Kerameikos (Esposito and Sanidas 2012). Most naming conventions in Classical cities refer to streets, as Hellmann (2012) has noted, rather than referencing areas, zones, or quarters, and this is likely how many urban areas would have been experienced by inhabitants – at street level, following road systems. This is implied in placenames, such as the "workshop on the road from the Basilica" at Aphrodisias (Smith 2011, 64–65). Other conventions juxtapose public monuments and everyday workshops. The "public workshops opposite the Bouleuterion" at Aphrodisias might be understood in this way (Smith 2011, 64–65). In these examples, it becomes clear that the placement of workshops and industries helped to construct a local understanding of place and community.

WORKSHOP STRUCTURES: ARCHITECTURAL VERNACULAR?

Given such topographical references to streets and urban monuments, for many city dwellers craft workshops would have been perceived in the cityscape, at street level. This raises the question of how the pottery workshop buildings appeared and were appreciated within the city's viewscapes, within which the facade and built environments of industry would sit alongside buildings of different functions, styles, and materials. For example, Dio Chrysostom's first-century-AD account of Prusa in Bithynia gives the impression that workshop structures were modest buildings of little architectural regard (Dio Chry., *Discourses* 40.8–9). Having offered to construct a monumental colonnaded street for his home city, Dio was both affronted and perplexed when the local populace protested against the removal of long-situated industry workshops to clear the area for his construction project, and ultimately, he was obliged to build his monument in another area of the city. In this instance, different segments of the urban community interestingly seem to have divergently valued their local industry works (Mayer 2012, 82–84), but what is of further significance here is Dio's description of the appearance of the workshops:

> hovels where even the blacksmiths were scarcely able to stand erect but worked with bowed head; shanties, moreover, in tumbledown condition, held up by props, so that at the stroke of the hammer they quivered and threatened to fall apart. And yet there were some who were distressed to see the signs of their former poverty and ill-repute disappearing, who, far from being interested in the columns which were rising, or in the eaves of the roof, or in the shops under construction in a different quarter, were interested only in preventing your ever feeling superior to that crew. (Dio Chry., *Discourses* 40.8–9; trans. Crosby 1962, 115–17)

Such structures were clearly, in his eyes as wealthy urban benefactor, unworthy of a thriving city center. Accounting for Dio Chrysostom's personal bias, his description of workshops hosting heavy industry implies that they were constructed in a "vernacular" style that contrasted with public monuments constructed by some benefactors of the time. The archaeological record of pottery workshops of the Hellenistic and Roman periods confirms that pottery workshops, at least, were modest structures – particularly in terms of their construction materials and the techniques of their building. The suburban pottery workshops at az-Zurrāba near Petra (Zayadine 1982, 382–84) and the Ketios Valley Workshops near Pergamon (Bounegru 2009, 75–79) were composed of mud-mortared fieldstone, while mudbrick (on a stone socle) was used for workshops at Sagalassos and Elusa (Arubas and Goldfus 2008a, 1715). These were utilitarian buildings constructed of common local materials. These were certainly modest structures, but were they so dissimilar to other building types (both public and private) that coexisted in a city?

In cases where it is possible to compare the workshops with other non-elite private structures, many ceramic workshop buildings appear to fit within local (modest) domestic building traditions, particularly in terms of materials. For example, in comparing Petra's az-Zanṭūr domestic neighborhood to the pottery workshops at az-Zurrāba, the house walls of the former are described as being composed of lightly worked fieldstone covered with plaster with occasional dressed sandstone elements (Stucky 1993, 44–46). In contrast, the workshop walls at az-Zurrāba were composed of unworked fieldstone, some walls were plastered, and some rooms were vaulted, with dressed sandstone voussoirs selectively employed (Zayadine 1982, 382–84). It seems that the workshops were in keeping with the local building tradition in general, although their construction may have been expedited through the greater use of undressed fieldstone. At Buto, Hellenistic housing found in the area of the kilns was composed of mudbrick (Ballet and Marouard 2012, 14–16) – construction methods similar to those used for the kiln structures and associated walls.

The architectural similarities between modest houses and pottery workshops are also reflected in the difficulty of archaeologically distinguishing work versus domestic functions. This distinction is often only accomplished when internal infrastructure is present, or when a detailed contextual study of artifact distributions is conducted. At Dura-Europos, for example, the vernacular architecture is such that it is difficult to establish from the building plans and construction styles alone whether the building was domestic, commercial, or productive in function (Baird 2007, 414). In an area of the city described as the *îlot des potiers* (Allara 1992), several kilns found within courtyards were identified as part of either workshop-houses, or as part of a workshop with nearby potter housing (Allara 1992, 108, 112). The function was impossible to discern from the building remains alone. Likewise, at Hierapolis, the two Frontinus Street houses dated to the fifth and sixth centuries AD are difficult to interpret.

They appear to have hosted domestic spaces with cooking facilities (Mastronuzzi and Melissano 2007, 549–51). However, two very large kilns (both approximately 3 m in diameter) were constructed immediately adjacent to, – and just steps away from the doorways of, – the house structures. Kiln spacers and a deposit of raw clay were also found in the northern unit, which might suggest that these structures had mixed domestic and work function (Mastronuzzi and Melissano 2007, 543, f. 2).[2] Using standing sections of architecture, reused materials, and mixed construction of small stone blocks interspersed with layers of fired brick, they are very much of the style common for contemporary housing found in other parts of the city (Mastronuzzi and Melissano 2007, 542). At Elkab, the ostraca found within the house-workshops seem to indicate mixed workshop and house areas, although in House B one-third of the rooms are of an unknown function, highlighting the difficulty in demarcating functional zones within the same structure (Hendrickx 1998, 1363). At Sagalassos, just east of the Neon Library, a building row in the second half of the fifth century AD accommodated a textile workshop, a workshop manufacturing molded wares, and a space thought to have been used for housing (Uleners and Poblome 2014; 2016; Poblome et al. 2015). Again, here modest housing units were constructed alongside and as part of the workshop areas.

At least as regards their locally sourced materials and locally vernacular architecture (and in some cases, even as regards their layouts), workshop structures seem to align with those of other types of modest private buildings. This is of further interest in that the building materials and techniques of the workshop structures sometimes contrasted those used to build kilns. At az-Zurrāba (Petra), the kilns were constructed entirely of brick, while the workshop structures were made of fieldstone (ʻAmr and al-Momani 1999, 176). At Sagalassos, the kilns were primarily fired brick and mud mortar, while the workshops were built of mudbrick on a stone socle. At Khirbet Baraqa, the workshop and corridor structures were composed of local worked kurkar stone that was then partially plastered and covered in barrel vaults, while the kilns were mudbrick construction (Gadot and Tepper 2003, 133). Because of the special demands of kiln architecture, the workshop structures follow divergent building styles that more closely align with local traditions.

Pottery workshops were also sometimes built into repurposed (existing) structures, perhaps further emphasizing their expedited, cost-minded, or

[2] The northern unit included spaces 1101, 181, 1060, 1053, and the southern unit included spaces 1072, 1048, 1095 (Mastronuzzi and Melissano 2007, 543, f. 2). The southern unit was clearly provisioned with an upstairs, the function of which is difficult to reconstruct, but a domestic function cannot be excluded.

otherwise ad hoc construction. This pattern of reusing structures is commonly observed in Late Antiquity, with many pottery workshops (as well as those of other crafts) found in the remains of earlier public buildings. These Late Antique "encroachments" (for further discussion, see Saradi 1998; 2006; Jacobs 2009; Murphy and Uytterhoeven 2023) present a rather stark contrast to the monumental buildings in which they are found. Late Antique ceramic workshops have been found in the public baths of Anemourion (Russell 2002) and Antiochia-ad-Cragum (Hoff et al. 2016), in Patara's *basilica thermarum* (Erkoç 2019, 230–31), as well as slightly later in the Bath-Gymnasium Complex of Sardis (Yegül 1986, 39–41). They appear in the hippodrome (Units E32, 40, 29) of Gerasa (Ostrasz and Kehrberg-Ostrasz 2020), in a shop in the north portico of Nysa's agora (İdil and Kadıoğlu 2008, 503–4), on the Frontinus Street of Hierapolis (Mastronuzzi and Melissano 2007), and in what was once an elite housing complex of Ephesos, Terrace House 2 (Ladstätter 2011, 14, f. 17). Kilns were also grafted into the remains of earlier buildings at the Molded-Wares Workshop Complex at Sagalassos (Murphy and Poblome 2016, 188) and at the Monastery of St. Jeremia at Saqqara (Ghaly 1992, 163–64).

In these cases, modestly sized structures composed of a series of mudbrick and fieldstone walls were built against and along solid ashlar faces; mosaic floors were cut through to build a furnace; and fragments of earlier bricks and stone masonry were used, all in order to fit these workshops into the shell of older buildings. Such a juxtaposition of private industry in once public architecture has been seen as a common feature of the period (Saradi 1998; 2006; Jacobs 2009; Lavan 2012). However, earlier, Roman-period kilns are also documented as having been inserted into standing sections of abandoned structures at Aḥihud (Avshalom-Gorni and Shapiro 2015, 70). At Palmyra, five pottery kilns dated between the first and third centuries AD were discovered just within the walls of what had been the *principia-forum* building (Krogulska 1985, 43; 1996). Many of these examples involve circular chambers built into rectangular rooms and required infilling between the outer curve of the chamber wall and the rectangular corner of the space. This is the case at the Sagalassos Molded-Wares Workshop Complex (Murphy and Poblome 2016, 188), Aḥihud (Avshalom-Gorni and Shapiro 2015, 66), and Allanoi (Yaraş 2003, 406). At the Monastery of St. Jeremia at Saqqara, a circular kiln (Kiln 121) was inserted into an earlier space and the earlier doorway was employed as the stoke hole (Ghaly 1992, 163–64). Many, but not all, of these are Late Antique renovations of earlier buildings.

When seen in the context of these earlier pottery workshops, these later "encroachments" might be understood as a continuation of a longer history in industrial vernacular building, a tradition that sometimes also incorporated all or parts of earlier structures and that was cost-minded, using techniques and materials also employed for domestic buildings. These workshop structures appear to have been part of a wider milieu of non-elite building traditions.

INDUSTRY STATUS AND VISIBILITY

The episode described by Dio Chrysostom – local protests against the removal of workshops at Prusa – suggests that some members of the urban community valued the placement of local industry and were willing to advocate on its behalf. While that instance was entangled in issues of urban development, there is reason to suspect that industries might also be valued for their reputation and the consequent status conveyed on the town. Ancient textual sources occasionally refer to highly specialized products of urban industry that were well regarded and closely associated with individual cities and regions. Kibyra's fine ironwork was described by Strabo (Strabo 13.4.17; Plin., *Nat. His.* 5.29.11; Özüdoğru 2018, 19), and the cities of Lycia were singled out for their quality textiles (Strabo VII, 578; Plin., *Nat. Hist.* 8. 190). Many of these industries continued into Roman and Late Antique times, and historical documents such as Diocletian's Price Edict verify that the products of these cities were greatly prized.[3] The collective presence of these well-regarded industries must have afforded their craftspeople some status locally.

Esteem of local industry might also be expressed in other ways, such as investment in urban infrastructure for industry. This is most notable in the case of urban water systems. While there are examples of private investment in workshop water supply, such as the private cistern constructed at Elaiussa Sebaste's amphora workshop (Borgia and Iacomi 2010, 1040–42), water supply to other workshops may have been drawn from the public supply. At Sagalassos, the city's eastern suburbs were crisscrossed with water piping and canals, and in the East Slope Tableware Workshop vertical terracotta piping was found in the corner of the workshop (Claeys and Poblome 2019). These waterlines likely connected to the water system running into the city. Similar situations have been observed for other urban industries. In the area of Tralleis' workshops (Sigillata Alanı) terracotta pipes were found and, while not clearly tapped by the workshops, water was provisioned to the industrial area through civic infrastructure (Civelek and Atıcı 2014, 429–31). At Petra, the az-Zurrāba workshops were in proximity to the Ain Musa wadi, but were also near an ancient, canalized reservoir to the city, and both have been described as possible water sources for the workshops (Zayadine 1986a, 258–60; 1986b, 185–86). These examples highlight the consumption of water

[3] Laodikaian wool and linen were among the costliest textiles; however, highly priced linen was also made at Tarsus, and wool was manufactured in the regions of Phrygia and Cappadocia (*Diocl. Edict* 25–28).

by workshops from urban collection and distribution systems, and also investment in such urban infrastructure that not only helped support local trades, but may also have been used to attract and sustain work activities to a particular part of town. Saliou (2012, 48) has even proposed that the provisioning of water for industry might have been politically motivated on the part of civic administrators, as the presence of workshops benefitted and profited the city through the exaction of rents.

While pottery is typically considered a lower-cost good that was widely produced and consumed, there are nonetheless occasional references to the desirability of pottery manufactured at particular centers. The cups of Pergamon were referenced by Pliny the Elder as being highly esteemed, and the pottery of Tralleis was also of note (Plin., *Nat. Hist.* 35.46). Another local industry famously cited in several Roman texts is that manufacturing "Rhosian ware" (*Rhosica vasa*, Ρωσικὸς κέραμος). Requested by Atticus from Cicero during the latter's governorship of Cilicia in 51–50 BC (Cic., Att. 6.1.13), these tablewares are thought to refer to ESA – a ware group manufactured in the region of Cilicia and Syria (Lund 2005; Lund et al. 2006b). There was therefore widely held recognition for the quality or desirability of at least some such pottery wares and, as Pliny noted (*Nat. Hist.* 35. 161), the work of these modest ceramic industries "brings nations fame" (Rackham 1952, 378–79).

As some pottery wares were closely associated with their place of production, well-regarded pottery might also provide visual references to its location of manufacture. There are (albeit rare) examples in which tablewares were stamped with the name of their home city; this is the case with two vessels found at Notion and stamped with ΕΚΚΑΙϹΡΗΑΣ (an ancient reference to Tralleis) (Domżalski 2014, 155–56, f. 6; Rotroff et al. 2018, 134). There is also an example of an ESC vessel stamped with the name of Pergamon and depicting a Capricorn; the Capricorn also appeared on contemporary civic coinage (Domżalski 2014, 155–56, f. 6). While still rare, such examples nonetheless seem to make explicit reference to their place of manufacture – perhaps advertising the already well-regarded products, but also referencing a meaningful association between the city and its pottery industry.

Beyond these limited textual references, it becomes more challenging to assess the local community status of urban industries identified archaeologically – and particularly for industries that were lesser-known to the ancient interregional market. However, Stissi has proposed that the continual location of Athens' Kerameikos along a major thoroughfare into and out of the Classical city reflected the status of the potters' work in the city and the importance of that work to its economy (Stissi 2012, 217; see also Lund 2015, 54–56). Indeed, like their earlier counterparts, many Roman workshops are described as being near major roads of their city. In Patara, workshops are found along and near the northern road into town (Varkıvanç 2001–2002;

Dündar 2015). Gerasa's hippodrome workshops, by the sixth/seventh centuries AD, framed either side of the major northern road into the town near an earlier monumental gate dedicated to Hadrian (Kehrberg and Ostrasz 1997, 169–70; Kehrberg 2009). At Soli-Pompeiopolis, a Late Antique amphora kiln and its production dump, sitting just 100 m from the harbor, would have been visible when entering the city's port and likely was also visible from the theater (Autret et al. 2010, 203). Workshops with associated domestic spaces were also found along roads. At Hierapolis, domestic spaces with pottery kilns were built over the commercial agora and encroached onto Frontinus Street, just outside the city wall (Mastonuzzi and Melissano 2007). The workshop-house structures of Dura-Europos were found in a major quarter of the city (Allara 1992; 1994). Pottery workshops in some cities could therefore be positioned in visible locales.

In other urban contexts, however, particularly those of the earlier Roman period, the placement of ceramic workshops was not quite so conspicuous. At Sagalassos, the city's eastern suburban workshops were situated in general proximity to the major cart road into town (Claeys and Poblome 2019, f. 2). However, the geophysical survey of the area shows that the major access way did not immediately connect to the workshop area (Martens et al. 2012), at least on roads that could be easily traversed with carts. Instead, it would have been necessary to follow the roads that wound around the theater to the workshop cluster. Moreover, the workshops were set on higher terraces, tucked behind a fringe of large tombs that ringed the area's lower slopes and terraces. In this way, the workshops would have been visibly concealed from the visitor entering the city from the east by the funerary monuments positioned on the lower terracing in front.

At Kibyra, there is a similar situation, whereby the tiering of monuments on different terraces was used to present a dramatic view of the city's stadion, theater, and *odeion*. The pottery workshops were situated on the far side of the city, and away from the main arteries to the city from the south. The Kibyra workshops were likewise upslope, on the highest hill of the city (at an elevation of 1,350 MASL). These workshops, manufacturing unguentaria and tableware, were identified from surface collections near the northwest necropolis, placing them behind the theater hill (Japp 2009; Kugler 2018). The large amphora workshop at Elaiussa-Sebaste is situated on the upper plateau in a residential quarter, and the narrow road leading to the complex is on a terraced slope (Borgia and Iacomi 2010, 1030–33). The impression one gets at these sites is that the terrain was used to conceal these workshops behind other, sometimes monumental and commemorative, features. While the smoke plumes of the kilns would have risen above this section of town, there is some reason to suspect that "hiding" the workshop structures was intentional, as similar strategic uses of terracing were also employed at cities, like Sagalassos, in the urban monumental center.

LOCATION OF PRODUCTION: TENSION BETWEEN PUSH-AND-PULL FACTORS

Regardless of an industry's visibility or consumer regard for its products, nearly all urban pottery industries were located in the peri-urban fringe of a city. This is the case at numerous sites, including Kibyra, Sagalassos, and Gerasa, as has already been discussed. This is also the case at Phokaia, where parts of several pottery workshops and kilns dated to the Hellenistic and Roman periods were uncovered in the modern Atatürk Quarter on the edge of the ancient city. A ceramic dump dated to the Roman period was also found to the north of the ancient city on the west side of the Çifte Kayalar Hill (Özyiğit 1994, 78, f. 1; Pekin 2015, 104). Peri-urban placement is also observed at Patara, where workshops dated between the Hellenistic and Late Antique periods were excavated to the north of the city on and around the Tepecik Acropolis; at least one of the workshops was on the northern road into and out of the city (Varkıvanç 2001–2002; Dündar 2015). At Buto in Egypt, the Hellenistic and Roman-period kilns were found on the northern slopes of the northern-most settlement mound (Kôm A) (Ballet 2007, 18). At Anemourion, surface material (e.g., wasters, bricks, kiln supports) was found in the northern edges of the city, and was thought to represent the Roman-period potters' quarter (Russell 2002, 225). At Tralleis, the Sigillata Alanı (thought to be a tablewares workshop area) was identified and partially excavated on the southwest slope of the ancient city (Civelek and Atıcı 2014, 429–31). At Porphyreon, the workshops were located on the periphery of the city (Wicenciak 2014, 104–21; Lund 2015, 55–56). Meanwhile, in the Byzantine town of Elusa (Negev), a pottery workshop manufacturing storage jars was situated on the outskirts of town close to the wadi, Naḥal Besor (Arubas and Goldfus 2008a, 1714–15; Bucking and Goldfus 2012).

In other cases, nucleated workshops are found a few kilometers from cities. As noted in Chapter 7, these might be better understood as suburban, rather than peri-urban, workshops. In the Ketios Valley, the Late Hellenistic / Early Imperial period tableware workshop cluster associated with the mountain city of Pergamon, the workshops are down in the valley below the city – separated physically from the urban core above. This is also the case with the workshops found at the foot of a rock face on the edge of Petra, between the modern village of az-Zurrāba and an ancient water reservoir to the city (Zayadine 1986a, 258; 1986b, 185–86). Near Jerusalem, the Hellenistic and Roman ceramic production was positioned approximately 4 km from the city wall (Arubas and Goldfus 2005, 11). The regularity across the region with which these workshop clusters are found separated from ancient urban centers is notable. Yet these differ from what might be referred to as a "village industry" (van der Leeuw 1977, 71, t. 1), as they seem to be part of the low density and gradual transition of the suburban zone into countryside that cannot be easily disassociated with the city (where the workers are sometimes thought to have lived).

PULL FACTORS: URBAN POPULATIONS AS REGULAR CONSUMERS

Cities offer any number of benefits for industries, and they often attract clusters of craftspeople. As discussed in Chapters 5 and 7, industry clusters offer interpersonal professional networks among craftspeople, facilitated professional association development, apprenticeship training, exchange of business knowledge, pools of human capital, and spillover work for large, commissioned orders (Venticinque 2010; 2016). Cities also provided concentrations of institutions (civic, religious, and later military) that might employ local crafts directly or provide infrastructural support to crafts and tradespeople, and urban professional associations might serve as intermediaries between collectives of craftspeople and authorities (van Nijf 1997; 2002) . Cities additionally provided a ready market to sell wares. It is generally held that in the Roman world most pottery was a relatively affordable commodity that could be widely marketed (Greene 2008). Ceramics are also thought to have had a limited use-life (David 1972; Shott 1996; Peña 2007, 58–60), meaning that there was a continual demand for these wares. Cities – as large and dense population centers – provided stable, regular, and proximate consumer markets for ceramic producers.

There were numerous means by which potters might reach consumers, and in cities wares could be marketed through well-established traders with specialized commercial shop spaces. The store-lined streets of Roman cities in the eastern Mediterranean attest to regular consumption by urban populations – including the consumption of local and imported ceramic wares – and a potter's wares might be marketed alongside both specialized ceramics and general goods. In Asia Minor, shops on the Cardo of Pisidian Antioch are thought to have sold ceramics, alongside glass and metal wares (Özhanlı 2014, 14), while at Dura-Europos the third-century Shop B8-G2 appears to have exclusively sold ceramic lamps (Baird 2007, 419). At Aizanoi, a Roman-period shop recently found in the agora appears to have specialized in oil lamps (Gerson 2021; Coşkun *forthcoming*).

A papyrus from Dura-Europos (*P. Dura.* 126) documents that, in at least one instance, ceramic production and sales were occurring in the same shop (Perkins 1959, 396–98; Baird 2007, 417). While most urban ceramic workshops tended to be spaces primarily dedicated to manufacturing, the distinction between production and sales is often difficult to discern archaeologically. The production and sale of small, molded objects, such as lamps or figurines, might occur in small shops in town. Indeed, lamp molds have been discovered in several shop contexts in cities. At Caesarea, an assemblage of molds and finished products was found in a shop thought to have been making lamps and figurines (or selling molds to potters) (Sussman 1980, 79; 2012), and lamp molds have been documented in many cities, including Laodikeia (Şimşek 2013, 490), Ephesos (Mitsopoulos-Leon 1985; Ladstätter 2011, 19–20), Shiḥin (Strange and Aviam 2017), Caesarea Maritima (Sussman 1980), and Sepphoris (Meyers et al. 1987, 277; Lapp 2016, 183).[4] Requiring (relatively) small quantities of clay and water, and necessitating minimal investment in infrastructure, manufacturing small items may have been better placed in downtown shops than other types of ceramic production. At Dura-Europos, a complete (two-part) lamp mold was found in a third-century-AD shop (G1–114/118) that sold ceramic wares, including molded wares (Baird 2007, 419–20). The shop lacked a kiln, suggesting that the small objects were transported to a kiln site for firing elsewhere.[5] This raises the likelihood that a commercially oriented shop might form small items that could be transported and fired off-site (see Chapter 2 for other contexts where kiln firing might be spatially separated from the workshop).

Commercial sales might also occur in larger pottery workshops with storage spaces. At Elusa (Negev), the smaller rooms of a workshop were thought to have been used for storage and possibly sales (Arubas and Goldfus 2008a, 1714–15; Bucking and Goldfus 2012, 48). A great variety of nonlocal pottery was found in House B at Elkab, leading the excavators to suppose that the small house-workshop (rooms a–c) was both producing pottery and also selling nonlocal pottery (Hendrickx 1998, 1365–66). There is a Rabbinic textual reference to purchasing production-damaged pottery for use by children (i.e., a "seconds" market) (Vitto 1986, 55); it is difficult to imagine that such pots were commonly distributed by middlemen or shopkeepers, and this transaction more likely occurred between potter and buyer. Another textually attested circumstance in which a vessel would be acquired at the workshop concerns vessels used in rituals in the Judaic tradition (and discussed in Chapter 4). In this case, the consumer was advised to watch the furnace overnight and collect the vessel directly from the kiln in order to avoid pollution (Mishnah Parah 5.1; Tosefta Parah 5.1; Vitto 1983–1984, 54).

4 Unusually, a ceramic kiln and glass furnace were found in the north portico of the agora at Nysa (İdil and Kadıoğlu 2008). However, the ceramic kiln (associated with amphorae and unguentaria) was positioned at the far end of the complex and the room was accessed on the opposite side of the building away from the other shop units.

5 While not within the urban center, a similar situation is also observed at Patara, where a fifth–sixth-centuries-AD ceramic workshop on the Tepecik Acropolis was identified as manufacturing lamps based on the high number of unused examples found in the workshop (Varkıvanç 2001–2002, 138–39, 145). This workshop also lacked a kiln on the immediate property, and it was suggested that the lamp workshop might have used a tile kiln located in the nearby necropolis area.

Integrated complexes hosting both production and commercial specialists might also occur. At Anemourion in the sixth and seventh centuries AD, the Small Baths (north of the palaestra) were repurposed, and in the rear service area a large pottery kiln was built. In another room of the Small Baths, a hoard of 700 unused lamps was found stacked atop a disused hypocaust floor. Ready for sale, the assemblage of lamps was thought to be part of a merchant's storage area (Russell 2002, 225). The appearance of many copper coins and lead weights, as well as high frequencies of both CRS and ARS ware imports, led the excavators to think that the bath complex was serving both production and commercial functions in different areas (Russell 2002, 226).

Workshops without storefronts may have involved middlemen distributors or local shopkeepers, yet direct producer-to-consumer exchanges might also have occurred without formal commercial space. To better understand these circumstances, it is helpful to consider the case modelled for Galilee's village production centers. Adan-Bayewitz (1993, 229) outlined six modes of distribution by which a pot might be acquired by a consumer in Galilee, based on textual sources (Table 4), involving direct sales between consumer and potter, centralized markets, and itinerant peddlers. In addition, market days (de Ligt 1988; 1993; Cohn 2011; Lavan 2012; Pitarakis 2012) are well documented across the region more broadly for both Roman and Late Roman periods. Topos markers sometimes indicate the sale spaces and workspaces of these tradespeople in public buildings and in marketplaces (Rouché 2004, inscriptions no. 187–233; Lavan 2012, 338–40). In addition to permanent and periodic markets, festivals might also draw in other occasional traders, thus providing opportunities to comparatively shop (de Ligt and de Neeve 1988, 398–99; for Rabbinic prohibitions on fairs, see Cohn 2011). In Talmudic sources, conversely, potters are described as peddling their own wares. Carrying their vessels – likely on a yoke or a carrying pole – to consumers would evidently have put the potters in direct contact with their buyers (Vitto 1986, 55–57, see also Adan-Bayewitz 1993, 230–33).

Archaeologically identifying these types of exchange is of course challenging, but distribution patterns have been compared with different models (Adan-Bayewitz 1993). Given the distances and quantities involved in the distribution

TABLE 4 *List of different modes of marketing pottery (from Adan-Bayewitz 1992, 229).*

(A) consumer at potter's workshop for purchase
(B) potter travels to the consumers to market ware (itinerate peddler to multiple sites)
(C) producer-potter travels to central marketplace to market wares
(D) producer-potter travels to sell to middleman
(E) a middleman acquires pot at workshop and peddles to multiple sites
(F) middleman acquires pottery from workshop and sells at central marketplace

of Kefar Ḥananya wares, for example, most distribution is thought to have been conducted at central markets, with either the potter carrying their own goods or traders taking them to market. This contrasts sales made at the production site or by itinerant middlemen traders, such as the short-distance peddlers described in sources as selling in four or five villages and returning home at night (Adan-Bayewitz 1993, 232). These other means may have also been contributing to the distribution of wares, but much less frequently (Adan-Bayewitz 1993, 232–33).

The archaeological and textual evidence of sales by potters highlights that the distribution of wares could be organized in all sorts of ways. For urban potters, the sales options and nature of encounter with buyers were diverse – e.g., informal sales of "seconds," lamp-making shopkeepers, and peddling potters. These different modes of distribution established different types of socioeconomic relationships between craftspeople and their local consumers. Moreover, these various commercial arrangements highlight how urban markets could be a major attraction for craftspeople, presenting not only a larger but a more regular consumer base. Altogether, cities presented an attractive location for potters and workshops.

PUSH FACTORS INFLUENCING LOCATION OF PRODUCTION

In opposition to the "pull" factors of urban markets and civic infrastructure, other factors may have encouraged the establishment of workshops in areas of town set apart from the monumental center and dense residential areas. In urban contexts, the remains of pottery workshops are often described by archaeologists as parts of potters' quarters or artisanal quarters, reinforcing the impression of a controlled segregation of industry works from other public and domestic space. A significant body of work has, however, disputed the idea that these clusters were the consequence of official zoning regulation imposed by urban authorities (Esposito and Sanidas 2012; see Sanidas 2020 for more detailed discussion of metalworking). What is becoming clear is that the placement of industry – and especially ceramic production – appears to have been directed by a number of factors, including cultural norms of neighborly relations, risk of legal liabilities, and religious proscriptions. Moreover, among different communities in different regions of the eastern Mediterranean, the reasoning for this distancing may have varied, but collectively these proscriptions and norms seem to have served to similarly and repeatedly push pottery production to the outskirts of town. Saliou has even suggested that pottery workshops rarely appear in these textual sources on account of the fact that they already adhered so closely to distancing norms and expectations that proscriptions were unnecessary (Saliou 2012, 47).[6]

[6] Saliou (2012, 47) notes that the omittance of pottery production is a peculiar feature of the textual record.

That pottery workshops may not have been particularly welcome neighbors is to some extent understandable. Most Roman and Late Roman pottery kilns were of a simple updraft design. In such kilns, firings can easily last many hours, and in some cases multiple days, typically reaching temperatures of 800 to 1,000 degrees centigrade. Moreover, the fire was kept large relative to the size of the kiln, and the use of cut wood and other combustibles (clippings, grasses, press cakes) could have produced significant smoke. With multiple ceramic workshops in simultaneous operation, smoke and fire risk must have been real concerns. The workshops in Patara, with possible evidence for a destruction event associated with fire, may provide corroborating archaeological evidence that fires did break out (Özüdoğru and Dökü 2007, 401). Moreover, the making of tablewares, storage vessels, or cooking pots necessitated large areas for drying vessels, storing fuel and clay and, in the case of large or complex forms, adequate spaces for storing and forming vessels in parts that would then be joined. These would have placed certain demands on property size. Finally, as we have seen in Chapter 7, these production processes can generate notable waste. These features (demands for workspace, unpleasant environmental conditions, fire risk, and waste generation) are all inherent to any full-time professional pottery workshop.

While typical of any sizable pottery workshop, these factors were not exclusive to potting, however, and this raises the question of how the placement of potting workshops compares with that of other pyrotechnological industries. In this respect, there is also some reason to suppose culturally recognized differences in furnace designs that may have influenced how pottery workshops were variously included in or excluded from the urban space. As mentioned in Chapter 6, there were terminological distinctions made in juridical texts between domestic hearths (*focus*) and artisanal furnaces (*furnus*), the latter of which included bakery and craft ovens (Saliou 2012, 41).[7] The classical Greek term, *kaminos* (κάμινος), similarly references industrial furnaces (Hasaki 2006, 222). While these terms do not align with the differing urban patterns of these artisanal and commercial pyrotechnologies, they do suggest a rather sophisticated understanding of furnace design. In contrast to pottery kilns, blacksmiths and glass furnaces appeared within city walls, and sometimes in surprisingly congested locations. Late Antique glass furnaces were found in shop spaces in the Sebasteion of Aphrodisias and in the cavea area of the theater at Side (Alanyalı 2013, 129–30), while Late Antique smithies have been identified in the Upper Agora of Sagalassos. A glass furnace was excavated in the colonnaded street of Tralleis (Akkan et al. 2016, 271) and another in the

[7] In everyday parlance, such distinctions might not be so closely maintained. Marichal (1988, 95) notes how the Latin terms *furnus* and *fornax*, for example, were incorrectly used on the kiln dockets of La Graufesenque (France).

lower city of Kelenderis (Zoroğlu et al. 2019, 77). Many of these examples are Late Roman in date, a period when industry becomes archaeologically more conspicuous in many cities (Sodini 2003; Zanini 2006). Moreover, the urban appearance of these furnaces also might be explained by their designs. While reaching very high temperatures (over 1,000 degrees centigrade), a smith or glass furnace is designed as an oven, wherein an intense but relatively small-sized fire was maintained, sometimes with the assistance of bellows and likely fueled by charcoal, which sustains a hotter and less smokey fire (than, for example, wood-fired pottery kilns). This may imply a cultural acceptance of "cleaner" furnaces within the city space.

Certainly, a preoccupation with air quality is evident in the ancient sources. Horace describes smoke as staining the buildings of Rome (Horace, *Odes* 3.29.11–12), and Tacitus refers to the air of Rome as *infamis aer* (Tac., *Hist.* 2.94; Hughes 1994, 126–27; Davies 2012, 69). In Greek, Roman, and Talmudic textual traditions, there were documented concerns about the polluting nature of some industries and how to deal with them. We also saw, in Chapter 3, the sometimes deleterious health effects of working with ceramic kilns. Rabbinic sources (Babylonian Talmud, Baba Kamma 82h; Zebahim 96a) state that furnaces should be kept outside of Jerusalem at a distance of fifty cubits (approximately 20 m) "on account of the smoke" (Vitto 1983–1984, 22; 1986, 59), and they (Mishnah Baba Bathra 2.9; Vitto 1986, 59; Tosefta Baba Bathra 10b–15b, 399, 1.10) state that tanneries, with their foul smells, should be on the east side of the city since the wind blows predominately from the northwest (Vitto 1983–1984, 22). Indeed, murex dye installations (a smelly industry, even by ancient standards) were found in Israel to have been situated downwind of settlements (Karmon and Spanier 1987; Bartosiewicz 2003, 184–85). At Khirbet 'Azzun, the pottery and glass kilns were both positioned along a major road to the regional city Apollonia and downwind of the settlement center (Erlich 2017, 193).

The Rabbinic texts express these stipulations as religious concerns (Green 2014), but similar apprehensions also are conveyed in Julian of Ascalon's treatise, *On the Laws or Customs in Palestine*. The text was written in the sixth century AD but is thought to have been influenced by earlier works (Saliou 1996, 27). Among his advice regarding building activity and avoiding damage to neighboring properties, Julian was concerned with issues of fire risk, as well as quality of air, land, and earth of neighboring properties (Hakim 2001, 7). In this regard, he advised distancing industry from neighboring buildings. These distances were determined by the type of industry involved, the height (i.e., number of storeys) of the buildings, the location of their windows and door openings, as well as the orientation of the buildings in relation to the kilns (Saliou 2012, 46, tab.3). Pottery kilns, specifically, were advised to be set apart approximately 1.70 m and 15.75 m from neighboring structures (Table 5).

TABLE 5 *Recommended distances between built structures and pottery kilns. (from Saliou 2012, 46, tab. 2).*

1.70 m	between a pottery kiln and a single-storey building with a closed facade toward the kiln, and located to the south or west
3.4 m	between a pottery kiln and a single-storey building with a closed facade toward the kiln, and located to the north or east
6.3 m	between a pottery kiln and a two- or three-storey building with windows overlooking the kiln, if the kiln is situated to the west or south of this earlier building
7.875 m	between a pottery workshop and and an earlier pottery workshop, if it is located to the north or east
10.5 m	between a pottery kiln and a two- or three-storey building with windows overlooking the kiln, if the kiln is located to the north or east of the earlier building
15.75 m	between a pottery workshop and and an earlier workshop, if the latter is located to the west or south

Distances calculated on the cubit conversion of 52.5 cm.

Of course, such advice was not necessarily followed, but it does illustrate contemporary concerns over the placement of workshops and furnaces, varying levels of concern regarding different industries, and measures that could be taken to encourage good neighborly relations.

Much like the Talmudic sources, Julian's interest in direction of buildings in relation to the kiln likely reflects a concern with the prevailing wind direction, such that wind would drive smoke (and conceivably also fire) away from town.[8] This is consistent with the archaeological evidence of several urban pottery clusters, where the local topography might direct the wind away from the settlement. In some cases, this could be highly localized; for example, at Buto (Egypt), wind was naturally funneled between mounds at the site (i.e., Kôm A and Kôm B) (Seton-Williams 1966, 163–65). More generally, the location of pottery kilns was such that smoke would be blown away from the central areas of several towns and cities,[9] and at Patara, Sagalassos, and Kibyra, the major workshop clusters tended to be situated at a higher elevation than other parts of the city (either on hills or upper terraces) – presumably helping to lift the smoke up and away from their urban cores. This upslope placement might reflect similar thinking to that used for constructing tall furnace chimneys in Spanish mining operations, described by Strabo (Strabo 3.2.8; Davies 2012, 74).

The role of urban authorities in directing this apparent clustering is very difficult to establish, and top-down mechanisms of zoning are not necessarily

[8] The use of prevailing wind direction to control industry smells is also known in other historical contexts (Bartosiewicz 2003, 181).

[9] Wind direction was observed using the program WindTracker.

the only means by which such concentrations of industry might occur. Davies has proposed for the city of Rome that: "This informal segregation [of unpleasant industries] does not suggest urban planning so much as the hierarchy of acceptable smells and wastes, calibrated according to the necessity of an industry or activity to everyday living" (2012, 69–70). Brimblecombe (1987) similarly has read the legal sources as advising socially neighborly behavior, rather than imposing a legally sanctioned urban zoning. In other Classical cities, this position is also supported by Esposito and Sanidas (2012), who understand ancient industry as developing within the urban fabric in more organic ways, rather than as having been mapped and formally zoned. Moreover, different cities, such as imperial capitals, might have particular institutional proscriptions specific to their status (Saliou 2012, 50). In Roman legal tradition, the pollution caused by workshop activities might also receive more than just neighborly reproach, and legal sources describe the responsibilities and liabilities of property owners. The *Corpus Iuris Civilis* of Justinian recognized that, if found negligent, workshops were potentially liable for any fires resulting from their work (*Digest of Justinian* 47.9.11). Thus, these risks may have helped encourage separation on the part of potters.

URBAN NEIGHBORLY RELATIONS

In negotiating these different expectations (and perhaps in some cases legal liabilities), it appears that potting activities were regularly relegated to the outskirts of the city. [10] This put them, therefore, in proximity to necropoleis, which also – according to many ancient traditions – were physically separated from the living space. Rome's Twelve Tables precluded human burials within the city's pomerium and restricted them to areas considered inappropriate for domiciles (Bodel 2000), and many centuries later, Horace still referenced urban development south of the Esquiline Gate where a cemetery was situated (Hor. *Sat.* 1.8; Edmunds 2009). As a consequence of such cultural expectations, there came to be a long association between necropoleis and the potting activity of a town or city across the classical world (for Archaic and Classical Greek workshops in proximity to cemeteries, see Stissi 2012, 214).

In Chapter 4, the significance of burials in kilns and in workshops was discussed; however, these were often in a wider context that placed human burials in proximity to workshops. Indeed, archaeological examples of urban fringe areas occupied by both necropoleis and potters are widely documented.

[10] Clay beds prevented easy percolation of water, making them poor soils for most agricultural use, and the pitted surface of quarries needed to be filled before building over the site. In fact, at Sagalassos, the points of clay extraction around the city have been identified and appear as deep ruts that required significant filling and levelling for later building.

At Gerasa, a cache of second-century-AD molds as well as lamps and figurines were found in a cave that was thought to have been an earlier Roman tomb; the ceramic objects were stored in the cave, and the associated work area of the ceramicist is considered to have been nearby (Iliffe 1945, 2). In later periods at Gerasa's hippodrome, following the abandonment of a workshop, two mass graves of individuals thought to have perished in the seventh-century-AD plague were interred in the structure (Ostrasz and Kehrberg 2020, 310–11). At Antandros, following erosional events that covered the first-century-AD necropolis, industry works were established in the fourth century (Polat et al. 2019, 263–65). Workshops in the vicinity of tombs are found at Patara (Özüdoğru and Dökü 2007, 400) and Porphyreon (Wicenciak 2016, 27–31). In Sagalassos' eastern suburbs, a monumental (*naiskos*) tomb was found to encroach into the plot of an earlier workshop area. At the Ketios Valley worksite (near Pergamon) between two phases of potting activity, the site was used for human burials (Bounegru 2014, 24). A Late Roman amphora kiln at Soli-Pompeiopolis was found in the vicinity of a necropolis outside the city (Autret et al. 2010, 204). Surface scatters of workshop waste at Kibyra were found below the area of the northwestern necropolis. The Roman-Byzantine pottery kiln found in the area of Roman-Byzantine tombs in the northeast suburbs of Abila (Jordan) also suggests a contemporary or close-to-contemporary use of the area (de Vreis and Bikai 1993, 491).

At Buto, in Egypt, human interments and cremation pyres were found throughout the workshop areas on Kôm A (Seton-Williams 1966; 1967; Ballet and Marouard 2012; Ballet et al. 2019); they both predate (third century BC) and postdate (Roman or Late Roman) the kilns there (Ballet et al. 2019, 62), while others were thought to be contemporary with workshop activity (Charlesworth 1972, 46).[11] At Buto, there is also evidence of a grave pyre (late third / early second centuries BC) for the cremation of at least three individuals and situated on the same Kôm as the Hellenistic and Roman pottery kilns (Ballet et al. 2019, 67–68). The appearance of crematoria in peri-urban areas has also been noted at Rome (Bodel 2000, 132–34). Given the concerns expressed elsewhere regarding air quality and fire risk, as well as the association between pottery kilns and necropoleis, this is perhaps not surprising. Yet the conditions of the remains evidence a fire of at least 600 degrees centigrade at Buto – less than that reached by the pottery kilns, but far surpassing that of a domestic oven (Ballet et al. 2019, 67–68). Thus, the area appears to have been occupied by multiple specialized pyrotechnological features of both industrial and funerary functions.

[11] A disused kiln discovered in the 1960s had several skulls in niches within the kiln; the human remains were thought to be placed there while other nearby workshops were active.

In some cases, the movement of property lines through time, such as at Sagalassos, Buto, and Antandros (Polat et al. 2019, 263–65), may reflect shifting lines in the competition over these busy peri-urban spaces. The association of a space with large-scale burning, whether of pottery in a kiln or a corpse on a pyre, may have reinforced the co-occupation of necropoleis and industry work. As noted in Chapter 4, there is also evidence from some workshops that the interaction between the workspace and the space of the dead was more intimate; an infant burial under the threshold of an active workshop in Gerasa's hippodrome (Kehrberg and Ostrasz 2020, 309) and the use of a kiln as a burial structure at Buto (Charlesworth 1967, 152; 1972, 46). It is difficult to determine the extent to which these associations with burial grounds might have influenced the wider cultural views on ceramic workshops over time. Nonetheless, understanding the patterns of workshop location, and the textual discussions surrounding ideal placements, illuminates how these workshops might have been perceived and engaged by the wider urban community.

SHIFTING INDUSTRIAL CITYSCAPES OVER TIME: LONG-TERM EFFECTS OF PUSH-AND-PULL FACTORS

Many Roman-period potting industries in cities continued in a particular part of town for centuries and over generations. More recent historical examples demonstrate that the existence of earlier workshops, particularly of shared or related crafts, encouraged the establishment of additional workshops (Wilson 2002; Goodman 2012, 303–7; 2013, 123–26); once established, successful industry clusters attracted further industry. The proscription preventing any additional potters setting up shop in Apolloniou Parembole District of Arsinoe (*SPP* IV p. 70–71 Coll. VII, IX, X) may represent an attempt to prevent such industry growth (Wipszycka 1971, 126–27). This sometimes paints a picture of rather entrenched industry spaces. However, even when long-established, the placement of pottery industries was not static, and if we take a longer-term view on the few cases where potting workshops can be documented from the Hellenistic period through Late Antiquity, it becomes possible to trace out changes in the ceramic production topographies of these cities. This longer-term perspective frames a period during which cities underwent real changes – particularly as regards their growing or receding sizes, shifting public and private areas, varying levels of development in building projects, and changing religious and cultural practices. Alongside those wider urban changes, the locations of workshops moved in concert.

These urban changes to local pottery workshops can be continually tracked from the Hellenistic period at some cities. In the city of Sagalassos, the earliest evidence of pottery production (dated to the Late Hellenistic period) was found beneath the Roman-period *odeion* (Waelkens and Poblome 2011, 78).

The location, at the heart of the city, and urban building projects from the Late Hellenistic and early Roman imperial periods, likely helped to push the industry to new areas of the city. At Sagalassos, by the first century BC, workshops are documented in the eastern suburban regions of the city, where they continued to operate for the next seven centuries. A similar story of urban development might also have occurred at Laodikeia where, in the Hellenistic period, a workshop was identified manufacturing lamps and mold-made bowls on Asopos Tepesi on the outskirts of the Hellenistic city (Şimşek and Bilgin 2018, 190–92). This area would later be incorporated into the urbanized areas of the larger Roman city.

The changing economic topographies of Asia Minor cities in the Late Hellenistic / Early Roman periods appears to have imposed new pressures and opportunities on some local workshops, whereby they were pushed away from the growing city. These examples demonstrate relatively short-lived Hellenistic-period workshops that, soon after abandonment, came to be incorporated into the urban built space. These may reflect the type of scenario described earlier involving Dio Chrysostom in the first century AD at his hometown of Prusa, where he attempted to acquire the properties of local blacksmiths and other industrial workshops for the construction of a new colonnaded street for the city (Dio Chry., *Discourses* 40.8–9; Mayer 2012, 82–84). While his acquisition of the properties failed at Prusa, such types of urban public works and building development might help to explain why Hellenistic workshops in other cities are found under Roman monuments.

Of course, growth and contraction of cities might not all result in the displacement of workshops. For example, Kibyra (Japp 2009), Sagalassos (Claeys and Poblome 2019), and Phokaia (Pekin 2015, 104) hosted industries for centuries in a particular location of the city. At Buto, a more than one-hectare area comprising a concentration of pottery kilns was found on the northern terraces of the northern-most site mound (Kôm A) (Ballet 2011). Already in the Hellenistic period, ceramic production appears to have taken place on the Kôm A; however, following the abandonment of a Hellenistic domestic quarter in the early first century BC, the evidence for production increases (Ballet and Marouard 2012, 14). Once established at the end of the first century BC/early first century AD, these kilns also operated in the vicinity of a Roman bath complex. After the baths ceased to function in the second half of the second century AD, the pottery workshops continued working until the third century on the mound, with some later kilns constructed with materials recovered from the building (Seton-Williams 1966, 166; Ballet 2011; Ballet and Marouard 2012). In this case, the workshops in the Roman period appear to have gradually expanded into these earlier settlement areas from a relatively early date.

LATE ANTIQUE CITIES AND URBAN INDUSTRY

Similar types of industry expansions into earlier settlement areas and relocation to new neighborhoods became much more common in cities in the eastern Mediterranean by Late Antiquity (fourth–seventh centuries AD). These patterns have been documented in other regions of the Late Antique world (Leone 2003, 269–73; Rogers 2011, 130–49; Underwood 2019, 156–58), but there appear to be some regional distinctions both in the timing and character of these changes, which reflect different trajectories of urban history (Murphy and Uytterhoeven 2023). In Asia Minor and the Near East, when industry and trade activities of all sorts became much more visible in the archaeological record of cities, their visibility was such that some scholars have seen it as reflecting a growing role and status of these social groups within their cities (Sodini 2003; Zanini 2006). Implications for social status aside, these archaeological contexts provide the clearest evidence for how industry locations moved in dialogue with other urban changes. While each urban story was unique, some common features of this process are observed at several sites. In numerous cities, new urban monuments were constructed in many of these cities, creating both new urban boundaries and new points of attraction. These had direct implications for the social practices and expectations of workshop location.

As we have seen, urban pottery workshops typically were found on the periurban fringes of the city. In Late Antiquity, however, the construction of new fortification walls often came to enclose a smaller, more densely built urban core (Kirilov 2007). This happened at cities across the eastern Mediterranean at different points in time, but the clearly demarcated fortification wall provides an index with which to track the relative placement of industries in relation to the perimeter walls. With the size of central urban areas reduced, this also meant the former pottery workshop clusters were now farther from the urban core. Thus, while some of the earlier industry quarters continued to host active workshops in their traditional part of town, other workshops are also at that time observed closer to the new boundary of the city, sometimes shadowing the new city perimeter. At Patara, Late Antique workshops appear along the northern road, where potters had been in operation since the Hellenistic period, but contemporaneously they also appear in the *basilica thermarum*[12] (Erkoç 2019, 230). These kilns were still extramural, but closer to the Late Antique city wall (İşkan and Şahin 2019, 332–43). At Phokaia, four ceramic kilns dated to the fifth and sixth centuries AD were found just behind the Temple of Athena (Özyiğit 2011, 485; 2016, 528; Pekin 2015, 104). At Ephesos, a cluster of workshops (smith, mill, stone saw, and potter), settled

[12] This had been described as part of the Harbor Baths complex in earlier publications.

in Terrace House 2 in Late Antiquity outside of the Late Antique city wall (Wefers and Mangartz 2011, 213). At Hierapolis, the partially destroyed commercial agora came to be positioned just outside the northern gate of the new Late Antique fortification wall, the ceramic workshops were part of the wider fifth-century-AD industrial conversion of the area to build the city wall (Arthur 2006, 117–18). At Kibyra, Late Antique (fourth–sixth-centuries-AD) ceramic workshops appear in the area around the *odeion*, closer to the new city wall that encircled the agora (Özüdoğru 2018, 39). Human burials also appear in the areas around the *odeion* (Özüdoğru 2018, 51).

It is clear that other activities (particularly funerary activities) on the edges of town were closely in dialogue with the workshop properties. In Late Antiquity, new types of buildings were established in the peri-urban fringes. Grave churches and shrines situated in the areas of revered burials acquired new ritual and community significance, and pottery workshops were perhaps not only being attracted to the newly defined urban center (with its markets and consumers), but also were being pushed away from the new peri-urban landmarks. This is seen at Patara, with the establishment of the Grave Church in the northern fringes of the city (Erkoç 2019, 230; İşkan and Şahin 2019, 332–43). At Kibyra, a temple situated north of the city's theater was converted into a church and near to the area of ceramic production (Özüdoğru 2018, 39).

Finally, occasional examples of ceramic workshops also began to appear within cities. At Laodikeia, Late Antique pottery workshop debris was found on the Stadium Street (Stadyum Caddesi), within the urban core of the city at that time (Şimşek 2013, 143; Şimşek and Bilgin 2018, 191–93). At several cities of Asia Minor, amphora workshops were found within the urban area. At Antiochia-ad-Cragum, a Late Roman 1 amphora workshop has been uncovered within the city wall, in the frigidarium of the Great Bath (Hoff et al. 2016, 4–6). An amphora and unguentaria workshop is thought to have been found in a late (possibly fourth and fifth centuries AD) shop space in the vicinity of the agora at Nysa (İdil and Kadioğlu 2008, 503–4). At Elaiussa-Sebaste, on a promontory with earlier Roman housing, the area came to be used for craft and production purposes in the late fourth through seventh centuries AD. This involved the establishment of an amphora workshop complex on the lower terraces. (Borgia and Iacomi 2010, 1030–33; Iacomi 2019), and oil and wine presses have also been found elsewhere in the city (Iacomi and Cassiani 2016). An early fifth- through early seventh-century-AD kiln was found near Soli-Pompeiopolis near a necropolis (Autret et al. 2010, 204–5). In earlier periods, such large container production tended to occur in more rural contexts in the countryside, yet kilns of this type, like presses, became common features in cities in Late Antiquity.

This was not a simple, uniform process, and one or more of these features might be observed at a given city. At some cities, it is possible to trace out several of these processes happening at once. At Sagalassos, for example, in the eastern suburbs (the traditional area of the Roman-period workshops), the Molded-Wares Workshop Complex was active from the fourth to the early sixth century AD (Murphy and Poblome 2016), and the East Slope Tableware Workshop was active until the mid fifth century AD (Murphy and Poblome 2014). However, in the second half of the fifth and early sixth centuries, molded ware production also occurred in the Library East location (Uleners and Poblome 2014, 89–90). This ceramic operation moved into a shared building alongside other industry work, including textile production; later, the pottery kilns were used for lime burning (Uleners and Poblome 2014; 2016). This location was outside but closer to the fourth-century-AD city wall and, for the first time in seven centuries, a pottery workshop appeared west of the city's theater. The movement of workshops closer to the urban core also corresponded with new building in the eastern suburbs, including the establishment of a Late Antique church just beyond the traditional workshop area (Murphy and Poblome 2016).

At Gerasa, the shifting locations are more difficult to trace, but there is some reason to suppose a similar process as observed elsewhere, with Roman-period (second-century-AD) production materials (molded objects and molds) found in what was thought to have been an earlier Roman-period rock-cut tomb. It is therefore assumed that this was likely in the cemetery on the outskirts of contemporary city (Iliffe 1945, 2; see also Kehrberg and Ostrasz 1997, 167, n. 1). Beginning in the third century AD, as we have seen, an industrial complex of pottery workshops and tanneries was found in the city's hippodrome (Kehrberg and Ostrasz 1997; Kehrberg 2009), a context that was outside the contemporary city wall. While these workshops were still active, late sixth-century-AD deposits associated with ceramic production were found intramurally in the Temple of Zeus (Rasson and Seigne 1989, 151). Byzantine-Ummayad ovens were found in the Temple of Artemis (Fisher 1938, 285; Watson 1989, 236), and a later Ummayad potters' quarter was established in the North Temple (Falkner 1986). These latter kiln sites were also within the city walls. While there are gaps in the phasing, it seems that the local industry moved from extramural placement of workshops in the vicinity of human burials, to a more mixed (intramural and extramural), and finally to a largely intramural placement.

The movement of workshops across the cityscape seems to have had real social consequences that resulted in the breakup of some earlier workshop clusters. New clusters were composed of not only pottery and ceramic workshops, but also a range of other industries. At Ephesos' Terrace House 2, a smith, mill, stone cutter, and potter were all neighbors in Late Antiquity (Wefers and Mangartz 2011, 213). At Hierapolis, the area that had been part of the commercial agora was occupied by ceramic kilns, as well as lime burning and stone cutting (Arthur 2006, 109–10, 117–18; Mastonuzzi and Melissano 2007). At Antiochia-ad-Cragum, the Great Bath was converted to industry use, and seven kilns have been found in the tepidarium, frigidarium, near the *natatio*, and in the north room (Hoff et al. 2018, 6–9). These included amphora kilns, a production dump in the latrines, and a glass furnace constructed in the palaestra (Can et al. 2015, 10; Hoff et al. 2016, 4–6; 2018, 6–9). At Nysa, in the North Portico of the Agora, shops were converted to heavy industry use, and an amphora and unguentaria kiln was found in a corner unit dating to the fourth and fifth centuries AD; next to the ceramic workshop, glass production was taking place (İdil and Kadioğlu 2008, 502–4). These new circumstances conceivably would have prompted the emergence of new social relations among local craftspeople. In fact, these new neighbors would not have offered much practical or logistical support, as they worked different materials and their furnaces often consumed different types of fuel (charcoal versus wood). Thus, these new industry clusters and neighborhoods would have been built on different types of industry relationship. That these new communities might form new collectives may be evidenced at Kibyra, where the establishment of new workshops appear in the vicinity of a newly constructed Late Antique bath complex that is thought to have serviced the neighboring worker community (Özüdoğru 2018, 34–35).

It seems that, in Late Antiquity, with new city walls and Christian monuments, pottery industries appear to have shifted and adapted to new urban realities, which in some cases would have helped to support transplanted workshops. Rather than isolated external communities or bubbles of industry, these workshop movements highlight just how interwoven these suburban industries were with their wider urban environments. Moreover, these shifting industrial spaces across the cities of the period had implications for the social lives of these craft communities, which ultimately resulted in the gradual break up of some of the earlier specialized potters' quarters. New workshops came to be implanted in earlier buildings, and new clusters were established, sometimes composed of multiple different industries. These movements of pottery workshops into new urban settings and alongside workshops often of other trades (and sometimes with associated domestic spaces) appear in many cities. This suggests that the specialized nature of some earlier industry neighborhoods was changing.

CONCLUSION

In the ancient world, workshops and industry facilities were part of most cities, and naming conventions of the time demonstrate a close association between economic and social geographies. The placement of industry within a cityscape has been understood as a reflection of cultural norms and expectations, as well as the status of particular industries within their local communities and economies. This was a relationship that often located ceramic workshops on the outskirts of the city and away from the households of both producers and consumers, yet in close proximity to other workshops and to necropoleis. There were pragmatic reasons for such placement, but these patterns would have implications for how clusters of pottery workshops developed over time. It also would have affected how these craftspeople distributed their wares and is probably reflected in the fact that few of the potteries from the region have architectural features that can be clearly interpreted as shopfronts, commercial areas, or domestic spaces. This is not to undervalue the place of these potting industries in their cities or to exclude other forms of interaction by potters with the city's inhabitants (e.g., occasional direct sales to passers-by, potters setting up stalls at local markets, directly selling to local shop keepers, distribution through local markets or shops). However, it would have spatially defined such relationships. Furthermore, the factors influencing the place of workshops were not static, and expectations between cities and their industries could change over time, such that workshops might move across the urban space.

CHAPTER NINE

CRAFTING COMMUNITIES: SOME FINAL THOUGHTS ON THE SOCIAL EXPERIENCE OF ROMAN WORKSHOPS

Like so many trades of the Roman world, we have relatively few textual references with which to reconstruct the activities, experiences, and lives of potters and ceramicists. However, the many preserved pottery workshops, kilns, and waste dumps – features easily distinguished from other types of crafts work – offer remarkable opportunities to more fully understand the lifeways of and social relations maintained by these everyday craftspeople. With so much emphasis on the economic organization of workshops and the contribution of workshops to regional trade, it is to some extent understandable that reports and analyses on workshop infrastructure and product repertoire have dominated the discussion. However, this scholarship comes at the expense of other research questions; those regarding social dynamics, the experience of labor, and work cultures of the Roman period. While the potential of these questions still remains too often underrealized, this book focuses attention on the sorts of evidence that otherwise only feature in the margins of scholarship, as footnotes or side discussions on daily life at a given workshop site. By drawing these types of scattered evidence from across the Roman East, this volume demonstrates that such approaches can be immensely fruitful to both archaeologists and social historians.

It is well understood that ceramic production in the Roman world was organized along multiple axes: at variable scales and differing intensities, taking place in various contexts (from the urban to rural), and coordinated by any number of actors (involved in private enterprise, civic estates, or households).

Relying on classificatory typological models of production has helped to organize our thinking on ancient ceramic workshops and has defined the way workshops are discussed and categorized since the 1980s. Yet there is no single model that captures the full variability in Roman workshop organization. Even in clusters of ceramic workshops, individual units were often arranged in variable ways for different types of workgroup and work process. The eastern Mediterranean (in particular Asia Minor, the Levant, and Egypt) has supplied case studies that are embedded in culturally, environmentally, and economically diverse contexts. Consequently, this book captures some of the local "flavor" and contextual diversity expressed in the material record of these industries. By looking at this set of workers – all specialized in transforming clay into ceramic goods – what is most striking is how different their working lives, craft traditions, and social experiences might have been across these eastern provinces.

The regions of Asia Minor, the Levant, and Egypt have framed the choice and selection of case studies presented in the volume. These regions had long traditions of pottery production, drawing on local resources and using kiln and wheel technologies already developed many millennia before the Roman era. In this sense, the eastern provinces contrast with other regions of the empire, where the introduction of new pyrotechnologies appears alongside other Roman cultural encounters. It also means that many local techniques and technological systems already existed across the Roman East, presenting a diverse industrial milieu by the time of political integration into the empire. As has been demonstrated, similar products made for a similar market might be manufactured according to different *chaînes opératoires* by different production centers. Kiln and wheel technologies reflect local traditions and embedded knowledge using local materials. The resilience of some such traditions to change is demonstrated in processes wherein innovations typically represent tweaks on existing traditions, rather than rapid and wholesale replacement of technological systems.

Moreover, in cases where major rupture appears within the technological and ceramic traditions of a locale, these can sometimes be related to abrupt social or economic changes – for example, the usurpation of a production site by an occupying military force, or the relocation of potters trained in a far-away ceramic tradition. The long duration of several of these ceramic industries also provides a view into how local craft communities might change over time. This is most notable in the rich evidence for Late Antiquity, when changing consumer demands encouraged innovations within a potter's repertoire, and when changes in cities influenced the placement of workshops. Thus, by investigating the technologies and methods of manufacture (factors so central to economic models), the local, community-based social influences become apparent. These local trends and technological choices are not so readily explained by economic rationalism or consumer-driven responses to market demand, but rather are better understood in contextualized, social terms.

TRACING RELATIONSHIPS

Acknowledging that some of the key metrics used to define the economics and organization of ancient production are inadequate to fully explain local production choices and workshop activities, means that new approaches to the material are needed. In response, this book spotlights sets of relationships that defined and articulated the social lives of these potters and ceramicists. In doing so, the important earlier contributions of economic and organizational studies can be augmented by those approaches with social insights. After all, the relationships that can be traced are richly complex and provide compelling evidence for what life could be like for craftspeople in the Roman East. These relationships can be seen to have tied potters to their material worlds, to their shared traditions and cultural practices, to their colleagues, and to their wider communities. It is by reconstructing these complex human, spatial, temporal, and material relationships that narratives of ancient working lives are more fully socialized.

The workshop, of course, was the nexus of working lives, and our entry point into workgroups and their activities. In some cases, these workgroups might be composed of family members, and they might involve multiple generations assigned to perform different tasks. In other cases, specialists with particular skills and performing special roles can be identified from the textual and archaeological records. Such workgroups likewise were not static, and could change with seasonal peaks of production and large commissions. Divisions of labor have long been seen as critical to the organization of production, but the performance of these roles surely resulted in particular working conditions and work schedules that affected personal well-being. The role of kiln operator, for example, seems to have required extended hours at the worksite, and the regular exposure to the kiln environment might even have had long-term health consequences: with this specialized work might have come specialized health issues. In addition to the daily cycles of potting, the archaeological evidence demonstrates that these workgroups engaged in other mundane, but shared, social activities – fishing, cooking, and dining together. The significance of the workshop and associated social relations in the lives of its workers might be further reflected through a range of ritual activities, and even final interment in kilns at death. The workshop was a social place with meaning constructed and maintained through such routine and shared experiences.

It is in some sense easier to reconstruct social dynamics within a workplace than among larger units of analysis, as modern excavations are typically limited to single buildings and thus are restricted to that scale of observation. However, it should not be surprising that social relationships also extended well beyond the workshop walls. Archaeologically, this has been best investigated at nucleated workshops, where multiple workplaces are seen to have operated collaboratively using shared resources and trade networks. However, workshop clusters also encourage competition and rivalries among neighboring potters making similar products, and negotiating one's place in such complex contexts has been shown to require active social and economic mediation strategies, including in the choice of one's products. Other craftspeople might also be part of the social network of potters. Evidence for the involvement of other artisanal specialists demonstrates a community of collaborating craftspeople, a community in which carpenters, builders, and metalsmiths might all contribute to making and sustaining key potting technologies like wheels and kilns. These cross-craft relationships were therefore critical in maintaining the ceramic industry. It is also clear that decisions concerning infrastructure could be made by actors from outside the workgroup – for example, property owners, other craftspeople, urban authorities. Potters were part of wide, rich, and complex social networks.

Workshops were also part of wider landscapes that shaped potters' spaces of experience. This is reflected in the material culture of the potters, whose tools were adapted from objects acquired in town and with items and raw materials retrieved from the wider countryside. Some of these spaces of experience were part of regular *taskscapes* that extended across the city and into the countryside. Even worksites used by a workgroup might be distributed across different parts of town. Most notably, a kiln might be separated from the workshop, requiring routine movement between worksites. The importance of the workshop as a *place* is more clearly evidenced in cities of the eastern provinces, where most workshop excavations have been conducted. In these urban contexts, the collective presence of a workshop cluster could be a vital part of the local economy and a major supplier of everyday goods. An industry cluster, particularly those active for many centuries, might come to be seen as a landmark in the local social geography. Yet ceramic workshops appear not to have made very good neighbors, and they often were positioned in accordance with cultural concerns about industry waste and smoke. Relegated to peri-urban areas of town, urban pottery workshops are found in association with necropoleis and funerary monuments – property uses that incurred similar cultural proscriptions. Over time, workshops can be seen to move in concert with their changing cityscape and with changing cultural expectations, particularly in Late Antiquity. These spaces of experience and social geographies of industry connected the work routines to the environment in ways that structured their place within the community and in society.

Many studies of Roman ceramic workshops have tended to focus on a single period of the workshop's occupation, particularly the final phase of activity. Yet with so many workshops in continual operation over several centuries (anywhere from two to eight generations), structures were subject to changes that reflected fluctuating economic circumstances of manufacturing as well as the changing career stages of potters. Indeed, from one generation to another, the workshop might witness major structural and organizational adjustments. These are observed with kiln renovations and revised layouts of workshop spaces. New potters were necessarily trained to sustain the workshop over so many generations, and small fingerprints impressed into clay attest to such scaffolded learning and on-the-job training. Imparting the workshop's traditions through intergenerational workgroups sustained the social life of the workplace, and the occasional human burial in a kiln or under a workshop floor conceivably continued these social bonds and associations with the workplace even in death. The workshop, far from being a static structure, was adapted in response to the changing careers and fortunes of its potters.

The occupations of potters and ceramicists, while not always aligning with modern conventions of industry, were to some extent defined by their products, and the unique role that pottery plays in archaeology – both in its uses for typo-chronological dating and in reconstructing trade networks – means that it is exceedingly well studied when compared to other craft products of the period. Such studies have understandably seen the relationship between pot and potter as embedded in the economic cycles of production, distribution, and consumption, whereby consumer practices and preferences are viewed as directing the functions and styles made by the potter. However, while consumer-driven demand surely affected product repertoire, more situated decision-making, reflecting local influences and ideas, can also be observed. Innovations in products might be inspired by the work of other craftspeople (glassworkers, woodworkers, metalworkers). Motifs found on local public art might be reproduced as decoration on a platter; a neighboring shopkeeper might sell imported tablewares that then spark new ideas on making local common wares. The relationships evidenced by such influences demonstrate an embeddedness of these potters in their local communities and in their local material worlds, as well as the rather casual way that new ideas could sometimes be incorporated into ceramic work.

Nonetheless, learning to make new forms certainly incurred adaptation costs in time and labor, and when innovative ideas were incorporated into an established tradition of potting, they were typically transferred through the technical know-how and experience of potters. Known gestures were adapted to execute new shapes; larger basins were made using a mental template of well-known and long-made cups. These transferals not only reduced failure rates, but also sustained learned practices and techniques within the tradition.

Thus, styles and repertoire of potters can be shown to have been influenced by both wider consumer trends as well as local inspirations, and then translated through familiar craft skills.

FINAL NOTE

The stories presented in this volume all involved workers who transformed clay into ceramic. The details of their craft – for example, the techniques, technologies, properties of materials, and the rhythms of production – all specifically concern the ceramic trade. Likewise, the wide range of economic sectors supplied by these industries, the varied contexts (urban and rural) in which they appear, the divergent scales at which they might operate makes the ceramic crafts in some respects unusual for the period. Nonetheless, the social dynamics (e.g., practices of craft tradition and innovation, apprenticeship and craft learning, competition and collaboration in small professional communities) offer perspectives from which to think through the evidence of other craft professions – particularly other occupations that can also be included among the textually "quiet" segments of Roman society. Furthermore, the stories of potters and their working lives should not be seen in isolation. The casual interactions documented between potters and other artisans and craftspeople also evidence their blended professional network. The experiences of potters in that regard must have affected the experiences of carpenters, glassworkers, and blacksmiths, and vice versa. In this sense, the worlds of Roman ceramicists both reflect the complexity of working lives in the period and were embedded in a rich world of artisans and craftspeople.

GLOSSARY OF SPECIALIZED POTTING TERMS

BAT: a disk (typically made in ceramic or wood) upon which clay can be formed into vessels or onto which wet vessels are placed to avoid distortions to the shape when being moved.

COMBUSTION CHAMBER (firebox): the lower chamber of a simple updraft kiln where the fire is stoked and from where the heat emanates.

FIRING CHAMBER: the upper chamber of a simple updraft kiln where the products are stacked.

JOLLY: a mold or other shaping form that is mounted onto a potter's wheel. The vessel is effectively thrown inside the mold giving a more consistent and sometimes more complex form.

KILN LINING: an application (often of mud plastering) across the interior of a kiln in order to protect the structure from extreme heat.

KNEADING: a technique of working natural clay by hand (similar to kneading bread). This technique serves to identify any large particulates, incorporate additives and water, and make the consistency of the clay more regular.

POTTER'S RIB: a type of potting tool that is used to form and finish vessels. They appear in many different shapes and materials and can be used to model, scrape, or polish.

SAGGAR (or cassette): A large, industrial vessel used to hold vessels (which will be marketed for sale) within the kiln. The saggar can serve to protect the vessels inside from irregular heat during firing, control the exposure to firing atmosphere in the kiln, and/or keep glazed vessels from fusing with other surfaces.

SETTLING BASIN (or levigation tank): large containers, either built structures or large vessels, designed to refine raw clay for use in production. This is achieved by suspending clay in water and allowing the clay particles and sediment to progressively settle.

SIMPLE UPDRAFT KILN: a type of kiln design in which the flame and heat are drawn upwards to a chimney situated at the top of the furnace. The interior shaft of the kiln is typically divided into a lower combustion chamber and an upper firing chamber.

TREADING: a technique of working natural clay by pushing with the heel or ball of the foot. This technique serves to identify any large particulates, incorporate additives and water, and make the consistency of the clay more regular.

TUBULAR DESIGN: the design of a kiln that incorporates piping, channels, or flues in order to introduce additional air into a kiln.

BIBLIOGRAPHY

Adams, W. Y. 1986. *Ceramic Industries of Medieval Nubia Vol. 1: Memoirs of the UNESCO Archaeological Survey of Sudanese Nubia.* Lexington: University Press of Kentucky.

Adan-Bayewitz, D. 1991. "Notes and News: Kefar Ḥananya, 1989." *Israel Exploration Journal* 41 (1/3): 176–211.

Adan-Bayewitz, D. 1993. *Common Pottery in Roman Galilee: A Study of Local Trade.* Tel Aviv: Bar-Ilan University Press.

Adan-Bayewitz, D. 1995. "A Lamp Mould from Sepphoris and the Location of Workshops for Lamp and Common Pottery Manufacture in Northern Palestine." In *The Roman and Byzantine Near East,* edited by J. H. Humphrey, 177–82. *JRA* Supplementary Series 14. Ann Arbor, MI: Journal of Roman Archaeology.

Agady, S., M. Arazi, B. Arubas, S. Hadad, E. Khamis, and Y. Tsafrir. 2002. "Byzantine Shops in the Street of the Monuments at Bet Shean (Scythopolis)." In *What Athens Has to Do with Jerusalem: Essays on Classical, Jewish and Early Christian Art and Archaeology in Honor of Gideon Foerster,* edited by L. V. Rutgers, 427–591. Leuven: Peeters.

Akkan, Y., A. Saraçoğlu, and A. Özver. 2016. "2015 Yılı Tralleis Antik Kenti restorasyon ve alt yapı çalışmaları." *Kazı Sonuçları Toplantısı* 38(1): 265–78.

Alanyalı, H. S. 2013. "Side 2011–2012 yılı çalışmaları / Archaeological Work at Side in 2011 and 2012." *ANMED Anadolu Akdenizi Arkeoloji Haberleri / ANMED News of Archaeology from Anatolia's Mediterranean Areas* 11: 121–33.

Albero Santacreu, D. 2017. "Interpreting Long-Term Use of Raw Materials in Pottery Production: A Holistic Perspective." *Journal of Archaeological Sciences Reports* 16: 505–12.

Allara, A. 1992. "L'Îlot des potiers et les fours à Doura-Europos: Etude préliminaire." *Syria* 69(1–2): 101–20.

Allara, A. 1994. "Osservazioni sulle fornaci per ceramica di Dura Europos sull'Eufrate." *Rivista di archeologia* 18: 129–34.

Allison, P. M., ed. 2006. *Archaeology of Household Activities.* London: Routledge.

Alston, R. 2001. *The City in Roman and Byzantine Egypt.* London: Routledge.

Amiran, R. 1956. "The Millstones and the Potter's Wheel." *Eretz-Israel: Archaeological, Historical and Geographical Studies* 4: 46–49. [in Hebrew]

Amiran, R., and D. Shenhav. 1984. "Experiments with an Ancient Potter's Wheel." In *Pots and Potters: Current Approaches in Ceramic Archaeology,* edited by P. M. Rice, 107–12. Los Angeles: Institute for Archaeology, University of California.

'Amr, K. 1986. "Instrumental Neutron Activation Analysis of Pottery and Clay from the Zurrabah Kiln Complex." *Annual of the Department of Antiquities of Jordan* 30: 319–28.

'Amr, K. 1987. *The Pottery from Petra: A Neutron Activation Study.* BAR-IS 324. Oxford: BAR.

'Amr, K. 1991. "The Petra National Trust Site Projects: Preliminary Reports on the 1991 Season at Zurrabah." *Annual of the Department of Antiquities of Jordan* 35: 313–25.

'Amr, K., and A. al-Momani. 1999. "The Discovery of Two Additional Pottery Kilns at az-Zurraba/Wadi Musa." *Annual of the Department of Antiquities of Jordan* 43: 175–94.

Andreau, J. 1999. *Banking and Business in the Roman World.* Cambridge: Cambridge University Press.

Annis, M. B. 1985. "Resistance and Change: Pottery Manufacture in Sardinia." *World Archaeology* 17(2): 240–55.

Annis, M. B. 2007. "La produzione della terracotta nel Campidano tra gli anni venti e gli anni ottanta del Novecento." In *Ceramiche: Storia, linguaggio e prospettive in Sardegna*, 119–260. Nuoro: Ilisso.

Antonaccio, C. 2005. "Excavating Colonization." In *Ancient Colonizations: Analogy, Similarity and Difference*, edited by H. Hurst and S. Owen, 97–113. London: Duckworth Publishing.

Apel, J. 2008. "Knowledge, Know-How and Raw Material: The Production of Late Neolithic Flint Daggers in Scandinavia." *Journal of Archaeological Method and Theory* 15 (1): 91–111.

Applebaum, H. A. 1992. *The Concept of Work: Ancient, Medieval, and Modern*. Albany: State University of New York Press.

Arnaoutoglou, I. 2002. "Roman Law and Collegia in Asia Minor." *Revue internationale des droits de l'antiquité* 43: 27–44.

Arnaoutoglou, I. 2011. "Craftsmen Associations in Roman Lydia: A Tale of Two Cities?" *Ancient Society* 41: 257–90.

Arnaoutoglou, I. 2016. "Hierapolis and Its Professional Associations: A Comparative Analysis." In *Urban Craftsmen and Traders in the Roman World*, edited by A. Wilson and M. Flohr, 278–300. Oxford: Oxford University Press.

Arnold, D. E. 1972. "Native Pottery Making in Quinua, Peru." *Anthropos* 67(5/6): 858–72.

Arnold, D. E. 1985. *Ceramic Theory and Cultural Process*. Cambridge: Cambridge University Press.

Arnold, D. E. 2006. "The Threshold Model for Ceramic Resources: A Refinement." In *Ceramic Studies: Papers on the Social and Cultural Significance of Ceramics in Europe and Eurasia Prehistoric to Historic Times*, edited by D. Gheorghiu, 3–9. BAR-IS 1553. Oxford: Archaeopress.

Arnold, P. 1966. "Die römischen Ziegeleien von Hunzenschwil-Rupperswil." *Jahresbericht / Gesellschaft Pro Vindonissa* 1965: 37–55.

Arthur, P. 2006. *Byzantine and Turkish Hierapolis (Pamukkale): An Archaeological Guide*. Istanbul: Ege Yayınları.

Arthur, P. 2007. "Form, Function and Technology in Pottery Production from Late Antiquity to the Early Middle Ages." In *Technology in Transition, A.D. 350–600*, edited by L. Lavan, E. Zanini, and A. Sarantis, 162–63. Leiden: Brill.

Arubas, B., and H. Goldfus. 1995. "The Kilnworks of the Tenth Legion Fretensis." In *The Roman and Byzantine Near East: Some Recent Archaeological Research*, edited by J. H. Humphrey, 96–107. *JRA* Supplementary Series 31. Ann Arbor, MI: Journal of Roman Archaeology.

Arubas, B., and H. Goldfus, eds. 2005. *Excavations on the Site of the Jerusalem International Convention Center (Binyanei Ha'uma): A Settlement of the Late First to Second Temple Period, the Tenth Legion's Kilnworks, and a Byzantine Monastic Complex*. *JRA* Supplementary Series 60. Portsmouth, RI: Journal of Roman Archaeology.

Arubas, B., and H. Goldfus. 2008a. "Elusa." In *The New Encyclopedia of Archaeological Excavations in the Holy Land, Vol. 5: Jerusalem*, edited by E. Stern, 1713–15. Jerusalem: Israel Exploration Society.

Arubas, B., and H. Goldfus. 2008b. "The Jerusalem International Convention Center." In *The New Encyclopedia of Archaeological Excavations in the Holy Land, Vol. 5: Jerusalem*, edited by E. Stern, 1828–30. Jerusalem: Israel Exploration Society.

Atik, N. 1995. *Die Keramik aus den Südthermen von Perge*. IstMitt-BH 40. Tübingen: Ernst Wasmuth Verlag.

Aubert J.-J. 1994. *Business Managers in Ancient Rome: A Social and Economic Study of Institores 200 B.C.–A.D. 250*. Columbia Studies in the Classical Tradition 21. Leiden: Brill.

Aubert, J.-J., and B. Sirks, eds. 2002. *Speculum Iuris. Roman Law as a Reflection of Social and Economic Life in Antiquity*. Ann Arbor: University of Michigan Press.

Auer, M. 2014. "Pottery in Western Noricum: Questions of Distribution and Group Identity." *RCRF Acta* 43: 765–70.

Auer, M. 2018. "Pottery Regions in Noricum. Evidence for Communities of Practice?" *RCRF Acta* 45: 467–76.

Autret, C., and N. Rauh. 2010. "Roman Amphora Production in Western Rough Cilicia." In *Olive Oil and Wine Production in Anatolia During Antiquity. International Symposium Proceedings (06–08 November 2008, Mersin, Turkey)*, edited by B. Fischer-Genz, Y. Gerber, and H. Hamel, 109–22. Istanbul: Research Center of Cilician Archaeology.

Autret, C., R. Yağcı, and N. Rauh. 2010. "An LRA 1 Amphora Kiln Site at Soli/ Pompeiopolis." *ANMED Anadolu Akdenizi Arkeoloji Haberleri / ANMED News of Archaeology from Anatolia's Mediterranean Areas* 8: 203–7.

Aviam, M. 2014. "'Kefar Hananya Ware' Made in Yodefat. Pottery Production at Yodefat in the First Century AD." In *Roman Pottery in the Near East: Local Production and Regional Trade. Proceedings of the Round Table Held in Berlin, 19–20 February 2010*, edited by B. Fischer-Genz, Y. Gerber, and H. Hamel, 139–46. Roman and Late Antique Mediterranean Pottery 3. Oxford: Archaeopress.

Avshalom-Gorni, D., and A. Shapiro. 2015. "A Pottery Workshop at Aḥihud and Its Relationship to the Jar Industry in the Northeastern Zevulun Valley and Western Galilee During the Roman Period." *'Atiqot* 83: 67–92.

Ayalon, E., and Y. Levy. 2011. "Ḥorbat Gelilot (el-Jelil): Excavations on the Fringes of a Roman-Byzantine-Period Village in the Sharon Plain." *'Atiqot* 66: 156–57.

Babraj, K., and H. Szymańska. 2010. "Marea or Philoxenite? Polish Excavations in the Mareotic Region 2000–2007." In *Lake Mareotis: Reconstructing the Past. Proceedings of the International Conference on the Archaeology of the Mareotic Region Held at Alexandria University, Egypt, 5th–6th April 2008*, edited by L. Blue and E. Khalil, 75–85. BAR 2113. Oxford: Archaeopress.

Badoud, N. 2015. *Le temps de Rhodes: Une chronologie des inscriptions de la cité fondée sur l'étude de ses institutions*. Vestigia 63. Munich: Beck.

Bailey, D. M. 1988. *A Catalogue of the Lamps in the British Museum II: Roman Lamps Made in Italy*. London: British Museum Publications.

Bailey, D. M. 1997. "Roman Pottery Lamps." In *Pottery in the Making: Ceramic Traditions*, edited by I. Freestone and D. Gaimster, 164–69. Washington, DC: Smithsonian Institution Press.

Baird, J. A. 2007. "Shopping, Eating and Drinking at Dura-Europos: Reconstructing Contexts." In *Objects in Context, Objects in Use: Material Spatiality in Late Antiquity*, edited by L. Lavan, E. Swift, and T. Putzeys, 413–37. Leiden: Brill.

Baldini Lippolis, I. 2005. "Private Space in Late Antique Cities: Laws and Building Procedures." In *Housing in Late Antiquity*, edited by L. Lavan, L. Özgenel, and A. Sarantis, 197–237. Late Antique Archaeology 3. Leiden: Brill.

Ballet, P. 2007. "The Graeco-Roman Pottery Workshops of Buto." *Egyptian Archaeology* 24: 18–19.

Ballet, P. 2011. "Les ateliers hellénistiques de Bouto (Tell el-Fara'in) et le 'décor surpeint' (Overpainted)." In *Under the Potter's Tree: Studies on Ancient Egypt Presented to Janine Bourriau on the Occasion of Her 70th Birthday*, edited by D. Aston, B. Bader, C. Gallorni, P. Nicholson, and S. Buckingham, 189–200. Orientalia Lovaniensa Analecta 204. Leuven: Peeters.

Ballet, P., F. Béguin, T. Herbich, G. Lecuyot, and A. Schmitt. 2007. "Recherches sur les ateliers hellénistiques et romains de Bouto (Delta)." In *Actes du Neuvième Congrès international des égyptologues, Grenoble, 6–12 Septembre 2004*, edited by J.-C. Goyon and C. Cardin, 133–43. Orientalia Lovaniensia Analecta 150. Leuven: Peeters.

Ballet, P., F. Béguin, G. Lecuyot, and A. Schmitt. 2006. "De nouvelles technologies céramiques à Bouto?" In *L'apport de l'Égypte à l'histoire des techniques: Méthodes, chronologie et comparaisons*, edited by B. Mathieu, D. Meeks, and M. Wissa, 15–30. Cairo: Institut Français d'Archéologie Orientale.

Ballet, P., F. Béguin, G. Lecuyot, and A. Schmitt. 2019. *Tell el-Fara'în-Buto VI:*

Recherches sur les ateliers romains de Bouto. Prospections et sondages (2001–2006). Archäologischen Veröffentlichungen 110. Wiesbaden: Harrassowitz.

Ballet, P., and F. Mahmoud. 1987. "Moules en terre cuite d'Eléphantine (Musée Copte): Nouvelles données sur les ateliers de la région d'Assouan, à l'époque byzantine et aux premiers temps de l'occupation arabe." *Bulletin de l'Institut Français d'Archéologie Orientale* 87: 53–72.

Ballet, P., F. Mahmoud, M. Vichy, and M. Picon. 1991. "Artisanat de la céramique dans l'Égypte romaine tardive et byzantine. Prospections d'ateliers de potiers de Minia à Assouan." *Cahiers de la céramique egyptienne* 2: 129–43.

Ballet, P., and G. Marouard. 2012. "Workshops and Urban Settlement in Buto." *Egyptian Archaeology* 40: 14–17.

Ballet, P., and A. Schmitt. 2019. "Première partie. Les prospections pédestres et géophysiques." In *Tell el-Fara'în-Buto VI: Recherches sur les ateliers romains de Bouto. Prospections et sondages (2001–2006)*, edited by P. Ballet, F. Béguin, G. Lecuyot, and A. Schmitt, 53–183. Archäologischen Veröffentlichungen 110. Wiesbaden: Harrassowitz.

Ballet, P., and M. Vichy. 1992. "Artisanat de la céramique dans l'Égypte hellénistique et romaine. Ateliers du Delta, d'Assouan et de Kharga." In *Ateliers de potiers et productions céramiques en Égypte. Actes de la table ronde (Le Caire, 26–29 novembre 1990) organisée par l'institut français d'archéologie orientale*, edited by P. Ballet, 109–19. Cahiers de la céramique egyptienne 3. Cairo: Institut français d'archéologie orientale.

Ballet, P., and T. von der Way. 1993. "Exploration archéologique de Bouto et de sa région (époques Romaine et Byzantine)." *Mitteilungen des Deutschen Archaologischen Instituts Abteilung Kairo* 99: 1–22.

Bangert, S. 2010. "The Archaeology of Pilgrimage: Abu Mina and Beyond." *Religious Diversity in Late Antiquity*, edited by D. Gwynn and S. Bangert, 291–327. Late Antique Archaeology 6. Leiden: Brill.

Barry, W. D. 1993. "Aristocrats, Orators, and the 'Mob': Dio Chrysostom and the World of the Alexandrians." *Historia: Zeitschrift fur alte Geschichte* 42(10): 82–103.

Bartosiewicz, L. 2003. "'There's Something Rotten in the State...': Bad Smells in Antiquity." *European Journal of Archaeology* 6(2): 175–95.

Baumgarten, Y. 1997. "Giv'ati Junction." *Excavations and Surveys in Israel* 19: 79–80.

Be'eri, R., and D. Levi. 2011. "Roman Period Workshops at the Crowne Plaza Hotel in Western Jerusalem." *Qadmoniot* 141: 35–39.

Be'eri, R., and D. Levi. 2012. "Excavations at the Jerusalem Crowne Plaza Hotel: Binyanē Ha-Umma." In *New Studies on Jerusalem* 18, edited by E. Baruch, Y. Levin, and A. Levy-Reifer, 203–10. Ramat Gan: Bar Ilan University.

Béguin, F., A. Schmitt, and P. Ballet. 2019. "Deuxième partie. Les sondages des secteurs P1, P1K, P2, P3 et P4." In *Tell el-Fara'în-Buto VI: Recherches sur les ateliers romains de Bouto. Prospections et sondages (2001–2006)*, edited by P. Ballet, F. Béguin, G. Lecuyot, and A. Schmitt, 53–183. Archäologischen Veröffentlichungen 110. Wiesbaden: Harrassowitz.

Bender Jøgensen, L. 2012. "Writing Craftsmanship? Vocabularies and Notation Systems in the Transmission of Craft Knowledge." In *Archaeology and Apprenticeship: Body Knowledge, Identity, and Communities of Practice*, edited by W. Wendrich, 240–54. Tucson: University of Arizona Press.

Benton, J. T. 2020. *The Bread Makers: The Social and Professional Lives of Bakers in the Western Roman Empire*. London: Palgrave MacMillan.

Bentz Høgseth, H. 2012. "Knowledge Transfer: The Craftmen's Abstraction." In *Archaeology and Apprenticeship: Body Knowledge, Identity, and Communities of Practice*, edited by W. Wendrich, 61–78. Tucson: University of Arizona Press.

Bergamasco, M. 1995. "Le Didaskalika nella ricerca attuale." *Aegyptus* 75: 95–167.

Bergamini, M., ed. 2007. *Scoppieto I: Il territorio e i materiali (lucerne, opus doliare, metalli)*. Borgo San Lorenzo: All'Insegna del Giglio.

Bergamini, M., ed. 2011. *Scoppieto II: I materiali*. Borgo San Lorenzo: All'Insegna del Giglio.

Berger, A. 1948. "A Labor Contract of A.D. 164: CIL, III, P.948, No. X." *Classical Philology* 43(4): 231–42.

Berlin, A. M. 2005. "Pottery and Pottery Production in the Second Temple Period." In *Excavations on the Site of the Jerusalem International Convention Center (Binyanei Ha'uma): A Settlement of the Late Late First to Second Temple Period, the Tenth Legion's Kilnworks, and a Byzantine Monastic Complex*, edited by B. Arubas and H. Goldfus, 28–60. *JRA* Supplementary Series 60. Portsmouth, RI: Journal of Roman Archaeology.

Bes, P. 2015. *Once upon a Time in the East: The Chronological and Geographical Distribution of Terra Sigillata and Red Slip Ware in the Roman East.* Roman and Late Antique Mediterranean Pottery Series. Oxford: Archaeopress.

Bevan, A. 2014. "Mediterranean Containerization." *Current Anthropology* 55(4): 387–418.

Bhabha, H. 2004. *The Location of Culture.* London: Routledge.

Billot, M.-F., J.-F. Billot, and D. Kassab Tezgör. 2010. "Les fours: Leur structure et le mode de construction." In *Les fouilles et le matériel de l'atelier amphorique de Demirci près de Sinope*, edited by D. Kassab Tezgör, 105–17. Varia Anatolica 22. Istanbul: Institut Français d'Études Anatoliennes.

Biswas, A. A. A., M. Kumar Saha, I. Hasan, M. Faisal, and J. Prokash. 2018. "Occupational Musculoskeletal and Respiratory Illness among Brick Kiln Industry Workers in Bangladesh." *Caspian Journal of Health Research* 3(3): 80–85.

Blakely, S. 2006. *Myth, Ritual and Metallurgy in Ancient Greece and Recent Africa.* Cambridge: Cambridge University Press.

Blitz, J. H. 2015. "Skeuomorphs, Pottery, and Technological Change." *American Anthropologist* 117(4): 665–78.

Blue, L., ed. 2010. *Lake Mareotis: Reconstructing the Past. Proceedings of the International Conference on the Archaeology of the Mareotic Region Held at Alexandria University, Egypt, 5th–6th April 2008.* Oxford: Archaeopress.

Boak, A. E. R. 1937. "The Organization of Gilds in Greco-Roman Egypt." *Transactions and Proceedings of the American Philological Association* 68: 212–20.

Bodel, J. 2000. "Dealing with the Dead: Undertakers, Executioners, and Potter's Fields in Ancient Rome." In *Disease and Death in the Ancient City*, edited by V. M. Hope and E. Marshal, 128–79. London: Routledge.

Bodel, J. 2011. "Slave Labour and Roman Society." In *The Cambridge World History of Slavery. Volume 1: The Ancient Mediterranean World*, edited by K. R. Bradley and P. Cartledge, 311–36. Cambridge: Cambridge University Press.

Bond, S. 2016. *Trade and Taboo: Disreputable Professions in the Roman Mediterranean.* Ann Arbor: University of Michigan Press.

Bonifay, M. 2004. *Etudes sur la céramique romaine tardive d'Afrique.* BAR-IS 1301. Oxford: Archaeopress.

Borchardt-Ott, A. V. 2001. "Die Anthropologische Untersuchung der Skelettreste aus Ofen 10." In *Die römischen Töpfereien von Haltern*, edited by B. Rudnick, 187–248. Mainz am Rhein: von Zabern.

Borgers, B., S. Willems, C. Dupuis, and R. Clotuche. 2021. "Technological Knowledge and Transfer of Roman Pottery Production in Civitas Nerviorum (Northern France, Central Belgium) during the 1st–3rd Centuries CE." *Journal of Archaeological Science: Reports* 38: 103061.

Borgia, E., and V. Iacomi. 2010. "Note preliminari su un complesso industriale per la produzione di anfore Late Roman I a Elaiussa Sebaste (Cilicia)." In *I luoghi e le forme dei mestieri e della produzione nelle province africane. Atti del XVIII Convegno di studio, Olbia, 11–14 Dicembre 2008*, edited by M. Milanese, P. Ruggeri, and C. Vismara, 1029–52. L'Africa Romana 18. Rome: Carocci.

Börker, C. 1978. "Der rhodische Kalender." *Zeitschrift für Papyrologie und Epigraphik* 31: 193–218.

Boschma, R. A. 2005. "Proximity and Innovation: A Critical Assessment." *Regional Studies* 39(1): 61–74.

Bounegru, O. 2003. "La Production des ateliers de ceramique de Pergame (vallee de Kestel):

Un aperçu general." In *Les ceramiques en Antatolie aux epoques hellenistique et romaine. Actes de la table ronde d'Istanbul, 22–24 mai 1996*, edited by C. Abadie-Reynal, 137–40, pl. LXXXVI–LXXXIX. Varia Anatolica 15. Paris: De Boccard.

Bounegru, O. 2009. "Die keramischen Werkstätte von Pergamon. Die Planimetrie." *PEUCE Serie Nouă* 7: 73–96.

Bounegru, O. 2014. "La production des ateliers de ceramique de Pergame (vallée de Kestel): Un Aperçu général." In *Late Hellenistic to Mediaeval Fine Wares of the Aegean Coast of Anatolia: Their Production, Imitation and Use*, edited by H. Meyza and K. Domżalski, 23–29. Warsaw: Neriton.

Bounegru, O., and S. Erdemgil. 1998. "Terra-Sigillata-Produktion in den Werkstätte von Pergamon-Ketiostal: Vorläufiger Bericht." *IstMitt* 48: 263–77.

Bourdieu, P. 1977. *Outline of a Theory of Practice*. Cambridge: Cambridge University Press.

Bowman, A. K. 1983. *The Oxyrhynchus Papyri. Volume L [Nos 3522–3600]*. London: Egypt Exploration Society.

Bradley, K. 1985. "Child Labour in the Roman World." *Historical Reflections* 12(2): 311–30.

Braekmans, D. 2011. The Archaic, Classical and Hellenistic Ceramics in the Later Territory of Sagalassos and Düzen Tepe: The Petrographic and Geochemical Evidence. Unpublished PhD thesis, University of Leuven.

Braekmans, D., P. Degryse, J. Poblome, B. Neyt, K. Vyncke, and M. Waelkens. 2011. "Understanding Ceramic Variability: An Archaeometrical Interpretation of the Classical and Hellenistic Ceramics at Düzen Tepe and Sagalassos (Southwest Turkey)." *Journal of Archaeological Science* 38: 2101–15.

Brand, Y. 1953. *Klei Haheres Besifrut Hatalmud (Ceramics in Talmudic Literature)*. Jerusalem: Mossad Harav Kook.

Brimblecombe, P. 1987. "The Antiquity of 'Smokeless Zones.'" *Atmospheric Environment* 21(11): 2485.

Brughmans, T., and J. Poblome. 2016. "Roman Bazaar or Market Economy? Explaining Tableware Distributions through Computational Modelling." *Antiquity* 350: 393–408.

Bucking, S., and H. Goldfus. 2012. "O. Elusa 2: Another Enigmatic Ostracon from the Pottery Workshop at Elusa in Byzantine Palestine." *Palestine Exploration Quarterly* 144(1): 47–66.

Cacho, S. F. 1995. "Las industrias derivadas de la pesca en la provincia romana de al Bética la alfarería de 'El Rinconcillo' (Algeciras, Cádiz)." *SPAL: Revista de preistorica y arqueologia* 4: 173–214.

Can, B., M. Hoff, R. Townsend, E. Erdoğmuš, and T. Howe. 2015. "Antiochia ad Cragum Arkeolojik Araştırma Projesi: 2014 Sezonu / The Antiochia ad Cragum Archaeological Research Project: 2014 Season." *ANMED Anadolu Akdenizi Arkeoloji Haberleri / ANMED News of Archaeology from Anatolia's Mediterranean Areas* 13: 8–14.

Carrié, J.-M. 2002. "Les associations professionnelles à l'époque tardive: Entre 'munus' et convivialité." In *Humana sapit: Études d'antiquités tardive offertes à Lellia Cracco Ruggini*, edited by J.-M. Carrié and R. Lizzi Testa, 309–32. Bibliothèque de l'Antiquité Tardive 3. Turnhout: Brepols.

Cau, M. A., P. Reynolds, and M. Bonifay, eds. 2011. *Late Roman Fine Wares: Solving Problems of Typology and Chronology*. Oxford: Archaeopress.

Charlesworth, D. 1967. "The Industrial Area (Jj 33/34, Kk 34)." In "The Tell el-Farâ'în Expedition, 1967" by M. V. Seton-Williams. *The Journal of Egyptian Archaeology* 53: 146–55.

Charlesworth, D. 1969. "Tell-Farâ'în: The Industrial Site." *The Journal of Egyptian Archaeology* 55: 23–30.

Charlesworth, D. 1972. "Tell-Fara'in Egypt: An Industrial Site in the Nile Delta." *Archaeology* 25(1): 44–47.

Civelek, A., and Ş. Atıcı. 2014. "2013 Yılı Tralleis kazıları: Sigillata alanı akıntı toprak kazı çalışmaları." *Kazı Sonuçları Toplantısı* 36(1): 429–31.

Claeys, J., and J. Poblome. 2019. "Meanwhile in Suburbia." In *Meanwhile in the Mountains: Sagalassos*, edited by P. Talloen, E. Torun, and M. Waelkens, 110–20. Istanbul: Yapı Kredi Yayınları.

Cline, R. H. 2019. "Amulets and the Ritual Efficacy of Christian Symbols." In *Oxford Handbook of Early Christian Archaeology*, edited by W. R. Caraher, T. W. Davis, and D. K. Pettegrew, 1–18. Oxford: Oxford University Press.

Cockle, H. 1981. "Pottery Manufacture in Roman Egypt: A New Papyrus." *Journal of Roman Studies* 71: 87–97.

Cohen-Weinberger, A., D. Levi, and R. Be'eri. 2020. "On the Raw Materials in the Ceramic Workshops of Jerusalem, before and after 70 C.E." *Bulletin of the American Schools of Oriental Research* 383: 33–59.

Cohn, Y. B. 2011. "The Graeco-Roman Trade Fair and the Rabbis." *Journal of the American Oriental Society* 131(2): 187–93.

Cool, H. E. M. 2006. *Eating and Drinking in Roman Britain*. Cambridge: Cambridge University Press.

Coşkun, G. 2024, "Aizanoi 2022." *Kazı Sonuçları Toplantısı* 43(5): 185–206.

Costello, J. G. 1997. "Brick and Tile Making in Spanish California with Related Old and New World Examples." In *The Prehistory and History of Ceramic Kilns*, edited by P. M. Rice, 195–217. Ceramics and Civilization 7. Westerville, OH: American Ceramics Society.

Costin, C. 1991. "Specialization: Issues in Defining, Documenting, and Explaining the Organization of Production." *Journal of Archaeological Method and Theory* 3: 1–56.

Coulon, G. 1994. *L'enfant en Gaule romaine*. Paris: Errance.

Coulson, W. D. E., and N. C. Wilkie. 1986. "Ptolemaic and Roman Kilns in the Western Nile Delta." *Bulletin of the American Schools of Oriental Research* 263: 61–75.

Crane, H. 1988. "Traditional Pottery Making in the Sardis Region of Western Turkey." *Muqarnas* 5: 9–20.

Crown, P. L. 2007. "Life Histories of Pots and Potters: Situating the Individual in Archaeology." *American Antiquity* 72(4): 677–90.

Csitneki, D. 2017. "Jerash Bowls: Fine Tableware from Jerash." In *Gerasa / Jerash From the Urban Periphery*, edited by A. Lichtenberger and R. Raja, 99–105. Aarhus: AUTRYK, Aarhus University.

Cuomo di Caprio, N. 1971–1972. "Proposta di classificazione delle fornaci per ceramica e laterizi nell'area italiana: Dalla preistoria a tutta l'epoca romana." *Sibrium* 11: 371–461.

Cuomo di Caprio, N. 1982. "Rassegna di fornaci per ceramica e laterizi." *Rivista di archeologia* 6: 88–100.

Cuomo di Caprio, N. 1992. *Fornaci e officine da vasaio tardo-ellenistiche*. Princeton: Princeton University Press.

Cuomo di Caprio, N. 2007. *Ceramica in archeologia: Antiche tecniche di lavorazione e moderni metodi di indagine*. Rome: L'Erma di Bretschneider.

Curtis, F. 1962. "The Utility Pottery of Bailén, Southern Spain." *American Anthropologist* 64(3): 486–503.

da Costa, K. 2010. "Economic Cycles in the Byzantine Levant: The Evidence from Lamps at Pella in Jordan." *Levant* 42(1): 70–87.

Daems, D., and J. Poblome. 2017. "The Pottery of Late Achaemenid Sagalassos: An Overview." *Journal of Hellenistic and Roman Material Culture* 6(1): 49–62.

Dauterman Maguire, E., H. P. Maguire, and M. J. Duncan-Flowers. 1989. *Art and Holy Powers in the Early Christian House*. Illinois Byzantine Studies 2. Urbana: University of Illinois Press.

Dardenay, A., and N. Laubry, eds. 2020. *Anthropology of Roman Housing*. Turnhout: Brepols.

D'Arms, J. H. 1980. "Senators' Involvement in Commerce in the Late Republic: Some Ciceronian Evidence." In *The Seaborne Commerce of Ancient Rome*, edited by J. H. D'Arms and E. C. Kopff, 77–89. *MAAR* 36. Ann Arbor: University of Michigan Press.

Darvill, T., and A. McWhirr. 1984. "Brick and Tile Production in Roman Britain: Models of Economic Organisation." *World Archaeology* 15(3): 239–61.

David, N. 1972. "On the Life Span of Pottery, Type Frequencies, and Archaeological Inference." *American Antiquity* 37(1): 141–42.

Davies, P. J. E. 2012. *Rome, Pollution and Propriety: Dirt, Disease and Hygiene in the Eternal City from Antiquity to Modernity*. Cambridge: Cambridge University Press.

de Certeau, M. 1984. *The Practice of Everyday Life*. Translated by S. Rendall. Berkeley: University of California Press.

Degryse, P., and J. Poblome. 2008. "Clays for Mass Production of Table and Common Wares, Amphorae and Architectural Ceramics at Sagalassos." In *Sagalassos VI: Geo- and Bio-archaeology at Sagalassos and in Its Territory*, edited by P. Degryse and M. Waelkens, 231–54. Leuven: Leuven University Press.

Delcroix, G., and J.-L. Huot. 1972. "Les fours dits "de potiers" dans l'Orient ancien." *Syria* 49: 35–95.

de Ligt, L. 1993. *Fairs and Markets in the Roman Empire: Economic and Social Aspects of Periodic Trade in a Pre-industrial Society*. Amsterdam: Gieben.

de Ligt, L., and P. W. de Neeve. 1988. "Ancient Periodic Markets: Festivals and Fairs," *Athenaeum* 66: 391–416.

Demierre, B. 2002. "Les fours à chaux en Grèce." *Journal of Roman Archaeology* 15: 282–96.

Desbat, A. 2001. *L'Atelier de potiers antique de la Rue du Chapeau Rouge à Vaise (Lyon 9e)*. Lyon: Ville de Lyon, Service archéologique municipal.

de Vreis, B., and P. Bikai. 1993. "Archaeology in Jordan." *American Journal of Archaeology* 97(3): 457–520.

Dietler, M. 2015. *Archaeologies of Colonialism: Consumption, Entanglement, and Violence in Ancient Mediterranean France*. Berkeley: University of California Press.

Dietler, M., and I. Herbich. 1989. "Tich Matek: The Technology of Luo Pottery Production." *World Archaeology* 21(1): 148–64.

Dio Chrysostom. 1946. *Discourses 37–60*. Translated by H. L. Crosby. Loeb Classical Library 376. Cambridge, MA: Harvard University Press.

Diosono, F. 2007. *Collegia: Le associazioni professionali nel mondo romano*. Rome: Quasar.

Dixneuf, D. 2011. *Amphores égyptiennes: Production, typologie, contenu et diffusion (IIIe siècle avant J.-C. -IXe siècle après J.-C.)*. Études Alexandrines 22. Alexandria: Centre d'études Alexandrines.

Dobosi, L. 2016. "Animal and Human Footprints on Roman Tiles from Brigetio." *Dissertationes archaeologicae ex instituto archaeologico, universitatis de Rolando Eötvös nominatae* 3 (4): 117–33.

Dodd, E. K. 2020. *Roman and Late Antique Wine Production in the Eastern Mediterranean: A Comparative Archaeological Study at Antiochia ad Cragum (Turkey) and Delos (Greece)*. Oxford: Archaeopress.

Doherty, S. K. 2015. *The Origins and Use of the Potter's Wheel in Ancient Egypt*. Oxford: Archaeopress.

Domżalski, K. 2014. "The Pitane Workshop and the Most Successful Export of Eastern Sigillata C." In *Late Hellenistic to Mediaeval Fine Wares of the Aegean Coast of Anatolia: Their Production, Imitation and Use*, edited by H. Meyza and K. Domżalski, 151–59. Travaux de l'Institut des cultures méditerranéennes et orientales de l'Académie Polonaise des Sciences. Warsaw: Éditions Neriton.

Drogou, S., ed. 2020. *Pottery Workshops: Craftsmen and Workshops*. Athens: Hellenic Ministry of Culture and Sports.

Dufaÿ, B., Y. Barat, and S. Raux. 1997. *Fabriquer de la vaisselle à l'époque romaine. archéologie d'un centre de production céramique en Gaule: La Boissière-École (Yvelines – France) (Ier et IIIe siècles après J.-C.)*. Versailles: Service archéologique départmental des Yvelines.

Dündar, E. 2015. "The Ceramics from Patara: Investigations, Production and Trade. Past Studies – Future Projections." In *Patara VII.1: From Sand into a City, 25 Years of Patara Excavations / Kum'dan Kent'e Patara Kazılarının 25 Yılı*, edited by H. İşkans and F. Işik, 199–227. Istanbul: Ege Yayınları.

Du Plessis, P. 2006. "Theory and Practice: New Perspectives on the Roman Law of Letting and Hiring." *The Cambridge Law Journal* 65(2): 423–37.

Dzierzykray-Rogalski, T., and C. Grzeszyk. 1991. "Les dermatoglyphes: Empreintes des lignes papillaires relevés sur les lampes de Kôm el-Dikka (Alexandrie)." *Cahiers de la céramique egyptienne* 2: 14–21.

Edmunds, L. 2009. "Horace's Priapus: A Life on the Esquiline (Sat. 1.8)." *The Classical Quarterly, New Series* 59(1): 125–31.

El-Ashmawi, F. 1998. "Pottery Kiln and Wine-Factory at Burg el-Arab." In *Commerce et artisanat dans l'Alexandrie hellénistique et romaine. Actes du colloque d'Athènes*, edited by J.-Y. Empereur, 55–64. Paris: de Boccard.

Ellis, S. J. R. 2018. *The Roman Retail Revolution: The Socio-economic World of the Taberna.* Oxford: Oxford University Press.

Emery-Barbier, A. 2010. "Actuelle et passee de la region de Sinope. Apports des analyses palynologiques et anthrocologiques du site de Demirci à la reconstitution de la couverture végétale au ier millénaire AD." In *Les fouilles et le materiel de l'atelier amphorique de Demirci pres de Sinope*, edited by D. Kassab Tezgör, 27–40. Varia Antolica 22. Istanbul and Paris: Institut français d'études anatoliennes.

Empereur, J.-Y. 1986. "Un atelier de Dressel 2-4 en Égypte au IIIe siècle de notre ère." In *Recherches sur les amphores grecques*, edited by J.-Y. Empereur and Y. Garlan, 599–608. *BCH* Suppl. 13. Paris: de Boccard.

Empereur, J.-Y., C. Kritzas, and A. Marangou. 1991. "Recherches sur les amphores crétoises II: Les centres de fabrication d'amphores en Crète centrale." *Bulletin de Correspondance Hellénique* 115(1): 481–523.

Empereur, J.-Y., S. Markoulaki, and A. Marangou. 1989. "Recherches sur les centres de fabrication d'amphores de Crète occidentale." *Bulletin de Correspondance Hellénique* 2: 551–80.

Empereur, J.-Y., and M. Picon. 1986a. "A propos d'un nouvel atelier de Late Roman C." *Figlina* 7: 143–46.

Empereur, J.-Y., and M. Picon. 1986b. "A la recherche des fours d'amphores." In *Recherches sur les amphores grecques*, edited by J.-Y. Empereur and Y. Garlan, 103–26. *BCH* Suppl. 13. Paris: de Boccard.

Empereur, J.-Y., and M. Picon. 1992. "La reconnaissance des productions des ateliers céramiques: L'exemple de la Maréotide." In *Ateliers de potiers et productions céramiques en Égypte. Actes de la table ronde (Le Caire, 26–29 novembre 1990) organisée par l' institut français d'archéologie orientale*, edited by P. Ballet, 145–49. Cairo: Institut français d'archéologie orientale.

Empereur, J.-Y., and M. Picon. 1998. "Les ateliers d'amphores du Lac Mariout." In *Commerce et artisanat dans l'Alexandrie hellénistique et romaine: Actes du colloque d'Athènes*, edited by J.-Y. Empereur, 75–91. Paris: de Boccard.

Erdkamp, P. M. 2001. "Beyond the Limits of the 'Consumer City'. A Model of the Urban and Rural Economy in the Roman World." *Historia: Zeitschrift für Alte Geschichte* 50(3): 332–356.

Erdkamp, P. 2016. "Seasonal Labour and Rural-Urban Migration in Roman Italy." In *Migration and Mobility in the Early Roman Empire*, edited by L. de Ligt and L. E. Tacoma, 33–49. Studies in Global Social History 23, Studies in Global Migration History 7. Leiden: Brill.

Erkoç, S. 2019. "The Harbor Bath." In *Patara: City, Harbor, Cult*, edited by H. İşkan, 214–33. Istanbul: Türkiye İş Bankası Kültür Yayınları.

Erlich, A. 2017. "A Roman Pottery Kiln at Khirbet 'Azzun (Ra'anana), Israel." *Levant* 49(2): 192–204.

Esposito, A., and G. M. Sanidas, eds. 2012. *"Quartiers" artisanaux en Grèce ancienne. Une perspective méditerranéenne.* Villeneuve d'Ascq: Presses universitaires du Septentrion.

Ettlinger, E. 1951. "Legionary Pottery from Vindonissa." *Journal of Roman Studies* 41: 105–11.

Falkner, R. K. 1986. "A Note on the Two Kilns from the British Excavations at the North Theatre." In *Jerash Archaeological Project 1981–1983 I*, edited by F. Zayadine, 450–59. Amman: Department of Antiquities of Jordan.

Faraone, C. A. 2001. "A Collection of Curses against Kilns (Homeric *Epigram* 13.7–23)." In *Antiquity and Humanity: Essays on Ancient Religion and Philosophy Presented to Hans Dieter*

Betz on His 70th Birthday, edited by A. Y. Collins and M. M. Mitchell, 435–49. Tübingen: Mohr Siebeck.

Feissel, D. 1985. "Deux listes de quartiers d'Antioche astreints au creusement d'un canal (73–74 après J.-C.)." *Syria* 62(1–2): 77–103.

Feldman, M. P. 2003. "Location and Innovation: The New Economic Geography of Innovation, Spillovers, and Agglomeration." In *The Oxford Handbook of Economic Geography*, edited by G. L. Clark, M. S. Gertler, and M. P. Feldman, 373–84. Oxford: Oxford University Press.

Felton, J. S. 1963. *Man, Medicine, and Work: Historic Events in Occupational Medicine*. Washington, DC: US Department of Health, Education, and Welfare.

Ferguson, J. R. 2008. "The When, Where, and How of Novices in Craft Production." *Journal of Archaeological Method and Theory* 15: 51–67.

Ferrazzoli, A. F., and M. Ricci. 2007. "Elaiussa Sebaste: Produzioni e consumi di una città della Cilicia tra V e VII secolo." In *LCRW 2, Late Roman Coarse Wares, Cooking Wares and Amphorae in the Mediterranean. Archaeology and Archaeometry*, edited by M. Bonifay and J. C. Treglia, 671–88. BAR-IS 1662. Oxford: Archaeopress.

Ferrazzoli, A. F., and M. Ricci. 2010. "Un centro di produzione delle anfore LR 1: Elaiussa Sebaste in Cilicia. Gli impiante, le anfore." In *LCRW 3, Late Roman Coarse Wares, Cooking Wares and Amphorae in the Mediterranean. Archaeology and Archaeometry*, edited by S. Menchelli, S. Santoro, M. Pasquinucci, and G. Guiducci, 815–26. BAR-IS 2185. Oxford: Archaeopress.

Fischer, A. 2007. "The Lives of Glass-Workers at Sepphoris." In *The Archaeology of Difference: Gender, Ethnicity, Class and the "Other" in Antiquity. Studies in Honor of Eric M. Meyers*, edited by D. R. Edwards and C. T. McCollough, 301–10. Annual of the American Schools of Oriental Research 60/61. Boston: American Schools of Oriental Research.

Fisher, C. S. 1938. *Gerasa City of the Decapolis: Description of the Site, the Temple of Artemis, Temple C, the "Forum" Buildings of the Christian Period, the Southwest Cemetery*. New Haven, CT: American Schools of Oriental Research.

Forbes, H. A. 1996. "The Uses of the Uncultivated Landscape in Modern Greece: A Pointer to the Value of the Wilderness in Antiquity?" In *Human Landscapes in Classical Antiquity: Environment and Culture*, edited by G. Shipley and J. Salmon, 68–97. London: Routledge.

Foxhall, L. 1998. "Snapping up the Unconsidered Trifles: the Use of Agricultural Residues in Ancient Greek and Roman Farming." *Environmental Archaeology* 1(1): 35–40.

Frankfurter, D. 2017. *Christianizing Egypt: Syncretism and Local Worlds in Late Antiquity*. Princeton: Princeton University Press.

Freu, C. 2015. "Labour Status and Economic Stratification: The Hierarchy of Wages in Egypt." *Journal of Roman Archaeology* 28: 161–77.

Freu, C. 2016. "Disciplina, Patrocinium, Nomen: The Benefits of Apprenticeship in the Roman World." In *Urban Craftsmen and Traders in the Roman World*, edited by M. Flohr and A. Wilson, 183–99. Roman Economy Project 2. Oxford: Oxford University Press.

Freu, C. 2018. "Writing Labor History Today: A Critical Note on the Case of the Roman Empire." *Annales. Histoire, Sciences Sociales* 73 (1): 157–78.

Frieman, C. J. 2013. "Innovation and Identity: The Language and Reality of Prehistoric Imitation and Technological Change." In *The Archaeology of Hybrid Material Culture*, edited by J. J. Card, 318–26. Center for Archaeological Investigations, Occasional Paper No. 39. Carbondale: Southern Illinois University Press.

Gadot, Y., and Y. Tepper. 2003. "A Late Byzantine Pottery Workshop at Khirbet Baraqa." *Tel Aviv* 30(1): 130–62.

Gager, J. 1992. "Businesses, Shops, and Taverns." In *Curse Tablets and Binding Spells from the Ancient World*, edited by J. Gager, 151–74. New York: Oxford University Press.

Gallimore, S. 2010. "Amphora Production in the Roman World: A View from the Papyri." *Bulletin of the American Society of Papyrologists* 47: 155–84.

Gandon, E., T. Nonaka, J. A. Endler, T. Coyle, and R. J. Bootsma. 2020a. "Traditional Craftspeople Are Not Copycats: Potter Idiosyncrasies in Vessel Morphogenesis." *PLoS ONE* 15(9): e0239362.

Gandon, E., T. Nonaka, R. Sonabend, and J. Endler. 2020b. "Assessing the Influence of Culture on Craft Skills: A Quantitative Study with Expert Nepalese Potters." *PLoS ONE* 15(10): e0239139.

Gandon, E., and V. Roux. 2019. "Cost of Motor Skill Adaptation to New Craft Traits: Experiments with Expert Potters Facing Unfamiliar Vessel Shapes and Wheels." *Journal of Anthropological Archaeology* 53: 229–39.

Gauß, W., G. Klebinder-Gauß, and C. von Rüden, eds. 2015. *The Transmission of Technical Knowledge in the Production of Ancient Mediterranean Pottery: Proceedings of the International Conference at the Austrian Archaeological Institute at Athens, 23rd–25th November 2012.* Vienna: Österreichisches Archäologisches Institut.

Gawlikowski, M., and A. Musa. 1986. "The Church of Bishop Marianos." In *Jerash Archaeological Project 1981–1983*, edited by F. Zayadine, 137–62. Amman: Department of Antiquities.

Genin, M. 2002. *Céramiques de La Graufesenque et autres productions d'époque romaine: Nouvelles recherches. Hommages à Bettina Hoffmann.* Montagnac: M. Mergoil.

Genin, M. 2007. *La Graufesenque, Millau, Aveyron: Volume 2.* Pessac: Éditions de la fédération aquitania.

George, M. 2006. "Social Identity and Dignity of Work in Freedmen's Reliefs." In *The Art of Citizens, Soldiers and Freedmen in the Roman World*, edited by E. D'Ambra and G. P. R. Métraux, 19–29. BAR-IS 1526. Oxford: Archaeopress.

Gerber, Y. 2001. "A Glimpse of the Recent Excavations on ez-Zantur/Petra: The Late Roman Pottery and its Prototypes in the 2nd and 3rd Centuries AD." In *La céramique byzantine et proto-islamique en Syrie-Jordanie (IVe–VIIe siècles apr. J.-C.). Actes du colloque tenu à Amman les 3, 4 et 5 décembre 1994*, edited by E. Villeneuve and P. M. Watson, 7–12. Bibliothèque Archéologique et Historique 159. Beirut: Institut français d'archéologie du proche Orient.

Gerber, Y. 2005. "Late Roman Coarse Ware from Petra, Jordan: Changes in Typology and Chemical Composition." In *Late Roman Coarse Wares I, Cooking Wares and Amphorae in the Mediterranean Archaeology and Archaeometry*, edited by J. M. Gurt, I. Esparraguera, J. Buxeda i Garrigós, and M. A. Cau Ontiveros, 725–26. BAR-IS 1340. Oxford: Archaeopress.

Gerber, Y. 2010. "Positively Byzantine – Or More of the Same? Chemical Continuity vs. Discontinuity of the 'Byzantine Pottery.'" In *LRCW3 Late Roman Coarse Wares, Cooking Wares and Amphorae in the Mediterranean Archaeology and Archaeometry. Vol. 2: Comparison between the Western and Eastern Mediterranean*, edited by S. Menchelli, S. Santoro, M. Pasquinucci, and G. Guiducci, 891–98. Oxford: Archaeopress.

Gerson, L. 2021. "Roman-Era Shops, Statues of Greek Deities Found in Ancient City in Turkey." *Smithsonian Magazine*, 16 November 2021. www.smithsonianmag.com/smart-news/roman-era-shops-statue-heads-found-in-ancient-city-in-turkey-180979071. Accessed 15 March 2024.

Getzov, N., D. Avshalom-Gorni, Y. Gorin-Rosen, E. J. Stern, D. Syon, and A. Tatcher. 2009. *Horbat Uza: The 1991 Excavations.* Jerusalem: Israel Antiquities Authority.

Ghaly, H. 1992. "Pottery Workshops of Saint-Jeremia (Saqqara)." In *Ateliers de potiers et productions céramiques en Égypte*, edited by P. Ballet, 161–71. Cahiers de la céramique égyptienne 3. Cairo: L'institut français d'archéologie orientale.

Giannopoulou, M. 2010. *Pithoi Technology and History of Storage Vessels through the Ages.* BAR-IS 2140. Oxford: Archaeopress.

Goldmann, H. 1950. *Excavation at Gözlü Kule. Tarsus I: The Hellenistic and Roman Periods.* Princeton: Princeton University Press.

Goodman, P. 2012. *The Roman City and Its Periphery: From Rome to Gaul*. Oxford: Routledge.

Goodman, P. 2013. "The Production Centres: Settlement Hierarchies and Spatial Distribution." In *Seeing Red: New Economic and Social Perspectives on Terra Sigillata*, edited by M. Fulford and E. Durham, 121–36. London: University of London.

Goren, Y. 2005. "Appendix: The Pottery Technology." In *Excavations on the Site of the Jerusalem International Convention Center (Binyanei Ha'uma): A Settlement of the Late Late First to Second Temple Period, the Tenth Legion's Kilnworks, and a Byzantine Monastic Complex*, edited by B. Arubas and H. Goldfus, 192–94. *JRA* Supplementary Series 60. Portsmouth, RI: Journal of Roman Archaeology.

Goren, Y., and P. Fabian. 2008. "The Oboda Potter's Workshop Reconsidered." *Journal of Roman Archaeology* 21(1): 340–51.

Gosselain, O. P. 1992. "Technology and Style: Potters and Pottery among Bafia in Cameroon." *Man* 27(3): 559–86.

Gosselain, O. P. 2008. "Thoughts and Adjustments in the Potter's Backyard." In *Breaking the Mould: Challenging the Past through Pottery*, edited by I. Berg, 67–79. BAR-IS 1861. Oxford: Archaeopress.

Gosselain, O. P. 2010. "Ethnographie compareé des trousses à outils de potiers au sud du Niger." *Bulletin de la Société préhistorique française* 107(4): 667–89.

Gosselain, O. P. 2016. "To Hell with Ethnoarchaeology!" *Archaeological Dialogues* 23(2): 215–28.

Goudineau, Ch. 1968. *Fouilles de l'École française de Rome à Bolsena (Poggio Moscini) IV. La céramique arétine lisse (1962–1967)*. Rome: MEFR.

Grawehr, M. 2006. *Petra, ez Zantur III: Ergebnisse der Schweizerisch-Liechtensteinischen Ausgrabungen. Pt. 2: Die Lampen der Grabungen auf ez Zantur in Petra*. Mainz: Verlag Philipp von Zabern.

Green, D. A. 2014. "Fragrance in the Rabbinic World." In *Smell and the Ancient Senses*, edited by M. Bradley, 146–57. London: Routledge.

Greene, K. 2008. "Learning to Consume: Consumption and Consumerism in the Roman Empire." *Journal of Roman Archaeology* 21: 64–82.

Grimes, W. F. 1930. *Holt, Denbighshire: The Works Depot of the Twentieth Legion at Castle-Lyons. The Magazine of the Honourable Society of Cymmrodorion*. London: Cymmrodor.

Gunneweg, J., and M. Balla. 2010. "Was the Qumran Settlement a Mere Pottery Production Center? What Instrumental Neutron Activation Revealed." In *Holistic Qumran: Trans-disciplinary Research of Qumran and the Dead Sea Scrolls*, edited by J. Gunneweg, A. Adriaens, and J. Dik, 39–61. Leiden: Brill.

Hakim, B. S. 2001. "Julian of Ascalon's Treatise of Construction and Design Rules from Sixth-Century Palestine." *Journal of the Society of Architectural Historians* 60(1): 4–25.

Hampe, R., and A. Winter. 1962. *Bei Töpfern und Töpferinnen in Kreta, Messenien, und Zypern*. Mainz: Römisch-Germanisches Zentralmuseum.

Hampe, R., and A. Winter. 1965. *Bei Töpfern und Zieglern in Süditalien, Sizilien und Griechenland*. Mainz: Römisch-Germanisches Zentralmuseum.

Handberg, S. 2011. "Amphora Fragments Re-used as Potter's Tools in the Rural Landscape of Panskoye." In *Pottery in the Archaeological Record: Greece and Beyond. Acts of the International Colloquium Held at the Danish and Canadian Institutes in Athens, June 20–22, 2008*, edited by M. L. Lawall and J. Lund, 62–66. Aarhus: Aarhus University Press.

Hankey, V. 1968. "Pottery-Making at Beit Shebab, Lebanon." *Palestine Exploration Quarterly* 100: 27–32.

Hansen Streily, A. 2000. "Early Pottery Kilns in the Middle East." *Paléorient* 26(2): 69–81.

Harizanov, A. 2016. "Drying the Pots: Facilities for Pre-firing Treatment of Ceramic Artefacts from the Roman Period in Bulgaria." *Instrumentum: Bulletin du group de travail européen sur l'artisanat et les productions manufacturées de l'antiquité à l'époque moderne* 43: 32–37.

Harper, D., and H. M. Lawson. 2003. "Introduction." In *The Cultural Study of Work*, edited by D. Harper and H. M. Lawson, 1–7. New York: Rowman and Littlefield Publishers.

Hartley, B. R. 2002. "Associations of Potters on Stamps from La Graufesenque." In *Céramiques de La Graufesenque et autres productions d'époque romaine: Nouvelles recherches. Homages à Bettina Hoffman*, edited by M. Genin and A. Vernhet, 133–38. Montagnac: Éditions Monique Mergoil.

Hartung, U., P. Ballet, F. Béguin, J. Bourriau, D. Dixneuf, A. von den Driesch, and P. French. 2007. "Tell el-Fara'in – Buto 9. Vorbericht." *Mitteilungen des Deutschen Archaologischen Instituts Abteilung Kairo* 63: 69–166.

Hartung, U., P. Ballet, F. Béguin, J. Bourriau, P. French, T. Herbich, and P. Kopp. 2003. "Tell el-Fara'in – Buto 8. Vorbericht." *Mitteilungen des Deutschen Archaologischen Instituts Abteilung Kairo* 59: 199–267.

Hasaki, E. 2002. "Ceramic Kilns in Ancient Greece: Technology and Organization of Ceramic Workshops." Unpublished PhD diss., University of Cincinnati.

Hasaki, E. 2006. "Ancient Greek Ceramic Kilns and Their Contribution to the Technology and Organization of the Potter's Workshops." In *Proceedings of the 2nd International Conference on Ancient Greek Technology*, edited by P. Tasios and C. Palyvou, 221–27. Athens: Texhniko Epimeletrio Elladas.

Hasaki, E. 2011. "Crafting Spaces: Studies of Spatial Organization in Pottery Workshops in Greece and Tunisia." In *Pottery in the Archaeological Record: Greece and Beyond. Acts of the International Colloquium Held at the Danish and Canadian Institutes in Athens, June 20–22, 2008*, edited by M. L. Lawall and J. Lund, 12–28. Aarhus: Aarhus University Press.

Hasaki, E. 2012. "Craft Apprenticeship in Ancient Greece: Reaching beyond the Masters." In *Archaeology and Apprenticeship: Body Knowledge, Identity, and Communities of Practice*, edited by W. Wendrich, 171–202. Tucson: University of Arizona Press.

Hasaki, E. 2021. *Potters at Work in Ancient Corinth: Industry, Religion, and the Penteskouphia Pinakes*. Hesperia Supplement 51. Princeton: American School of Classical Studies at Athens.

Hasaki, E., ed. n.d. The WebAtlas of Ceramic Kilns in Ancient Greece. University of Arizona. https://atlasgreekkilns.arizona.edu. Accessed October 10, 2024.

Hasaki, E., and C. Raptis. 2016. "Roman and Byzantine Ceramic Kilns in Greece (1st–15th c.) Continuities and Changes in Kiln Typology and Spatial Organization of Production." In *Archeologia delle produzioni ceramiche nel mondo antico: Spazi, prodotti, strumenti e tecniche*, edited by N. Cucuzza, B. M. Giannattasio, and S. Pallecchi, 209–29. Rome: Ariccia.

Hawkins, C. 2012. "Manufacturing." In *The Cambridge Companion to the Roman Economy*, edited by W. Schiedel, 175–94. Cambridge: Cambridge University Press.

Hawkins, C. 2016. *Roman Artisans and the Urban Economy*. Cambridge: Cambridge University Press.

Hawthorne, J. 1997. "Post Processual Economics: The Role of African Red Slip Ware Vessel Volume in Mediterranean Demography." In *TRAC 96: Proceedings of the Sixth Annual Theoretical Roman Archaeology Conference, Sheffield 1996*, edited by K. Meadows, C. Lemke, and J. Heron, 29–37. Oxford: Oxbow.

Hayes, J. 1972. *Late Roman Pottery*. Rome: British School at Rome.

Hayes, J. 1997. *Handbook of Mediterranean Roman Pottery*. Norman: University of Oklahoma Press.

Hayes, J. 2001. "Late Roman Fine Wares and Their Successors: A Mediterranean Byzantine Perspective (with Reference to the Syro-Jordanian Situation)." In *La céramique byzantine et proto-islamique en Syrie-Jordanie (IVᵉ–VIIᵉ siècles apr. J.-C.)*, edited by E. Villeneuve and P. M. Watson, 275–82. Beirut: Institut français d'archéologie du proche Orient.

Heilmeyer, W. D. 2004. "Ancient Workshops and Ancient 'Art.'" *Oxford Journal of Archaeology* 23(4): 403–15.

Hellmann, M.-C. 2012. "Quartiers ou rues? La notion de quartier économique spécialisé dans le monde grec: Comparaison des données textuelles et archéologiques." In *"Quartiers" artisanaux en Grèce ancienne: Une perspective méditerranéenne*, edited by A. Esposito and G. Sanidas, 23–38. Villeneuve d'Ascq: Presses universitaires du Septentrion.

Hendrickx, S. 1998. "Habitations de potiers à Elkab à l'époque romaine." In *Egyptian Religion. The Last Thousand Years. Part II: Studies Dedicated to the Memory of Jan Quaegebeur*, edited by W. Clarysse, A. Schoors, and H. Willems, 1353–76. Leuven: Peeters.

Henein, N. H. 1997. *Poterie et potiers d'Al-Qasr: Oasis de Dakhla.* Cairo: Institut français d'archéologie orientale.

Herzfeld, M. 2004. *The Body Impolitic: Artisans and Artifice in the Global Hierarchy of Value.* Chicago: University of Chicago Press.

Hines, B. 2012. "Romano-British Kiln Building and Firing Experiments: Two Recent Kilns." *Journal of Roman Pottery Studies* 15: 26–38.

Hirschfeld, Y. 1997. "Farms and Villages in Byzantine Palestine." *Dumbarton Oaks Papers* 51: 33–71.

Hite, J. M., and W. S. Hesterly. 2001. "The Evolution of Firm Networks: From Emergence to Early Growth of the Firm." *Strategic Management Journal* 22(3): 275–86.

Hodos, T. 2009. "Local and Global Perspectives in the Study of Social and Cultural Identities." In *Material Culture and Social Identities in the Ancient World*, edited by S. Hales and T. Hodos, 3–31. Cambridge: Cambridge University Press.

Hoff, M., B. Can, R. Townsend, T. Howe, A. Kızılarslanoğlu, and G. Dobos. 2018. "Antiochia ad Cragum Excavations: 2016 and 2017 Seasons / Antiochia ad Cragum 2016 ve 2017 Yılları Kazı Çalışmaları." *ANMED Anadolu Akdenizi Arkeoloji Haberleri / ANMED News of Archaeology from Anatolia's Mediterranean Areas* 16: 1–14.

Hoff, M., R. Townsend, E. Erdoğmuş, B. Can, and T. Howe. 2016. "Antiochia ad Cragum Arkeolojik Araştırma Projesi: 2015 Sezonu / The Antiochia ad Cragum Archaeological Research Project: 2015 Season." *ANMED Anadolu Akdenizi Arkeoloji Haberleri / ANMED News of Archaeology from Anatolia's Mediterranean Areas* 14: 1–8.

Holwerda, J. H., and W. C. Braat. 1946. *De Holdeurn bij Berg en Dal. Centrum van pannenbakkerij en aardewerk-industrie in den Romeinschen tijd.* Leiden: Brill.

Homès-Fredericq, D., and H. J. Franken, eds. 1986. *Pottery and Potters: Past and Present. 7000 Years of Ceramic Art in Jordan.* Tübingen: Attempto Verlag.

Hope, C. 1978. "Dakhleh Oasis Project: Report on the Study of the Pottery and Kilns." *The Journal of the Society for the Study of Egyptian Antiquities* 9: 187–201.

Hope, C. 1982. "Concerning Egyptian Potter's Wheels." *Journal of the Society for the Study of Egyptian Antiquities* 12: 13–14.

Hübner, G. 1993. *Die Applikenkeramik von Pergamon: Eine Bildersprache im Dienst des Herrscherkultes.* Berlin: de Gruyter.

Hudson, J. 1997. "Urban Pottery Workshops in North Africa." In *Pottery in the Making: Ceramic Traditions*, edited by I. Freestone and D. Gaimster, 134–39. Washington, DC: Smithsonian Institution Press.

Hudson, N. 2006. "Dining in the Late Roman East." Unpublished PhD diss., University of Minnesota.

Hughes, J. D. 1994. *Environmental Problems of the Greeks and Romans: Ecology in the Ancient Mediterranean.* 2nd ed. Baltimore: Johns Hopkins University Press.

Humphreys, O. J. 2018. "Craft, Industry and Agriculture in a Roman City: The Iron Tools from London." Unpublished PhD diss., University of Reading.

Iacomi, V. 2008. "Some Notes on Late-Antique Oil and Wine Production in Rough Cilicia (Isauria) in the Light of Epigraphic Sources: Funerary Inscriptions from Korykos, LR1 Amphorae Production in Elaiussa Sebaste and the Abydos Tariff." In *Olive Oil and Wine Production in Anatolia during Antiquity. Symposium Proceedings, 06–08 November 2008, Mersin, Turkey*, edited by Ü. Aydınoğlu and A. Şenol, 19–32. Mersin: Research Centre of Cilician Archaeology.

Iacomi, V. 2019. "Before Final Abandonment: Some Notes on Post-residential Use of Private Spaces from the Domestic District of Elaiussa-Sebaste in the Late Early Byzantine Period (mid VII c. AD)." In *ΣΕΒΑΣΤΗ Studies in Honour of Eugenia Equini Schneider*, edited by A. Polosa, H. A. Kızılarslanoğlu, and M. Oral, 307–16. Istanbul: Ege Yayınları.

Iacomi, V., and V. Cassiani. 2016. "La Cilicia/Isauria tra IV e metà VII secolo: Insediamenti, produzioni e attività economiche. Nuove considerazioni alla lucedei più recenti studi sulla regione." *Landscape Archaeology Conference Proceedings 2014*, 1–11. https://dx.doi.org/10.5463/lac.2014.3.

İdil, V., and M. Kadıoğlu. 2008. "2007 Yılı Nysa Kazı ve Restorasyon Çalışmaları." *Kazı Sonuçları Toplantısı* 30(3): 499–520.

Iliffe, J. H. 1945. "Imperial Art in Transjordan: Figurines and Lamps from a Potter's Store at Jerash." *Quarterly of the Department of Antiquities of Palestine* 11: 1–26.

Ingold, T. 1993. "The Temporality of the Landscape." *World Archaeology* 25(2): 152–74.

Ingold, T. 2007. "Materials against Materiality." *Archaeological Dialogues* 14(1): 1–16.

Ingold, T. 2010. "The Textility of Making." *Cambridge Journal of Economics* 34(1): 91–102.

İşkan, H., and F. Şahin. 2019. "Grave Church and Its Cemetery." In *Patara: City, Harbor, Cult*, edited by H. İşkan, 332–43. Istanbul: Türkiye İş Bankası Kültür Yayınları.

Israel, Y. 1993. "Ashqelon." *Excavations and Surveys in Israel* 12: 100–105.

Israel, Y. 1995. "Survey of Pottery Workshops, Nahal Lakhish-Nahal Besor." *Excavations and Surveys in Israel* 14: 106–7.

Israel, Y. 1997. "Khirbet Irza." *Excavations and Surveys in Israel* 16: 80–81.

Israel, Y., and T. Erickson-Gini. 2013. "Remains from the Hellenistic through the Byzantine Periods at the 'Third Mile Estate,' Ashqelon." *'Antiqot* 74: 167–222.

Jackson, M, M. Zelle, L. Vandeput, and V. Köse. 2012. "Primary Evidence for Late Roman D Ware Production in Southern Asia Minor: A Challenge to 'Cypriot Red Slip Ware.'" *Anatolian Studies* 62: 89–114.

Jacobs, I. 2009. "Encroachment in the Eastern Mediterranean between the Fourth and the Seventh Century AD." *Ancient Society* 39: 203–43.

Jaffe, A. B., M. Trajtenberg, and R. Henderson. 1993. "Geographic Localization of Knowledge Spillovers as Evidenced by Patent Citations." *The Quarterly Journal of Economics* 108(3): 577–98.

Japp, S. 2009. "The Local Pottery Production of Kibyra." *Anatolian Studies* 59: 95–128.

Japp, S. 2014. "Sigillata of Pergamon: Eastern Sigillata C. Problems of Classification and Chronology." In *Late Hellenisic to Mediaeval Fine Wares of the Aegean Coast of Anatolia: Their Production, Imitation and Use*, edited by H. Meysa, 11–21. Warsaw: Neriton.

Johnson, B. L., and L. E. Stager. 1995. "Ashkelon: Wine Emporium of the Holy Land." In *Recent Excavations in Israel: A View to the West. Reports on Kabri, Nami, Miqne-Ekron, Dor and Ashkelon*, edited by S. Gitin, 95–109. Archaeological Institute of American Colloquia and Conferences Papers No. 1. Dubuque, IA: Kendall-Hunt Publishing.

Johnston, A. W. 1985. "A Greek Graffito from Arezzo." *Oxford Journal of Archaeology* 4(1): 119–24.

Joshel, S. R. 1992. *Work, Identity, and Legal Status at Rome: A Study of the Occupational Inscriptions*. Norman: University of Oklahoma Press.

Joshi, S. K., and I. Dudani. 2008. "Environmental Health Effects of Brick Kilns in Khatmandu Valley." *Khatmandu University Medical Journal* 6(1): 3–11.

Kamp, K. A., N. Timmerman, G. Lind, J. Graybill, and I. Natowsky. 1999. "Archaeology Discovering Childhood: Using Fingerprints to Find Children in the Archaeological Record." *American Antiquity* 64 (2): 309–15.

Karmon, N., and E. Spanier. 1987. "Archaeological Evidence of the Purple Dye Industry from Israel." In *The Royal Purple and the Biblical Blue: Argaman and Tekhelet. The Study of Chief Rabbi Dr. Isaac Herzog on the Dye Industries in Ancient Israel and Recent*

Scientific Contributions, edited by E. Spanier, 147–58. Jerusalem: Keter.

Kassab Tezgör, D. 2010. *Les fouilles et le materiel de l'atelier amphorique de Demirci près de Sinope: Recueil de travaux*. Paris: Institut français d'études anatoliennes – Georges Dumézil.

Kassab Tezgör, D., and İ. Tatlıcan. 1998. "Fouilles des ateliers d'amphores a Demirci pres de Sinop en 1996 et 1997." *Anatolia Antiqua* 6: 423–42.

Kehrberg, I. 2007. "Gerasa as Provider for Roman Frontier Stations: A View Seen from Late Roman Potters' Waste at the Hippodrome and the Upper Zeus Temple." *Studies in the History and Archaeology of Jordan* 9: 31–48.

Kehrberg, I. 2009. "Byzantine Ceramic Production and Organizational Aspects of Sixth Century AD Pottery Workshops at the Hippodrome of Jarash." *Studies in the History and Archaeology of Jordan* 10: 493–512.

Kehrberg, I. 2011. "The Complexity of Ancient Lamps: Archaeological Contexts, Material Assemblages, and the Chronology of Lamp Types." In *Lampes antiques du Bilad es Sham. Jordanie, Syrie, Liban, Palestine. Ancient lamps of Bilad es Sham. Actes du colloque de Pétra-Amman (6–13 Novembre 2005)*, edited by D. Frangié and J.-F. Salles, 127–47. Paris: De Boccard.

Kehrberg, I. 2016. "Pottery and Glass Sherd-Tools from Roman and Byzantine Workshops at the Gerasa Hippodrome and other Sites: A Reappraisal," *Studies in the History and Archaeology of Jordan* 12: 411–30.

Kehrberg, I. 2020. "Pottery and Glass Sherd-Tools from Roman and Byzantine Workshops at the Gerasa Hippodrome and Other Sites: A Reappraisal of Earlier Findings." In *The Hippodrome of Gerasa: A Provincial Roman Circus*, edited by A. A. Ostrasz and I. Kehrberg-Ostrasz, 411–30. Oxford: Archaeopress.

Kehrberg, I., and A. A. Ostrasz. 1997. "A History of Occupational Changes at the Site of the Hippodrome of Gerasa." *Studies in the History and Archaeology of Jordan* 6: 167–73.

Kehrberg, I., and A. A. Ostrasz. 2020. "Ancient Burials at the Hippodrome of Gerasa / Jerash." In *The Hippodrome of Gerasa: A Provincial Roman Circus*, edited by A. A. Ostrasz and I. Kehrberg-Ostrasz, 307–13. Oxford: Archaeopress.

Kelepeshi, C., D. Braekmans, D. Daems, J. Poblome, E. Vassilieva, and P. Degryse. 2024. "From Hellenistic Slipped Tableware to Roman Imperial Sagalassos Red Slip Ware: A Petrographic and Geochemical Study." *Journal of Archaeological Science: Reports* 53: 104390.

Kelly, S. E., and T. Arden. 2016. "Craft Specialization and the Comparative Advantages of Gender." In *Gendered Labor in Specialized Economies: Archaeological Perspectives on Female and Male Work*, edited by S. E. Kelly and T. Arden, 3–26. Boulder: University Press of Colorado.

Killick, M. 1987. "Nabataean Pottery." In *Udhruh: A Caravan City and Desert Oasis*, edited by A. Killick, 7–8. Romsey: Hants.

Killick, M. 1990. "Les Nabatéens à Udhruh." *ARAM Periodical* 2(1–2): 249–52.

Kirilov, C. 2007. "The Reduction of the Fortified City Area in Late Antiquity: Some Reflections on the End of the 'Antique City' in the Lands of the Eastern Roman Empire." In *Post-Roman Towns, Trade and Settlement in Europe and Byzantium. Vol. 2: Byzantium, Pliska and the Balkans*, edited by J. Henning, 3–23. Berlin: De Gruyter.

Kloppenborg, J. S., and S. G. Wilson. 1996. *Voluntary Associations in the Greco-Roman World*. London: Routledge.

Knappett, C. 2002. "Photographs, Skeuomorphs, and Marionettes: Some Thoughts on Mind, Agency and Object." *Journal of Material Culture* 7(1): 97–117.

Kramer, C. 1997. *Pottery in Rajasthan: Ethnoarcheology in Two Indian Cities*. Washington, DC: Smithsonian Institution Press.

Krause, R. A. 1985. *The Clay Sleeps: An Ethnoarchaeological Study of Three African Potters*. Tuscaloosa: University of Alabama Press.

Kristensen, S. B. 2017. "Cooking up Culture: Production Traditions in Late Roman-Byzantine Locally Produced Cooking

Ware." In *Gerasa / Jerash: From the Urban Periphery*, edited by A. Lichtenberger and R. Raja, 75–81. Aarhus: University of Aarhus Press.

Krogulska, M. 1985. "A Ceramic Workshop in the Western Quarter of Palmyra." *Studia Palmyreńskie* 8: 43–68.

Krogulska, M. 1996. "Palmyrenian Pottery of the Second Century A.D." *Palmyra and the Silk Road*. 339–53. Damascus: Directorate General of Antiquities and Museums Syrian Arab Republic.

Kruit, N., and K. A. Worp. 2000. "Geographical Jar Names: Towards a Multi-disciplinary Approach." *APF* 46: 65–146.

Kugler, K. 2018. "A Ceramic Production Site in the Kibyratis: A Contribution to the Problematic Identification of Local Ceramic Workshops." In *Symposium Proceedings of Uluslararası Genç Bilimciler Buluşması II: Anadolu Akdenizi Sempozyumu 04–07 Kasım 2015 / International Young Scholars Conference II: Mediterranean Anatolia 04–07 November 2015*, edited by T. Kahya, A. Özdizbay, N. Tüner Önen, and M. Wilson, 479–504. Antalya: AKMED.

Kunze-Götte, E. 1999. *Die Nekropole von der Mitte des 6. Bis zum Ende des 5. Jahrhunderts. Kerameikos 7, 2*. Munich: Hirmer.

Künzl, E., and T. Weber. 1990. "Das spätantike Grab eines Zahnarztes zu Gadara in der Dekapolis mit einem Anhang zur Anthropologie des Skelettmaterials von Dieter Butz und Winfried Henke." *DM* 5: 81–118.

Ladstätter, S. 2007. "Mode oder politisches Manifest? Überlegungen zur Übernahme römischen Formenguts in der frühkaiserzeitlichen Keramik von Ephesos." In *Neue Zeiten – Neue Sitten: Zu Rezeption und Integration römischen und italischen Kulturguts in Kleinasien*, edited by M. Meyer, 203–19. Vienna: Phoibos.

Ladstätter, S. 2011. "Bizans Döneminde Ephesos: Büyük bir Kentin Tarihinde son Sayfa." In *Bizans Döneminde Ephesos*, edited by F. Daim and S. Ladstätter, 3–27. Istanbul: Ege.

Ladstätter, S., and R. Sauer. 2005. "Late Roman C-Ware und Lokale Spätantike Feinware aus Ephesos." In *Spätantike und mittelalterliche Keramik aus Ephesos*, edited by F. Krinzinger, 143–201. Vienna: Verlag der Österreichischen Akademie der Wissenschaften.

Laes, C. 2008. "Child Slaves at Work in Roman Antiquity." *Ancient Society* 38: 235–83.

Lapp, E. 2016. *Sepphoris II: The Clay Lamps from Ancient Sepphoris: Light Use and Regional Interactions*. Sepphoris Excavation Reports 2. University Park, PA: Eisenbrauns.

Laubenheimer, F., ed. 2001. *20 ans de recherches à Sallèles d'Aude*. Paris: Presses universitaires Franc-Comtoises.

Lauwers, V., P. Degryse, and M. Waelkens. 2007. "A Ceramic Tool for the Glass-Blower." *Oxford Journal of Archaeology* 26(2): 193–200.

Lavan, L. 2012. "From Polis to Emporion? Retail and Regulation in the Late Antique City." In *Trade and Markets in Byzantium*, edited by C. Morrisson, 333–78. Dumbarton Oaks Byzantine Symposia and Colloquia. Washington, DC: Dumbarton Oaks.

Leach, B. 1949. *A Potter's Book*. New York: Transatlantic Arts.

Lechtman, H. 1977. "Style in Technology: Some Early Thoughts." In *Material Culture: Styles, Organization, and Dynamics of Technology*, edited by H. Lechtman and. R. Merrill, 3–20. St. Paul, MN: West Publishing.

Lechtman, H., and A. Steinberg. 1979. "The History of Technology: An Anthropological Point of View." In *The History and Philosophy of Technology*, edited by G. Bugliarello and B. Doner, 135–60. Chicago: University of Illinois Press.

Lecuyot, G., and A. Schmitt. 2019. "II.3 secteurs P3 et P4. Les fours et le mur de clôture." In *Tell el-Fara'în-Buto VI: Recherches sur les ateliers romains de Bouto prospections et sondages (2001–2006)*, edited by P. Ballet, F. Béguin, G. Lecuyot, and A. Schmitt, 150–83. Wiesbaden: Harrassowitz.

Leibner, U. 2010. "Arts and Crafts, Manufacture and Production." In *The Oxford Handbook of Jewish Daily Life in Roman Palestine*, edited by C. Hezser, 264–96. Oxford: Oxford University Press.

Leidwanger, J. 2017. "From Time Capsules to Networks: New Light on Roman Shipwrecks in the Maritime Economy." *American Journal of Archaeology* 121(4): 595–619.

Lemonnier, P. 1986. "The Study of Material Culture Today: Toward an Anthropology of Technical Systems." *Journal of Anthropological Archaeology* 5: 147–86.

Lemonnier, P. 1992. *Elements for an Anthropology of Technology*. Ann Arbor: Museum of Anthropology, University of Michigan.

Leone, A. 2003. "Topographies of Production in North African Cities during the Vandal and Byzantine Periods." In *Theory and Practice in Late Antique Archaeology*, edited by L. Lavan and W. Bowden, 257–87. Late Antique Archaeology 1. Leiden: Brill.

Leroi-Gourhan, A. 1993. *Gesture and Speech*. Translated by A. Bostock Berger. Cambridge, MA: MIT Press.

Levi, D., and R. Be'eri. 2010. "Excavations in the Crown Plaza Hotel (Binyanei Ha'uma)." In *New Studies in the Archaeology of Jerusalem and Its Region (Collected Papers IV)*, edited by D. Amit, O. Peleg-Barkat, and G. D. Stiebel, 119–29. Jerusalem: Israel Antiquities Authority; Hebrew University of Jerusalem, Institute of Archaeology.

Levi, D., and R. Be'eri. 2011. "Jerusalem, Binyanē Ha-Umma. Preliminary Report." *Hadashot Arkheologiyot: Excavations and Surveys in Israel* 123.

Levi, D., and R. Be'eri. 2017. "The Potter's Workshops at Binyane Ha-Umma as a Tool for Understanding Historical and Cultural Changes in Jerusalem from the Second Century BCE to the Second Century CE." In *New Studies in the Archaeology of Jerusalem and its Region (Collected Papers XI)*, edited by Y. Gadot, Y. Zelinger, K. Cytryn-Silverman, and J. Uziel, 124–43. Jerusalem: Israel Antiquities Authority; Hebrew University of Jerusalem, Institute of Archaeology.

Lichtenberger, A. 2016. *Terakotten aus Beit Nattif: Eine Untersuchung zur religiösen Alltagspraxis im spätantiken Judäa*. Contextualizing the Sacred 7. Turnhout: Brepols.

Lis, C., and H. Soly. 2012. "Chapter 2. The Roman Empire: Continuity and Change." In *Worthy Efforts: Attitudes to Work and Workers in Pre-industrial Europe*, edited by C. Lis and H. Soly, 54–98. Studies in Global Social History 10. Leiden: Brill.

Lis, C., and H. Soly. 2016. "Work, Identity and Self-Representation in the Roman Empire and the West-European Middle Ages: Different Interplays between the Social and the Cultural." In *Work, Labour, and Professions in the Roman World*, edited by K. Verboven and C. Laes, 262–89. Impact of Empire 23. Leiden: Brill.

Liu, J. 2005. "Local Governments and Collegia: A New Appraisal of the Evidence." In *A Tall Order: Writing the Social History of the Ancient World: Essays in Honor of William V. Harris*, edited by W. V. Harris, J.-J. Aubert, and Z. Várhelyi, 285–316. Munich: K. G. Saur.

Liu, J. 2017. "Group Membership, Trust Networks, and Social Capital: A Critical Analysis." In *Work, Labour, and Professions in the Roman World*, edited by K. Verboven and C. Laes, 201–26. Impact of Empire 23. Leiden: Brill.

Loebert, H. W. 1984. "Types of Potters' Wheels and the Spread of the Spindle Wheel in Germany." In *The Many Dimensions of Pottery: Ceramics in Archaeology and Anthropology*, edited by S. E. van der Leeuw and A. C. Pritchard, 203–30. Amsterdam: University of Amsterdam Press.

Loeschcke, S. 1912. "Sigillata-Töpfereien in Tscandarli: Bericht über die Ergebnisse einer Versuchsgrabung im Jahre 1911." *Mitteilungen des Kaiserlich Deutschen Archäologischen Instituts* 37: 344–407.

London, G. 1989. "Past and Present: Village Potters in Cyprus." *Biblical Archaeologist* 52(4): 219–29.

London, G. 2000. "Continuity and Change in Cypriot Pottery Production." *Near Eastern Archaeology* 63(2): 102–10.

Loney, H. 2007. "Prehistoric Italian Pottery Production: Motor Memory, Motor Development and Technological Transfer." *Journal of Mediterranean Archaeology* 20(2): 183–207.

Lund, J. 2005. "An Economy of Consumption: The Eastern Sigillata A Industry in the Late Hellenistic Period." In *Making, Moving, and Managing: The New World of Ancient Economies, 323–31 BC*, edited by Z. H. Archibald, J. K. Davies, and V. Gabrielsen, 233–51. Oxford: Oxbow Books.

Lund, J. 2009. "Engendering the Potters of Hellenistic and Roman Cyprus." In *Medelhavsmuseet. Focus on the Mediterranean, no. 5. Proceedings from the International Conference "Finds and Results from the Swedish Cyprus Expedition 1927–1931: A Gender Perspective," March 31–April 2, 2006, Medelhavsmuseet, Focus on the Mediterranean 5*, edited by S. Houby-Nielsen, K. Slej, K. Göransson, and S. Häggman, 165–70. Stockholm: Medelhavsmuseet.

Lund, J. 2014. "Pots and Politics: Reflexions on the Circulation of Pottery in the Ptolemaic and Seleucid Kingdoms." In *Pottery, Peoples and Places*, edited by P. G. Bilde and M. L. Lawall, 297–305. Black Sea Studies 16. Aarhus: Aarhus University Press.

Lund, J. 2015. *A Study of the Circulation of Ceramics in Cyprus from the 3rd Century BC to the 3rd Century AD.* Gösta Enbom Monographs, Volume 5. Aarhus: Aarhus University Press.

Lund, J. 2016. "Eastern Sigillata A Ware: The Riddle of the Stamps." In *Ηχάδιν, Honorary Volume for Stella Drougou / ΗΧΑΔΙΝ: ΤΙΜΗΤΙΚΟΣ ΤΟΜΟΣ ΓΙΑ ΤΗ ΣΤΕΛΛΑ ΔΡΟΥΓΟΥ. ΤΟΜΟΣ Ι*, edited by M. Giannopoulou and C. Kallini, 831–40. Athens: Ministry of Culture.

Lund, J., D. Malfitana, and J. Poblome. 2006a. "General Introduction." In *Old Pottery in a New Century: Innovating Perspectives on Roman Pottery Studies. Atti del convegno internazionale di studi Catania, 22–24 aprile 2004*, edited by D. Malfitana, J. Poblome, and J. Lund, 19–26. Catania: Istituto per i Beni Archeologici e Monumentali.

Lund, J., D. Malfitana, and J. Poblome. 2006b. "Rhosica Vasa Mandavi (Cic., Att. 6.1.13) towards the Identification of a Major Ceramic Tableware Industry of the Eastern Mediterranean: Eastern Sigillata A." *Archeologia classica* 57: 491–507.

Lynch, K. M. 1995. "Desperately Seeking Faustus." *The Biblical Archaeologist* 58(2): 115.

Mackensen, M. 1993. *Die spätantiken Sigillata- und Lampentöpfereien von El Mahrine (Nordtunesien): Studien zur nordafrikanischen Feinkeramik des 4. bis 7. Jahrhunderts.* Münchner Beiträge zur Vor- und Frühgeschichte 50. Munich: Beck.

Mackensen, M. 1998. "Centers of African Red Slipped Ware Production in Tunisia from the Late 5th to the 7th Century." In *Ceramica in Italia: VI–VII secolo*, edited by L. Sagui, 23–40. Florence: Giglio.

Magen, Y. 2002. *The Stone Vessel Industry in the Second Temple Period: Excavations at Ḥizma and the Jerusalem Temple Mount.* Jerusalem: Israel Exploration Society.

Magen, Y., and Y. Peleg. 2006. "Back to Qumran: Ten Years of Excavation and Research, 1993–2004." In *Qumran: The Site of the Dead Sea Scrolls. Archaeological Interpretations and Debates. Proceedings of a Conference Held at Brown University, November 17–19, 2002*, edited by J.-B. Humbert, J. Zangenberg, and K. Galor, 55–113. Leiden: Brill.

Maggetti, M., and G. Galetti. 1993. "Die Baukeramik von Augusta-Raurica: Eine mineralogische-chemisch-technische Untersuchung. Zur Herstellung und Verbreitung der in Kaiseraugst produzierten Ziegel der Legio Prima Martia," *Jahresberichte aus Augst und Kaiseraugst* 14: 199–225.

Magness, J. 2002. *The Archaeology of Qumran and the Dead Sea Scrolls.* Grand Rapids, MI: Eerdmans.

Magness, J. 2011. Aelia Capitolina: A Review of Some Current Debates about Hadrianic Jerusalem. In *Unearthing Jerusalem: 150 Years of Archaeological Research in the Holy City*, edited by K. Galor and G. Avni, 313–24. University Park, PA: Eisenbrauns.

Maguire, E. D., H. Maguire, and M. J. Duncan-Flowers. 1989. *Art and Holy Power in the Early Christian House.* Chicago: University of Illinois Press.

Mahmoud, F. 1992. "Les argiles dans l'Égypte actuelle leur destination artisanale et industrielle. Quelques données." *Cahiers de la céramique égyptienne* 3: 183–88.

Majcherek, G., and A. el-Shennawi. 1991. "Tell el-Haraby: A Newly Discovered Kiln-Site." *Bulletin de liason du groupe international d'étude de la céramique égyptienne* 15: 5–7.

Malafouris, L. 2008. "At the Potter's Wheel: An Argument *for* Material Agency." In *Material Agency: Towards a Non-anthropocentric Approach*, edited by C. Knappett and L. Malafouris, 19–36. New York: Springer.

Malafouris, L. 2013. "Becoming One with the Clay." *How Things Shape the Mind: A Theory of Material Engagement*, 207–26. Cambridge, MA: MIT Press.

Manacorda, D., and S. Pallecchi, eds. 2012. *Le Fornaci romane di Giancola (Brindisi)*. Bari: Edipuglia.

Marichal, R. 1988. *Les grafittes de La Graufesenque*. Gallia supplément 47. Paris: Éditions du Centre national de la recherche scientifique.

Maritan, L., F. Tourtet, G. Meneghin, C. Mazzoli, and A. Hausleiter. 2017. "Technological Transfer? Comparative Analysis of 2nd–3rd/4th century CE "Late Roman" Pottery from Taymāʾ, Saudi Arabia, and Petra, Jordan." *Journal of Archaeological Science: Reports* 12: 712–25.

Martens, F., B. Mušič, J. Poblome, and M. Waelkens. 2012. "The Integrated Urban Survey at Sagalassos." In *Urban Landscape Survey in Italy and the Mediterranean*, edited by F. Vermeulen, G.-J. Burgers, S. Keay, and C. Corsi, 84–93. Oxford: Oxbow.

Martin, R. 1965. *Manuel d' architecture grecque. Pt. 1: Les matériaux*. Paris: Picard.

Martin, S. D. 2001. "Imperitia: The Responsibility of Skilled Workers in Classical Roman Law." *American Journal of Philology* 122(1): 107–29.

Martorelli, R. 1999. "Riflessioni sulle attività produttive nell'età tardoantica ed altomedievale: Esiste un artigianato "ecclesiastico"?" *Revista di archeologi cristiana* 75(1/2): 571–96.

Mason, J. R. B., and K. 'Amr. 1990. "A Study of Nabataean Pottery Manufacturing Techniques: An Experiment for Reconstructing the Production of Fine Bowls." *ARAM Periodical* 2(1/2): 287–307.

Mastronuzzi, G., and V. Melissano. 2007. "Le case bizantine sul lato ovest dell'Agorà (Regio I)." In *Hierapolis di Frigia I: Le attività delle campagne di scavo e restauro 2000–2003*, edited by F. D'Andria and M. Piera Caggia, 541–81. Istanbul: Ege Yayınları.

Matson, F. R. 1966. "Power and Fuel Resources in the Ancient Near East." *The Advancement of Science* 23(109): 146–53.

Matson, F. R. 1973. "The Potters of Chalkis." In *Classics and the Classical Tradition: Essays Presented to Robert E. Dengler on the Occasion of His Eightieth Birthday*, edited by E. Borza and R. W. Currubba, 117–42. University Park: Pennsylvania State University.

Mayer, E. 2012. *The Ancient Middle Classes: Urban Life and Aesthetics in the Roman Empire, 100 BCE–250 CE*. Cambridge, MA: Harvard University Press.

Mayerson, P. 1992. "The Gaza 'Wine' Jar (Gazition) and the 'Lost' Ashkelon Jar (Askalônion)." *Israel Exploration Journal* 42: 76–80.

Mayerson, P. 2000. "The Economic Status of Potters in P. Oxy. L 3595–3597 & XVI 1911, 1913." *The Bulletin of the American Society of Papyrologists*. 37(1): 97.

Mayet, F., and F. Picon. 1986. "Une sigillée phocéenne tardive (Late Roman C Ware) et sa diffusion en Occident." *Figlina* 7: 129–46.

Mees, A. 2002. *Organisationsformen römischer Töpfer-Manufakturen am Beispiel von Arezzo und Rheinzabern unter Berücksichtigung von Papyri, Inschriften und Rechtsquellen*. Monographien Römisch-Germanisches Zentralmuseum 52. Mainz: Verlag des Römisch-Germanischen Zentralmuseums.

Meyers, E., E. Netzer, and C. Meyers. 1987. "Sepphoris (Ṣippori), 1986 (I): Joint Sepphoris Project." *Israel Exploration Journal* 37: 275–78.

Meyer-Schlichtmann, C. 1988. *Die pergamenische Sigillata aus der Stadtgrabung von Pergamon*. Pergamenische Forschungen 6. Berlin: de Gruyter.

Meyza, H. 2000. "Early Eastern Sigillata A from Paphos, Cyprus." In *Acts of the Fifth International Conference on Hellenistic Pottery, Chania, April 1997 / Πρακτικά Ε' Επιστημονικής Συνάντησης για την Ελληνιστική Κεραμεική*, edited by S. Drougou, 237–44. Athens: Archaeological Resources and Expropriations Fund.

Mikati, R. 2003. "Faustus the Early Roman Lamp Maker Visits Beirut: Evidence of a Tyre-Based Production." In *Nouveautés Lychnologiques*, edited by L. Chrzanovski, 175–180. Hauterive: LychnoServices.

Miller, S. G. 1991. "Terracotta Figurines: New Finds at Ilion, 1988–1989." *Studia Troica* 1: 39–68.

Mitsopoulos-Leon, V. 1985. "Töpferateliers in Ephesos." In *Pro Arte Antiqua. Festschrift für Hedwig Kenner 2*, edited by W. Alzinger, 247–51. Vienna: A. F. Koska.

Möller, H. 2017. "Ceramics in Context: Interpreting Life through Pottery." In *Gerasa / Jerash from the Urban Periphery*, edited by A. Lichtenberger and R. Raja, 59–65. Aarhus: Aarhus University.

Möller, H. 2024. *Ceramic Finds (Roma to Early Islamic Times): Final Publications from the Danish-German Jerash Northwest Quarter Project*. Turnhout: Brepols.

Monteix, N. 2010. *Les lieux de métier boutiques et ateliers d'Herculaneum*. Rome: École française de Rome.

Monteix, N., and N. Tran, eds. 2011. *Les savoirs professionnels des gens de métier: Études sur le monde du travail dans les sociétés urbaines de l'empire romain*. Collection du Centre Jean Bérard 37. Naples: Centre Jean Bérard.

Murphy, E. A. 2015. "Socially Embedded Work Practices and Production Organization in the Roman Mediterranean: Beyond Industry Lines." *Journal of Mediterranean Archaeology* 28 (2): 221–39.

Murphy, E. A. 2016. "Roman Workers and Their Workplaces: Some Archaeological Thoughts on the Organization of Workshop Labor." In *Work, Labour, and Professions in the Roman World*, edited by K. Verboven and C. Laes, 133–47. Impact of Empire 23. Leiden: Brill.

Murphy, E. A. 2017. "Rethinking Standardisation through Late Antique Sagalassos Ceramic Production: Tradition, Improvisation and Fluidity." In *Materialising Roman Histories*, edited by M. Pitts and A. Van Oyen, 101–22. Oxford: Oxbow.

Murphy, E. A., H. Goldfus, and B. Arubas. 2018. "The Jerusalem X Legio Fretensis Kilnworks: Contextualizing the Ceramic Manufacture of 'Legionary Wares.'" *OJA* 37(4): 443–66.

Murphy, E. A., and J. Poblome. 2011. "Producing Pottery vs. Producing Models: Interpreting Workshop Organization at the Potters' Quarter of Sagalassos." In *Pottery in the Archaeological Record: Greece and Beyond. Acts of the International Colloquium Held at the Danish and Canadian Institutes in Athens, June 20–22, 2008*, edited by M. L. Lawall and J. Lund, 29–36. Aarhus: Aarhus University Press.

Murphy, E. A., and J. Poblome. 2012. "Technical and Social Considerations of Tools from Roman-Period Ceramic Workshops at Sagalassos (Southwest Turkey): Not Just Tools of the Trade?" *Journal of Mediterranean Archaeology* 25(2): 197–217.

Murphy, E. A., and J. Poblome. 2016. "A Late Antique Ceramic Workshop Complex: Evidence for Workshop Organisation at Saglassos (Southwest Turkey)." *Anatolian Studies* 66: 185–99.

Murphy, E. A., and J. Poblome. 2017. "From Formal to Technical Styles: Production Challenges and Economic Implications of Changing Tableware Styles in Roman to Late Antique Sagalassos." *American Journal of Archaeology* 121(1): 61–84.

Murphy, E. A., and J. Poblome. 2021. "Intramuros: Cross-Industry Practices and Networks in 6th-Century Sagalassos." *Journal of Urban Archaeology* 3: 101–16.

Murphy, E. A., and I. Uytterhoeven. 2023. "Late Antique Industry in the Urban Public and Private Spaces of Asia Minor." *Adalya* 25: 137–59.

Negev, A. 1974. "Corrigenda: Nabataean Sigillata." *Revue Biblique* 81(3): 422.

Nenna, M. D., and P. T. Nicholson. 2013. "Faience Technology." In *Working in Memphis: The Production of Faience at Roman Period Kom Helul*, edited by P. T. Nicholson, 133–46. London: Egypt Exploration Society.

Neuburger, A. 1930. *The Technical Arts and Sciences of the Ancients*. Translated by H. L. Brose. New York: McMillan.

Nevitt, L. C. 2010. *Domestic Space in Classical Antiquity*. Cambridge: Cambridge University Press.

Neyt, B., D. Braekmans, J. Poblome, J. Elsen, M. Waelkens, and P. Degryse. 2012. "Long-Term Clay Raw Material Selection and Use in the Region of Classical/Hellenistic to Early Byzantine Sagalassos (SW Turkey)." *Journal of Archaeological Science* 39(5): 1296–305

Nicholson, P. T. 2011. "'I'm Not the Saggar-Maker, I'm the Saggar-Maker's Mate...': Saggar Making and Bottom Knocking in Stoke-on-Trent as a Guide to Early Saggar Technology." In *Under the Potter's Tree: Studies on Ancient Egypt Presented to Janine Bourriau on the Occasion of Her 70th Birthday*, edited by D. Aston, B. Bader, C. Gallorini, P. T. Nicholson, and S. Buckingham, 703–22. Leuven: Peeters.

Nicholson, P. T. 2013. *Working in Memphis: The Production of Faience at Roman Period Kom Helul*. London: Egypt Exploration Society.

Nicholson, P. T., and H. L. Patterson. 1985a. "The Ballas Pottery Project." *Anthropology Today* 1(2): 16–18.

Nicholson, P. T., and H. L. Patterson. 1985b. "Pottery Making in Upper Egypt: An Ethnoarchaeological Study." *World Archaeology* 17(2): 222–39.

Nicholson, P. T., and H. L. Patterson. 1989. "Ceramic Technology in Upper Egypt: A Study of Pottery Firing." *World Archaeology* (21)1: 71–86.

Nicholson, P. T., and E. Peltenburg. 2000. "Egyptian Faience." In *Ancient Egyptian Materials and Technology*, edited by P. T. Nicholson and I. Shaw, 177–94. Cambridge: Cambridge University Press.

Nicklin, K. 1979. "The Location of Pottery Manufacture." *Man New Series* 14(3): 436–58.

Oked, H. S. 2001. "'Gaza Jars': A Chronicle and Economic Overview." In *Ashkelon: A City on the Seashore*, edited by A. Sasson, Z. Safrai, and N. Sagiv, 227–50. Tel Aviv: Mikhlala ha-aqademit Ashqelon.

Orlandos, A. 1966. *Les Matériaux de Construction et la Technique Architecturale des Anciens Grecs: Vol. 1*. Paris: de Boccard.

Ortiz, S. 2002. "Work, The Division of Labour and Co-operation." In *Companion Encyclopedia of Anthropology*, edited by T. Ingold, 891–910. London: Routledge.

Orton, C., P. Tyers, and A. Vince. 1993. *Pottery in Archaeology*. Cambridge Manuals in Archaeology. Cambridge: Cambridge University Press.

Ostrasz, A. A. 1989. "The Hippodrome of Gerasa: A Report on Excavations and Research 1982–1987." *Syria* 66 (1–4): 51–77.

Ostrasz, A. A., and I. Kehrberg-Ostrasz, eds. 2020. *The Hippodrome of Gerasa: A Provincial Roman Circus*. Oxford: Archaeopress.

Outschar, U. 1991. "Exportorientierte Keramikproduktion auch noch im spätantiken Ephesos?" *Rei Cretariae Romanae Fautorum Acta* XXIX (XXX): 317–27.

Oxe, A., H. Comfort, and P. M. Kenrick. 2000. *Corpus vasorum Arretinorum: A Catalogue of the Signatures Shapes and Chronology of Italian Sigillata*. 2nd ed. Bonn: Habelt.

Özhanlı, M. 2014. "Pisidia Antiokheiası Kazısı 2013 / Excavations at Pisidian Antioch in 2013." *ANMED Anadolu Akdenizi Arkeoloji Haberleri / ANMED News of Archaeology from Anatolia's Mediterranean Areas* 12: 14–19.

Oziol, T. J. 1993. *Le lampes au musée de la Fondation Pierides*. Nicosia: Zavallis Litho.

Özüdoğru, Ş. 2018. "Geç Antikçağ'da Kibyra / Cibyra in Late Antiquity." *Cedrus* 6: 13–64.

Özüdoğru, Ş. and E. Dökü. 2007. "Patara Seramik Fırınları / Pottery Kilns in Patara." In *IV. Uluslararası Katllımlı Seramik, Cam, Emaye Sir ve Boya Semineri (26–28 Kasım 2007)*. Istanbul: Türk Seramik Derneği Yayını.

Özüdoğru, Ş., and E. Dündar. 2007. "Kibyra Geç Roma: Erken Doğu Roma Dönemi Mühürlü Unguentariumları." *Olba* 15: 145–78.

Özyiğit, Ö. 1994. "The City Walls of Phokaia." *Revue des Études Anciennes* 96(1–2): 77–109.

Özyiğit, Ö. 2011. "2010 Yılı Phokai Kazı Çalışmaları." *Kazı Sonuçları Toplantısı* 33(2): 481–504

Özyiğit, Ö. 2016. "2015 Yılı Phokaia Kazı Çalışmaları." *Kazı Sonuçları Toplantısı* 38(2): 519–38.

Özyiğit, Ö. 2017. "2016 Yılı Phokaia Kazı Çalışmaları." *Kazı Sonuçları Toplantısı* 39(2): 111–28.

Papadopoulos, S. 1995. "L'organisation de l'espace dans deux ateliers de potiers traditionnels de Thasos." *Bulletin de correspondance hellénique* 119(2): 591–606.

Parker, S. T. 2000. "The Roman Aqaba Project: The 1997 and 1998 Campaigns." *Annual of the Department of Antiquities of Jordan* 44: 373–94.

Patlagean, E. 1977. *Pauvreté économique et pauvreté sociale à Byzance, 4e–7e siècles*. Paris: Mouton.

Peacock, D. P. S. 1982. *Pottery in the Roman World: An Ethnoarchaeological Approach*. London: Longman.

Peacock, D. P. S., F. Bejaoui, and N. B. Lazreg. 1990. Roman Pottery Production in Central Tunisia. *Journal of Roman Archaeology* 3: 59–84.

Pekin, A. V. 2015. *Foça Tarihi / The History of Phokaia*. Istanbul: Ege Yayınları.

Peña, J. T. 2007. *Roman Pottery in the Archaeological Record*. Cambridge: Cambridge University Press.

Peña, J. T., and M. McCallum. 2009. "The Production and Distribution of Pottery at Pompeii: A Review of the Evidence. Part 1: Production." *American Journal of Archaeology* 113 (1): 57–79.

Perkins, A. 1959. *The Excavations at Dura-Europos Conducted by Yale University and the French Academy of Inscriptions and Letters: Final Report V, Part I*. New Haven, CT: Yale University Press.

Perlman, I., J. Gunneweg, and J. Yellin. 1986. "Pseudo-Nabataean Ware and Pottery of Jerusalem." *Bulletin of the American Schools of Oriental Research* 262: 77–82.

Pfaffenberger, B. 1992. "Social Anthropology of Technology." *Annual Review of Anthropology* 21: 491–516.

Piccolpasso, C. 1934. *Arte del Vasaio / The Three Books of the Potter's Art*. Translated by B. Rackham and A. van de Put. London: Victoria and Albert Museum.

Pitarakis, B. 2012. "Daily Life in the Marketplace in Late Antiquity and Byzantium." In *Trade and Markets in Byzantium*, edited by C. Morrisson, 399–428. Dumbarton Oaks Byzantine Symposia and Colloquia. Washington, DC: Dumbarton Oaks.

Pitts, M. 2008. "Globalizing the Local in Roman Britain: An Anthropological Approach to Social Change." *Journal of Anthropological Archaeology* 27: 493–506.

Pitts, M., and M. J. Versluys, eds. 2015. *Globalisation and the Roman World: World History, Connectivity and Material Culture*. Cambridge: Cambridge University Press.

Poblome, J. 1999. *Sagalassos Red Slip Ware: Typology and Chronology*. Studies in Eastern Mediterranean Archaeology 2. Turnhout: Brepols.

Poblome, J. 2012. "'Our Daily Bread' at Ancient Sagalossos." In *INDVSTRIA APIVM L'Archéologie: Une démarche singulière, des pratiques multiples. Hommages à Raymond Brulet*, edited by M. Cavalieri, 81–94. Leuven: Presses Universitaires de Louvain.

Poblome, J. 2014. *Het Leven van elke dag in het antieke Sagalassos*. Leuven: Peeters.

Poblome, J., O. Bounegru, P. Degryse, W. Viaene, M. Waelkens, and S. Erdemgil. 2001. "The Sigillata Manufactories of Pergamon and Sagalassos." *Journal of Roman Archaeology* 14: 143–65.

Poblome, J., D. Braekmans, B. Mušič, M. Van Der Enden, B. Neyt, B. De Graeve, and P. Degryse. 2013. "A Pottery Kiln underneath the Odeon of Ancient Sagalassos: The Excavation Results, the Table Wares and Their Archaeometrical Analysis." In *Networks in the Hellenistic World According to the Pottery in the Eastern Mediterranean and Beyond*, edited by H. Fenning and C. Römer-Strehl, 175–86. BAR-IS 2539. Oxford: Archaeopress.

Poblome, J., P. Degryse, W. Viaene, R. Ottenburgs, M. Waelkens, R. Degeest, and J. Naud. 2002. "The Concept of a Pottery Production Centre: An Archaeometrical

Contribution from Ancient Sagalassos." *Journal of Archaeological Science* 29(8): 873–82.

Poblome, J., and N. Firat. 2011. "Late Roman D: A Matter of Open(ing) or Closed Horizons?" In *Late Roman Fine Wares: Solving Problems of Typology and Chronology*, edited by M. A. Cau, P. Reynolds, and M. Bonifay, 49–55. Oxford: Archaeopress.

Poblome, J., H. Uleners, I. Uytterhoeven, E. Marinova, and B. De Cupere. 2015. "The 2012 to 2014 Excavation Campaigns at Site LE, Sagalassos: The Structural Remains and General Phasing." *Anatolica* 41: 203–40.

Polat, G., Y. Polat, K. Yağız, S. Çokoğullu, E. Açar, E. Baysu, E. Kıraç, M. Çobanoğulları, and İ. Ürün. 2019. "Antandros 2017–2018 Yılı Kazıları." *Kazı Sonuçları Toplantısı* 41(2): 259–76.

Prachner, G. 1980. *Die Sklaven und Freigelassenen im arretinischen Sigillatagewerbe*. Wiesbaden: Franz Steiner.

Princeton University Environmental Heath and Safety. 2022. "Ceramics." https://ehs.princeton.edu/health-safety-the-campus-community/art-theater-safety/art-safety/ceramics.

Pyatt, F. B., A. J. Pyatt, C. Walker, T. Sheen, and J. P. Grattan. 2005. "The Heavy Metal Content of Skeletons from an Ancient Metalliferous Polluted Area in Southern Jordan with Particular Reference to Bioaccumulation and Human Health." *Ecotoxicology and Environmental Safety* 60: 295–300.

Rabinowitz, A. 2001. "Lease of Part of a House and Workshop." *The Bulletin of the American Society of Papyrologists* 38(1/4): 51–62.

Rackham, H., trans. 1952. *Pliny. Natural History. Volume IX: Books 33–35*. Loeb Classical Library 394. Cambridge, MA: Harvard University Press.

Rajala, U., and P. Mills, eds. 2017. *Forms of Dwelling: 20 Years of Taskscapes in Archaeology*. Oxford: Oxbow.

Rasson, A.-M., and J. Seigne. 1989. "Une citerne byzantino-omeyyade sur le sanctuaire de Zeus." *Syria* 66(1–4): 117–51.

Rauh, N. K., C. Autret, and J. Lund. 2013. "Amphora Design and Marketing in Antiquity." In *Kauf, Konsum und Märkte, Wirtschaftswelten im Fokus von der römishen Antike bis zur Gegenward*, edited by M. Frass, 145–82. Philippika: Marburgeraltertumskundliche Abhandlungen 59. Wiesbaden: Harrassowitz Verlag.

Reay, B. 2005. "Agriculture, Writing, and Cato's Aristocratic Self-Fashioning." *Classical Antiquity* 24(2): 331–61.

Reynolds, P. 2005. "Levantine Amphorae from Cilicia to Gaza: A Typology and Analysis of Regional Production Trends from the 1st to 7th Centuries." In *Roman Coarse Wares, Cooking Wares and Amphorae in the Mediterranean I: Archaeology and Archaeometry Conference Papers Held at Barcelona, 14–16th March 2002*, edited by J. M. Gurt i Esparraguerra, J. Buxeda i Garrigós, and M. A. Cau Ontiveros, 563–611. BAR-IS 1340. Oxford: Archaeopress.

Rhodes, D. 1968. *Kilns: Design, Construction, and Operation*. Philadelphia: Chilton Book Co.

Ricci, M. 2007. "Elaiussa Sebaste: Context, Production and Commerce." In *Çanak: Late Antique and Medieval Pottery and Tiles in Mediterranean Archaeological Contexts (BYZAS 7)*, edited by B. Böhlendorf-Arslan, A. O. Usyat, and J. Witte-Orr, 169–80. Istanbul: Deutsches Archäologisches Institut.

Rice, P. M. 1981. "Evolution of Specialized Pottery Production: A Trial Model." *Current Anthropology* 22(3): 219–40.

Rice, P. M. 1987. *Pottery Analysis: A Sourcebook*. Chicago: University of Chicago Press.

Rice, P. M. 2015. *Pottery Analysis: A Sourcebook*. 2nd ed. Chicago: University of Chicago Press.

Rieger, A.-K., and H. Möller. 2011. "Kilns, Commodities and Consumers: Greco-Roman Pottery Production in Eastern Marmarica (Northwestern Egypt)." *Archäologischer Anzeiger* (1): 141–70.

Rieth, A. 1960. *5000 Jahre Töpferscheibe*. Konstanz: Jan Thorbecke Verlag.

Riggsby, A. M. 2010. *Roman Law and the Legal World of the Romans*. New York: Cambridge University Press.

Rodziewicz, E. 2011. "Wine Production and Trade in Late Roman Alexandria."

In *Alexandrie médiévale 4: Études alexandrines vol. 24*, edited by C. Décobert, J.-Y. Empereur, and C. Picard, 39–56. Alexandria: Centre d'études alexandrines.

Rodziewicz, M. 1998. "Classification of Wineries from Mareotis." In *Commerce et artisanat dans l'Alexandrie hellénistique et romaine*, edited by J.-Y. Empereur, 27–36. Actes du colloque d'Athènes. Paris: de Boccard.

Rogers, A. 2011. *Late Roman Towns in Britain: Rethinking Change and Decline*. Cambridge: Cambridge University Press.

Rogl, C. 2014. "Mouldmade Relief Bowls from Ephesos: The Current State of Research." In *Pottery, Peoples and Places: Study and Interpretation of Late Hellenistic Pottery*, edited by P. G. Bilde and M. L. Lawall, 113–39. Aarhus: Aarhus University Press.

Romanowska, I., A. Lichtenberger, and R. Raja. 2021. "Trends in Ceramic Assemblages from the Northwest Quarter of Gerasa/Jerash, Jordan." *Journal of Archaeological Science: Reports* 36: 102778.

Rosen, G. 1958. *A History of Public Health*. New York: MD Publications.

Rosenthal-Heginbottom, R. 2005. "The 1968 Excavations." In *Excavations on the Site of the Jerusalem International Convention Center (Binyanei Ha'uma): A Settlement of the Late Late First to Second Temple Period, the Tenth Legion's Kilnworks, and a Byzantine Monastic Complex*, edited by B. Arubas and H. Goldfus, 229–82. *JRA* Supplementary Series 60. Portsmouth, RI: Journal of Roman Archaeology.

Rosenthal-Heginbottom, R. 2015. "Factory Lamps 'Firmalampen' in the Levant, Strata." *Bulletin of the Anglo-Israel Archaeological Society* 33: 119–46.

Roth, R. 2007. *Styling Romanization: Pottery and Society in Central Italy*. Cambridge: Cambridge University Press.

Rotroff, S. I. 2006. "The Introduction of the Moldmade Bowl Revisited: Tracking a Hellenistic Innovation." *Hesperia* 75(3): 357–78.

Rotroff, S. I. 2013. *Industrial Religion: The Saucer Pyres of the Athenian Agora*. *Hesperia* Supplement 47. Princeton, NJ: American School of Classical Studies at Athens.

Rotroff, S. I., M. Daszkiewicz, G. Schneider, and R. Owen. 2018. "Eastern Sigillata at Sardis: Evidence for a Local Industry." *Bulletin of the American Schools of Oriental Research* 380: 133–204.

Rotroff, S. I., and A. Oliver. 2003. *The Hellenistic Pottery from Sardis: The Finds through 1994*. Cambridge, MA: Harvard University Press.

Roueché, C. 1989. *Aphrodisias in Late Antiquity*. Journal of Roman Studies Monograph 5. London: Society for the Promotion of Roman Studies.

Roueché, C. 2004. *Aphrodisias in Late Antiquity: The Late Roman and Byzantine Inscriptions*. Rev. 2nd ed. King's College London. http://insaph.kcl.ac.uk/ala2004.

Roux, V. 2019. *Ceramics and Society: A Technological Approach to Archaeological Assemblages*. New York: Springer.

Roux, V., and D. Corbetta. 1989. *The Potter's Wheel: Craft Specialization and Technical Competence*. New Delhi: Oxford and IBH Publishing.

Roux, V., and P. de Miroschedji. 2009. "Revisiting the History of the Potter's Wheel in the Southern Levant." *Levant* 41 (2): 155–73.

Rowlandson, J., ed. 1998. *Women and Society in Greek and Roman Egypt: A Sourcebook*. Cambridge: Cambridge University Press.

Ruffing, K. 2008. *Die berufliche Spezialisierung in Handel und Handwer: Untersuchungen zu ihrer Entwicklung und zu ihren Bedingungen in der römischen Kaiserzeit im östlichen Mittelmeerraum auf der Grundlage der griechischen Inschriften und Papyri*. Pharos 24. Rahden: Marie Leidorf.

Ruffing, K. 2016. "Driving Forces for Specialization: Market, Location Factors, Productivity Improvements." In *Urban Craftsmen and Traders in the Roman World*, edited by A. Wilson and M. Flohr, 115–31. Oxford: Oxford University Press.

Russell, J. 1995. "The Archaeological Context of Magic in the Early Byzantine Period." In *Byzantine Magic*, edited by H. Maguire, 35–50. Washington, DC: Dumbarton Oaks.

Russell, J. 2002. "Anemourion." In *The Economic History of Byzantium: From the Seventh through the Fifteenth Century*, edited by A. E. Laiou, 221–28. Washington, DC: Dumbarton Oaks.

Rye, O. S. 1981. *Pottery Technology: Principles and Reconstruction*. Washington, DC: Taraxacum.

Rye, O. S., and C. Evans. 1976. *Traditional Pottery Techniques of Pakistan: Field and Laboratory Studies*. Washington, DC: Smithsonian Institution Press.

Safrai, Z. 1992. "Urbanization and Industry in Mishnaic Galilee." In *Galilee in the Second Temple and Mishnaic Periods. Volume 1: Life, Culture, and Society*, edited by D. A. Fiensy and J. R. Strange, 272–296. Minneapolis: Fortress Press.

Saliou, C. 1994. *Les lois des bâtiments: Voisinage et habitat urbain dans l'empire romain*. BAH Beyrouth 116. Beirut: Institut français d'archéologie du Proche-Orient.

Saliou, C. 1996. *Le traité d'urbanisme de Julien d'Ascalon: Droit et architecture en Palestine au VIe siècle*. Paris: de Boccard.

Saliou, C. 2012. "Artisanats et espace urbain dans le monde romain: Droit et projets urbains (Ier siècle av. J.C.–VIe siécle ap. J.-C.)." In *"Quartiers" artisanaux en Grèce ancienne: Une perspective méditerranéenne*, edited by A. Esposito and G. Sanidas, 39–55. Villeneuve d'Ascq: Presses universitaires du Septentrion.

Saller, R. P. 2011. "The Roman Family as Productive Unit." In *A Companion to Families in the Greek and Roman Worlds*, edited by B. Rawson, 116–28. Malden, MA: Wiley-Blackwell.

Sanidas, G. M. 2020. "Le ville infecte? origines et gestion des nuisances artisanales urbaines dans l'Athènes classique: L'exemple des grandes fonderies de bronze." *MÉFR* 132(2): 277–88.

Saradi, H. 1998. "Privatization and Subdivision of Urban Properties in the Early Byzantine Centuries: Social and Cultural Implications." *Bulletin of the American Society of Papyrologists* 35(1/2): 17–43.

Saradi, H. 2006. *The Byzantine City in the Sixth Century: Literary Images and Historical Reality*. Athens: Society of Messenian Archaeological Studies.

Saxenian, A. 1994. *Regional Advantage: Culture and Competition in Silicon Valley and Route 128*. Cambridge, MA: Harvard University Press.

Schaad, D. 2007. *La Graufesenque (Millau, Aveyron): Vol. 1. Condatomagos une agglomération de confluent en territoire rutène IIe s. a.C.–IIIe s. p.C.* Bordeaux: Éditions de la Fédération Aquitania.

Schaad, D., and A. Vernhet. 2007. "Chaiptre 2: Les données archéologiques de La Graufesenque." In *La Graufesenque (Millau, Aveyron): Vol. 1. Condatomagos une agglomération de confluent en territoire rutène IIe s. a.C.–IIIe s. p.C.*, edited by D. Schaad, 61–218. Bordeaux: Éditions de la Fédération Aquitania.

Schaer, A. 2005. "Aktuelle Ausgrabungsergebnisse aus den römischen Legionsziegeleien von Hunzenschwil (AG)." *Jahresbericht/Gesellschaft Pro Vindonissa* 2005: 41–51.

Schmid, S. G. 1995. "Nabataean Fine Ware Pottery and the Destructions of Petra." *Studies in the History and Archaeology of Jordan* 5: 637–47.

Schmid, S. G. 1997. "Nabataean Fine Ware Pottery and the Destructions of Petra in the Late First and Early Second Century AD." *Studies in the History and Archaeology of Jordan* 6: 413–20.

Schmid, S. G. 2000. *Petra – Ez Zantur II: Ergebnisse der schweizerisch-liechtensteinischen Ausgrabungen, Teil 1. Die Feinkeramik der Nabatäer: Typologie, Chronologie und kulturhistorische Hintergründe*. Mainz: Verlag Philipp von Zabern.

Schmid, S. G. 2007. "Nabataean Pottery." In *The World of the Nabataeans: Volume 2 of the International Conference "The World of the Herods and the Nabataeans" Held at the British Museum, 17–19 April 2001*, edited by K. D. Politis, 309–26. Stuttgart: Franz Steiner.

Schmidt, P. R. 2009. "Tropes, Materiality, and Ritual Embodiment of African Iron Smelting Furnace as Human Figures." *Journal of Archaeological Method and Theory* 16: 262–82.

Schmitt, A. 2019. "Troisième Partie. Aspects Techniques des Productions de Buoto." In *Tell El-Fara'in-Buto VI: Recherches sur les ateliers romains de Bouto. Prospections et sondages (2001–2006)*, edited by P. Ballet, F. Béguin, G. Lecuyot, and A. Schmitt, 185–98. Wiesbaden: Harrassowitz.

Scholl, T. 1995. "Kilns of the Ptolemaic Period at Tell Atrib." *Hellenistic and Roman Pottery in the Eastern Mediterranean: Advances in Scientific Studies*, edited by H. Meyza and J. Młynarczyk, 423–30. Warsaw: Polish Centre of Mediterranean Archaeology, Warsaw University.

Seeley, F., and J. Drummond-Murray. 2005. *Roman Pottery Production in the Walbrook Valley: Excavations at 20–28 Moorgate, City of London, 1998–2000*. London: Museum of London Archaeology Service.

Seifert, M. 1993. "Pottery Kilns in Mainland Greece and on the Aegean Islands." *Revista di Archeologia* 17: 93–105.

Sennett, R. 2008. *The Craftsman*. New Haven, CT: Yale University Press.

Seton-Williams, M. V. 1966. "The Tell-Farâ'în Expedition, 1966." *The Journal of Egyptian Archaeology* 52: 163–71.

Seton-Williams, M. V. 1967. "The Tell-Farâ'în Expedition, 1967." *The Journal of Egyptian Archaeology* 53: 146–55.

Shaikh, S., A. A. Nafees, V. Khetpal, A. A. Jamali, A. M. Arain, and A. Yousuf. 2012. "Respiratory Symptoms and Illnesses among Brick Kiln Workers: A Cross Sectional Study from Rural Districts of Pakistan." *BMC Public Health* 12: 999.

Shepard, A. O. 1965. *Ceramics for the Archaeologist*. Washington, DC: Carnegie Institution of Washington.

Shimada, I. 2007. *Craft Production in Complex Societies: Multicraft and Producer Perspectives*. Salt Lake: University of Utah Press.

Shott, M. J. 1996. "Mortal Pots: On Use Life and Vessel Size in the Formation of Ceramic Assemblages." *American Antiquity* 61(3): 463–82.

Sillar, B. 1997. "Reputable Pots and Disreputable Potters: Individual and Community Choices in Present-Day Pottery Productions and Exchanges in the Andes." In *Not So Much a Pot, More a Way of Life*, edited by C. G. Cumberpatch and P. W. Blinkhorn, 1–20. Oxford: Oxbow Books.

Şimşek, C. 2013. *Laodikeia (Laodicea ad Lycum). Laodikeia Çalışmaları 2*. Istanbul: Ege Yayınları.

Şimşek, C., and M. Bilgin. 2018. "Laodikeia Geç Antik Çağ Seramikleri (Late Antique Pottery of Laodikeia)." In *Geç Antik Çağ'da Lykos Vadisi ve Çevresi / The Lykos Valley and Neighbourhood in Late Antiquity*, edited by C. Şimşek and T. Kaçar, 175–99. Istanbul: Ege Yayınları.

Slane, K.W. 1997. "The Fine Wares." In *Tel Anafa II, 1: The Hellenistic and Roman Pottery*, edited by S. C. Herbet, 247–393. *JRA* Supplementary Series 10. Ann Arbor, MI: Journal of Roman Archaeology.

Smith, P. E. 2006. "Children and Ceramic Innovation: A Study in the Archaeology of Children." *Archeological Papers of the American Anthropological Association* 15: 65–76.

Smith, R. R. R. 2011. "Marble Workshops at Aphrodisias." In *Roman Sculpture in Asia Minor: Proceedings of the International Conference to Celebrate the 50th Anniversary of the Italian Excavations at Hierapolis in Phrygia, Held on May 24–26, 2007, in Cavallino (Lecce)*, edited by F. D'Andria and I. Romeo, 61–76. Portsmouth, RI: Journal of Roman Archaeology.

Sodini, J.-P. 2003. "Archaeology and Late Antique Social Structures." In *Theory and Practice in Late Antique Archaeology*, edited by L. Lavan and W. Bowden, 25–56. Late Antique Archaeology 1. Leiden: Brill.

Sorenson, O., and P. G. Audia. 2000. "The Social Structure of Entrepreneurial Activity: Geographic Concentration of Footware Production in the United States, 1940–1989." *American Journal of Sociology* 106 (2): 424–62.

Spencer, A. J. 1997. "Dynastic Egyptian Pottery." In *Pottery in the Making: World Ceramic Traditions*, edited by I. Freestone and D. Gaimster, 44–49. Washington, DC: Smithsonian Institution Press.

Sperduti, A. 1997. "Life Conditions of a Roman Imperial Age Population: Occupational Stress Markers and Working Activities in Lucus Feroniae (Rome, 1st–2nd c. AD)." *Human Evolution* 12(4): 253–67.

Stark, M. T., ed. 1998. *The Archaeology of Social Boundaries*. Washington, DC: Smithsonian Press.

Steinmann, L. 2020. "Finds from Miletus XXXII: Clay Rings from the Sanctuary of Dionysos in Miletus." *Archäologischer Anzeiger* 2020(1): 1–49.

Stern, E. M. 2008. "Glass Production." In *The Oxford Handbook of Engineering and Technology in the Classical World*, edited by J. P. Oleson, 520–47. Oxford: Oxford University Press.

Stillwell, A. N. 1948. *The Potter's Quarter: Corinth Results of Excavations Conducted by the American School of Classical Studies at Athens. Volume XV, Part I*. Athens: American School of Classical Studies at Athens.

Stissi, V. 2012. "Giving the *Kerameikos* a Context: Ancient Greek Potters' Quarters as Part of the *Polis* Space, Economy and Society." In *"Quartiers" artisanaux en Grèce ancienne: Une perspective méditerranéenne*, edited by A. Esposito and G. Sanidas, 201–32. Villeneuve d'Ascq: Presses universitaires du Septentrion.

Strange, J. R. 2019. "Shiẖin – 2013." *Hadashot Arkheologiyot: Excavations and Surveys in Israel* 131.

Strange, J. R., and M. Aviam. 2017. "Shiḥin Excavation Project: Oil Lamp Production at Ancient Shiḥin." *Strata: Bulletin of the Anglo-Israel Archaeological Society* 35: 63–99.

Stucky, R. 1993. "Das nabatäische Wohnhaus und das urbanistische System der Wohnquartiere in Petra." In *Arabia Antiqua*, edited by A. Invernizzi and J.-F. Salles, 37–53. Serie Orientale Roma 70. Rome: Instituto Italiano per il Medio ed Estremo Oriente.

Sussman, V. 1980. "Moulds for Lamps and Figurines from a Caesarea Workshop." *Atiqot* 14: 76–79.

Sussman, V. 2012. *Roman Period Oil Lamps in the Holy Land: Collection of the Israel Antiquities Authority*. BAR-IS 2447. Oxford: Archaeopress.

Sutton, A. 2020. "Resistance Is Futile? Ceramic Technology and Social Change in Later Iron Age and Early Roman Britain: Silchester Ware as a Case Study." *Britannia* 51: 53–82.

Swan, V. 2021. The Pottery Kilns of Roman Britain by Vivien Swan. https://romankilns .net/.

Swan, V. G. 1984. *The Pottery Kilns of Roman Britain*. London: Her Majesty's Stationary Office.

Swift, E. 2009. *Style and Function in Roman Decoration: Living with Objects and Interiors*. London: Routledge.

Swift, E. 2017. *Roman Artefacts and Society: Design, Behaviour, and Experience*. Oxford: Oxford University Press.

Talloen, P., and J. Poblome. 2005. "What Were They Thinking Of? Relief Decorated Pottery from Sagalassos. A Cognitive Approach." *Les mélanges de l'école française de Rome: Antiquité* 117(1): 55–81.

Talloen, P., and J. Poblome. 2019. "The Age of Specialiation. Dionysus and the Production of Wine in Late Antiquity: A View from Sagalassos (SW Turkey)." *Olba* 27: 413–42.

Tandon, S., S. Gupta, S. Singh, and A. Kumar. 2017. "Respiratory Abnormalities among Occupationally Exposed, Non-smoking Brick Kiln Workers from Punjab, India." *The International Journal of Occupational and Environmental Medicine* 8: 166–73.

Tekkök, B. 2004. "The Pottery Workshops at Eceabat in Northwest Anatolia: The Hellenistic and Roman Traditions Continue." In *Ethnoarchaeological Investigations in Rural Anatolia: Volume 1*, edited by T. Takaoğlu, 97–114. Istanbul: Ege Yayınları.

Temin, P. 2013. *The Roman Market Economy*. Princeton, NJ: Princeton University Press.

Terrenato, N. 1998. "The Romanization of Italy: Global Acculturation or Cultural Bricolage?" In *TRAC 97*, edited by C. Forcey, J. Hawthorne, and R. Witcher, 20–27. Oxford: Oxbow.

Toll, N. P. 1943. *The Excavations at Dura-Europos, Final Report IV: The Green Glazed Pottery*. New Haven, CT: Yale University Press.

Tomasevic-Buck, T. 1982. *Die Ziegelbrennöfen der Legio I Martia in Kaiseraugst/AG und die Ausgrabungen in der Liebrüti 1970–1975 (Archäologischer Führer durch Augst/Kaiseraugst Band 1).* Augst: Römermuseum Augst.

Tran, N. 2007. "La mention épigraphique des métiers artisanaux et commerciaux en Italie centro-méridionale." In *Vocabulaire et expressions de l'économie dans le monde antique*, edited by J. C. Andreau and V. Bordeaux, 119–41. Paris: de Boccard.

Tran, N. 2013. *Dominus tabernae: Le statut de travail des artisans et des commerçants de l'Occident romain (Ier siècle av. J.-C.–IIIe siècle ap. J.-C.).* BÉFAR 360. Rome: École Française de Rome.

Tran, N. 2016. "Ars and Doctrina: The Socioeconomic Identity of Roman Skilled Workers (First Century BC–Third Century AD)." In *Work, Labour, and Professions in the Roman World*, edited by K. Verboven and C. Laes, 246–61. Impact of Empire 23. Leiden: Brill.

Trombley, F. 1987. "Korykos in Cilicia Trachis: The Economy of a Small Coastal City in Late Antiquity (Saec. V–VI): A Précis." *The Ancient History Bulletin* 1(1): 16–23.

Uleners, H., and J. Poblome. 2014. "Sagalassos'ta Beklenmedik Bir Keşif: Yeni Bir Keramik Atölyesi / A New and Unexpected Potters' Workshop at Sagalassos." *ANMED Anadolu Akdenizi Arkeoloji Haberleri / ANMED News of Archaeology from Anatolia's Mediterranean Areas* 12: 87–93.

Uleners, H., and J. Poblome. 2016. "Sagalassos LE Alanı 2015 Yılı Kazıları / The 2015 Excavation Campaign at Site LE, Sagalassos." *ANMED Anadolu Akdenizi Arkeoloji Haberleri / ANMED News of Arhcaeology from Anatolia's Mediterranean Areas* 14: 129–36.

Ulrich, R. B. 2007. *Roman Woodworking.* New Haven, CT: Yale University Press.

Underwood, D. 2019. *(Re)using Ruins Public Buildings in the Cities of the Late Antique West, A.D. 300–600.* Brill: Leiden.

Vamos, P. 2010. "Types of Pottery Kilns in Aquincum." *Rei Cretariae Romanae Favtorvm Acta* 41: 67–74.

Vamos, P. 2012. "Some Remarks on Military Pottery in Aquincum." *Acta Archaeologica Academiae Scientiarum Hungaricae* 63: 395–406.

van den Brink, E. C. M., C. Commenge, A. Cohen-Weinberger, T. Schick, H. Khalaily, and M. Sade. 2016. "XI/ / Lod (Newe Yaraq): A Late Roman Pottery Kiln and Pottery Neolithic A (Jericho IX/Lodian) Remains." *Atiqot* 85: 1–36.

van der Enden, M., J. Poblome, and P. Bes. 2014. "From Hellenistic to Roman Imperial in Pisidian Tableware: The Genesis of Sagalassos Red Slip Ware." In *Late Hellenistic to Mediaeval Fine Wares of the Aegean Coast of Anatolia: Their Production, Imitation and Use*, edited by H. Meyza and K. Domżalski, 81–93. Travaux de l'Institut des Cultures Méditerranéennes et Orientales de l'Académie Polonaise des Science 1. Warsaw: Neriton.

van der Leeuw, S. E. 1977. "Towards a Study of the Economics of Pottery Making." In *Ex Horreo*, edited by B. L. Beek, R. W. Brant, and W. Gruenman van Watteringe, 68–76. Amsterdam: University of Amsterdam Press.

van Minnen, P. 1986. "Urban Craftsmen in Roman Egypt." *Münsterische Beiträge zur Antiken Handelsgeschichte* 6: 31–88.

van Nijf, O. 1997. *The Civic World of Professional Associations in the Roman East.* Amsterdam: J.C. Gieben.

van Nijf, O. 2002. "Collegia and Civic Guards: Two Chapters in the History of Sociability." In *After the Past: Essays in Ancient History in Honour of H. W. Pleket*, edited by W. Jongman and M. Kleijwegt, 305–40. Leiden: Brill.

Van Oyen, A. 2012. "Knowledge Systems in the Production of Terra Sigillata: Moving Beyond the Local/Global Paradox." In *TRAC 2011: Proceedings of the Twenty First Theoretical Roman Archaeology Conference, Newcastle 2011*, edited by M. Duggan, F. McIntosh, and D. J. Rohl, 48–59. Oxford: Oxbow.

Van Oyen, A. 2015. "Actor-Network Theory's Take on Archaeological Types: Becoming, Material Agency and Historical Explanation." *Cambridge Archaeological Journal* 25: 163–78.

Varinlioğlu, G. 2011. "Trades, Crafts, and Agricultural Production in Town and Countryside in Southeastern Isauria." In *Archaeology and the Cities of Asia Minor in Late Antiquity*, edited by O. Dally and C. Ratté, 173–88. Ann Arbor: University of Michigan Press.

Varkıvanç, B. 2001–2002. "Patara'da bir Seramik İşliği." *Adalya* 5: 137–52.

Venticinque, P. F. 2010. "Family Affairs: Guild Regulations and Family Relationships in Roman Egypt." *Greek, Roman and Byzantine Studies* 50: 273–94.

Venticinque, P. F. 2016. *Honor among Thieves: Craftsmen, Merchants, and Associations in Roman and Late Roman Egypt*. Ann Arbor: University of Michigan Press.

Verboven, K. 2002. *The Economy of Friends: Economic Aspects of Amicitia and Patronage in the Late Republic*. Brussels: Latomus.

Verboven, K. 2011a. "Resident Aliens and Translocal Merchant Collegia in the Roman Empire." In *Frontiers in the Roman World*, edited by O. Hekster and T. Kaiser, 322–48. Leiden: Brill.

Verboven, K. 2011b. "The Freedman Economy of Roman Italy." In *Free at Last! The Impact of Freed Slaves on the Roman Empire*, edited by S. Bell and T. Ramsby, 88–109. London: Bristol Classical Press.

Verboven, K. 2014. "Attitudes to Work and Workers in Classical Greece and Rome." *Tijdschrift voor economische en sociale geschiedenis* 11: 67–87.

Verboven, K. 2016. "Guilds and the Organisation of Urban Populations during the Principate." In *Work, Labour, and Professions in the Roman World*, edited by K. Verboven and C. Laes, 173–202. Impact of Empire 23. Leiden: Brill.

Verboven, K., and C. Laes, eds. 2016. *Work, Labour, and Professions in the Roman World*. Impact of Empire 23. Leiden: Brill.

Verhagen, P., and M. Gazenbeek. 2006. "The Use of Predictive Modeling for Guiding the Archaeological Survey of Roman Pottery Kilns in the Argonne Region (Northeastern France)." In *GIS and Archaeological Site Location Modeling*, edited by M. Mehrer and K. Wescott, 447–59. Boca Raton, FL: CRC Press.

Vermoere, M., S. Six, J. Poblome, P. Degryse, E. Paulissen, M. Waelkens, and E. Smets. 2003. "Pollen Sequences from the City of Sagalassos (Pisidia, Southwest Turkey)." *AnatSt* 53: 161–73.

Versluys, M. J. 2014. "Understanding Objects in Motion: An Archaeological Dialogue on Romanization." *Archaeological Dialogues* 21(1): 1–20.

Vickers, M. 1994. "Nabataea, India, Gaul, and Carthage: Reflections on Hellenistic and Roman Gold Vessels and Red-Gloss Pottery." *American Journal of Archaeology* 98(2): 231–48.

Vickers, M., and D. Gill. 1994. *Artful Crafts: Ancient Greek Silverware and Pottery*. Oxford: Clarendon Press.

Vis, B. N. 2009. *Built Environments, Constructed Societies: Inverting Spatial Analysis*. Leiden: Sidestone Press.

Vitto, F. 1980. "Notes and News." *Israel Exploration Journal* 30(3/4): 205–39.

Vitto, F. 1983–1984. "A Look into the Workshop of a Late Roman Galilean Potter." *Bulletin of the Anglo-Israel Archaeological Society* 1983–4: 18–22.

Vitto, F. 1986. "Potters and Pottery Manufacture in Roman Palestine." *Bulletin of the Institute of Archaeology (University College London)* 23: 47–64.

Vitto F., M.W. Prausnitz, R. Rosenthal, M. Hershkovitz, J. Elgavish, E. Stern, S. M. Paley, Y. Porath, M. Zohar, Y. Shiloh, K. G. O'Connell, D. G. Rose, J. D. Seger, A. Kloner, R. Cohen, and W. G. Dever. 1980. "Notes and News." *Israel Exploration Journal* 30 (3/4): 205–39.

Vokaer, A. 2013. "Pottery Production and Exchange in late Antique Syria (Fourth–Eight Century A.D.): A Study of Some Imported and Local Wares." In *Local Economies? Production and Exchange of Inland Regions in Late Antiquity*, edited by L. Lavan, 567–606. Late Antique Archaeology 10. Leiden: Brill.

Vossen, R. 1984. "Towards Building Models of Traditional Trade in Ceramics: Case Studies from Spain and Morocco." In *The Many Dimensions of Pottery: Ceramics in Archaeology and Anthropology*, edited by S. E. van der Leeuw and A. C. Pritchard, 338–97. Amsterdam: University of Amsterdam Press.

Vroom, J. 2007. "The Archaeology of Late Antique Dining Habits in the Eastern Mediterranean: A Preliminary Study of the Evidence." In *Objects in Context, Objects in Use*, edited by L. Lavan, E. Swift, and T. Putzeys, 313–61. Late Antique Archaeology 5. Leiden: Brill.

Vroom, J. 2019. "Medieval Ephesos as a Production and Consumption Centre." In *Ephesos from Late Antiquity until the Late Middle Ages: Proceedings of the International Conference at the Research Center for Anatolian Civilizations, Koç University, Istanbul, 30th November–2nd December 2012*, edited by S. Ladstätter and P. Magdalino, 231–56. Vienna: Verlag Holzhausen GmbH.

Waelkens, M. 1977. "Phyrgian Votive and Tombstones as Source of the Social and Economic Life in Roman Antiquity." *Ancient Society* 8: 277–315.

Waelkens, M. 1986. *Die Kleinasiatischen Türsteine: Typologische und Epigraphische Untersuchungen der Kleinasiatischen Grabreliefs mit Scheintür*. Mainz am Rhein: von Zabern.

Waelkens, M., and Poblome, J. 2011. *Sagalassos. City of Dreams*. Tongeren: Openbaar Kunstbezit Vlaanderen.

Waliszewski, T., and M. Gwiazda. 2015. "Porphyreon through the Ages: The Fading Archaeological Heritage of the Lebanese Coast." *Journal of Eastern Mediterranean Archaeology and Heritage Studies* 3(4): 330–48.

Wallace-Hadrill, A. 1996. *Houses and Society in Pompeii and Herculaneum*. Princeton, NJ: Princeton University Press.

Watson P. 1989. "Jerash Bowls: Study of a Provincial Group of Byzantine Decorated Fine Ware." *Syria* 66 (1–4): 223–61.

Weber, A. 1928. *Theory of the Location of Industries*. Translated by C. J. Friedrich. Chicago: University of Chicago Press.

Wefers, S., and F. Mangartz. 2011. "Ephesos Bizans Dönemi Atölyeleri." In *Bizans Döneminde Ephesos*, edited by F. Daim and S. Ladstätter, 213–28. Istanbul: Ege Yayınları.

Weksler-Bdolah, S. 2016. "A Villa and a Pottery Kiln from the Late Roman-Byzantine Periods at 'En Ya'al (Naḥal Refa'im), Jerusalem." *Atiqot* 87: 107–10.

Wendrich, W. 2006. "Body Knowledge: Ethnoarchaeological Learning and the Interpretation of Ancient Technology." In *L'apport de l'Égypte à l'histoire des techniques*, edited by B. Mathieu, D. Meeks, and M. Wissa, 267–75. Cairo: Institut français d'archéologie orientale.

Wendrich, W. 2012. "Archaeology and Apprenticeship: Body Knowledge, Identity, and Communities of Practice." In *Archaeology and Apprenticeship: Body Knowledge, Identity, and Communities of Practice*, edited by W. Wendrich, 1–19. Tucson: University of Arizona Press.

Wenger, E. 1998. *Communities of Practice: Learning, Meaning, and Identity*. Cambridge: Cambridge University Press.

Westermann, W. L. 1914a. "Apprentice Contracts and the Apprentice System in Roman Egypt." *Classical Philology* 9(3): 295–315.

Westermann, W. L. 1914b. "Vocational Training in Antiquity." *The School Review* 22 (9): 601–10.

Whitehouse, D. 1977. "Kangan: Una fabbrica tradizionale di ceramiche nell'Iran meridionale." In *Atti X: Convegno internazionale della ceramica, Albisola, 26–29 maggio, 1977*, 41–64. Albisola: Centro ligure per la storia della ceramica.

Wicenciak, U. 2016. *Porphyreon: Hellenistic and Roman Pottery Production in the Sidon Hinterland*. Translated by M. Stępień and I. Zych. Warsaw: Polish Centre of Mediterranean Archaeology, University of Warsaw.

Wickham, C. 2006. *Framing the Early Middle Ages: Europe and the Mediterranean 400–800*. Oxford: Oxford University Press.

Wilfong, T. 2008. "A Coptic Account of Pottery from the Kilns of Psabt (P.Lond. Copt. 1.695)." *Bulletin of the American Society of Papyrologists* 45: 247–59.

Willet, R. 2018. "Early Imperial Tableware in Roman Asia Minor: A Perspective on the Diachronic Patterns and Morphological Developments." *Internet Archaeology* 50. https://doi.org/10.11141/ia.50.17.

Wilson, A. 2002. "Urban Production in the Roman World: The View from North Africa." *Papers of the British School at Rome* 70: 231–73.

Wilson, A., and M. Flohr, eds. 2016. *Urban Craftsmen and Traders in the Roman World.* Oxford: Oxford University Press.

Winslow, D. 2009. "The Village Clay: Recursive Innovations and Community Self-Fashioning among Sinhalese Potters." *Journal of the Royal Anthropological Institute* 15(2): 254–75.

Wipszycka, E. 1971. "Les impôts professionnels et la structure de l'industrie dans l'Egypte romaine. A propos de la Κοπὴ Τριχός." *The Journal of Juristic Papyrology* 16–17: 117–30.

Wissemann, M. 1984. "Die Spezialisierung des römischen Handels." *Münstersche Beiträge zur Antiken Handelsgeschichte* 3(1): 116–24.

Worp, K. A. 2011. "Female Professionals in the Hellenistic World." In *"Palabras bien dichas": Estudios filológicos dedicados al P. Pius Ramon Tragan*, 77–87. Barcelona: Publicaciones de l'Abadia de Montserrat.

Wrabetz, J. F. 1977. "A New Serenus Stamping from Sardis and the Origins of the Eastern Sigillata B Ware." *Harvard Studies in Classical Philology* 81: 195–97.

Yannai, E. 2012. "A Byzantine Pottery Kiln Complex at Yavne." *Qadmoniot: A Journal for the Antiquities of Eretz-Israel and Bible Lands* 144: 94–103.

Yaraş, A. 2003. "Allianoi Geç Antik Çağ Seramik Fırınları / Allianoi Late Antique Age Ceramic Ovens." In *Uluslararası Eskişehir Pişmiş Toprak Sempozyumu Bildiriler Kitabı / III. International Eskişehir Terra Cotta Symposium Proceedings Book*, 404–10. Eskişehir: Eskişehir Tepebaşı Belediyesi.

Yaylalı, A. 2007. "2006 Yılı Tralleis Antik Kenti Kazı ve Restorasyon Çalışmaları." *Kazı Sonuçları Toplantısı* 29(1): 555–78.

Yegül, F. K. 1986. *The Bath-Gymnasium Complex at Sardis.* Archaeological Exploration of Sardis Reports 3. Cambridge, MA: Harvard University Press.

Zabehlicky-Scheffenegger, S. 2003. "C. Sentius and His Commercial Connections." In *Les céramiques en Anatolie aux époques hellénistiques et romaines: Actes de la table ronde d'Istanbul, 23–24 mai 1996*, edited by C. Abadie-Reynal, 117–19. Varia Anatolica 15. Istanbul: Institut Français d'Études Anatoliennes.

Zamek, J. 1999. *What Every Potter Should Know.* Iola, WI: Krause Publications.

Zanini, E. 2006. "Artisans and Traders in the Early Byzantine City: Exploring the Limits of Archaeological Evidence." In *Social and Political Life in Late Antiquity*, edited by C. Machado, A. Gutteridge, and A. Bowden, 373–411. Late Antique Arcaheology 3. Leiden: Brill.

Zayadine, F. 1981. "Recent Excavations and Restorations of the Department of Antiquities (1979–80)." *Annual of the Department of Antiquities of Jordan* 25: 341–53.

Zayadine, F. 1982. "Recent Excavations at Petra (1979–81)." *Annual of the Department of Antiquities of Jordan* 26: 365–93.

Zayadine, F. 1986a. "Ein Töpfereikomplex am Rand von Petra." In *Petra: Neue Ausgrabungen und Entdeckungen*, edited by M. Lindner, 258–67. Munich: Delp.

Zayadine, F. 1986b. "Petra." In *Pottery and Potters, Past and Present: 7000 Years of Ceramic Art in Jordan*, edited by D. Homès-Fredericq and H. J. Franken, 182–89. Austellungskatologe der Universität Tübingen Nr. 20. Tübingen: University of Tübingen.

Zevulun, U., and Y. Olenik. 1979. *Function and Design in the Talmudic Period.* Tel Aviv: Haaretz Museum.

Zimmer, G. 1985. "Römischen Handwerker." In *Aufstieg und Niedergang der Römischen Welt: Geschichte und Kultur Roms im Spiegel der neueren Forschung*, edited by H. Temporini and W. Haase, 205–28. Berlin: de Gruyter.

Zoroğlu, L. 1989. "Some Roman Names on Eastern Sigillata A from Samosata." In *The Eastern Frontier of the Roman Empire: Proceedings of a Colloquium Held at Ankara in September 1988*, edited by H. French and C. S.

Lightfoot, 573–79. BAR-IS 553. Oxford: Archaeopress.

Zoroğlu, K. L., R. Bozkurttan, and B. Özdemir. 2019. "Kelenderis 2018 Yılı Kazı ve Onarım Çalışmaları." *Kazı Sonuçları Toplantısı* 41(3): 63–86.

Zuskin, E., J. Mustajbegovic, E. N. Schachter, J. Kern, J. Doko-Jelinic, and J. Godnic-Cvar. 1998. "Respiratory Findings in Workers Employed in the Brick-Manufacturing Industry." *Journal of Occupational and Environmental Medicine* 40(9): 814–20.

INDEX

For EU product safety concerns, contact us at Calle de José Abascal, 56–1°, 28003 Madrid, Spain or eugpsr@cambridge.org.

www.ingramcontent.com/pod-product-compliance
Lightning Source LLC
LaVergne TN
LVHW081937200926
848484LV00009B/2454

9781009514606